Social Computing in Homeland Security:
Disaster Promulgation and Response

Amy Wenxuan Ding
University of Illinois, USA

INFORMATION SCIENCE REFERENCE

Hershey · New York

Director of Editorial Content:	Kristin Klinger
Senior Managing Editor:	Jamie Snavely
Managing Editor:	Jeff Ash
Assistant Managing Editor:	Carole Coulson
Typesetter:	Chris Hrobak
Cover Design:	Lisa Tosheff
Printed at:	Yurchak Printing Inc.

Published in the United States of America by
Information Science Reference (an imprint of IGI Global)
701 E. Chocolate Avenue, Suite 200
Hershey PA 17033
Tel: 717-533-8845
Fax: 717-533-8661
E-mail: cust@igi-global.com
Web site: http://www.igi-global.com

and in the United Kingdom by
Information Science Reference (an imprint of IGI Global)
3 Henrietta Street
Covent Garden
London WC2E 8LU
Tel: 44 20 7240 0856
Fax: 44 20 7379 0609
Web site: http://www.eurospanbookstore.com

Library of Congress Cataloging-in-Publication Data

Ding, Amy Wenxuan,
  Social computing in homeland security : disaster promulgation and response / by Amy Wenxuan Ding.
     p. cm.
  Includes bibliographical references and index.
  Summary: "This book presents a theoretical framework addressing how to enhance national response capabilities and ready the public in the presence of human-made or natural disasters"--Provided by publisher.
  ISBN 978-1-60566-228-2 (hardcover) -- ISBN 978-1-60566-229-9 (ebook)
  1. Emergency management. I. Title.
  HV551.2. D54 2009
  363.34--dc22
                       2008037979

British Cataloguing in Publication Data
A Cataloguing in Publication record for this book is available from the British Library.

Table of Contents

Section I
Threat Warning and Psychological Warfare

Unit I
From Threat Warning to Information Perception and Public Response

Unit II
Psychosocial Aspect and Social Dynamics: A Mathematical Modeling Approach

Chapter III
Psychosocial Effects: A Silent Influence... **32**

Chapter IV
Individual Reactions and Psychological Impact **45**

Chapter V
Disaster Promulgation and Collective Behaviors... **52**

Section II
Improving Response Capability to Counter the Threat

Unit III
Forming Situation Awareness for First Decisions and Lifesaving

Foreword

Since before the days of Archimedes, scientists have assisted their nations in dealing with war. They have also improved the ability of societies to cope with the vagaries of Nature with safer and more robust transportation, dams, waterways, and buildings. By and large, their contributions have been in the physical domain of physics, chemistry, and engineering. In the current era, we are faced with what may be a long-term threat of terrorism intended to cause massive disruption and perhaps massive deaths. To this must be added potential threats such as the rapid emergence of new and lethal strains of influenza. A characteristic feature of these threats is that success in avoiding or coping with them will depend fundamentally on individual and collective human behavior. This is not new, of course, as illustrated by how important such matters were in the dark days of World War II. Something similar in spirit but very different in detail may be needed in the years ahead. How can today's science help to harness citizen power in response to crisis?

Professor Amy Ding's book is remarkable for addressing this very issue, and by exploiting modern science involving human cognition, decision making, and behavior. She not only describes relevant concepts, but uses mathematics and computer simulation to apply the concepts pragmatically. Much of the book is therefore quite technical, as befits its text-book nature. Readers, however, will be motivated by its being organized around real, important, and all-too-familiar problems such as: How can the broad "situational awareness" of the public be improved to help avert or respond quickly and effectively to threats? How can government, private institutions, and the public cooperate effectively in times of un-expected events and potential chaos? It turns out that science, mathematics, and modeling can actually help answer such questions! We need not just fall back on common intuition, which is often quite wrong. At the same time, we can systematically build better intuition.

Some people doubt that much can be done to prepare for turbulent circumstances, but that simply is not true. A more subtle skepticism (based on recent experience) is that governments can be trusted only to do things poorly. In fact, however, local, state, and national governments are intensely concerned about how best to prepare for and deal with crises of the sort discussed in this book. Great dedication and enormous resources are going into such matters. This book helps to inform those efforts and is spot-on in its attention to such concrete matters as how government information can be structured and communicated so as to be maximally valuable. The prescriptions are not in the form of foolish detailed plans that would fall apart as real events proved to be different from those anticipated, but rather about tools and organizational approaches that would prove useful for rapid adaptation, and about building systems and organizations so as to be flexible in what they can do and robust to shock. In effect, the book is laying out elements of a strategy to allow for flexibility, adaptiveness, and robustness (FARness)—attributes highlighted by me and other researchers concerned with planning under uncertainty.

It is one thing to agree with this type of philosophy; it is quite another to identify practical steps to pursue it. Here the book laudably translates the challenges into what I think of as concrete "engineering problems," such as how to characterize, communicate, and reinforce information to the public, or how first responders can sensibly (although by no means "optimally") allocate their resources rapidly amidst confusion. Addressing such problems can benefit greatly from science-based principles and from clever at-the-time use of heuristics and tools to assist assessment, decision, and action. Professor Ding's book attempts to teach such principles and approaches to practical problem-solving. It is an unusual and welcome contribution.

Paul K. Davis
Principal Researcher, RAND Corporation
Professor of Policy Analysis, Pardee RAND Graduate School

Paul K. Davis *is a principal researcher at the RAND Corporation and a professor of policy analysis in the Pardee RAND Graduate School. His work is interdisciplinary and he has published extensively on: strategic planning and resource allocation under uncertainty; decision science and human decision making; advanced methods of modeling, simulation; and counterterrorism. Dr. Davis has served on many panels of the National Research Council and Defense Science Board. He has a BS from the University of Michigan and a PhD in chemical physics from the Massachusetts Institute of Technology. Before joining RAND, he was a senior executive in the Office of the Secretary of Defense (Program Analysis and Evaluation).*

Preface

Throughout human history, certain events (e.g., scientific inventions, wars) may change the development of history. However, *any* event can assist in human knowledge accumulation. People acquire experience or learn lessons from an event; sometimes the event may even prompt knowledge development and new knowledge generation. Entering the 21st Century, the world has experienced a sequence of major events, unlike any before, that have promoted worldwide research into disaster planning and responses by homeland security. The September 11, 2001, attacks in the United States attracted international attention to the problem of countering terrorism and its broader security implications. The outbreak of severe acute respiratory syndrome (SARS) in 2003 and the subsequent emergence of another novel disease (i.e., bird flu epidemic), both without known countermeasures, also focused the world's attention on health preparations in response to a potential threat of a new influenza pandemic. The tsunami disaster in December 2004 affected several countries in Southeast Asia and further promoted a widespread discussion about establishing threat warning systems to protect the public and save lives. These are just some typical examples. Yet all such severe events catalyze a national push for homeland security research, which presents us with unique opportunities to identify and mitigate not only our own vulnerabilities but also a range of difficult decision problems for which there are no easy answers.

Little information about homeland security research was published prior to 2000, and the learning curve has been very steep for all parties involved in developing programs to counter terrorism. The World Health Organization even describes terrorism as a "public health issue" (WHO, 2001a) and exhorts countries to "strengthen their capacity to respond to the consequences of the use of biological or chemical weapons" (WHO, 2001b).

This book presents recent scientific research work based on human cognitive theory, together with mathematical modeling and computer simulation, designed to address various homeland security issues, ranging from public threat warning advisories to response-side capability building. The themes emerging from this research include the difficulties inherent to quickly realizing sudden and unexpected events and ascertaining their nature and severity, designing effective threat warning advisories, quantifying public reactions to and confidence in warning advisories, assessing psychosocial impacts on social productivity, the vital need to identify the potential involvement of HazMat materials and surveillance reactions, and the critical importance of first decisions in achieving successful disaster prevention and/or mitigation.

The goal of the book is therefore to recognize how to enhance national and social response capabilities in the presence of human-made or natural disasters. It addresses critical issues involved in completing the "Universal Task List" for major events represented by the Homeland Security National Planning Scenarios (FEMA, 2008), as well as achieving specific capabilities that all levels of government should possess to respond effectively to threats or incidents. The book consists of 13 distinctive chapters, each focusing on a specific topic that falls under the theme of protecting people and enhancing response capabilities. Critical shifts—moving from discussing adversary-side behavior phenomena to exploring our response capability enhancement and from using case analysis or statistics to employing dynamic cognitive modeling with computer simulation—represent two important features of this book. Because speed is critical in saving lives, and organizing an effective and efficient response in a timely manner is crucial in response to any unexpected disaster, this book provides scientific backup for generating such responses. Meanwhile, it may serve as a textbook for students to learn problem solving using cognitive modeling and computer simulation in the new field of homeland security research.

CONTENTS AND ORGANIZATION

Two major players emerge in the face of a sudden disaster or threat. One is the protégé (i.e., the public), and the other is the protector (i.e., the response forces). Thus, the topics covered herein are organized into two parts. Section I focuses on the protégé side, examining public reactions and psychosocial effects of disasters; Section II pertains to the protector, exploring how to increase response capabilities using limited existing resources. We describe each part in detail next.

Section I: Threat Warning and Psychological Warfare

Human history indicates that human survival depends on the ability to mount a successful response to threats. A disaster—whether terrorism like the 9/11 attack in 2001 or a natural event like Hurricane Katrina in 2005—can cause tremendous damage to both physical entities (e.g., buildings, roads, factories) and humans (e.g., sickness, death). To achieve effective protection and preparation in advance, the dissemination of early warnings to the public regarding impending disasters or notification of what is happening and then advising appropriate responses to the hazard can save lives and reduce possible damages. In *Making the Nation Safer*, the U.S. National Research Council calls for efforts to disseminate information about terrorism-related threats to the public "that is clear, placed in context, repeated, and authoritative" (U.S. National Research Council [NCR], 2002, p. 272). So, Section I is further divided into two units. Unit I explores how humans attend to stimuli and thus clarifies what constitutes an effective warning advisory. Damages from a terrorist attack or a natural disaster usually are limited to the scene of the attack/disaster itself, but such an act also influences an audience far beyond the victims. In turn, Unit II examines and quantifies how a disaster event may impair people's mindsets.

Unit I: From Threat Warning to Information Perception. This unit contains two chapters. Because awareness is a perceived pattern of physical energy, in Chapter I, we examine how to capture attention and thereby investigate how humans react to threat warnings. An effective warning alert must first capture people's attention, as well as be understandable and have a specific and unique meaning, which will enable it to motivate people to take appropriate protective actions.

In Chapter II, we investigate how threat warnings may affect public confidence. To quantify the dynamics of public perceptions of the information content of threat warnings, we present a theoretical model that details the nature of the warning frequency and its associated public response and confidence. Our analyses suggest that security advisory systems must take into account the rise and fall of public credibility and attention to warnings and then be designed accordingly. In our view, a dynamic and predictive model can offer great help.

Unit II: Psychosocial Aspect and Social Dynamics. Terrorism has often been conceptualized as a form of psychological warfare, and certainly terrorists have waged such campaigns through different means. Direct physical attacks not only cause physical damages to the target population but also transmit messages to people, beyond the immediate victims, that cause them to feel they are vulnerable as individuals, anywhere and anytime. Indirect psychological threats create fear and anxiety. For example, after the September 11, 2001 terrorist attack, terrorists often released threatening videos before important U.S. holidays (e.g., Independence Day, Thanksgiving, Christmas) to threaten the public with potential hazard attacks. If a threat involves the possible release of a biological agent, the targeted population experiences worry and fear. The characteristics of such threats, such as the uncertainty about whether or when the threat will become a real attack, the difficulty of determining the scope of the attack, and the possibility of contagion, may heighten the level of fear and anxiety, resulting in additional psychosocial damages. Moreover, responders may be influenced and concerned about their personal health. Such threat-induced psychological effects influence the effectiveness of response efforts. In three chapters, Unit II therefore focuses on ways to model psychological damages and their associated social dynamics.

In Chapter III, we explore the formation procedure and mechanism for psychosocial effects of disasters, as well as identify key components critical to their formation. When a large-scale disaster occurs suddenly, the affected populations, including both direct victims and those secondarily involved (e.g., first responders, caregivers, care providers, educators), are many in number. Therefore, there is an urgent need for real-time modeling that estimates the potential psychosocial impacts of a disaster during the disaster while also examining and recognizing how they affect response efforts (NRC, 2006). We target this research gap in Chapter IV, by modeling how people react to an unexpected disaster or threat and thus quantifying the potential psychosocial effects a person may experience. Specifically, we analyze the working procedure of brain components that are in charge of human memory and decision making. We then use differential dynamics to model how a person generates a response decision when facing a threat. With this approach, we can measure individual-level psychosocial consequences of a disaster event and project the range and severity of the possible psychosocial consequences during the course of the disaster.

The actions or anxiety moods of others may directly affect a person's attitude, especially when the situation is ambiguous and difficult to assess. For example, the observed actions undertaken by others may suggest the situation is more severe. Because fear and beliefs can be shared by people, when observable anxiety with somatic symptoms is initiated, it tends to be imitated by the wider population and might become a social trend. In Chapter V, we quantify disaster-induced possible collective anxiety. Analytic solutions project the range and severity of the possible psychosocial consequences of a disaster and suggest the extent to which these consequences influence effective behavioral responses. We also analyze possible targeting interventions and resource allocations and suggest methods for measuring the efficiency of such policy interventions.

In applying our proposed models to examine the potential psychosocial influence of an infectious disease like SARS, we demonstrate that the model's predictions are highly consistent with observed empirical data. Therefore, we consider this work a first step in developing mathematical models to understand the psychosocial effects of a disaster and how such impacts may affect social productivity. Planning for behavioral health responses in advance is urgent and necessary. In our view, dynamic systems theory and mathematical modeling can lead to important advancements in planning for such responses.

Section II: Improving Response Capability to Counter the Threat

In Section II, we turn our attention to capability building in response to any sudden emergency. A response usually involves at least two different levels of responders: incident commanders and frontline responders. Unit III in Section II therefore explores how incident commanders and frontline responders can quickly realize the occurrence of a sudden unexpected attack and thereby start a response immediately. For incident commanders, we discuss how to generate effective initial decisions, even with limited information and under time pressures. For frontline responders, specifically firefighters and health care workers, we consider how to generate incident-specific response operations to respond to a chemical or biological attack, including infectious disease. Unit IV addresses issues involved in enhancing the resilience of the critical infrastructure, including those associated with border patrol, cyber security, and financial stability.

Unit III: Forming Situation Awareness for First Decisions and Lifesaving. Disasters, whether natural or human-made, can strike at any time. However, forecasting such events is very hard. If 9/11 had been foreseeable, it would have been prevented. Therefore, disaster often hits us unawares, and the two central components of response are situation awareness and hazard identification. If an unexpected incident occurs suddenly, it does not automatically indicate that responders will be immediately aware of its occurrence. In some cases, awareness may be quick, such as in the case of an explosion, but in other situations, awareness may take longer. For example, if an incident involves the release of a biological agent or radiological materials, it might not be recognized for several days, until the people exposed develop symptoms and seek treatment in hospitals. If there are only a small number of cases, they may not even attract attention, and if the symptoms are common and look like a natural disease, it again may not prompt an investigation. Therefore, a time delay may exist between the time of the attack and the time the responders realize it.

The ability to detect the occurrence of an attack quickly is a critical factor for generating an effective response to any unexpected emergency situation. Existing research focuses on different response preparations, assuming that both the occurrence of an incident and the type of the incident are known. In reality, however, unless the incident generates obvious signs, such as an explosion accompanied by audible sounds and a visible blast, or eyewitnesses on the scene directly experience the event, awareness comes only some time later when signs or symptoms suggest what might have happened.

In Chapter VI, we explore the possibility of realizing that an event has occurred and ascertaining the nature and severity of the event. We consider emergencies caused by five types of incidents: explosives, chemical, biological, radiological, and nuclear (denoted ECBRN). By examining the characteristics of these five types of incidents, we identify possible markers that might improve awareness.

Because a reaction to any unexpected incident initiates only after awareness of its occurrence, in most cases, there is no time to think of a detailed strategic plan or analyze the state of the situation and the magnitude of the hazards involved, which already exist, before taking action. This set of urgent circumstances and time pressures indicates that generating an effective response is not an easy task, for either the incident commanders or the frontline responders. Chapter VII addresses capability issues related to incident commanders, whereas Chapters VIII and IX examine those related to frontline responders.

Because decisions made in the very first minutes and hours are critical to successful damage control, the prevention of casualties and structural losses, and, ultimately, the overall resolution of the disaster (Hendmerson, 2001; Pesik et al., 1999), in Chapter VII, we discuss factors that affect decision making during the early stage of an incident and explore how existing decision theories, such as classical rational expectation (or maximization) and behavioral decision making, are of limited use in a disaster. Today's threats may not match yesterday's preparations, so we identify heuristics to help incident commanders generate initial decisions. In addition, we present an incident command support system that incorporates onsite response and hospital command structures into a unified system, so that onsite responders (e.g., fire chief), EMS staff, and health care professionals can work together and communicate.

The incident command support system addresses several issues: What are the response directions? What does an incident commander need to do *now* to control the situation? What are the most import tasks? What are the capabilities required to perform these key tasks? Which task should be performed first? How much capability is available? How should these available resources and capabilities be allocated to make the most difference in controlling the situation?

When a disaster occurs, most response activities can be classified roughly into two branches, depending on location. One branch refers to activities implemented at the site of the incident, which we label onsite response, including pre-hospital rescue. The other branch refers to hospital responses. In this book, we consider two classes of first responders: firefighters and hospital staff.

When a disaster involves nuclear or radiological material, radiation contamination is easy to detect with relatively inexpensive equipment that can confirm a radioactive release. However, quickly identifying the release of toxic chemicals or recognizing an infectious disease outbreak is very difficult. Therefore, in Chapter VIII, we introduce a computer-supported chemical substance discovery system, which we imagine as a portable, digitized fire chief that can assist firefighters in identifying agents on the basis of only limited or observed symptoms and thereby generate an incident-specific response operation in a short time. Recognizing the type of agent involved has clear implications for both rescue actions and pre-hospital treatment. For example, it helps responders implement an appropriately specific plan that includes decontamination efforts. Without detailed laboratory and animal testing, response commanders would lose a basic method for receiving the information they need to make correct judgments and wise decisions. However, most laboratory testing requires special equipment, and the sample must be taken within two hours after the exposure—conditions that are not easy to meet, because the special equipment rarely is available in either fire departments or doctors' offices. If a release is covert, collecting a sample within two hours also may not be possible. Moreover, many chemical agents do not generate biological symptoms in the human body, so no simple blood test or other diagnostics can return results within the time required for effective intervention. Our effort in Chapter VIII attempts to generate a simple method for quick identification and response.

In Chapter IX, we model routine care functions in a hospital as a patient care system and show how a similar system could be used for real-time data analysis to provide an early alert for a potential disease outbreak, regardless of whether it is natural or human-made. In addition, if an incident occurs, the exposed or injured people rapidly seek care, which means they may not wait to find facilities designed by existing response plans. Thus, every health care facility must be able to organize an effective response quickly; speed is critical in life saving. A means to employ existing healthcare capacities quickly to generate a "dual-use" response infrastructure therefore becomes an urgent issue, because many of the capabilities required to respond to a large-scale chemical or biological attack also are required to respond to naturally occurring disease outbreaks. We introduce a hospital emergency support system to help hospital managers organize an effective response and discuss its application to the avian influenza virus and related health consequences to identify the effectiveness of several public health interventions that may be able to halt a pandemic in its earliest stages.

Finally, in Chapter X, we consider ways to channel evacuees quickly during an emergency situation. Although incident commanders and others assume that people will act rationally—hear a warning, realize the danger based on the warning, and leave when told to do so—more often, people do not do as emergency commanders expect. In an emergency, urgency creates a sense of uncertainty and forces people to act to escape from the danger. Congestion occurs. We therefore propose a mathematical model with algorithms to help incident commanders organize at-risk populations and evacuate them from potentially dangerous environments to safer areas during an emergency. Specifically, we present a computer support system, the *Emergency Evacuation Command System*, with a simulation. Compared with two benchmark cases (i.e., random self-evacuation and herding behavior), the proposed method can rescue people at risk and move them to safe area in a much shorter time and without congestion.

Unit IV: Enhancing the Resilience of Critical Infrastructure: Border Patrol, Cyber Security and Financial Stability. Since an incident area could be in cyber domain, financial zone, or other areas where critical assets are critical for national security, economic stability, and public safety, in this fourth unit, we focus on three major areas: border patrol, cyber security, and financial sustainability. Protecting critical infrastructure components, such as securing energy networks, gas pipelines, reservoirs, or the coastline, requires an effective and efficient inspection and patrol system. In Chapter XI, using border patrol management as an example, we consider the design of an effective and efficient inspection and patrol system that can help avoid an emergency similar to Northeast Blackout of 2003.

Chapter XII, which we entitle "Weaponizing the Internet and the YouTube War," discusses how terrorists can exploit the Internet as a propaganda tool and generate cyber fear. The modern Internet penetrates all levels of society, such that information flows continuously and seamlessly across political, ethnic, and religious divides. Although the Internet infrastructure officially consists of software and hardware, these elements form a global cyberspace that remains open to the world and available to anyone, anywhere, assuming they have sufficient capability to exploit those opportunities. Because of the global nature of cyberspace, it provides a new platform on which terrorists can wage battles. In this chapter, we model the Internet structure, identify its inherent vulnerabilities, and suggest response methods. We show that the inherent vulnerability of the Internet infrastructure itself permits malicious activities to flourish and perpetrators to remain anonymous. Managing threat and reducing vulnerability in cyberspace is a particularly complex challenge because of the number and range of users. We analyze the course of war in cyberspace and propose that the Internet should have the ability to implement self-awareness mechanisms to sense/identify harmful contents exhibiting in various computer codes.

Lastly, we turn our attention to the financial zone to explore an issue of how to maintain financial stability, a key component of homeland security. Certain non-terrorist events that reach catastrophic levels can have significant implications for homeland security, such as the modern financial crisis. If the International Monetary Fund is correct, the credit crisis that began in 2007 could turn out to be the most expensive financial crisis in history, measured in dollar terms of $945 billion in losses (Guha, 2008; Strauss, 2008). Under increasing strain, more and more companies are reaching distressed debt levels, averaging 10 defaults per month (Oakley, 2008). In Chapter XIII, we propose a new methodology to provide an early warning of financial distress and thus avoid collapse. We assert that simple models using limited information can capture the essential dynamics of an individual firm's credit risk. Existing conventional models share one fundamental and key assumption: the possible market outcomes follow known probability distributions which do not change over time. That is, if the variables of interest have probabilities, then these probabilities are known to modelers in advance. For example, suppose someone plans to build a model to describe a firm's operating performance and forecast its earning trend. Using this modeling assumption, he would specify that the present state of the firm's performance follows a single and known probability distribution. Giving this setting, the possible earning states at a given future date can be obtained as a calculable probability of each such future state's occurrence, conditional on the present state. Recognizing that no one has a perfect foresight or can fully pre-specify changes overtime, we argue that each company has its own characteristics, so its corresponding probability distribution of the variables of interest cannot be predetermined. In contrast to those conventional models, our proposed individual-level adaptive model can capture individual firm characteristics and determine the actual distribution(s) exhibited in the firm's own data. Using only two pieces of information about the firm, we generate strong predictions. An empirical study using real-world data illustrates the greater predictive power of the proposed model compared with current conventional economic models.

FEATURES AND MAJOR STRENGTHS

The novelty of this book lies in our mathematical treatments, which incorporate human cognitive theory and computer simulation into the emerging area of homeland security research. Specifically, the book:

- Establishes a theoretical foundation for developing effective emergency response mechanisms;
- Explores critical response capabilities and details how a set of dynamic models may be used against threats and to mitigate diseases;
- Incorporates cognitive and security theories with mathematical modeling to enhance response capabilities;
- Provides scientific backup for security policy planning and command, disaster mitigation and counterterrorism, and training; and
- Contains models, methods, and solution steps that are the foremost creative and innovative.

The book also features the following strengths:

- *Concrete matters.* This book focuses on problem solving, addressing *how* to perform each specific task. For example, it:
  - Presents anti-threat warning and information perception theory;
  - Offers a real-time model of public confidence in warning advisories;
  - Lays the foundation for a comprehensive theory of human and social behavior in emergency situations;
  - Presents a new approach to model collective anxiety using differential dynamics for the first time in social science;
  - Develops strategies and interventions for different levels of response forces - incident commanders and frontline responders - in recognizing and responding to unexpected biological, chemical and radiological threats; and
  - Establishes theoretical models and new approaches about
    - ➢ Emergency evacuation
    - ➢ Border patrol and securing coastline
    - ➢ Countering cyber threat
    - ➢ Early warning of finical crisis.

Modern threats are not the same as those for which societies have prepared in the past, so increasing our capability to generate effective, event-specific, and real-time response strategies is very important for both incident commanders and frontline responders. This book presents methods and step-by-step guidelines to achieve that goal.

- *Cutting-edge theories applied to practice.* The topics in the book cross different traditional disciplinary fields, including theories ranging from cognition to social psychology to decision making to disease control to economics to computer science to nonlinear dynamical system theory. The cutting-edge theories we develop are applied throughout the book. For example, we show that both rational expectation and behavioral economic decision theories are inappropriate in a setting that the decision maker has never encountered before, in which information is limited and unclear, and time is urgent.
- *Filling the gaps.* In each chapter, we identify existing issues or gaps, and propose (new) methods to address them. For example, little research in warning theory quantifies the impact of threat warnings on public confidence. Thus, in Unit I, we describe the process of human "attention" and explain the dynamics of public perceptions of threat information using differential dynamics. A mathematical model captures the effectiveness of warning advisories and corresponding public confidence levels, combined, for the first time, with cognitive science. In Unit II, we acknowledge extensive research that attempts to estimate the economic impacts and long-term psychological effects (i.e., PSDT) of a disaster, but to the best of our knowledge, no studies apply mathematical equations to study psychosocial effects or their impact on the effectiveness of public responses in terms of social productivity (Stein et al., 2004). Few published reports about the psychological impact of disease outbreaks adopt a survey approach or present summarized results at an aggregate level. Because individuals likely have different emotional and behavioral reactions to the same threat, survey results suggest only the level of importance and cannot account for how individual-level psychosocial damage develops, nor understand its underlying dynamic processes. Therefore, the modeling effort proposed herein offers a first step in developing mathematical models of the impacts of a threat on people's minds during the disaster. Complete modeling at both individual- and population-levels, as well as the shift from a statistical to a dynamic mathematical model to evaluate psychosocial concerns, enable us to understand how people dynamically respond to a disaster event, suggest more effective responses including resource allocations and targeting interventions, and help reduce the occurrence of long-term psychological damages.

Recognizing that no one has perfect knowledge or can predetermine future changes perfectly, we introduce approaches to generate effective decisions. Specifically, using the credit crisis as a test example, our proposed method sheds new light on a firm's risk evaluation, a task that has relied on conventional, aggregate-level models for decades.
- *Realistically limited information and resources.* Because limited resources and human cognition capabilities exist in reality, we present a set of capabilities-based processing models that can help responders generate response capabilities suitable for a wide range of threat and hazards. For example, in preparing to respond to terrorist attacks on a health care facility, the current approach recommends proactively educating health care providers about the clinical management of different type of injuries caused by bombings and biological, chemical, radiological, and nuclear incidents. Yet such education is expensive, and even if health care providers initially receive training to care for these ECBRN-related injuries, assuming that these incidents do not become a more frequent

and unfortunate reality, the education must be repeated regularly to ensure current knowledge and clinical competency. In addition, many EMS systems and hospitals lack the capacity to care for any patients beyond their usual volume. The costs of increasing these facilities' capacity in both EMS and hospital systems may be substantial. We instead propose a system to illustrate how existing hospital routine care functions might be integrated to generate rapid responses.

In addition, to help onsite responders identify chemical terrorism, we present a method that functions with only limited information. Furthermore, we examine how to generate an effective and efficient border patrol that can reduce and prevent escalating illegal crossings, even given limited resources.

Our hope is that the publication of this book will accelerate the spread of new ideas currently emerging in scientific literature. The book therefore features theoretical contributions and system developments that pertain to a more general topic: how to increase response capabilities to a wide range of unexpected emergencies. The clear explanations make the models and methods accessible, operational and implementable. It is intended to play three roles and serve three distinct audiences:

- A scientific text on modeling homeland security and disaster responses for academic researchers and scholars. This book provides valuable resources in the field of research into modeling human and social dynamical behavior, as well as state-of-the-art approaches to the new area of homeland security. It promotes the application of formal models in cognitive science and social science.
- A college textbook introducing the applications of mathematics and cognitive theory in the new field of homeland security and related fields for undergraduate seniors and graduate students.
- A handbook for policymakers, executives, and administrators at different levels of local, state, and federal government agencies all over the world who are involved in emergency response and management.

REFERENCES

Guha, K. (2008). IMF points to high cost of global credit crisis. *Financial Times*, *4*, April 7, 2008.

Hendmerson, D. A. (2001). The threat of bioterrorism and the spread of infectious diseases. *U.S. Congressional Hearing*, September 5, 2001.

Oakley, D. (2008). Distressed debt levels rise to five-year peak. *Financial Times*, *25*, April 8, 2008.

Pesik, N., Kein, M., & Rie Sampson, T. (1999). Do U.S. emergency medicine residency programs provide adequate training for bioterrorism? *Annals of Emergency Medicine*, *34*, 173-176.

Strauss, D. (2008). OECD predicts subprime losses to hit $420 billion. *Financial Times*, *4*, April 16, 2008.

U.S. Federal Emergency and Management Agency [FEMA] (2008). *National Response Framework*. Retrieved March 16, 2008, from http://www.fema.gov/NRF.

U.S. National Research Council [NRC] (2002). *Making the nation safer: The role of science and technology in countering terrorism*. Washington, DC: National Academies Press.

U.S. National Research Council [NRC] (2006). *Facing hazards and disasters: Understanding human dimensions*. Committee on Disaster Research in the Social Sciences: Future Challenges and Opportunities. Washington DC, US: National Academies Press.

World Health Organization [WHO] (2001a). Terrorism branded 'New disease' at Health Ministers meeting. *Press Release*, September 24, 2001. Retrieved March 2003, from http://www.paho.org/English/DPI/pr010924.html.

World Health Organization [WHO] (2001b). Countries need to plan effectively for 'Deliberate Infections'–WHO leader urges health ministers. Press Release, September 24, 2001. Retrieved March 2003, from http://www.paho.org/English/DPI/pr010924.html.

Acknowledgment

I would like to thank Professor Paul Davis of Rand Corporation and Pardee RAND Graduate School, who read the manuscript and wrote the Foreword for this book. Appreciation and gratitude is also due to three anonymous reviewers of this book for the valuable comments and suggestions.

Special thanks go to the publishing team at IGI Global, whose contributions throughout the whole process from inception of the initial idea to final publication have been invaluable. In particular to Lindsay Johnston and Kristin Klinger, whose enthusiasm motivated me to initially accept their invitation for taking on this project and to Rebecca Beistline, who continuously supported and kept the project on schedule.

Last but not least, I also would like to thank my parents and my husband. Without their unconditional support, love and encouragement, this book would not be possible.

Amy Wenxuan Ding, PhD
Chicago, Illinois, USA
August 2008

Introduction

OBJECTIVE

Entering the 21st Century, the world has experienced a sequence of major events, unlike anything before, that has promoted worldwide research into disaster responses in homeland security. The 9/11 terrorist attacks in the United States attracted international attention to the problem of countering terrorism and its broader security implications. The outbreak of severe acute respiratory syndrome (SARS) in 2003 and the subsequent emergence of another novel disease (i.e., bird flu epidemic) posed significant and ongoing hazards. In addition, naturally occurring geological hazards, such as the most destructive natural disaster, Hurricane Katrina in 2005, and the 2008 SiChuan killer earthquake in China, showed that generating effective incident responses is both urgent and important.

We also remain vulnerable to incidents involving industrial hazards, infrastructure failures, and financial crisis (HSC, 2007). For example, an estimated 50 million people across eight states in the United States and the Canadian province of Ontario were left without electrical power in August 2003 when a utility firm in Ohio (U.S.) experienced problems that induced a chain reaction of events, leading to power outages that lasted several days in some places. This incident, the "Northeast Blackout of 2003," cost roughly US$6 billion and caused at least 265 power plants to shut down (CNN, 2003; NYISO, 2004; Parks, 2003). The recent credit crunch offers another example; its resulting effect has spread from Wall Street to the broader economy. If the International Monetary Fund is correct, the resulting credit crash could be the most expensive in history, measured in dollar terms, at $945 billion (Guha, 2008; Strauss, 2008). Such non-terrorist events also can have significant implications for homeland security.

Severe events catalyze national pushes for homeland security research, which presents us with unique opportunities to identify and mitigate not only our own vulnerabilities but also a range of difficult decision problems for which there are no easy answers. This mission calls for a National Response Framework, which requires rapid assessments of emerging threats/incidents, taking actions to prevent and/or mitigate threats, ensuring safety, and recovering from incidents that occur (FEMA, 2008). As its inherent principle, such a framework attempts to save lives, mitigate suffering, and protect properties. The task is challenging because little information about homeland security research was published prior to 2000, and the learning curve has been very steep for all parties involved in developing programs to counter threats. However, revolutionary advances in the areas of computing capabilities, communications, remote sensing, and modeling for mission-system analysis now enable sharing and analysis of information, faster than ever before. It is imperative that such science and technological advances be harnessed to aid the incident/threat response and thereby reduce losses of life and property.

This book presents recent scientific research into modeling homeland security using advanced science and technology. It addresses critical issues involved in completing the "Universal Task List" for major events represented by the Homeland Security National Planning Scenarios (FEMA, 2008), as well as achieving specific capabilities that all levels of government should possess to respond effectively to threats or incidents. These issues include the inherent difficulties of designing effective threat warning advisories, quantifying public reactions to and confidence in warning advisories, assessing psychosocial impacts of disasters, quickly realizing sudden and unexpected events and ascertaining their nature and severity, the vital need to identify the potential involvement of HazMat materials and surveillance reactions, and the critical importance of first decisions in achieving successful disaster prevention and/or mitigation.

DEFINITION

The modern threats we face include actual or potential emergencies or all-hazard events that range from accidents and natural disasters to actual or potential terrorist attacks. As defined by the White House (HSC, 2007), homeland security is the concerted effort to prevent attacks, reduce vulnerability to terrorism, and minimize the damages and recover from attacks that occur. Part of the "minimize the damage" component entails the need for effective responses to damages or catastrophes. The term "response" is defined as immediate actions to save lives, protect property and the environment, and meet basic human needs.

In this context, we define a *disaster* as an unexpected and sudden occurrence that threatens a society, causes human suffering, or damages goods such as buildings, communication systems, infrastructures, living environments, and so on. According to this definition, society, humans, and goods are affected entities, and the force behind the occurrence is the causer or source of the disaster. The causer can be human-made or natural.

If an incident occurs, a force or power by the causer acts on the affected entities and produces an effect, namely, the disaster. When the causer activates this force, two results may occur. First, the affected entities may suffer physical and/or chemical changes due to the power of the causer, such that their physical structures or functions get damaged—for example, property damage or physical casualties. Second, the causer might not create any direct physical damage but instead cause other consequences, such as psychosocial effects. Therefore, the effect of an incident involves a dual role: causing directly visible physical damages and indirectly threatening people's mindsets (i.e., a threat). Because of the dual role, the resulting disaster area may span physical areas, such as the economic or geographic area declared to be in a state of emergency by proclamation of a governor (or resolution of the legislature), an area in the cyber domain (particularly the Internet) or the financial zone, and the indirect physical area, such as people's mindsets or psychosocial effects. When assessing disaster promulgation, we therefore need to consider both the direct physical damage and indirect psychosocial effects.

The terms "threat," "incident," and "disaster" are used interchangeably in this book.

THE PROCEDURE OF A RESPONSE

The National Response Framework has established a foundation for how the nation should conduct incident responses (FEMA, 2008). The entire operation procedure of a response, as shown in Figure 0.1, includes actions ranging from initial notification about an incident to preparation of the final disaster after-action report.

The procedure follows eight basic steps:

1. **Notification.** When an incident occurs, one of local responders, such as the local police, fire fighters, emergency medical services, public health and medical providers, emergency management, environmental response professionals, and others in the community, arrives on scene and reports the event. The local emergency operation center is activated.

2. **Report to state and local governments.** The local government reports to the state governor, who activates the state's emergency plan and ensures that all appropriate state and local actions have been taken. The state and local governments always take the lead in response and recovery. During response, they organize and integrate their capabilities and resources to protect the public and mitigate the incident. If a state anticipates that its resources are insufficient, the governor can request assistance from the federal government and/or other states.

3. **Governor's request for a Presidential emergency or major disaster declaration.** A request is sent to the FEMA (Federal Emergency Management Agency) regional office. The FEMA regional administrator evaluates the damage and requirements for federal assistance and makes a recommendation to the FEMA Administrator. The FEMA Administrator, acting through the Secretary of Homeland Security, recommends a course of actions to the President.

4. **Presidential declaration.** Concurrent with a Presidential declaration of a major disaster or emergency, a joint disaster field office is established, which operates 24 hours per day, as needed, or by a schedule sufficient to sustain federal operations.

5. **Activation response teams and other resources.** The emergency response team (ERT) begins its operations and mission assignments. The ERT is the principal interagency group that supports the disaster field office in coordinating the overall federal disaster operation.

6. **Implementation of emergency support functions (ESFs).** Emergency support functions act quickly to determine the impact of the disaster on their own capabilities and to identify, mobilize, and deploy resources to support response activities in the affected area.

7. **Execute recovery operations.** After immediate response missions and lifesaving activities conclude, emergency teams are demobilized, and the emphasis shifts from response to recovery operations. The Human Services and Services Support branches of the ERT assess recovery needs and relevant timeframes for program delivery. They coordinate assistance programs to help individuals, families, and businesses meet basic needs and return to self-sufficiency.

8. **After-action report.** Following a disaster, the field office submits an after-action report to the headquarters of the Department of Homeland Security (DHS), detailing any problems encountered, key issues affecting federal performance, and lessons learned.

The emergency response team (ERT) contains four sections: operations, emergency management, logistics, and administration sections (see Figure 0.2).

Operations section. This section provides the central coordination point among federal and state agencies and voluntary organizations that provide response operations and manage the activities of various emergency teams. It consists of four branches: Emergency Services, Human Services, Services & Support, and Communications. As Figure 0.2 shows, the 15 emergency support functions are organized functionally within each branch to provide a coordinated approach and ensure the seamless delivery of assistance to disaster survivors and the affected state.

Emergency management section. This section performs tasks such as issuing mission assignments and collecting, processing, analyzing, and disseminating information about disaster operations to support planning and decision making at both the field operations and headquarters levels.

Logistics section. This section plans, organizes, and directs logistics operations, including control and accountability for supplies and equipment; resource ordering; delivery of supplies, equipment, and services to the disaster field office and other field locations; resource tracking, facility location, set-up, space management, building services, and general facility operations; transportation coordination; administrative services such as mail management and reproduction; and customer assistance.

Administration section. Finally, this section is responsible for personnel functions and employee services. Personnel functions cover disaster reservist deployment, obtaining local hires, arranging billeting, and processing payroll. Employee services include providing for emergency response team personnel health and safety, overseeing access to medical services, and ensuring the security of personnel, facilities, and assets.

THE EMERGENCY SUPPORT FUNCTIONS (ESF)

To generate effective responses, the number, type, and sources of resources must capable of expanding rapidly to meet the needs associated with a given incident. Therefore, response actions are implemented according to emergency support functions (ESFs)—that is, functions that must be performed to respond successfully to any emergency or disaster. The framework contains 15 ESFs, each of which is headed by

Figure 0.1. How the nation conducts all-hazards responses (Source: FEMA, 2008)

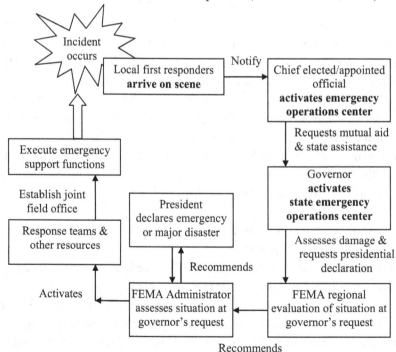

Figure 0.2. The detailed response organization

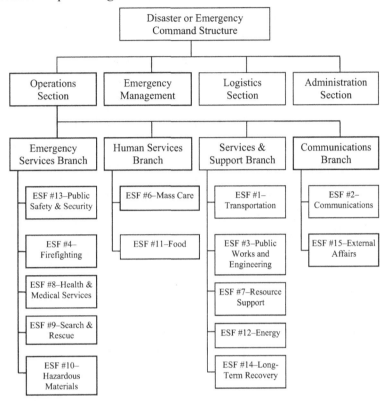

a primary agency designated on the basis of its authorities, resources, and capabilities in the particular functional area. Table 0.1 displays the designation matrix of the ESFs by primary agencies.

In a disaster or emergency, the DHS issues a mission assignment to give a primary agency responsibility for the necessary work to be performed on a reimbursable basis. When an ESF is activated in response to an incident, the primary department is responsible for:

1. Providing staff for the operation functions.
2. Activating and sub-tasking support departments.
3. Working with appropriate private sector organizations to maximize the use of all available resources.
4. Supporting and keeping other ESFs and organizational elements informed of ESF operational priorities and activities.
5. Executing contracts and procuring goods and services as needed.
6. Ensuring financial and property accountability for ESF activities.
7. Conducting planning sessions during non-emergency periods for the purpose of developing policy, plans, and procedures for coordinating the state-level response to a disaster with respect to that particular ESF.
8. Coordinating the development of an ESF that governs the functions of the various organizations assigned to that ESF during activation.

Table 0.1. Emergency support function designation matrix (FEMA, 2008)

ESF / Agency	Transportation	Communications	Public Works and Engineering	Firefighting	Emergency Management	Mass Care	Resources Support	Health and Medical Services	Search and Rescue	Hazardous Materials	Agriculture & Natural Resources	Energy	Public Safety & Security	Long-Term Community Recovery	External Affair
USDA				P							P			P	
DOD			P						P						
DOE												P			
HHS								P							
DHS		P	P		P	P	P		P					P	P
DOT	P														
ARC						P									
EPA										P					
GSA							P								
DOI									P						
DOJ													P		
HUD														P	
SBA														P	

Notes: P = Primary agency, responsible for coordination of the ESF.
USDA = U.S. Department of Agriculture
DOD = U.S. Department of Defense
DOE = U.S. Department of Energy
HHS = U.S. Department of Health and Human Services
DHS = U.S. Department of Homeland Security
DOT = U.S. Department of Transportation
ARC = The Arc
EPA = U.S. Environment and Protection Agency
GSA = U.S. General Services Administration
DOI = U.S. Department of the Interior
DOJ = U.S. Department of Justice
HUD = U.S. Department of Housing and Urban Development
SBA = Small Business Administration

9. During emergency activation, coordinating the flow of messages into and out of the ESF group, providing direction and control for the ESF group, and coordinating the activities of that ESF with the activities of other ESF groups.

10. Compiling documentation relative to the ESF's groups' activities during the emergency.

Of these 15 ESFs, the fifth (Emergency Management) is responsible for supporting the overall activities of the federal government for domestic incident management, from hazard mitigation and preparedness to response and recovery. Thus, this function is listed separately from the other 14 ESFs (see Figure 0.2), which can be grouped under the operation section of the emergency response team (ERT). On the basis of their defining roles and responsibilities in disaster or emergency response operation, these 14

ESFs further may be classified into four categories: emergency services, human services, services and support, and communications. A short description of each function appears next.

Emergency Services Branch. The core operations for disaster control and rescue, this area provides five emergency supports functions that are essential to responding to incidents such as explosions (ESF#4), infectious diseases or bioterrorism (ESF#8), and chemical, radiological, and/or nuclear incidents (ESF#10). In addition, ESF#9 and ESF#13 pertain to rescues and public safety.

ESF#4–Firefighting. Support for the detection and suppression of wildland, rural, and urban fires resulting from or occurring coincidentally with an incident that requires a coordinated federal response for assistance.

ESF#8–Public Health & Medical. Health surveillance and assessment of public health/medical needs, including the medical needs of members of the "at risk" or "special needs" population described in the pandemic and all-hazards preparedness act, as well as behavioral health needs (i.e., both mental health and substance abuse considerations) for victims and response workers.

ESF#9–Search & Rescue. Specialized lifesaving assistance (structure collapse search and rescue, waterborne search and rescue, inland/wilderness search and rescue, aeronautical search and rescue) when activated for incidents or potential incidents requiring a coordinated federal response.

ESF#10–Hazardous Materials. Federal support in response to an actual or potential discharge and/or uncontrolled release of oil or hazardous materials; for a chemical, biological, or radiological weapons of mass destruction incident, provides technical specialist(s) to offer scientific and technical expertise.

ESF#13–Public Safety and Security. Supports incident management planning activities and preincident actions required to mitigate threats and hazards. Identifies the need to analyze other potential factors (e.g., modeling and forecasting crowd size, impact of weather, other conditions) that may affect resource allocations and requisite actions affecting public safety and security. Provides basic law enforcement assistance to federal, state, tribal, and local agencies during incidents. Provides expertise and coordination for security planning efforts and technical assessments, including vulnerability assessments, risk analyses, and surveillance.

Human Service Branch. The area that provides services in the post-incident recovery phase consists of two ESFs.

ESF#6–Mass Care. Disaster services to help disaster victims, including shelters, emergency first aid, bulk distribution of emergency items, special needs populations, and housing assistance.

ESF#11–Agriculture & Natural Resources. Controls and eradicates (as appropriate) any outbreak of a highly contagious or economically devastating animal/zoonotic (i.e., transmitted between animals and people) disease or outbreak of an economically devastating plant pest or disease. Ensures the safety and security of the commercial food supply, provides for the safety and well-being of household pets during an emergency response or evacuation situation, and offers nutrition assistance.

Services and Support Branch. Through its five ESFs, this area provides management services in the post-incident response and recovery phases.

ESF#1–Transportation. Supports the management of transportation systems and infrastructure during domestic threats or in response to incidents. Carries out U.S. Department of Transportation's statutory responsibilities, including regulating transportation, managing national airspace, and ensuring the safety and security of the national transportation system.

ESF#3–Public Works & Engineering. Provides infrastructure protection and emergency repair, executes emergency contract support for life-saving and life-sustaining services, and provides engineering services and construction management.

ESF#7–Resource Support. Comprehensive national disaster logistics planning, management, and sustainment capability that meets the needs of disaster victims and responders.

ESF#12–Energy. Collects, evaluates, and shares information about energy system damage and estimations of the impact of energy system outages within affected areas, as well as facilitates the restoration of damaged energy systems and components.

ESF#14–Long-Term Community Recovery. Conducts social and economic community impact assessments, provides analyses and reviews of mitigation program implementation, and offers long-term community recovery assistance to states, tribes, local governments, and the private sector.

Communications Branch. To operate all communications services for control centers and operations forces during the incident and furnish information to the public, this area relies on two ESFs.

ESF#2–Communications. National security and emergency preparedness communications and information technology services, cyber security issues that result from or occur in conjunction with incidents, and oversight of communications within the federal incident management and response structure.

ESF#15–External affairs. Ensures that sufficient federal assets are deployed to the field during incidents. Missions include:
- Design emergency alert system (EAS) to send important emergency information quickly to the nation using radio, television, and cable systems.
- Design mobile emergency response support to provide mobile telecommunications, operations support, life support, and power generation assets for the onsite management of all hazard activities.
- Design national preparedness network capable of reaching large portions of the public in an impacted area with survival and recovery information before, during, and after catastrophic events.

- When commercial broadcast is impaired in an area, set up recovery radio support on an hourly basis through a pool feed.

KEY TASKS IN RESPONSE ACTIONS

During a response, ESFs provide a critical mechanism to coordinate functional capabilities and resources provided by federal departments and agencies, along with certain private-sector and nongovernmental organizations. The ESFs are assigned to different federal departments or agencies and maintained by the federal government. Hence, the ESFs are activated and executed when the state governor's request is granted and the joint field office is established. During the initial stage, when local first responders notify local and state governments of the occurrence of an incident, the ESFs are not immediately activated.

According to the National Response Framework (FEMA, 2008), incidents should be handled at the lowest jurisdictional level (i.e., local responders). The federal government provides supplemental assistance when the consequences of a disaster *exceed* state and local capabilities. In such a setting, local and state responders must have their own response functions to control the incident before waiting for the arrival of the federal ESFs. When responding to an incident that involves the use of toxic chemicals, biological agents, or radiological materials, local response capabilities are critical in both emergency response and disaster control.

Yet realizing the occurrence of an incident represents another critical issue. The response procedure illustrated in Figure 0.1 implies that local responders are immediately aware of the incident when it occurs, though in reality, an unexpected incident may occur suddenly, in which case local responders may not be immediately aware of the occurrence. For example, if an incident involves the release of a radiological material or biological agent, it must be unexpected and occur suddenly and covertly, or a deterrent action would have been taken in advance to prevent it. Furthermore, the occurrence might not be recognized for several days, that is, until the people exposed develop symptoms and seek treatment in hospitals. If the cluster of affected cases is small, it may not even attract attention. Alternatively, if the symptoms are common and look like a natural disease, the incident may not prompt an investigation. Therefore, a time delay may exist between the time of the incident and the time the responders realize it. One of the most serious considerations for local emergency responders therefore must be how to realize the occurrence of a sudden, unexpected incident quickly and thereby start an immediate response.

In this sense, the real response procedure is far more complex than the one displayed in Figure 0.1. In this monograph, we explore key tasks related to the six phases of effective response: threat warning and communications, understanding the psychology of threat and the readiness to act, realizing incident occurrence, gaining situation awareness, frontline response, and unity of effort through unified command. The relationship among these key tasks, emergency support functions (ESFs), and the book chapters is depicted in Figure 0.3.

Threat warning and communications. To achieve effective protection and preparation in advance, early warnings must be disseminated to the public about impending threats or current situations, as well as advice about appropriate responses to the hazard, which can save lives and reduce possible damages. Information can be transmitted instantly via the Internet and the 24/7 news channels. Although timely information is valuable, it also can be overwhelming. Therefore, Chapters I and II address basic questions about which factors characterize the effectiveness of a warning alert and why knowledge of threat warnings, public perceptions, and reactions is important. Without effective communication, the bias toward action will be ineffective at best, and perilous at worst.

Figure 0.3. Managing an incident/disaster

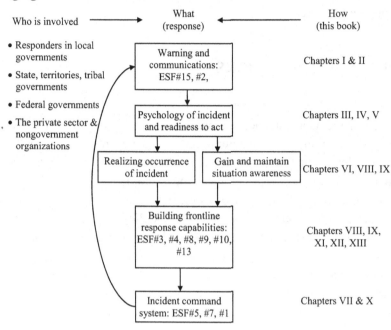

Well-developed public information, education strategies, and communication plans help ensure that life-saving measures, evacuation routes, threat and alert systems, and other public safety information get coordinated and communicated to numerous diverse audiences in a consistent, accessible, and timely manner. Chapters I and II pertain to ESF#15 and ESF#2.

Psychology of incident and readiness to act. Threat information can impair people because it works directly on human mindsets. The resulting effect can produce either negative or positive impacts. In a war situation, for example, the two sides often conduct media campaigns or operations before actual military combat begins. They convey selected information and indicators to their counterparts and attempt to influence people's emotions, consciousness, and attitudes. These operations further attempt to deter and threaten adversaries and obtain the support of friendly or neutral target audiences. After the September 11 terrorist attack, terrorists often released threatening videos before important U.S. holidays (e.g., Independence Day, Thanksgiving, Christmas) to threaten the public with potential hazard attacks. If a threat involves the possible release of a biological agent, the targeted population experiences worry and fear. The characteristics of such threats, such as uncertainty about whether or when the threat will become a real attack, the difficulty of determining the scope of the attack, and the possibility of contagion, may heighten the level of fear and anxiety, resulting in additional psychosocial damages. Moreover, responders may be influenced and concerned about their personal health. Such threat-induced psychological effects influence the effectiveness of response efforts. In Chapters III, IV, and V, we analyze the working procedure of brain components that are in charge of human memory and decision making. We then use differential dynamics to explore how people react to a threat or disaster event.

Because beliefs and/or fear can be shared, the actions or moods of others may directly affect a person's attitude, especially when the situation is ambiguous and difficult to assess. In addition, threat information can be either amplified or filtered through its circulation. Amplified information increases the atmosphere of anxiety and fear, which may create a fertile ground for rumors and misconceptions, whereas filtered or attenuated information may lower people's guards, perhaps resulting in unnecessary damages. We quantify possible collective behavior to measure how a population may be affected and how such influence challenges the effects of response. Chapters III, IV, and V relate to ESF#6 and ESF#14.

Realizing incident occurrence. If an unexpected incident occurs suddenly, the event does not automatically indicate that responders are immediately aware of the occurrence. The ability to detect the occurrence of an attack quickly is a critical factor for generating an effective response to any unexpected emergency situation. Existing research focuses on different response preparations, assuming that both the occurrence of an incident and its type are known. In reality however, unless the incident generates obvious signs, such as an explosion accompanied by audible sounds and a visible blast, or eyewitnesses on the scene directly experience the event, awareness comes only some time later, when signs or symptoms suggest what might have happened. Therefore, a time delay may exist between the time of the incident and the time the responders realize it. In Chapter VI, we explore the question of when it is possible to realize an event has occurred and how to ascertain the nature and severity of the event. On the basis of the DHS's classification of 15 planning scenarios, we consider emergencies caused by five types of incidents: explosives, chemical, biological, radiological, and nuclear (denoted ECBRN). We examine the characteristics of these five types of incidents and identify possible markers that might improve awareness. Because the timeframe for response is also key to whether control is successful, we examine the dynamics and timeline for each type of incident and suggest ways to help recognize or detect it and thus reduce the time delay of awareness.

Gaining situation awareness. For an effective response, responders must continuously monitor events, refine their ability to access the situation, and rapidly provide accurate and accessible information to decision makers. Chapters VI, VIII, and IX address situation assessments regarding five type of incidents: explosion, chemical, biological (including infectious disease), radiological, and nuclear. Chapter VII contains a more general discussion of situation assessments, including determining the event time, place, witnesses, and the affected geographical area; recognizing how many people are threatened, affected, exposed, injured, or dead; and identifying whether critical infrastructures have been affected, such as power, water supplies, sanitation, telecommunications, or transportation.

Frontline response. Frontline responders normally include personnel on the scene of an incident, or first responders, such as law enforcement, firefighters, emergency medical services, and so on. These people execute response strategies and perform associated tasks. Usually, when a disaster occurs, the response activities or tasks take place at the incident site or somewhere near it, though some disasters, such as infectious disease outbreaks or biological attacks, may move the battleground to hospitals or other sites distant from the event source because of the delayed awareness. Therefore, response activities may differ depending on the location of the battle. In Chapter VIII, we consider how to increase the capability to respond to chemical terrorism. Specifically, we introduce a computer-supported chemical substance discovery system—like a portable, digitized fire chief—that can assist firefighters in their response to incidents involving hazard materials and thereby generate an incident-specific response operation under severe time pressures. Chapter IX presents a hospital emergency support system that integrates existing health care routine functions within a real-time data analysis and thus suggests early alerts for potential disease outbreaks, regardless of whether it is natural or human-made. In addition, if an incident occurs, the exposed or injured people rapidly seek care, which means they may not wait to find facilities designed by existing response plans. Thus, every health care facility must be able to organize an effective response quickly; speed is critical in saving lives. A means to employ existing health care capacities quickly to generate a "dual-use" response infrastructure therefore becomes an urgent issue, because many of the capabilities required to respond to a large-scale chemical or biological attack also are required to respond to naturally occurring disease outbreaks. The proposed hospital emergency support system supports this purpose.

As mentioned previously, an incident area could be in cyber domain, financial zone, or other area. In Chapter XI, using border patrol as an example, we consider the design of an effective and efficient inspection and patrol system that can help avoid an emergency similar to Northeast Blackout of 2003. Terrorists also seek sanctuary in the cyber domain, particularly the Internet, because of its geographically unbounded and largely unconstrained space, and use it to create and disseminate propaganda, recruit new members, raise funds, and plan operations. The Internet thus has become a training ground on which terrorists acquire instruction, once possible only through physical training camps, and a weapon to generate cyber fear.

In Chapter XII, we examine the role of the Internet as a battlefield and analyze the course of war in cyberspace. We model the Internet structure, identify its inherent vulnerabilities, and suggest response methods. The inherent vulnerability of the Internet infrastructure permits malicious activities to flourish and perpetrators to remain anonymous. Therefore, we propose that the Internet should have the ability to implement self-awareness mechanisms that sense and identify harmful contents exhibited in various computer codes.

Finally, we turn our attention to the financial zone to explore ways to maintain financial stability, a key component of homeland security. In Chapter XIII, we explore how to use an individual firm's data to provide early warnings of financial distress and thus avoid collapse. Specifically, we assert that simple models using limited information can capture the essential dynamics of an individual firm's credit risk. These chapters relate to emergency support functions #3, #4, #8, #9, #10, and #13.

Unity of effort through a unified command. The efficiency and effectiveness of response operations requires a unified command system that coordinates different levels of response activities. As the incident unfolds, the on-scene incident commander must develop and update an incident action plan, revising courses of actions based on changing circumstances. Because the incident commander is the individual responsible for all response activities, including developing strategies and tactics and ordering and releasing resources, his or her decisions are critical. A reaction to any unexpected incident initiates only after awareness of its occurrence, so in most cases, the incident commander lacks time to think of a detailed strategic plan or analyze the state of the situation and the magnitude of the hazards involved, which already exist, before taking action. This set of urgent circumstances and time pressures indicates that generating an effective decision is not an easy task for the incident commander. Modern threats also may not match yesterday's preparations, so in Chapter VII, we discuss factors that affect decision making during the early stages of an incident. We identify heuristics to help incident commanders generate initial decisions and present an incident command support system that incorporates onsite response and hospital command structures into a unified system, so that onsite responders (e.g., fire chief), EMS staff, and health care professionals can work together and communicate.

The incident command support system thus addresses several issues: What are the response directions? What does an incident commander need to do *now* to control the situation? What are the most import tasks? What are the capabilities required to perform these key tasks? Which tasks should be performed first? How much capability is available? How should these available resources and capabilities be allocated to make the best differences in controlling the situation?

In Chapter X, we also consider ways to channel crowd population quickly during an emergency situation. Although incident commanders and others assume that people will act rationally—hear a warning, realize the danger based on the warning, and leave when told to do so—more often, people do not do as emergency commanders expect. In an emergency, urgency creates a sense of uncertainty and forces people to act to escape from the danger. Congestion normally occurs. We present a computer support system, the Emergency Evacuation Command System, to help incident commanders organize at-risk populations and evacuate them from potentially dangerous environments to safer areas during an emergency. These two chapters relate to emergency support functions # 5, #7, and #1.

The following chapters address these key tasks one by one. We show how advances in science and technology can help deploy key tasks. Topics involved in these tasks cross traditional disciplinary fields, including computational and social sciences. Thus, the book title refers to social computing in homeland security. From an information-processing perspective in the homeland security research area, social computing pertains to disaster informatics and its impact on different social entities, including people and physical properties. The technical infrastructure of social computing encompasses communication, the Internet, and all different types of computing software and systems. Many emergency support functions rely on information technology functions, such as direction and control, warning and communication, disaster analysis and assessment, and so on. Thus, information technology has significant mutual importance for successful threat promulgation and response.

REFERENCES

CNN (2003). *Major power outage hits New York, other large cities*. Retrieved August 14, 2003, from http://www.cnn.com/2003/US/08/14/power.outage/.

Guha, K. (2008). IMF points to high cost of global credit crisis. *Financial Times, 4*, April 7, 2008.

New York Independent System Operator [NYISO] (2004). NYISO interim report on the August 14, 2003 blackout. Retrieved January 15, 2004, from http://www.hks.harvard.edu/hepg/Papers/NYISO.blackout.report.8.Jan.04.pdf

Parks, B. (2003). Transforming the grid to revolutionize electric power in North America. U.S. Department of Energy. In *Proceedings of Edison Electric Institute's Fall 2003 Transmission, Distribution and Metering Conference*, October 13, 2003.

Strauss, D. (2008). OECD predicts subprime losses to hit $420 billion. *Financial Times*, April 16, 2008.

U.S. Federal Emergency and Management Agency [FEMA] (2008). *National Response Framework*. Retrieved March 16, 2008, from http://www.fema.gov/NRF.

U.S. Homeland Security Council [HSC] (2007). *National Strategy for Homeland Security*. Washington DC: Homeland Security Council.

Section I
Threat Warning and Psychological Warfare

Unit I
From Threat Warning to Information Perception and Public Response

INTRODUCTION

Human history indicates that human survival depends on the ability to mount a successful response to threats. A disaster—whether terrorism like the 9/11 attack in 2001 or a natural event like Hurricane Katrina in 2005—can cause tremendous damage to both physical entities (e.g., buildings, roads, factories) and humans (e.g., sickness, death). To achieve effective protection and preparation in advance, the dissemination of early warnings to the public regarding impending disasters or notification of what is happening, and advising appropriate responses to the hazard can save lives and reduce possible damages. In *Making the Nation Safer*, the U.S. National Research Council called for efforts to disseminate information about terrorism-related threats to the public "that is clear, placed in context, repeated, and authoritative" (U.S. National Research Council [NCR], 2002, p. 272).

Several studies explore various factors that are important for risk-related communication process (Fischhoff, 2003; Guttelling & Wiegman, 1996; Kasperson & Stallen, 1991; Mileti et al., 2003; Ropeik & Slovic, 2003). Although this literature stream provides a strong foundation for terrorism-related risk communications, many questions remain: What factors characterize the effectiveness of a warning alert? If the success of a warning is measured by the actions people take, how does warning frequency affect public response? Is it true that the more often warnings are heard, the more likely they are to be believed and acted upon? To address these questions and understand what constitutes an effective warning advisory, we begin by exploring the process of human attention to stimuli. An effective warning alert should first capture people's attention, be understandable, and have a specific and unique meaning, which will enable it to motivate people to take appropriate protective actions. We present a theoretical model to explore the dynamics of public perception of the information content of anti-threat warnings in order to uncover the nature of warning frequency and its associated public response and confidence. Our analyses suggest that security advisory systems must take into account the rise and fall of public credibility and attention to warnings and be designed accordingly. In our view, a dynamic and predictive model can offer great help.

REFERENCES

Fischhoff, B. (2003). Assessing and communicating the risks of terrorism. In *Science and technology in a vulnerable world* (pp. 51-64). American Association for the Advancement of Science. MA: Washington, DC.

Guttelling, J. M. & Wiegman, O. (1996). *Exploring risk communication.* Dordrecht: Klewer Academic Publishers.

Kasperson, R., & Stallen, P. J. M. (1991). *Communication risk to the public: International perspectives.* Boston: Klewer.

Mileti, D. S. Sorensen, J., Vogt, B., & Sutton, J. (2003). *Warning America. Report to the Federal Emergency Management Agency.* Boulder, CO: National Hazards Center, Institute of Behavioral Science, University of Colorado.

Ropeik, D. & Slovic, P. (2003). Risk communication: A neglected tool in protecting public health. *Risk in Perspective*, 11(2), Harvard Center for Risk Communication, Cambridge, MA.

U.S. National Research Council [NRC] (2002). *Making the nation safer: The role of science and technology in countering terrorism.* Washington, DC: National Academies Press.

Chapter I
Attention Capture and Effective Warning

INTRODUCTION

The term "attention" in psychology is defined as (1) the act or state of attending, especially by applying the mind to an object of sense or thought, and (2) a condition of readiness for such attention (Attention, 2007).

Drawing on research carried out for decades in psychology that explores the human attention mechanism to understand a variety of attentional phenomena, such as attention to dimensions and objects, selective listening, task switching, and so forth (e.g., Bundersen, 1990; Heinke & Humphreys, 2003; Logan, 2002; Luce, 1963; Ratcliff, 1978; Ratcliff et al. 1999; Reeves & Sperling, 1986; Shepard, 1957; Shih & Sperling 2002), we examine how attention might be captured and thus identify factors that characterize the effectiveness of a warning advisory. In this context, we use attention to describe awareness, a concentration of the mind on a single object, and a state of consciousness characterized by such concentration and the capacity to maintain selective concentration. Asking a person to pay attention to something implies that the person is aware of this "something" first, and then concentrates his or her mind on it. Therefore, we begin our discussion by defining awareness in this section.

AWARENESS AS A PERCEIVED PATTERN OF PHYSICAL ENERGY

Nothing exists except atoms and empty space: everything else is opinion.
— Democritus (ca. 400 BC)

The nature of awareness is a process in which the body functions as a sensory organism filled with receptors that perceive everything outside the body. Everything outside the body is the environment, which itself represents a pattern of physical energies that directly affect receptors (Landauer, 1991; Clare & Halligan, 2006; Styles, 2006). For example, the visual environment provides a changing pattern of radiant energies that act on the retina. A sound is a changing pattern of vibrations transmitted to auditory receptors.

Awareness varies in its sensory quality and intensity. Sensory quality measures the degree to which a person can discriminate an outside stimulus. For example, a person sees a red box and can determine whether the red is bright; another person feels pain in a finger and can discriminate that pain as sharp. Thus, humans possess different forms and ranges of sensitivity that match biologically significant variations in environmental energies. Even when the quality is constant, a pain experience may be heavy or light. Therefore, sensory intensity indicates the degree to which a stimulus signal is strong or weak. Empirical observations and existing evidence from neurophysiology suggest that any momentary quality of awareness involves the activity of nerve fibers at a specific locus in the material brain (Boring, 1933; Clare & Halligan, 2006). That is, human brains sense qualitative differences in structure or function when they receive a stimulus and can feel the corresponding energy changes, which enables them to react appropriately. These nerve signals move to the central nervous system and brain cortex, where (1) a concept of "knowing" about the occurrence of a stimulus forms, (2) a difference in excitation occurs, or (3) a difference emerges on which discriminatory behavior can be established.

Nervous systems are limited in their qualitative and intensive coverage of physical energies that abound in the environment. That is, all sensory systems in people's body have some type of thresholds for perceiving or sensing a stimulus. For a change in the environment to be perceived, the incremental increase or decrease in physical energy of the target environment, applied to the receptors of the body, must be greater than a certain minimal threshold. For example, if the light illumination of a room constantly varies by small amount, these changes may not be noticed by an occupant.

Awareness thus reflects a reaction of people's bodies; specifically, the receptors under the body's surface react to various forms of energies in its external and internal environments. If attention implies or includes awareness, can one's attention be captured?

ATTENTION CAPTURE

Using human visual perception as an example, we illustrate how attention is captured. In our discussion, we do not consider, however, how each nerve tissue or materials in the fiber may be excited by a stimulus.

The human eye is designed such that light waves fall on the retina, where their energy is translated into electrical form, presumably by means of photochemical substances in the rods and cones. Impulses generated in this manner in the receptors appear in electroretinograms. The interaction between a photon of light and the retina causes the molecule to go through isomerization, which then changes the membrane potential of the rod or cone. The rods or cones excite the bipolar cells, which in turn excite the ganglion cells. After the ganglion cells are excited, the electrical signals travel over the optic nerve to the optic chiasm. Through a series of transmissions, as the signal is transmitted to the upper layer of cortex, the information from both eyes mixes to create a binocular vision. Therefore, any object in the environment or an outside signal perceived by a vision system can be considered light waves with energy. These light waves are converted into electrical signals that cause the brain cortex to generate consciousness and make appropriate judgments or reactions (see Figure 1.1).

Similarly, theories of hearing (e.g., place theory, rate theory) suggest that an auditory message comes down to patterns of impulses in the auditory cortex (Beament, 2003). The frequency of these energy changes excites nerve fibers in auditory system, which senses signals and transmits them to the brain cortex to achieve consciousness or meanings, as shown in Figure 1.1.

Figure 1.1 A physical–chemical sense: abstract form

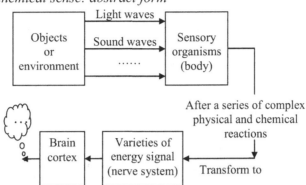

We adopt a simple example to illustrate this working procedure. Suppose we draw five rectangles vertically on a big sheet of yellow paper. Each rectangle uses a different color, as shown in Figure 1.2 (left side): red, orange, yellow, blue, and green. We can show this graph to one reader. Suppose that the visual optical flow moves from left to right when this reader views the graph displayed in Figure 1.2 . A person with a normal color vision (i.e., without color blindness) perceives four rectangles in red, orange, blue, and green and can discriminate these colors but cannot discern the yellow box on the yellow background. This example indicates that a person with normal (color) vision is able to perceive color changes. That is, people have differential sensitivities to color changes. For simplicity, if we assume there is no other noise signal to interfere with our observation in viewing these rectangles, the perception processes in viewing the yellow and blue rectangles can be illustrated as in Figure 1.2(a) and (b), respectively. The horizontal axis in both (a) and (b) represents the duration of receiving visual signals (i.e., moving to view each rectangle from left to right), whereas the vertical axis indicates the intensity of a perceived visual signal. The unit for the vertical axis is **Lux**, commonly used in photometry as a measure of the intensity of light, such that wavelengths are weighted according to the luminosity function, a standardized model of human brightness perceptions. The unit for the horizontal (V) axis can be any conventional time unit, such as a second, minute, hour, or day.

Figure 1.2(a) indicates that a yellow spectrum signal is observed, denoted as $L = f(Y)$ (where f is some function, and Y represents the energy of a yellow wave); however, a reader cannot distinguish whether this yellow spectrum signal comes from the yellow background of the paper or a yellow rectangle. If the reader is unaware of the existence of the yellow rectangle in advance, the yellow rectangle is actually invisible. If we replace the yellow rectangle with a blue one, the visual system perceives two different color spectrum signals: yellow and blue (one from yellow paper, and one forming the blue rectangle), with different wavelengths, denoted $L = f(Y)$ and $L = f(B)$, respectively. Through a series of chemical and physical reactions with energy transformation, the nerve system perceives energy changes (i.e., a chemical sense) in the difference between the two stimuli, yellow and blue.

How can such chemical sense be rendered observable? An analogous operation using calculus can provide a satisfying answer. The basic principle is simple: To see a change in the energy of each color, we take the first derivative of the signal curves obtained in both (a) and (b) of Figure 1.2 with respect to the corresponding yellow and blue energy signals. The results displayed in Figure 1.3, (a) and (b). Note that when a yellow rectangle appears on yellow paper, all information received is the wavelength of yellow (i.e., yellow signal from both the background and the rectangle). Thus, the nerve system can-

Figure 1.2 Mechanism of color perception

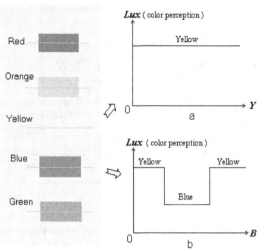

not sense any change in neural energy, as shown in Figure 1.3(a). When a blue rectangle is placed on a yellow paper, the two different wavelengths representing yellow and blue are perceived. Because of the background yellow paper, nerve receptors would not sense any energy change when receiving a yellow signal again but would have a noticeable neural activity when receiving a blue stimulus. Figure 1.3(b) reflects such effects.

To see and capture this noticeable difference—a term we use to represent an average point at which the viewer just perceives a difference between two stimuli, such as yellow and blue—we take the derivative from the results obtained in Figure 1.3. This calculation produces Figure 1.4, which shows how to capture different portions of the visible spectrum. The magnitude of the noticeable difference also is measured by **Lux** (i.e., the intensity of light which represents the density/strength of its energy).

Figure 1.3 Sense energy changes of each color

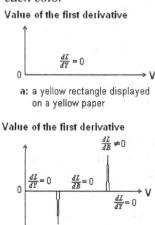

Figure 1.4 Energy changes causing awareness

Value of the second derivative

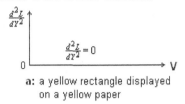

a: a yellow rectangle displayed
on a yellow paper

Value of the second derivative

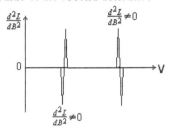

b: a blue rectangle displayed
on a yellow paper

Figure 1.4(a) reflects that the yellow rectangle displayed on yellow paper is invisible, whereas Figure 1.4(b) shows that the left and right edges of the blue rectangle on the yellow paper can be extracted, given our assumption that the visual optical flow moves from left to right when viewing Figure 1.2 on the yellow paper.

This example suggests that (1) a noticeable difference cannot be perceived and captured when the stimuli received are the same, (2) a noticeable difference occurs at the point that energy changes exist, and (3) the noticeable difference garners attention and awareness. Therefore, a constant invariant signal gradually loses its power of stimulation and cannot capture people's attention. Similarly, when viewing or hearing a warning, if the warning signal received today is the same as the ones before, the same results will hold. That is, no noticeable change occurs, people will not pay attention. Because the objective of issuing a warning is to inform people at risk in advance, if those people do not recognize a warning or do not attend to the warning signal, the warning loses its natural desired effects. Therefore, warnings should be designed to capture people's attention, which we consider the first key characteristic of an effective warning.

WARNING CONTENT AND DESIGNING EFFECTIVE WARNING

Issuing a warning involves a single instantaneous action, but the warning signal itself entails a continuous process. Suppose a warning is heard by person A at time t_0 and that there are no other similar signals before t_0. The warning as an outside stimulus to the receptors of person A will cause a noticeable change in neural energy at t_{0+}, from which person A gets a signal: "There is an alarm." But if this warning signal lasts for a while, the noticeable difference gradually decreases to zero, because person

A gets used to the signal. If we assume that the noticeable difference becomes zero at time t_1, then $(t_1 - t_0)$ is the time period during which the signal stimulus has an effect, as shown in Figure 1.5. That is, $(t_1 - t_0)$ represents the duration time for an effective stimulation. After t_1, even if the warning signal still issues an alarm, its stimulation effect becomes useless, because people's nerve systems have become accustomed to the signal, and the signal is unable to get nervous systems excited.

Therefore, when issuing warnings to the public, if authorities want to issue the warning continuously to ensure they reach those who may not have heard the warning before or to indicate the severity of a threat, they should issue the warnings at different time intervals to achieve an effective stimulation each time.

Notice that we assume that no other similar signals exist when a warning is issued. However, a variety of noises may co-occur in the real world, so a warning signal must be distinct and not appear as another common repetition, which enables people to recognize or understand it when they hear or view the warning. In many places, sirens are used to alert the public, but if that alarm sounds, does it signal that the public should stay at home or go somewhere else? Therefore, a warning should consist of two components: an alert signal and its associated meaning. The associated meaning contains information about the purpose of the alert. Both components reflect the desired effects that the authorities expect to achieve. To achieve such effects, a warning must not only capture the public's attention but also be understandable by the general public, regardless of race, beliefs, education, disability, financial status, culture, or language. Thus, being understandable represents the second characteristic of an effective warning.

Figure 1.5. Continuous warning and attention decay

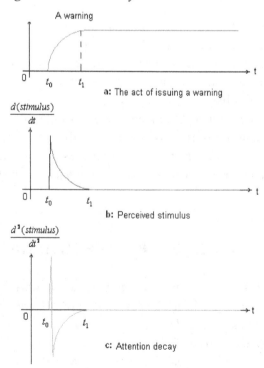

The third important factor requires providing a distinct and unique meaning. As shown in Table 1.1, the meaning of the warning prompts the public to realize that something may happen or is happening that is important enough for them to note and think about. An effective warning does far more than just alert the public to an impending threat; it also provides pertinent information about the nature of the threat, the potential target location, the risk in the affected area, and potential protective actions or ways to reduce damages that will help them make appropriate preparations against the threat.

In addition, the duration of a warning should be clear, so that the public knows when the threat is going to end and they can resume their normal activities.

Finally, to be effective, a warning must be issued from a trustworthy and credible source, such as certain government officials or other appropriate authorities. This final point may be the most important factor. Figure 1.6 summarizes the basic characteristics that an effective warning should possess.

Table 1.1. A warning advisory for the public

Threat Information	
Type of threats	Biological threat, bombing
Risk	Low, high, severe
When	Possible time and date period
Where	Potential target location
Impact area	Geographic regions, industry sectors
Duration	How long the threat will last
Recommended Actions	
Protective actions	Citizen guidance
Ways to reduce impact	
Contact points for further information and assistance	

Figure 1.6. Basic characteristics of an effective warning

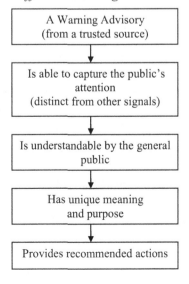

Recent public health emergencies such as the anthrax-letter attacks in October 2001 and the 2003 SARS epidemic have clearly demonstrated that the public's response clearly depends in part, on the following factors: (1) the type of public health information given to them, (2) the perceived and actual reliability and scientific "soundness" of such information, (3) source of the information, and (4) the timeliness of the information.

DISCUSSION AND FUTURE WORK

In their efforts to achieve effective warnings, many researchers have explored ways to frame warning messages and identify protocols to disseminate them effectively to and with federal agencies, state and local governments, and the public (CRS, 2004; GAO, 2004; PPW, 2004). Their research suggests the need to develop standard terminology to construct warning messages. According to research reports from the U.S. General Accounting Office [GAO] (2004) and the Partnership for Public Warning [PPW] (2002), the message should be clear and use simple, easily understood words without multiple or confusing meanings.

Research also suggests that warnings should reach those at risk, regardless of their location, the time of day, or their possible disabilities or special needs. The development of new technologies, in addition to traditional methods such as sirens, television alerts, and newspapers to disseminate warning messages, means that electronic media, such as the Internet, e-mail, wireless mobile networks, text messages, and GPS systems, also might be used for such purposes. For example, a sudden overnight intensification of a hurricane is the nightmare faced by storm forecaster because people are sleeping. Within a decade, a new internet-based storm warning system will be available to wake up residents in the middle of the night by sounding the alarm on a cell phone when a hurricane or tornado threatens (Reuters, 2008). In fact, electronic media technology has been used in disaster management. When wildfires have raged across southern California in October 2007, an emergency alter system which connects to Californian schools, colleges and universities has been used to deliver warnings and instructions to students, staff and parents across threatened areas. During the crisis, the system has delivered more than 6 millions messages including 2.7 millions voice messages, 1.15 millions e-mail, and text message that have reached 393,000 people with 4 percent of messages missing their targets (*Financial Times*, 2008). In addition, the U.S. Department of Homeland Security's Federal Emergency Management Agency (FEMA) also launches a Digital Emergency Alter System (DEAS) pilot in the National Capital Region (FEMA, 2004). Through the use of high speed wireless digital broadcasts, it is expected this system is able to provide a digital backbone that can improve the effectiveness and efficiency of the current emergency alert system. An open research question remains though: How will warnings reach the public if there is a power outage? Sirens may remain a good and necessary channel. However, currently siren is not covered in all areas in U.S. and only urban areas tend to be well covered.

Another challenge for the issuing authorities is when a warning should be issued to the right place at the right time. If a warning is issued too late, the public may not have enough time to make appreciate preparations. Taking a tornado warning as an example, if a storm moves at a somewhat sluggish 20 miles an hour and forecasters get spotter reports of a funnel cloud or see its telltale signature on their radar while it's still 10 miles out, they can post a warning that gives people a 30-minute heads up. But if a storm roars along at 60 miles an hour, that leaves 10 minutes between a warning and the storm's arrival.

Box 1.1.

```
*********************************************************************
TSUNAMI BULLETIN NUMBER 002
PACIFIC TSUNAMI WARNING CENTER/NOAA/NWS
ISSUED AT 0204Z 26 DEC 2004

THIS BULLETIN IS FOR ALL AREAS OF THE PACIFIC BASIN EXCEPT
ALASKA - BRITISH COLUMBIA - WASHINGTON - OREGON - CALIFORNIA.

................ TSUNAMI INFORMATION BULLETIN................

ATTENTION: NOTE REVISED MAGNITUDE.

THIS MESSAGE IS FOR INFORMATION ONLY. THERE IS NO TSUNAMI WARNING
OR WATCH IN EFFECT.

AN EARTHQUAKE HAS OCCURRED WITH THESE PRELIMINARY PARAMETERS

 ORIGIN TIME - 0059Z 26 DEC 2004
 COORDINATES -  3.4 NORTH   95.7 EAST
 LOCATION    - OFF W COAST OF NORTHERN SUMATERA
 MAGNITUDE  - 8.5

EVALUATION
 REVISED MAGNITUDE BASED ON ANALYSIS OF MANTLE WAVES.
 THIS EARTHQUAKE IS LOCATED OUTSIDE THE PACIFIC. NO DESTRUCTIVE
 TSUNAMI THREAT EXISTS FOR THE PACIFIC BASIN BASED ON HISTORICAL
 EARTHQUAKE AND TSUNAMI DATA.

 THERE IS THE POSSIBILITY OF A TSUNAMI NEAR THE EPICENTER.

THIS WILL BE THE ONLY BULLETIN ISSUED FOR THIS EVENT UNLESS
ADDITIONAL INFORMATION BECOMES AVAILABLE.

THE WEST COAST/ALASKA TSUNAMI WARNING CENTER WILL ISSUE BULLETINS
FOR ALASKA - BRITISH COLUMBIA - WASHINGTON - OREGON - CALIFORNIA.

*********************************************************************
```

Source: Warning message form the U.S. National Oceanic and Atmospheric Administration (NOAA). Available at http://www. prh.noaa.gov/ptwc/olderwmsg.

So, issuing a warning to the right place at the right time may not be easy to achieve. For example, when the Indian Ocean earthquake occurred on December 26, 2004, the Pacific Tsunami Warning center of the U.S. National Oceanic and Atmospheric Administration (NOAA) actually detected the earthquake and issued an alert to Pacific Islands (see Box 1.1) saying that there may be a possibility of a Tsunami at the epicenter. However, the tragedy is that this information was not communicated to the Indian Ocean region. The NOAA officers say that they did not have the addresses of the appropriate officials.

Several other interesting questions, such as how the public will respond to antithreat warnings and how warning frequency affects public responses, remain open as well. In next chapter, we explore these issues.

REFERENCES

Attention (2007). *Merriam-Webster online*. Retrieved May 5, 2007, from http://www.m-w.com/dictionary/attention.

Beament, J. (2003). *How we hear music*. Rochester, NY: Boydell Press.

Boring, E. G. (1933). *Dimensions of consciousness*. New York: Appleton-Century-Crofts, Inc.

Bundesen, C. (1990). A theory of visual attention. *Psychological Review, 97*, 523-547.

Bundesen, C. (2002). A general theory of visual attention. In L. Bäckman & C. von Hofsten (Eds.), *Psychology at the turn of the millennium: Vol. 1. Cognitive, biological, and health perspectives*, 179–200. Hove, UK: Psychology Press.

Clare, L., & Halligan, P. (2006). Pathologies of awareness: Bridging the gap between theory and practice, The Special Issue of the *Journal of Neuropsychological Rehabilitation*, August.

Financial Times (2008). Cascade that can help avert disaster. *Financial Times*, January 20, 2008.

Heinke, D., & Humphreys, G. W. (2003). Attention, spatial representation, and visual neglect: simulating emergent attention and spatial memory in the selective attention for identification model (SAIM). *Psychological Review, 110*, 29–87.

Kiang, N. Y. S. (1969). *Discharge patterns of single auditory fibers*. MIT Research Monograph 35, Cambridge, MA.

Landauer, R. (1991). Information is physical. *Physics Today, 44*, 23-29.

Logan, G. D. (2002). An instance theory of attention and memory. *Psychological Review, 109*, 376–400.

Luce, R. D. (1963). Detection and recognition. In R. D. Luce, R. R. Bush, & E. Galanter (Eds.), *Handbook of mathematical psychology*, 103–89. New York: Wiley.

Mileti, D. S., & O'Brien, P. (1992). Warning during disaster: normalizing communication risk. *Social Problems, 39*(1), 40-55.

Nigg, J. M. (1993). Risk communication and warning systems. In *Proceedings of the International Conference on Natural Risk and Civil Protection*, 209-236. Commission of European Communities, Belgirate, Italy.

Ratcliff, R. (1978). A theory of memory retrieval. *Psychological Review, 85*, 59–108.

Ratcliff, R., van Zandt, T., & McKoon, G. (1999). Connectionist and diffusion models of reaction time. *Psychological Review, 106*, 261–300.

Reeves, A., & Sperling, G. (1986). Attention gating in short-term visual memory. *Psychological Review, 93*, 180–206.

Reuters (2008), *U.S. aims to give wake-up alerts on storms*. February 12, 2008.

Shepard, R. N. (1957). Stimulus and response generalization: A stochastic model relating generalization to distance in psychological space. *Psychometrika, 22,* 325–45

Shih, S-I., & Sperling, G. (2002). Measuring and modeling the trajectory of visual spatial attention. *Psychological Review, 109,* 260–305.

Styles, E. (2006). *The psychology of attention.* 2nd ed. United Kingdom: Psychology Press.

The Partnership for Public Warning [PPW] (2002). Developing a unified all hazards public warning system. A report by the workshop on *Effective Hazard Warnings*, February, 2002. Retrieved January 3, 2003, from http://www.PartnershipforPublicWarning.org/.

Trettin, L., & Musham, C. (2000). Is trust a realistic goal of environmental risk communication? *Environment and Behavior, 32*(3), 410-426.

U.S. Congressional Research Services [CRS] (2004). *Homeland Security Advisory System: possible issues for congressional oversight.* January 29, 2004. Washington, DC: Congressional Research Services.

U.S. Federal Emergency Management Agency [FEMA] (2004). DHS lunches digital emergency alert system pilot for the national capital region. New Release, October 21, 2004. Retrieved October 23, 2004, from http://www.fema.gov/news/newsrelease_print.fema?id=14924.

U.S. General Accounting Office [GAO] (2004). *Homeland Security–Risk communication principles may assist in refinement of the Homeland Security Advisory System.* Retrieved January 3, 2005, from http://www.gao.gov/cgi-bin/getrpt?gao-04-538T.

Chapter II
Dynamics of Public Perception and Confidence

INTRODUCTION

To guard against potential terrorist attacks and protect the public and infrastructure, the U.S. Department of Homeland Security (DHS) and related authorities usually issue threat warning advisories to the public when there is a potential threat (CRS, 2004; DHS, 2001; PPW, 2004). The warning advisory relies on a five-color system (see Figure 2.1) that represents levels of risk related to a potential terror attack. Each threat level has a corresponding list of recommended actions that the public should take to reduce the likelihood or impact of a potential attack. Therefore, when a warning advisory is issued, authorities hope the public will follow the advisories, which are listed on the DHS's Citizen Guidance on the Homeland Security Advisory System Web page, and take the recommended actions (Citizen, 2001; Federal, 2001). For example, as of December 31, 2007, the country remained at an elevated risk (i.e., code yellow) for a terrorist attack. At this threat level, the public should take the following 12 actions:

1. Develop a family emergency plan. Share it with family and friends, and practice the plan. Visit www.Ready.gov for help creating a plan.
2. Create an "Emergency Supply Kit" for your household.
3. Be informed. Visit www.Ready.gov or obtain a copy of "Preparing Makes Sense, Get Ready Now" by calling 1-800-BE-READY.
4. Know how to shelter-in-place and how to turn off utilities (power, gas, and water) to your home.
5. Examine volunteer opportunities in your community, such as Citizen Corps, Volunteers in Police service, Neighborhood Watch or others, and donate your time.
6. Consider completing an American Red Cross first aid or CPR course, or Community Emergency Response Team (CERT) course.
7. Review stored disaster supplies and replace items that are outdated.
8. Be alert to suspicious activity and report it to proper authorities.
9. Ensure disaster supply kit is stocked and ready.
10. Check telephone numbers in family emergency plan and update as necessary.
11. Develop alternate routes to/from work or school and practice them.
12. Continue to be alert for suspicious activity and report it to authorities.

Figure 2.1. Color-coded threat level advisory system

(Source: Homeland Security Advisory System, http://www.dhs.gov/dhspublic/.)

If the code yellow alert appears every day, it implies the warning advisory is issued every day, so the public needs to perform these 12 actions every day until the warning is off. The question that arises is whether these 12 actions actually are being reviewed and repeated as necessary by the public and taken every day, given the continuation of the code yellow alert. We randomly interviewed 25 households living in the Chicagoland area and asked (1) whether they knew the current threat level of the warning advisory and (2) whether they performed all the recommended actions that corresponded to the current threat level. For question (1), 9 households answered no, and 16 said they believed the alert was code yellow, because they had not heard of any change in the alert level. Regarding question (2), none of them performed the 12 recommendations associated with code yellow every day. When asked why, they mentioned that they followed the recommendations the first time the warning was issued. However, after several months, they became accustomed to the warning and felt that there was no difference between completing all recommendations or only some of them. Gradually, they stopped following the 12 recommendations, even though the code yellow alert remained in effect.

If we were to measure the effect of a warning advisory by examining whether the public responds by taking the recommended actions, the data from our small survey seem to suggest continuous warnings may not generate the desired effect in terms of stimulating the public's response. We know that antithreat warnings can help save lives and reduce the costs of potential disasters, but warning about terrorist threats differs from familiar warnings about severe weather. Warnings about severe weather do not change whether the weather event will occur. That is, the severe weather will come, regardless of whether a warning is issued. In contrast, warnings about terrorist threats may prompt terrorists to alter their targets, thereby escaping legal justice but still causing grave harm. Issuing an antithreat warning thus may result in a change in the occurrence of a potential threat. In addition, if the potential threat does not materialize each time the warning is issued, and no public notice indicates that the warning is over, the public may gradually lose attention and ignore warnings, which would mean they would fail to perform the required recommendations. If this failure occurs frequently, it may gradually erode the credibility of the warning advisory system and public confidence (McCarthy, 2005). In this chapter, we develop differential equations to model the relationship between warning frequencies and their associated public response and confidence. In so doing, we develop ways to preserve public confidence in the warning advisory system while maintaining its effectiveness.

This chapter is organized as follows: First, we describe the problem setting and the model formulation, which quantifies the interaction of the warning rate and the resulting level of public response and confidence. Second, we examine the properties of the model and its qualitative behavior through graphical analysis. Third, we develop an analytical solution of the model to investigate how to determine warning frequency in each threat level. Fourth, we discuss the major contributions and limitations of this research, as well as avenues for further research.

PROBLEM SETTING AND MODEL

According to the DHS, authorities issue warnings to inform different levels of government agencies to take appropriate protective measures and alert the public that there may be some type of threat to the United States, so the public needs to take informed actions as well (CRS, 2004; DHS, 2001; GAO, 2004). In this chapter, we focus on the public's response. That is, we do not discuss how different levels of government agencies react to threat warnings. The term "response," as used herein, refers to the public taking the recommended actions listed by the DHS Citizen Guidance after a warning is issued. If the public does something other than these required actions, their response is counted as zero, because the purpose of the Homeland Security Advisory System (HSAS) is to inform the public and suggest they perform specific tasks (CRS, 2004).

Problem Setting

We define a threat event as one that can cause authorities to issue warning(s). When a decision to issue a warning is made, it normally covers the entire nation or a target region for a certain period of time. The target region is then in a threat state. For example, since its establishment in March 2002, the HSAS national threat level has remained at an elevated alert state with a code yellow warning, with the exception of five periods during which the administration raised it to high alert and issued a code orange warning. We assume that the public consists of people who can understand the language used in the warning message after hearing or reading the warning and that the public is aware that each threat level has an associated list of recommended actions. Our research problem can therefore be described as follows:

Given a threat state e (i.e., $\forall e \in E$, where E denotes a set of threat states, and a threat state corresponds to a threat level in HSAS), for which warnings would be issued for a target region r (i.e., $\forall r \in R$, where R denotes a set of target regions), we model how the warning rate influences effectiveness in terms of public response and confidence in the target region r.

A Model

For a particular threat state e, a corresponding maximum number of possible action items is recommended by DHS (see Appendix A). The public may incur time, labor, or monetary costs to perform each recommended action item. We use the term "task-load" to label such costs. Similar to other studies in economics, we can use money or time to measure task-load. Because the task-load required to complete every particular action item may differ for each individual, we let $P_{e,max}$ denote the average task-load needed for the targeted population to complete all the action items recommended for state e by the DHS. Note that the subscript "max" in $P_{e,max}$ refers to the maximum number of possible action items listed for the corresponding threat state e. We define $p_e(t)$ as the amount of the task-load that the public completes at time t in state e (i.e., number of action items the public undertakes). When people understand and trust a warning, they are more likely to take these recommended protective actions. In other words, if people take action and respond, they likely trust the warning information. From this point of view, $p_e(t)$ also indicates public confidence in the warning system.

Let the duration of a warning be τ. The unit for τ is any convenient unit of time, such as an hour, day, or week. If the duration of a warning can be treated as the continuous issuance of the same type of warning signal, we can let $w_e(t) = t/\tau$, which represents the number of warnings issued at time t in state e. Because the authorities control warning frequency, the warning is an outside stimulus to the public. Theoretically, authorities can issue endless warnings in state e, but intuitively, the duration cannot last forever, and the public's tolerance is limited. Because there exists a maximum possible duration time of warnings that the public can tolerate, we letn $W_{e,max}$ represent this maximum value. In other words, this value reflects the maximum number of warnings that can be issued in state e without eroding the effectiveness of the warning system and public confidence.

As we discussed in Chapter I, a warning should capture people's attention. If people do not recognize a warning about an impending threat, they will not respond. If a response occurs, the amount of the task-load the public can actually complete (i.e., number of action items the public can undertake) is also subject to the public's capability. Humans have physical and mental limitations, so a change in the amount of the task-load completed per unit time in state e (i.e., change in the number of action items performed per unit time in state e) is proportional to the available capabilities of the targeted population. Let α be a positive proportionality constant that indicates the degree to which the public perceives the warning information; then, we determine the following differential equation:

$$\frac{dp_e}{dt} = \alpha \, [P_{e,\max} - p_e(t)],$$

where α is the attention coefficient.

We add to the model by assuming that authorities may increase the warning frequency to indicate the severity of the threat state or reach those who may have ignored previous warnings. The average of the marginal increment in stimulating the public to perform recommended actions is also proportional to how many warnings the public can tolerate in state e. That is,

$$\frac{\frac{dp_e}{dt}}{w_e} \propto [W_{e,\max} - w_e(t)].$$

Combining these two equations leads to

$$\frac{dp_e}{dt} = \alpha \left[P_{e,\max} - p_e(t) \right] + \beta \left[W_{e,\max} - w_e(t) \right] w_e(t),$$

where β is a positive constant indicating whether the content of the warning message is clear about the nature of the threat and thus is labeled the quality coefficient. The public wants specific information about a threat and details on which to base their decisions. The more detailed a warning message, the better the chance that the public will react and take appropriate actions.

An issued warning also should provide motivation for people to take informed action(s), and the public should have the ability to act on such warning information. When they know of a warning, people decide whether the impending threat is relevant or if they are at risk. If relevant, they likely determine which informed action items they are required to perform and whether they have the ability to complete this required task-load. A change in the number of warnings issued per unit time in state e may be affected by the available capability the public possesses to complete the required task-load, as well as the extent to which the threat is geared to the public's immediate concerns. That is, if people think they are not at risk, they may not respond. The most effective warnings will be those whose contents are the most relevant.

If we let the nonnegative constant γ be a measure of perceived threat risk—that is, the extent to which the warning is geared to the public's immediate and relevant concerns (e.g., geographical proximity of the threat to nearby residents versus those living in a faraway town)—we can derive another differential equation:

$$\frac{dw_e}{dt} = \gamma \left(P_{e,\max} - p_e(t) \right),$$

where γ is the concern coefficient. Those at risk are more concerned than those who are not.

Combining these equations together, we obtain the following differential equation system that captures the relationship between the warning rate and the public's response and confidence:

$$\begin{cases} \dfrac{dp_e}{dt} = \alpha \left[P_{e,\max} - p_e(t) \right] + \beta \, w_e(t) \left[W_{e,\max} - w_e(t) \right] & \text{(2-1)} \\[2ex] \dfrac{dw_e}{dt} = \gamma \left[P_{e,\max} - p_e(t) \right] & \text{(2-2)} \end{cases}$$

subject to the initial conditions $w_e(0) = 0$, $p_e(0) = 0$, and the nonnegative constants α, β, and γ.

The term $P_{e,\max} - p_e(t)$ measures the potential increase in the targeted population's ability to respond to the warning. This term defines the difference between the maximum capability of the public to respond and its current capability at t. The term $W_{e,\max} - w_e(t)$ measures how many more warnings can be issued before reaching the saturation point, $W_{e,\max}$. This term therefore also indicates that an increasing number of warnings does not mean an absolute increase in the efficiency of the warning system.

The physical interpretation of equation (2-1) is that the public's marginal response and confidence is directly proportional to the public's attention to the warning information, the potential increase in its ability to respond, and how many more warnings can be issued without reducing the effectiveness of the warning system.

Equation (2-2) states that the marginal effect of the warning increases with both increasing relevance and increasing capability, because humans have both physical and mental limitations. The more relevant the warning, the greater the marginal effect will be.

Now, we need to determine how our model system behaves to understand the relationship of $w_e(t)$ and $p_e(t)$ with time t. Therefore, we examine the qualitative behavior of the model through phase analysis and then investigate the quantitative behavior by finding an analytic solution of the model system.

MODEL BEHAVIOR

Our model system is nonlinear, due to the presence of the $w_e^2(t)$ term in equation (2-1). It would be interesting to discover whether the system behaves periodically, which represents an important characteristic for understanding any mathematical model. For example, a triangle function y1 = sin(x) is a periodic function, so we can infer that the behavior of y1 will repeat in each cycle with x. We plot the path of the points $(p(t), w(t))$ in the $p - w$ plane, with t as the parameter that varies over the solution interval $0 < t < \infty$. Both $p(t)$ and $w(t)$ should be greater than or equal to zero, such that their corresponding physical meanings make sense. We use the phase plane to explore the changing behavior of $p(t)$, which pertains to the public response and confidence resulting from the changes in $w(t)$, the number of warnings issued.

Properties of the Model System

Finding 1. Equations (2-1) and (2-2) define a family of nonclosed, nonperiodic orbits for $p(t)$, with $w(t) > 0$.

PROOF. Suppose there exists a cycle; it must have $\frac{\partial}{\partial p}(\frac{dp}{dt}) + \frac{\partial}{\partial w}(\frac{dw}{dt}) = 0$ in the system. Therefore, we have

$$\frac{\partial}{\partial p_e}(\frac{dp_e}{dt}) + \frac{\partial}{\partial w_e}(\frac{dw_e}{dt}) = \frac{\partial}{\partial p_e}[\alpha\,(P_{e,\max} - p_e(t)) + \beta\,w_e(t)(W_{e,\max} - w_e(t))]$$

$$+ \frac{\partial}{\partial w_e}[\gamma\,(P_{e,\max} - p_e(t))]$$

$$= -\alpha < 0.$$

In turn, we conclude that the orbit of the system (2-1) and (2-2) does not have cycles, which proves Finding 1.

This property is very important, because it indicates that the public response and confidence, $p_e(t)$, does not behave periodically with $w_e(t)$, the number of warnings issued.

Finding 2. $\alpha \propto \gamma$. A relevant warning captures the attention of people at risk.

PROOF. We can rewrite equations (2-1) and (2-2) as

$$\frac{dp_e(t)}{dw_e(t)} = \frac{\alpha}{\gamma} + \frac{\beta\, W_{e,\,max} \times w_e(t) - \beta\, [w_e(t)]^2}{\gamma [P_{e,\,max} - p_e(t)]},$$

which yields

$$\frac{dp_e(t)}{dw_e(t)} - \frac{\beta\, W_{e,\,max} \times w_e(t) - \beta\, [w_e(t)]^2}{\gamma [P_{e,\,max} - p_e(t)]} = \frac{\alpha}{\gamma}. \tag{2-3}$$

Obviously, equation (2-3) is nonhomogeneous, because the right-hand side is not equal to zero. If we let $\dfrac{\alpha}{\gamma} = C$, then $\alpha = C\gamma$, which suggests that the relevance of the content of a warning issued to the public influences how the public reacts to the warning signal.

Model Interpretation

Because $p_e(t)$ does not behave periodically with $w_e(t)$ (i.e., Finding 1), one of our concerns surrounds how public responses change with the number of warnings issued for a given threat state. We therefore analyze the steady-state predicted by the model using a graphical analysis. To draw a phase plane of our model system, we must find the critical points of the model system, which occur where $\dot{p}(t) = 0$ and $\dot{w}(t) = 0$. Setting the right-hand sides of both equations (2-1) and (2-2) to zero, we have

$$\begin{cases} \alpha\, [P_{e,\,max} - p_e(t)] + \beta\, w_e(t)[W_{e,\,max} - w_e(t)] = 0 & \tag{2-4} \\ \gamma\, [P_{e,\,max} - p_e(t)] = 0 & \tag{2-5} \end{cases}$$

We then solve equations (2-4) and (2-5) for p_e and w_e simultaneously. Equation (2-5) is satisfied whenever $p_e = P_{e,\,max}$. If $p_e = P_{e,\,max}$, Equation (2-4) holds if $w_e = 0$ or $w_e = W_{e,\,max}$. Equation (2-4) will be satisfied if each of the bracketed terms vanishes. That is, if both $p_e = P_{e,\,max} = 0$ hold, equation (2-4) is satisfied; if $p_e = P_{e,\,max}$ and $w_e = W_{e,\,max}$, equation (2-4) also holds. Thus, we obtain two critical points, $(p_e, w_e) = (P_{e,\,max}, W_{e,\,max})$ and $(p_e, w_e) = (P_{e,\,max}, 0)$, in the phase plane.

Point $(P_{e,\,max}, 0)$ indicates that the public has completed the required task-load in state e without a warning, which implies a well-trained target population in a heightened state of readiness. Thus, no warning is necessary. Currently, the public obtains official threat alerts about terrorist attacks only from HSAS. That is, HSAS is the only means of disseminating threat and advisory information regarding terrorist attacks. From this point of view, even if the public already resides at a heightened state of readiness, at least one warning signal must be issued for notification. Otherwise, the public will not know of the existence of an impending threat. Therefore, we do not discuss the case of $(P_{e,\,max}, 0)$.

Instead, we focus our graphical analysis on point $(P_{e,\,max}, W_{e,\,max})$, the single point of interest for the system of equations (2-1) and (2-2). The pertinent behavior for investigation is what happens to the solution trajectories in the vicinity of the critical point $(P_{e,\,max}, W_{e,\,max})$. Let us draw the system's phase plane and analyze the directions of dp_e/dt and dw_e/dt in the plane. Although $w_e(t)$ and $p_e(t)$ represent the number of warnings issued and their corresponding public response, respectively, it may be helpful to think of the trajectories as the paths of a moving particle in the $p_e - w_e$ plane. Graphically, we can draw a short line of the proper slope through each of many points (p_e, w_e) in the $p_e - w_e$ plane, which creates a direction field/map (see Figure 2.2). A solution curve of the model system is tangent to the direction line at each point through which the curve passes, and the direction field offers a visual representation of the family of possible solution curves to the system of equations (2-1) and (2-2). Because we are only interested in area where $p_e \geq 0$ and $w_e \geq 0$, we provide a brief description of how we sketch the phase graph of the system in the first quadrant in the vicinity of the critical point $(P_{e,\,max}, W_{e,\,max})$.

The $p_e - w_e$ plane can be divided into four areas according to the relationship between p_e and $P_{e,\,max}$, as well as the relationship between w_e and $W_{e,\,max}$ (see Figure 2.2a).

Area 1: $p_e < P_{e,\,max}$ and $w_e < W_{e,\,max}$.

In this area, $(P_{e,\,max} - p_e) \geq 0$, $(W_{e,\,max} - w) \geq 0$, and $w_e \geq 0$. When Δt increases, we get the response increment

$$\Delta p_e = \Delta t \, [\alpha \, (P_{e,\,max} - p_e) + \beta \, w_e (W_{e,\,max} - w_e)] \geq 0.$$

Therefore, Δp_e increases with time t, and the direction of $\dfrac{\Delta p_e}{\Delta t}$ will be ⟹.

Similarly, we can have $\Delta w_e = \Delta t \, [\gamma(P_{e,\,max} - p_e)] \geq 0$, which indicates that Δw_e also increases with time t, and the direction of $\dfrac{\Delta w_e}{\Delta t}$ will be ⇑

Combining these two directions, we know that as time t increases, the combined direction of Δp_e and Δw_e will be ⬈, as shown with a single arrow in Figure 2.2b.

Area 2: $0 < p_e < P_{e,\,max}$ but $w_e > W_{e,\,max}$.

If the authorities continuously issue a warning in state e, then $\Delta t > 0$, and the warning increment $\Delta w_e > 0$. Thus, we would have $\dfrac{dw_e}{dt} = \dfrac{\Delta w_e}{\Delta t} > 0$. As time t increases, the changing direction of $\dfrac{\Delta w_e}{\Delta t}$ is ⇑.

Because $\dfrac{dw_e}{dt} > 0$, we know that $\gamma \, (P_{e,\,max} - p_e(t)) > 0$ from equation (2-2). This finding implies that $(P_{e,\,max} - p_e(t)) > 0$ must exist, because γ is positive. Suppose that $w_e(T) = W_{e,\,max}$ at time $t = T$; then, $p_e(T) = P_{e,\,max}$. This result means that people have completed the required task-load when $t = T$. When $t = T + \Delta t$, we have

$$w_e(T + \Delta t) = W_{e,\,max} + \Delta w_e > 0.$$

Because $\dfrac{dw_e}{dt} = \dfrac{w_e(T + \Delta t) - w_e(T)}{\Delta t} = \dfrac{\Delta w_e}{\Delta t} > 0$, from equation (2-2), we can infer that $\gamma[P_{e,\,max} - p_e(T + \Delta t)] > 0$ holds. In turn, $[P_{e,\,max} - p_e(T + \Delta t)] > 0$, because γ is positive. Thus, we have

Figure 2.2. Phase portrait of the system

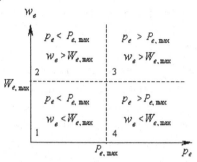

(a) The first quadrant: four possible situations

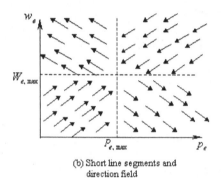

(b) Short line segments and direction field

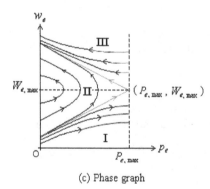

(c) Phase graph

$$\frac{dp_e}{dt} = \frac{p_e(T + \Delta t) - p_e(T)}{\Delta t}$$

$$= \frac{p_e(T + \Delta t) - P_{e,\max}}{\Delta t}$$

$$< 0.$$

That is, with time increasing, the changing direction of Δp_e is ⟸. The combined direction of Δp_e and Δw_e will be ⬃, as shown with the single arrow in Figure 2.2b.

Figure 2.2c displays the trajectories in the vicinity of the critical point $(P_{e,\max}, W_{e,\max})$, in which the arrows indicate the directions that solutions to p_e move as w_e increases.

Because the trajectories are nonperiodic, nonclosed curves, they show that, under the assumption of the system (i.e., $p_e(t)$ and $w_e(t) \geq 0$, $p_e(t) \leq P_{e,max}$), $p_e(t)$ increases when $w_e(t)$ increases in region I of Figure 2.2c. Increasing the number of warnings will stimulate the public to take the recommended actions, which helps build public confidence in the warning system. But when $w_e(t)$ exceeds $W_{e,max}$, $p_e(t)$ will decrease with $w(t)$ (see region II). That is, once $w_e(t) > W_{e,max}$, $p_e(t)$ will change direction immediately and enter region II. When this shift happens, the public's enthusiasm for responding decreases as the number of alerts increases, such that public response gradually decreases to the point of inaction if too many similar alerts of the same type of threat are issued; too many alerts also decrease public confidence in the warning system. Similarly, in region III of Figure 2.2c, increasing $w_e(t)$ leads to the decrease of $p_e(t)$. In other words, if the number of warnings is greater than $W_{e,max}$, public response and confidence decrease with time t. The solution trajectories of the system support the evidence from our small sample survey, which indicates that continuously issuing the same type of threat warnings may not generate the desired effect in terms of stimulating the public response.

The phase plane suggests that the $W_{e,max}$ for each event state plays an important role in public response and confidence. We are interested in determining an appropriate $W_{e,max}$ for each event state so that the proper number of warnings can be issued without eroding the effectiveness of the warning system or the level of public confidence in it. We therefore investigate the quantitative solution to the model presented next.

DETERMINING WARNING FREQUENCY IN EACH THREAT LEVEL

We begin by reanalyzing equation (2-3):

$$\frac{dp_e(t)}{dw_e(t)} - \frac{\beta W_{e,max} \times w_e(t) - \beta [w_e(t)]^2}{\gamma [P_{e,max} - p_e(t)]} = \frac{\alpha}{\gamma}. \tag{2-3}$$

As we mentioned previously, this equation is nonhomogeneous because the right-hand side is not equal to zero. Because the general solution to the nonhomogeneous equation is the sum of the complementary solution and any particular solution, we must find the complementary solution to the associated homogeneous equation of equation (2-3).

To obtain the associated homogenous equation, we set the left-hand side of equation (2-3) to equal zero. That is,

$$\frac{dp_e(t)}{dw_e(t)} - \frac{\beta W_{e,max} \times w_e(t) - \beta [w_e(t)]^2}{\gamma [P_{e,max} - p_e(t)]} = 0. \tag{2-6}$$

Extending equation (2-6) gives us

$$\gamma [P_{e,max} - p_e(t)] dp_e(t) = [\beta W_{e,max} \times w_e(t)] \, dw_e(t) - \beta [w_e(t)]^2 \, dwe(t). \tag{2-7}$$

Integrating both sides of equation (2-7) from 0 to t yields

$$-\frac{\gamma}{2}[p_e(t)]^2 + \gamma\,P_{e,\max}[p_e(t)] + [\frac{\gamma\,p_e^2(0)}{2} - \gamma\,P_{e,\max} \times p_e(0)] =$$

$$-\frac{\beta}{3}[w_e(t)]^3 + \frac{\beta W_{e,\max}}{2}[w_e(t)]^2 + [\frac{\beta\,w_e^3(0)}{3} - \frac{\beta W_{e,\max}}{2} \times w_e^2(0)].$$

Next, substituting the initial conditions $w_e(0) = 0$ and $p_e(0) = 0$ into this equation gives us

$$3\gamma[p_e(t)]^2 - 6\gamma P_{e,\max}[p_e(t)] = 2\beta[w_e(t)]^3 - 3\beta W_{e,\max}[w_e(t)]^2 \qquad (2\text{-}8)$$

Solving for p(t),

$$p_e(t) = P_{e,\max} \pm \sqrt{P_{e,\max}^2 + \frac{2\beta}{3\gamma}[w_e(t)]^3 - \frac{\beta}{\gamma}\,W_{e,\max}[w_e(t)]^2}\;.$$

Because $0 \le p_e(t) \le P_{e,\max}$, we take the "–" sign when determining a feasible solution. Therefore,

$$p_e(t) = P_{e,\max} - \sqrt{P_{e,\max}^2 + \frac{2\beta}{3\gamma}[w_e(t)]^3 - \frac{\beta}{\gamma}\,W_{e,\max}[w_e(t)]^2}\;. \qquad (2\text{-}9)$$

Equation (2-9) thus defines the solution trajectories of Equation 2-6 in the phase plane.

Let S_c denote equation (2-9). We borrow existing methods for solving constant-coefficient, nonhomogeneous linear equations (Giordano & Weir, 1994) and assume that we can apply this approach to a nonlinear situation. The general solution to the system of equation (2-3) thus equals the sum of the general solution of equation (2-6) and any particular solution of equations (2-1) and (2-2). Because the two critical points we have obtained are also two particular solutions to the system of equations (2-1) and (2-2), the format of the general solution to our model system can be written as

$$\begin{bmatrix} p_e(t) \\ w_e(t) \end{bmatrix} = S_c + \begin{bmatrix} P_{e,\max} \\ W_{e,\max} \end{bmatrix}, \qquad (2\text{-}10)$$

or
$$\begin{bmatrix} p_e(t) \\ w_e(t) \end{bmatrix} = S_c + \begin{bmatrix} P_{e,\max} \\ 0 \end{bmatrix}. \qquad (2\text{-}10)'$$

Note that S_c is given implicitly, and there is no general solution procedure for solving nonlinear equations. Thus, in the next section, we provide an approximation approach for finding the closed form of the general solution to our model system.

Solving for equations (2-9) and (2-10) in the vicinity of the critical point $(P_{e,\max}, W_{e,\max})$, that is, letting $p_e(t) = P_{e,\max}$, we get

$$P^2_{e,\max} + \frac{2\beta}{3\gamma}[w_e(t)]^3 - \frac{\beta}{\gamma}W_{e,\max}[w_e(t)]^2 = 0.$$

Because $w_e(t) = W_{e,\max}$ at the point $(P_{e,\max}, W_{e,\max})$, we substitute it into this equation and obtain the following constraint relation:

$$W^3_{e,\max} = \frac{3\gamma}{\beta}P^2_{e,\max}.$$

(2-11)

Theoretically, after authorities decide the degree of risk (γ) of a threat event and the suggested actions they expect the public to take in state e, they can use equation (2-11) to calculate the corresponding $W_{e,\max}$, that is, the maximum number of allowable warnings that can be issued in state e.

THE GENERAL SOLUTION USING LINEAR APPROXIMATION

As we noted previously, our model system is nonlinear. To solve it, the common approach linearizes the nonlinear equation approximately according to its associated nonhomogenous linear equation and then solves this nonhomogenous linear equation to get a general solution (Giordano & Weir, 1994). Because the critical point $(P_{e,\max}, W_{e,\max})$ is the one in which we are interested in this chapter, let $x(t) = p_e(t) - P_{e,\max}$, and $y(t) = w_e(t) - W_{e,\max}$. In turn,

$$\begin{aligned}
\frac{dx}{dt} &= \frac{\partial x}{\partial p_e} \cdot \frac{dp_e}{dt} \\
&= \frac{\partial}{\partial p_e}[p_e(t) - P_{e,\max}] \cdot \frac{dp_e}{dt} \\
&= \alpha[P_{\max} - p_e(t)] + \beta w_e(t)[W_{e,\max} - w_e(t)] \\
&= \alpha[-x(t)] + \beta[y(t) + W_{e,\max}] \cdot [-y(t)],
\end{aligned}$$

and

$$\begin{aligned}
\frac{dy}{dt} &= \frac{\partial y}{\partial w_e} \cdot \frac{dw_e}{dt} \\
&= \frac{\partial}{\partial w_e}[w_e(t) - W_{e,\max}] \cdot \gamma[P_{e,\max} - p_e(t)] \\
&= \gamma[P_{e,\max} - p_e(t)] \\
&= \gamma[-x(t)].
\end{aligned}$$

Rewriting these equations, we have

$\dot{x}(t) + \alpha\, x(t) + \beta\, W_{e,\max}\, y(t) = -\beta\, y^2(t)$, and   (2-12)

$\dot{y}(t) + \gamma\, x(t) = 0$.   (2-13)

Because equation (2-12) is a nonlinear differential equation, we approximate it with its associated homogenous linear equation. Now the system of equations (2-12) and (2-13) becomes

$$\dot{x}(t) \simeq -\alpha\, x(t) - \beta\, W_{e,\max}\, y(t) \quad \text{, and}$$

$$\dot{y}(t) = -\gamma\, x(t).$$

Or,

$$\begin{bmatrix} \dot{x}(t) \\ \dot{y}(t) \end{bmatrix} = \begin{bmatrix} -\alpha & -\beta\, W_{e,\max} \\ -\gamma & 0 \end{bmatrix} \cdot \begin{bmatrix} x(t) \\ y(t) \end{bmatrix}.$$ (2-14)

To find a general solution, we need to determine the eigenvalues for equation (2-14):

$$|\,A - \lambda E\,| = \begin{vmatrix} -\alpha - \lambda & -\beta\, W_{e,\max} \\ -\gamma & 0 - \lambda \end{vmatrix}$$

$$= -\lambda\,(-\alpha - \lambda) - \gamma\,\beta\, W_{e,\max}$$

$$= 0.$$

Therefore, $\lambda^2 + \alpha\lambda - \beta W_{e,\max}\gamma = 0$. Solving for it, we have

$$\lambda_{1,2} = -\frac{\alpha}{2} \pm \sqrt{(\frac{\alpha}{2})^2 + \beta\,\gamma\, W_{e,\max}} \ ,$$

so the general solution to equation (2-14) is

$$\begin{bmatrix} x(t) \\ y(t) \end{bmatrix} = c_1 \begin{bmatrix} a_1 \\ b_1 \end{bmatrix} e^{\lambda_1 t} + c_2 \begin{bmatrix} a_2 \\ b_2 \end{bmatrix} e^{\lambda_2 t} \ ,$$

where a_1, b_1, a_2, b_2, c_1, and c_2 are constants. The general solution to the linear approximated system of the original equations (2-1) and (2-2) is then

$$\begin{bmatrix} p_e(t) \\ w_e(t) \end{bmatrix} = \begin{bmatrix} k_1 \\ k_2 \end{bmatrix} e^{\lambda_1 t} + \begin{bmatrix} m_1 \\ m_2 \end{bmatrix} e^{\lambda_2 t} + \begin{bmatrix} P_{e,\max} \\ W_{e,\max} \end{bmatrix},$$ (2-15)

where $\begin{bmatrix} k_1 \\ k_2 \end{bmatrix} = \begin{bmatrix} c_1\, a_1 \\ c_1\, b_1 \end{bmatrix}$, and $\begin{bmatrix} m_1 \\ m_2 \end{bmatrix} = \begin{bmatrix} c_2\, a_2 \\ c_2\, b_2 \end{bmatrix}.$

DISCUSSION AND FUTURE WORK

Effective antithreat warnings can save lives and reduce the costs of potential disasters. However, if the potential threat does not materialize each time the warning is issued and the authorities fail to issue a public notice that the warning is over; if the warnings are issued too frequently; or if a warning lasts forever, the public may gradually come to ignore these warnings, which results in a lack of performance of the required recommendations, as suggested by our survey data. If this situation occurs frequently, it may result in a failure to respond in any real emergencies, as in the story of the boy who cried wolf.

In this chapter, we have constructed a differential equation model to understand how warning frequency influences effectiveness in terms of public response and confidence. We model the effectiveness of a warning advisory in terms of whether the warning (1) captures the public's attention, (2) is geared toward the public's immediate and relevant concerns (i.e., degree of risk), and (3) prompts people to follow the advisories listed in the guidelines that correspond to each threat level and then take the suggested actions.

The qualitative behavior in our model system predicts that the number of warnings about a particular threat state can reach a threshold, after which they erode the effectiveness of the warning system and public confidence. Below this threshold value, increasing the number of reliable warnings can improve the credibility and effectiveness of the warning system. However, once past the threshold, more warnings continue to decrease the public response and lower public confidence. When this scenario exists, the impacts of warnings have the opposite effect than that intended. If too many alerts in the same threat state are issued or a single warning is repeated for a long time, the public gradually loses attention and ignores all warnings. Our model's prediction is consistent with the result from our small survey.

We derive a formula for calculating the warning threshold for each threat state. The threshold value is constrained by the perceived risk of threat and the public's capability to respond. Because threats do not always materialize, the authorities should give detailed explanations for any warning that proves false to prevent public distrust. Such efforts would increase flexibility in the number of effective warnings that authorities can issue.

On a Sudden Catastrophic Event

Our model relies on a setting that assumes a state e (i.e., threat level) at which warnings are issued. That is, the model is threat state specific. For example, in an elevated risk state, authorities issue a code yellow warning, but at a high risk level, they provide a code orange warning. Thus, code yellow and code orange represent two warning signals and two different threat states—elevated and high, respectively. We use the subscript e to indicate different individual states (or threat levels), such that in our model, e can be an elevated, high, or severe risk state.

As in the study of more general dynamic systems (i.e., economic, biological, or electrical areas), we use a continuous system approach in the form of a set of differential equations to study human social behavior. However, continuous social behavior may be interrupted by a sudden, catastrophic, noncontinuous event. In this scenario, our model system likely would undergo a sudden switch from one equilibrium state to another, as shown in Figure 2.3. An outside force may cause the system to make such a sudden jump, such as if the model system resides in a particular state (e.g., low risk threat level), but then authorities suddenly raise the threat level from low to elevated risk because of events similar to September 11. In this case, the model system would switch to a new state, labeled elevated risk or code yellow, and in

Figure 2.3. System switching behavior due to a sudden catastrophe

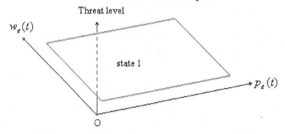

(a) The current threat level is state 1

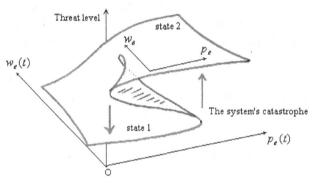

(b) The authorities raise the threat level to state 2

Notes: Figure 2.3a shows that the system resides in a particular state (e.g., threat level is state 1), and then the authorities suddenly raise the threat level to state 2, which makes the system undergo a sudden switch from state 1 to state 2, as shown in Figure 2.3b.

this new state, the system of equations (2-1) and (2-2) could display the public response with varying warning rates. The increased threat level, as a force outside the public, makes the system jump from a low to an elevated risk state. In addition, the public does not know how authorities determine the level of the risk state. If we assume the determination is based on factors unknown to the public but known by the authorities, we can use a function G $(v_1, v_2, \cdots, v_m)$ to represent the decision, where $v_1, v_2, \cdots, v_m$ are the various factors. Then we can conclude that our model system would experience a sudden state jump when the function G is suddenly added to the system.

We focus on public response and confidence. Further research might also study how government agencies determine the change of the threat state, that is, the explicit quantitative expression of the function G $(v_1, v_2, \cdots, v_m)$, as suggested by the U.S. General Accounting Office (2004).

Recommended Actions

The success of a warning depends on the actions people take. In our model, we assume that the public is aware that each threat level has a related list of recommended actions, as described in the DHS Citizen Guidance. People living in different geographic areas may have different requirements, such as cities with economic and symbolic value or places with hazardous facilities, so the recommended actions in different geographic areas may differ. Additional research could explore what type of action items and how many items the public needs to perform depending on their different target areas and threat state.

Attention Coefficient α

In our model, we treat the attention coefficient α as a constant. In the real world, it may vary with time t, because human bodies and minds may become fatigued over time. Thus, the attention coefficient α can be modeled as a function of time.

Suppose that the public's attention at time t_0 is α_0, and at time t, it is $\alpha(t)$. When $t = t_0$, $\alpha(t) = \alpha_0$. If we let $\Delta\alpha$ be an incremental amount/quantity of attention in Δt, then $-\Delta\alpha$ indicates a decay quantity in Δt.

Because humans experience fatigue over time, the change in attention per unit time is proportional to both the duration time of the attention-focused period and the intensity of attention that people expend during that time. Thus, within a Δt interval, we have

$$-\Delta\alpha \propto \Delta t \times [t\,\alpha(t)].$$

Rewriting it gives

$$-\frac{\Delta\alpha}{\alpha} = q \times \Delta t \times t,$$

where q is a constant. Then, taking the limit as $\Delta t \to 0$, we find

$$\lim_{\Delta t \to 0}\left(-\frac{\Delta\alpha}{\alpha}\right) = -\frac{d\alpha}{\alpha} = q\,t\,dt.$$

Solving this equation under the condition that α changes from α_0 to $\alpha(t)$ as time changes from t_0 ($= 0$) to t, we have

Figure 2.4. A decay curve of attention

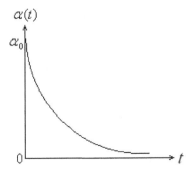

$$\alpha(t) = \alpha_0 \cdot e^{-\frac{q}{2}t^2}.$$

(2-16)

When $t \uparrow$, then $t^2 \uparrow\uparrow$, which causes $\alpha(t) \downarrow$. Therefore, attention decreases with t, as shown in Figure 2.4.

Threat Warning Interpretation

When hearing a threat warning, people may have different interpretations. According to Goffman (1974), a person could form frames (i.e. basic cognitive structures) to capture meanings of communication text and generate a definition and/or moral evaluation. This means people use frames to interpret the world and communicate about it (Entman, 1993). Therefore, if the threat warning information is unclear, people with different background may generate different frames, resulting in conflicting interpretations. To overcome this conflicting interpretation concerning threats, the warning messages should be clear and use simple, easily understood words without multiple or confusing meanings. As shown in Table 1.1 (in Chapter I), an appropriate warning message should include the type of the threat, the possible occurrence time, the potential target location, the duration of the threat warning, and the recommended protective actions.

REFERENCES

Citizen Guidance (2001). *Citizen guidance on the Homeland Security Advisory System*. Retrieved January 3, 2003, from http://www.dhs.gov/dhspublic/.

Congressional Research Services [CRS] (2004). Homeland Security Advisory System: Possible issues for congressional oversight. *Congressional Research Services*. Washington , DC, January 29, 2004.

Entman, R. M. (1993). Framing: Toward clarification of a fractured paradigm. *Journal of Communication*, *43*(4), 51-8.

Federal Guidance (2001). *Guidance for federal departments and agencies*. Retrieved January 3, 2003, from http://www.dhs.gov/dhspublic/.

General Accounting Office (2004). Homeland Security–Risk communication principles may assist in refinement of the Homeland Security Advisory System. *The U.S. General Accounting Office report on the Homeland Security Advisory System*. Retrieved December 12, 2004, from http://www.gao.gov/cgi-bin/getrpt?gao-04-538T.

Giordano, F. R., & Weir, M. D. (1994). *Differential equations: A modeling approach. Reprinted with correction*. New York: Addison-Wesley Publishing Company.

Goffman, E. (1974). *Frame analysis: An essay on the organization of experience*. London: Harper and Row.

McCarthy, M. (2005). Building an enduring capability for homeland security science and technology. *DHS Technology Conference*, Boston, MA.

PPW (2004). The Homeland Security Advisory System: Threat codes & public responses. *PPW testimony before the House Subcommittee on National Security, Emerging Threats and International Relations.* Retrieved November 18, 2004, from http://www.PartnershipforPublicWarning.org.

U.S. Department of Homeland Security [DHS] (2001). *The Homeland Security Advisory System.* Retrieved January 3, 2003, from http://www.dhs.gov/.

APPENDIX: CITIZEN GUIDANCE ON THE HOMELAND SECURITY ADVISORY SYSTEM

 READY.GOV
From The U.S. Department of Homeland Security.

Citizen Guidance on the Homeland Security Advisory System

Risk of Attack	Recommended Actions for Citizens
GREEN Low Risk	➡ Develop a family emergency plan. Share it with family and friends, and practice the plan. Visit www.Ready.gov for help creating a plan. ➡ Create an "Emergency Supply Kit" for your household. ➡ Be informed. Visit www.Ready.gov or obtain a copy of "Preparing Makes Sense, Get Ready Now" by calling 1-800-BE-READY. ➡ Know how to shelter-in-place and how to turn off utilities (power, gas, and water) to your home. ➡ Examine volunteer opportunities in your community, such as Citizen Corps, Volunteers in Police Service, Neighborhood Watch or others, and donate your time. ➡ Consider completing an American Red Cross first aid or CPR course, or Community Emergency Response Team (CERT) course .
BLUE Guarded Risk	➡ *Complete recommended steps at level green.* ➡ Review stored disaster supplies and replace items that are outdated. ➡ Be alert to suspicious activity and report it to proper authorities.
YELLOW Elevated Risk	➡ *Complete recommended steps at levels green and blue.* ➡ Ensure disaster supply kit is stocked and ready. ➡ Check telephone numbers in family emergency plan and update as necessary. ➡ Develop alternate routes to/from work or school and practice them. ➡ Continue to be alert for suspicious activity and report it to authorities.
ORANGE High Risk	➡ *Complete recommended steps at lower levels.* ➡ Exercise caution when traveling, pay attention to travel advisorie. ➡ Review your family emergency plan and make sure all family members know what to do. ➡ Be Patient. Expect some delays, baggage searches and restrictions at public buildings. ➡ Check on neighbors or others that might need assistance in an emergency.
RED Severe Risk	➡ *Complete all recommended actions at lower levels.* ➡ Listen to local emergency management officials. ➡ Stay tuned to TV or radio for current information/instructions. ➡ Be prepared to shelter-in-place or evacuate, as instructed. ➡ Expect traffic delays and restrictions. ➡ Provide volunteer services only as requested. ➡ Contact your school/business to determine status of work day.

Developed with input from the American Red Cross.

Unit II
Psychosocial Aspect and Social Dynamics:
A Mathematical Modeling Approach

The September 11, 2001, terrorist attack on the United States presented a new kind of threat. Damage to certain targets with strong symbolic meaning created fear and generated high levels of anxiety among a large population. Research involving post-disaster analyses, such as post-traumatic stress disorder (PTSD) analysis in the past 15–20 years, shows that in addition to physical property damage, a disaster event, whether natural or human-made, affects people's mindsets and may result in different levels of psychological damage (Briere et al., 2000; Norris et al., 2002a, 2002b; National Research Council [NRC], 2006). Although disaster-induced negative psychological outcomes may take time to develop, psychosocial effects start immediately after a disaster occurs, and fear and anxiety are common phenomena observed.

Threat information can impair people because it works directly on human mindsets. The resulting effect can produce either negative or positive impacts. In a war situation, for example, the two sides often conduct media campaigns or operations before actual military combat begins. They convey selected information and indicators to their counterparts and attempt to influence people's emotions, consciousness, and attitudes. These operations further attempt to deter and threaten adversaries and obtain the support of friendly or neutral target audiences. After the September 11 terrorist attack, terrorists often released threatening videos before important U.S. holidays (e.g., Independence Day, Thanksgiving, Christmas) to threaten the public with potential hazard attacks. If a threat involves the possible release of a biological agent, the targeted population experiences worry and fear. The characteristics of such threats, such as uncertainty about whether or when the threat will become a real attack, the difficulty of determining the scope of the attack, and the possibility of contagion, may heighten the level of fear and anxiety, resulting in additional psychosocial damages. Moreover, responders may be influenced and concerned about their personal health. Such threat-induced psychological effects influence the effectiveness of response efforts.

In this unit, we analyze the working procedure of brain components that are in charge of human memory and decision making. We then use differential dynamics to explore how people react to a threat or disaster event.

Because beliefs and/or fear can be shared, the actions or moods of others may directly affect a person's attitude, especially when the situation is ambiguous and difficult to assess. In addition, threat information can be either amplified or filtered through its circulation. Amplified information increases the atmosphere of anxiety and fear, which may create a fertile ground for rumors and misconceptions, whereas filtered or attenuated information may lower people's guards, perhaps resulting in unnecessary damages. We quantify possible collective behavior to measure how a population may be affected and how such influence challenges the effects of response. The analytic solutions project the range and severity of the possible psychosocial consequences of a disaster and suggest the extent to which these consequences influence effective behavioral responses.

In applying our proposed models to examine the potential psychosocial influences of an infectious disease, like SARS, we demonstrate that the model's predictions are highly consistent with observed empirical data. Thus, we consider this work a first step in developing mathematical models to understand the psychosocial effects of a disaster and how such impacts may affect social productivity. Planning for behavioral health responses in advance is urgent and necessary. In our view, dynamic systems theory and mathematical modeling can lead to important advances in planning for such responses.

The remainder of this unit is organized as follows: We describe the formation mechanism of the psychosocial effects in Chapter III, then introduce the modeling procedure and explore how people response to a disaster event in Chapter IV. Finally, we examine the population level psychosocial effects in Chapter V.

REFERENCES

Briere, J., & Elliott, D. M. (2000). Prevalence, characteristics, and long-term sequelae of natural disaster exposure in the general population. *Journal of Traumatic Stress, 13*(4), 661-679.

National Research Council [NRC], (2006). *Facing hazards and disasters: Understanding human dimensions.* Committee on Disaster Research in the Social Sciences: Future Challenges and Opportunities. Washington DC, US: National Academies Press.

Norris, F. H., Friedman, M. J., & Watson, P. J. (2002a). 60,000 disaster victims speak: Part II. Summary and implication of disaster mental health research. *Psychiatry, 65*(3), 240-260.

Norris, F. H., Friedman, M. J., Watson, P. J., Byrne, C. M., Diaz, E., & Kaniasty, K. (2002b). 60,000 disaster victims speak. Part I. An empirical review of the empirical literature, 1981-2001. *Psychiatry, 65*(3), 207-239.

Chapter III
Psychosocial Effects:
A Silent Influence

TWO POSSIBLE EFFECTS OF A DISASTER

According to the American Red Cross, a disaster is an occurrence, such as a hurricane, tornado, storm, flood, high water, wind-driven water, tidal wave, earthquake, drought, blizzard, pestilence, famine, fire, explosion, volcanic eruption, building collapse, transportation wreck, or other situation, that causes human suffering or creates human needs that the victims cannot alleviate without assistance. Basically, this definition covers all natural, conventional disasters. Since the attacks of September 11th, 2001, terrorist-related threats or attacks represent a newly realized danger to the public. For example, before September 11, 2001, Americans did not worry much about terrorism; after the attacks, they worried intensely. In this context, we define a *disaster* as an occurrence that threatens a society, causes human suffering, or damages goods such as buildings, communication systems, infrastructures, living environments, and so forth. In this definition, society, humans, and goods are called affected entities, and the force behind the occurrence is the causer or source of the disaster. The causer can be human-made or a natural force.

If a disaster occurs, a force or power by the causer acts on the affected entities and produces an effect, namely, the disaster. When the causer activates this force, two results may occur. First, the affected entities may suffer physical and/or chemical changes due to the power of the causer, such that their physical structures or functions get hurt—for example, property damage or physical casualties. Second, the causer might not create any direct physical damage but cause other consequences, which we call psychosocial effects. Usually, the latter effect is associated with the former when the causer activates its power. For example, the 1995 terrorist attack, during which Sarin nerve gas was released into the Tokyo subway system, not only caused physical casualties to people onsite but also produced a wave of mass anxiety in nearby areas. However, the latter result can play a threatening role, depending on type of the causer. For example, if the causer is a biological agent used as a threat, the targeted population would experience worry and fear. The associated characteristics, such as the uncertainty about whether, or when, a threat will become a real attack, the difficulty in determining the scope of the attack, and the possibility of contagion, may even heighten the level of fear and anxiety, resulting in additional psychosocial damages. Based on the 1995 Sarin gas attack in Tokyo, research suggests

Figure 3.1. Two forms of potential damages

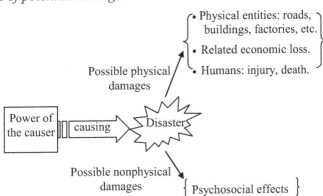

that a similar biological threat, if it materialized, would produce four psychological casualties for every one physical casualty, though the estimated ratio of psychological to physical casualties ranges from 4 to 1 to as high as 50 to 1 (Demartino, 2002).

Figure 3.1 sketches the two possible effects of a disaster: physical and nonphysical damages. If we consider the formation of the former audible or visible, then the formation of the latter is silent or invisible. Physical damages are usually obvious when a disaster occurs; for example, if a tornado touches down, the damages appear immediately. Thus, the physical impacts of a disaster tend to receive more attention and greater study because of their obvious consequences. By applying complex statistical methodology with predefined probability distributions for the key input variables, many studies have estimated possible death tolls, property damage, and dollar costs as a means to predict the potential effects of a disaster in advance and suggest appropriate preparations (Garrett, 2005; Karesh & Cook, 2005; Meltzer et al., 1999; Mileti, 1999; NRC, 2006; *Washington Post*, 2005). To help create emergency response plans, the U.S. Department of Homeland Security (DHS) has developed 15 national planning scenarios relating to possible terrorist attacks, disease outbreaks, and natural disasters (Lipton, 2005). Assessments and predictions surrounding these 15 scenarios focus mainly on estimating potential damages to properties and their related economic costs. Similarly, the National Earthquake Hazard Research Program (NEHRP)–sponsored "Second Assessment of Research on Natural Hazards" concentrates on dollar losses from a wide array of natural hazards, severe weather-related events, and earthquakes.

The latter effects, though silent, have powerful public implications as well. A disaster can impair people's physical bodies and minds; possible effects range from common signs such as fear and anxiety to fatigue and sadness, depression, or possible stress disorders. The worst potential consequence is a psychiatric disorder, which can occur after experiencing or witnessing life-threatening events, such as military combat, natural disasters, terrorist incidents, serious accidents, or violent personal assaults. Such disorders significantly impair a person's daily life. Therefore, people exposed to a disaster display different reaction and symptom levels during and/or after the disaster, such that some are more affected than others, depending on the nature of the event and the characteristics of the persons who have experienced or witnessed it (Koopman et al., 1995; NSW, 2000).

Possible psychosocial effects usually emerge immediately rather than long after the actual disaster, and fear and anxiety represent common reactions to imminent threats and actual disaster events (Bartholomew & Victor, 2004; Clark, 2002, 2003; Johnson, 1987; Quarantelli & Dynes, 1972). Fear can affect a person's behavior. Immediately following September 11, 2001, many people were afraid to fly, and domestic air travel declined 8.7 percent in May 2002 compared with the previous year (Air Transport Association, 2002). The 2004 water scare event in Washington DC provides another example of how anxiety and fear about an event can affect the public's response. In early 2004, reports indicated that drinking water in Washington DC contained high concentrations of lead, so the District of Columbia's Water and Sewer Authority recommended that residents let water run for 1–2 minutes prior to using it for drinking or cooking. However, many residents let their water run for approximately 10 minutes, which represents an inappropriate response (Davis, 2004). In the months following the 9/11 terrorist attacks, anthrax cases caused not only widespread fears about bioterrorism but also collective anxiety nationwide. In the wake of extensive bioterrorism fears, thousands of people bought the broad-spectrum antibiotic ciprofloxacin hydrochloride. A public survey conducted by Harvard School of Public Health indicates that 5 percent of Americans had purchased an antibiotic and that 20 percent had taken the drugs prophylactically (Public Survey, 2001).

Research into the outbreak of severe acute respiratory syndrome (SARS) in 2003 shows that disaster-induced psychosocial effects influence the effectiveness of response efforts, such as disaster control procedures, rescue processes, and participation by health care workers and others. The outbreak of SARS in 2003 led to psychological distress among both health care workers and the general public because of the stigmatization of groups perceived to be at high risk and general fears about safety and health (Bai et al., 2004; HSC, 2006; Maunder et al., 2006; Nickell et al., 2004; Tam et al., 2004). Nickell and colleagues (2004), in their survey investigating the psychosocial impacts of SARS on health care workers involved with SARS-affected patients or hospitals during and after the 2003 outbreak, reveal that of 1,988 health care workers, 40.7 percent showed some degree of concern about personal health (i.e., fear of contagion), 24 percent were extremely concerned about their personal health, and another 29 percent indicated the presence of emotional distress. Before the virus had been identified, SARS was an infection of unknown cause, unknown mode of transmission, global spread, and high mortality (CDC, 2003). Such characteristics increase people's perceived risks and heighten the level of fear and anxiety associated with being contaminated; even the psychological well-being of medical professionals could not avoid being affected, because such a disaster could threaten their lives as well (Straus et al., 2004).

These studies demonstrate that at the time of a disaster event, many people experience fear and anxiety. In this sense, a disaster event's physical damage and the results of mass fear and anxiety represent a terrible reality with the potential to cause great public health and economic burdens. Yet no models predict how psychosocial effects challenge the effectiveness of response efforts to mitigate the disaster (Garrett, 2005; Stein et al., 2004).

Psychosocial effects include not only fear and anxiety during the disaster but other psychopathologies as well, particularly depressive symptoms, such as decreased self-efficacy, impaired work performance, startle responses, and feelings of helplessness or sadness. Sometimes, the effects may cause a long-term consequence, namely, post-traumatic stress disorder (PTSD) (Bolton et al., 2000; Sharan et al., 1996). People who suffer from PTSD often relive the experience through nightmares and flashbacks, have difficulty sleeping, and feel detached or estranged. Therefore, to prepare better and protect the public, we must understand how a threat or disaster event affects people's minds and how individual-level anxiety and stress spread. In turn, we can build a model that describes how a threat or disaster influences behavior and reactions.

FORMATION PROCEDURE OF THE PSYCHOSOCIAL EFFECTS

When they face a threat or danger, the amygdala in humans' midbrains receives input on the conscious level from the cortex and sets off a chain of events that result in a rapid release of oxytocin, vasopressin, and a corticotropin-releasing hormone, which in turn activates the sympathetic nervous system (Alen et al., 1993; Cannon, 1932). In response, the adrenal glands produce adrenaline and, through a different pathway, cortisol, both of which prepare the body for fight or flight. Thus, without weighing pros and cons, the amygdala can make a quick decision to prompt immediate actions, such as fight or flight, when the person perceives a threat. Meanwhile, the hippocampus, a seahorse-shaped area in the midbrain, receives information from the cortex and combines the encountered event, such as the source or context surrounding the encounter, with separate features of past experiences into an integrated memory picture in the brain that helps the person make rational decisions. In a typical brain, the hippocampus works in conjunction with the amygdala to connect memory with emotion and make rational decisions. Therefore, a person's reaction to a threat is influenced by his or her experiences in memory.

If a human-made or natural disaster occurs in a targeted area, it can be treated as an external force acting on people in that area. Analogous to an information wave field or magnetic field, a disaster field forms, such that people in that area may be affected to various degrees (see Figure 3.2).

People in that area may be exposed to the disaster event as direct victims or eyewitnesses. Without having any connection to or communication with others, a person has only two base inputs to guide his or her reaction: the information reflected by the disaster event itself (i.e., the person's direct observation of the disaster) and information from the person's memory (i.e., knowledge or experience). These two types of information provide a base for the initial analysis we have described. During the course of the disaster, imagine that the person can observe others' behaviors and reactions or receive information from the mass media (e.g., newspaper, television, the Internet) or through word-of-mouth social communications. Then, the base inputs increase to include "one's own direct observation," "one's memory information," "other people's behavior or reactions," "information from the mass media," and/or "word-of-mouth social communication." The first two represent *individualized information*, whereas the latter three are labeled *social influence information*. Thus, a person's reaction to a disaster can be influenced by either individual or social influence information, or both together.

Figure 3.2. A disaster field

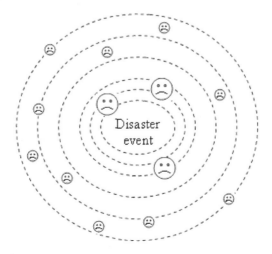

Those who are not physically in the disaster area receive disaster information only from social influence information. They interpret and incorporate it with their own memory information, which produces individualized information about the disaster.

Figure 3.3 displays how disaster information gets disseminated through two sources. One source is eyewitnesses or people experienced the disaster. These people may pass along or share their individualized information with others through social connections. Thus, the disaster information is disseminated or broadcast in terms of individualized information. The second source is social influence information. Through these two sources, disaster information, accompanied by personal feelings and interpretations, gets transmitted from one person to another. Note that transmission procedures run parallel to each other rather than as a sequence. On the basis of this information, each receiver, regardless of whether he or she is directly or indirectly affected by a disaster, generates a reaction. Each person's behavior then may be observed by others, which makes it a component of the social influence information, and may affect others' behavior or reactions. These behaviors eventually may accumulate and become collective behavior.

As a result of information dissemination, fear and subjective risk perceptions get transmitted as well. Sometimes, media reports prompt broad transmissions. For example, Orson Welles's famous radio show *The War of The Worlds*, broadcast in 1938, led many radio listeners to experience fear and rush out of their homes to escape the so-called "Gas Raid from Mars" (*The New York Times*, 1938). The psychological effects of a disaster thus clearly have social aspects and are transitive among different people. We therefore use the term "psychosocial effects" to describe the psychological effects of a disaster and its associated social characteristics. To prevent or reduce the negative impact of psychosocial effects, we must identify key components that are critical to their formation.

Figure 3.3. Information flow of disaster promulgation

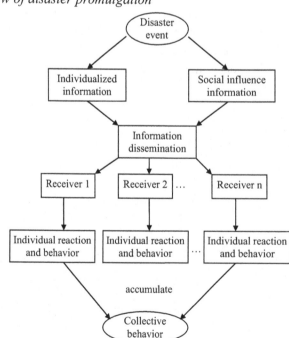

KEY COMPONENTS

Our analysis in the previous section suggests that several key components play important roles in forming psychosocial effects. The first and most obvious is the disaster event itself, or the causer, which can be human-made or a natural force. If the disaster event can be predicted in advance, an action to destroy the causer or prevent its occurrence provides the best way to avoid psychosocial effects. An early warning advisory to the public also can ensure appropriate preparations, which may decrease nervousness—forewarned is forearmed. If the disaster event occurs suddenly, implementing an effective onsite response immediately can help control the disaster. We discuss this issue more in Chapter VI. Meanwhile, providing timely information to the public about what is happening, the characteristics of the disaster, and its scope, as well the response actions undertaken, can help reduce anxiety.

The second component is the media: eyewitnesses of the disaster or mass media. As the information carrier, the particular medium transmits not only the information about the disaster with different interpretations but also descriptions about emotional and behavioral reactions to the disaster information. The medium also acts as an information disseminator, or source, that spreads information. Previous research on risk communication indicates that information can be either amplified or filtered through its circulation (Kasperson et al., 2003). Amplified information increases the atmosphere of anxiety and fear, which may create a fertile ground for rumors and misconceptions. Filtered or attenuated information may lower people's guard, perhaps resulting in unnecessary damages. Thus, providing accurate and objective information about the situation during the disaster is very important (Freudenburg, 1996).

The third component is information circulation. With different types of dissemination channels, disaster-related information spreads more quickly and thus may affect broad geographic areas. In the past, people got information through face-to-face communications or traditional news media, such as newspapers, radio, or television. Thus, the information-spreading area largely depended on the coverage areas of those media channels. Today, globalization and the telecommunications revolution, especially the emergence of the World Wide Web, have made the acquisition of information much easier. New technologies enable information to travel faster than ever before and reach all over the world within a very short time. Information transmission thus has increased exponentially in volume, variety, and velocity, which also speeds the spread of possible emotional reactions, such as fear and anxiety.

The fourth component refers to people's behaviors and reactions. When a person knows about a disaster event, knowledge about disaster characteristics alone is not enough to motivate a reaction. Instead, the information must be translated into a notion of pending danger. A series of processes in the amygdala, the hippocampus, and the brain cortex generates a reaction when the danger or threat is sensed and recognized. Different people with different educational and cultural backgrounds may undergo different life experiences, so even if they receive the same information, different people may have different interpretations, which will result in different reactions and behaviors.

Finally, the fifth component is convergent behavior. Social observers and philosophers have long recognized imitation as important in human society (Machiavelli, 1514; Hoffer, 1955). Within minutes of birth, human infants mimic the observed facial expressions of adults. As we grow older, we continue to be influenced by the observed actions of others, from simple recreation choices to wider lifestyles. That is, people tend to converge on similar behavior in what is known as "herding" behavior. The simplest reason for such behavior is that people generally face similar decision problems. When facing a threat, everyone confronts the same problem: Am I in danger? If so, how should I avoid it and what actions I should take? If a person does not know what actions to take, he or she likely follows others' actions.

Convergent behavior results when these reactions are similar, even if the information received is different. Thus, individual behavior may accumulate and become collective behavior.

Identifying these five key components enable us to understand how the psychosocial effects form and thus determine ways to prevent their occurrence or target each component to reduce its potential impacts. Extensive research focuses on (1) the second component, that is, developing and delivering a message about the danger in a pending emergency or in general from a risk expert to the general public, an area called risk communication (Cutter, 1995; Lundgren, 1994); (2) the fourth component, pertaining to how and which factors, such as gender, age, culture, or race, affect risk perceptions and evaluations (Sjöberg, 2000); and (3) the fifth component, or the possible long-term consequence of psychosocial effects, such as PTSD (NRC, 2006). In this study, we focus particularly on the fourth and fifth components and build mathematical models to understand how people react when facing a threat (Chapter IV). We then model macro-level psychosocial effects in the targeted population to analyze its effects on levels of social productivity (Chapter V).

Before introducing our mathematical modeling efforts, we first must identify the characteristics of the psychosocial effects and then briefly review current research.

CHARACTERISTICS OF THE PSYCHOSOCIAL EFFECTS

As we show in Figure 3.1, a disaster event may generate two possible impacts: physical and nonphysical. Unlike the physical impacts, which occur immediately when the disaster event hits the targeted area, nonphysical impacts—that is, the psychosocial effects—can happen before, during, and after the actual disaster event. Psychosocial effects can start earlier, last longer, and influence more widely and thus exhibit the following characteristics: long continuance, accumulation, and widespread transmissibility.

Long continuance. Nonphysical impacts of a disaster can impair people because they work directly on human mindsets. Thus, the psychosocial effects can play a role even before the actual occurrence of an event, which means they exhibit a preceding character. Furthermore, these effects can produce either negative or positive impacts, depending on the objectives. In a war situation, for example, the two sides often conduct media campaigns or operations before the actual military combat begins. They convey selected information and indicators to their counterparts and attempt to influence people's emotions, consciousness, and attitudes. These operations further attempt to deter and threaten adversaries and obtain the support of friendly or neutral target audiences. After the September 11 terrorist attacks, terrorists often released threatening videos before important U.S. holidays (e.g., Independence Day, Thanksgiving, Christmas) to threaten the public with potential hazard attacks. For example, when July 4, 2002, approached and news reports warned of the possibility of terrorist activity, gun sales on July 3, 2002, rose 32 percent higher than the FBI had predicted for that date (Wilson, 2002). Uncertainty about whether the attacks threatened would actually occur and whether the public perceived itself as at risk likely increased the level of general anxiety. Research on risk perception indicates that such uncertainty causes fear; the more uncertain we are, the more afraid we are (Slovic et al., 1979, 1980).

Disaster-induced psychosocial effects also appear during the disaster period and can last for months or years after a disaster event. Examining the possible psychiatric impacts of missile attacks on Israel during the 1992 Gulf War, Bleich and colleagues (1992) find that 773 civilians were taken to 12 different hospitals at the time of the attacks, and 43 percent of them as psychological casualties. Meanwhile, during the attacks, the Israeli population suffered a reported 250 percent increase in the risk of clinical depression (Lomranz et al. 1994). In addition, several studies have assessed how major accidents, such as the Three Mile Island nuclear power station accident in the United States in 1979, the Chernobyl nuclear disaster in the Soviet Union in 1986, and so forth, which may be considered similar to a terrorist attack, affect the public's mindset (Baum, et al. 1983; Houts, et al. 1988; Mould, 2000; UNDP, 2002). These studies indicate that many people remain fearful and anxious about whether they had been exposed to radiation at the time of the event. Some displayed chronic stress syndromes, depression and anxiety, and mood disorder symptoms several years after the events.

Furthermore, the long-term psychosocial impacts of a disaster have been reported and studied widely in public health literature (Clark, 2002; Johnson, 1987; Norris et al., 2002a, 20002b; NSW, 2000; Quarantelli & Dynes, 1972; Udwin et al., 2000; Ursano et al., 1996). For example, Ohbu and colleagues (1997) find that approximately 60 percent of the patients who presented at St. Luke's International Hospital following the 1995 Sarin gas attack in Tokyo suffered from PTSD symptoms that had persisted for longer than six months. The old saying, "Once bitten by a snake, one shies at a coiled rope for the next ten years," reflects the long continuance character.

Accumulation. Because the psychosocial effects of a disaster occur in people's minds, information, including feelings and experiences of historical events, may remain in memory. When a person faces another disaster or a threat, those past experience may come back to mind. Research indicates that previous experience with disaster events does not have a positive effect on the survival behavior of affected people; rather, it induces negative effects, and people with prior psychological distress histories suffer a much greater risk of being retraumatized by a new experience. People carry forward the combination of events and their impacts through time, inscribed in their memory, their sense of self, and their behavior. Thus, a disaster-/threat-induced psychosocial damage is both cumulative and summative (Kammerer & Mazelis, 2006).

Widespread with transmissibility. Relied through information dissemination, the psychosocial effects of a disaster can spread, unlike the direct physical damages, which are mainly confined to the disaster area and surrounding areas. Because feeling can be shared, emotional consequences get transmitted from one person to another. In the 1995 Sarin gas attack in Tokyo, for example, more than 4,500 members of the Tokyo population who were not in the subway at the time of the attack were labeled "psychological casualties" because they presented with symptoms unrelated to direct exposure to Sarin gas (Kawana, et al. 2001).

CURRENT PROGRESS

Studies examining the impacts of a potential disaster may be categorized into two tracks. The first focuses on economic analyses and attempts to estimate or predict the potential property losses and dollar costs of a disaster in advance (Garrett, 2005; Karesh & Cook, 2005; Meltzer et al., 1999; Mileti, 1999; *The Washington Post*, 2005). These analyses usually apply statistical methodology with predefined probability distributions of the key input variables to forecast possible death tolls, property damages, and dollar costs (NRC, 2006). The second track examines the possible long-term psychological consequences of a disaster, specifically PTSD, by conducting post-disaster follow-up case analyses. That is, after a disaster, researchers survey the affected population to examine their post-impact reactions, then keep tracking them for several years in an attempt to understand the factors related to increased or decreased risk for PTSD, which ideally helps affected people recover from their disaster distress (Clark,

2002; Johnson, 1987; Norris et al., 2002a, 20002b; NSW, 2000; Quarantelli & Dynes, 1972; Udwin et al., 2000; Ursano et al., 1996). For example, a survey study conducted in the immediate aftermath of the September 11 terrorist attacks revealed that 44 percent of the national sample reported experiencing substantial psychological distress, both in the cities where the attacks occurred and across the country (Schuster et al., 2002).

In a related area, "risk analysis and management," researchers identify factors that may govern risk evaluations and perceptions, such as the perceived catastrophic potential of the hazard and the perceived lack of control over the situation, which play major roles in determining the magnitude of a risk (Hermand, et al, 2003). Certain kinds of hazards and accidents, such as nuclear power hazards and terrorism risks, lead to widespread, strong concerns. That is, people appear more afraid of risks that are catastrophic and threaten to kill many people all at once in one place than those that are chronic and kill people over time in scattered locations. Using experiments and survey data, several studies examine the factors that affect perceptions of terrorism risks (Fischhoff et al., 2003; Lerner et al., 2003; Sjöberg, 2004; Sunstein, 2003; Viscusi & Zeckhauser, 2003). For example, people are more tolerant of risks that have been become familiar to them such as car versus planes. Studies find differences in risk perception or tolerance along ethnic, age, and gender lines. However, these studies do not detail the procedure by which people process risk perceptions in their minds when facing a threat or disaster. However, understanding how people process information represents a vital aspect of understanding their behavioral responses.

Fewer published reports about the psychological impact of disease outbreaks adopt a survey approach or present summarized results at an aggregate level. Because people likely have different emotional and behavioral reactions to the same threat, survey results suggest only the level of importance and cannot account for how individual-level psychosocial damage develops, nor understand its underlying dynamic processes. Therefore, in Chapters IV and V, we target this research gap by developing mathematical models of the impacts of a threat on people's minds during a disaster. This approach enables us to measure the individual-level psychosocial consequences of a disaster event and project the range and severity of the possible psychosocial consequences during the disaster; in turn, we can estimate population-level social productivity and response efforts.

Although extensive research estimates the economic impacts and long-term psychological effects (i.e., PSDT) of a disaster, to the best of our knowledge, no studies apply mathematical equations to describe psychosocial effects or explore their impact on the effectiveness of public responses in terms of social productivity (Stein et al., 2004). Modeling at both individual and population levels, with a concomitant shift from a statistical to a dynamic mathematical model, will enable us to understand how people dynamically respond to disaster events, suggest more effective responses, and help reduce the occurrence of long-term psychological damages.

REFERENCES

Air Transport Association [ATA], (2002). Passenger traffic down 8.7 percent in May. Press release June 18, 2002. Retrieved January 8, 2003, from http://www.airlines.org/public/news/display2asp?nid=5539.

Alen, M. T., Stoney, C. M., Owens, J. F., & Matthews, K. A. (1993). Hemodynamic adjustments to laboratory stress: the influence of gender and personality. *Psychosomatic Medicine, 55*, 505-517.

Bai, Y., Lin, C. C., Chen, J. Y., Chue, C. M., & Chou, P. (2004). Survey of stress reactions among health care workers involved with the SARS outbreak. *Psychiatry Service, 55*, 1055-1057.

Bartholomew, R. E., & Victor, J. S. (2004). A social-psychological theory of collective anxiety attacks: the "Mad Gasser" reexamined. *The Sociological Quarterly, 45*(2), 229-248.

Baum, A., Gatchel, R. J., & Schaeffer, M. A. (1983). Emotional, behavioral, and physiological effects of chronic stress at Three Mile Island. *Journal of Consulting and Clinical Psychology, 51*, 565-572.

Bleich, A., Dycian, A., Koslowsky, M., Solomon, Z., & Wiener, M. (1992). Psychiatric implications of missile attacks on a civilian population: Israeli lessons from the Persian Gulf War. *Journal of the American Medical Association, 268*, 613-615.

Bolton, D. O'Ryan, D., Udwin, O., Boyle, S., & Yule, W. (2000). The long-term psychological effects of a disaster experienced in adolescence: II: General psychopathology. *Journal of Child Psychology and Psychiatry, 41*(9), 513-523.

Cannon, W. B. (1932). *The wisdom of the body.* New York: Norton.

Chen, W. Y., & Bokka, S.(2005). Stochastic modeling of nonlinear epidemiology. *Journal of Theoretical Biology, 234*, 455-470.

Clark, L. (2002). Panic: Myth or reality? *Contexts,* Fall, 21-26.

Clark, L. (2003). Conceptualizing responses to extreme events: The problem of panic and failing gracefully. In L. B. Clark (ed.) *Terrorism and Disaster: New Threats, New Ideas. Research in Social Problems and Public Policy* (11) (pp. 123-141). Amsterdam: Elsevier.

Cutter, S. L. (1995). *Living with risk.* New York: Edward Arnold Publisher.

Davis, T. (2004). Public confidence down the drain: The federal role in ensuring safe drinking water in the District of Columbia. Open statement presented at a hearing before the House Committee on Government Reform, March 5, 2004. Washington, DC.

Demartino, R. M. (2002), Bioterrorism: what are we afraid of and what should we do? Paper presented to *the Biosecurity 2002 Conference,* November. Las Vegas.

Fischhoff, B., Gonzalez, R. M., Small, D. A., & Lerner, J. S. (2003). Judged terror risk and proximity to the World Trade Center. *Journal of Risk and Uncertainty, 26*, 131-151.

Freudenburg, W. R., Coleman, C. L., Gonzalez, J., & Hegeland, C. (1996). Media coverage of events: analyzing the assumptions. *Risk Analysis, 16*, 31-42.

Garrett, L. (2005). The next pandemic? *Foreign Affairs, 84*(4), 3-23.

Hermand, D., Karsenty, S., Py, Y., Guillet, L., & Chauvin, B. et al. (2003). Risk target: an interactive context factor in risk perception. *Risk Analysis, 23*, 821-833.

Hoffer, E. (1955). *The passionate state of mind,* aphorism 33. New York: Harper.

Homeland Security Council [HSC]. (2006). *National strategy for pandemic influenza: Implementation plan.* Washington DC: US Homeland Security Council.

Houts, P., Cleary, P., & Hu, T. (1988). *The Three Mile Island crisis: psychological, social and economic impacts on the surrounding population.* University Park: Pennsylvania State University Press.

Jaeger, C. C., Renn, O., Rosa, E. A., & Webler, T. (2001). *Risk, uncertainly, and rational action.* Earthscan Publications Ltd.

Kammerer, C. A., & Mazelis, R. (2006). Trauma and retraumatization. Retrieved Decemebr 12, 2006, from http://www.gainscenter.samhsa.gov/atc/pdfs/papers/trauma.pdf.

Karesh, W. B., & Cook, R. A. (2005). The human-animal link. *Foreign Affairs, 84*(4), 38-50.

Kasperson, J. X., Kasperson, R. E., Pidgeon, N., & Slovic, P. (2003). The social amplification of risk: Assessing fifteen years of research and theory. In N. Pidgeon, R. E. Kasperson, & P. Slovc (Eds.), *The social amplification of risk* (pp. 13-46). Cambridge, England: Cambridge University Press.

Kermack, W. O., & McKendrick, A. G. (1927). A contribution to the mathematical theory of epidemics. *Proceedings of the Royal Society of London, A, 115*(772), 700-721.

Koopman, C., Classen, C. C., Cardena, E., & Spiegel, D. (1995). When disaster strikes, acute stress disorder may follow. *Journal of Traumatic Stress, 8*(1), 29-46.

Lerner, J. S., Gonzalez, R. M. Small, D. A., & Fischhoff, B. (2003). Effects of fear and anger on perceived risks of terrorism: A national field experiment. *Psychological Science, 14*, 144-150.

Lomranz, J., Hobfoll, S., Johnson, R., Eyal, N., & Zermach, M. (1994). A nation's response to attack: Israelis' depressive reactions to the Gulf War. *Journal of Traumatic Stress, 7*, 59-73.

Lundgren, R. (1994). *Risk communication: A handbook for communicating environmental, safety and health risks.* Columbus, Ohio: Battelle Press.

Machiavelli, N. (1514). *The prince.* Cambridge, England: Cambridge University Press.

Maunder, R. G., Lancee, W. J., Balderson, K. E., Bennett, J. P., Borgundvaag, B., Evans, S., & Fernandes, C. M. B. et al. (2006). Long-term psychological and occupational effects of providing hospital healthcare during SARS outbreak. *Emerging Infectious Diseases, 12*(12), 1924-1932.

Meltzer, M. I., Cox, N. J., & Fukuda, K. (1999). The economic impact of pandemic influenza in the United States: Priorities for intervention. *Emerging Infectious Diseases, 5*(5), 659-671.

Mileti, D. S. (1999). *Design for future disasters: a sustainable approach for hazards research and application in the United States.* Washington, DC: Joseph Henry Press.

Mould, R. F. (2000). *Chernobl record. The Definitive history of the Chernobyl catastrophe.* Bristol, Institute of Physics Publishing.

National Research Council [NRC], (2006). *Facing hazards and disasters: Understanding human dimensions.* Committee on Disaster Research in the Social Sciences: Future Challenges and Opportunities. Washington DC, US: National Academies Press.

Nickell, L. A., Crighton, E. J., Tracy, C. S., Al Enazy, H., Bolaji, Y., & Hanjrah, S. et al. (2004). Psychosocial effects of SARS on hospital staff: survey of a large tertiary case institution. *Canadian Medical Association Journal, 170*, 793-798.

North, C. S., Kawasaki, A., Spitznagel, E. L., & Hong, B. A. (2004). The course of PTSD, major depression, substance abuse, and somatization after a natural disaster. *The Journal of Nervous and Mental Disease, 192*(10), 1-7.

North, C. A., Nixon, S. J., Shariat, S., Mallonee, S., McMillen, J. C., Spitznagel, E. L., & Smith, E. M. (1999). Psychiatric disorders among survivors of the Oklahoma City bombing. *Journal of the American Medical Association, 282*(8), 755-762.

Ohbu, S., Yamashina, A., Takasu, N., Yamguchi, T., Murai, T., & et al. (1997). Sarin poisoning on Tokyo subway. Retrieved February 12, 2005, from http://www.sma.org/smj/97june3.htm.

Public Survey (2001), Survey project on American's response to biological terrorism. *International Communications Research*, Harvard School of Public Health and Robert Wood Johnson Foundation. October 24-28, 2001.

Quarantelli, E. I., & Dynes, R. R. (1977). Response to social crisis and disaster. *Annual Review of Sociology, 3*, 23-49.

Schlenger, W. E., Caddell, L., Ebert, B. K., & Jordan, K. M. (2002). Psychological reactions to terrorist attacks: findings from the national study of Americans' reactions to September 11. *Journal of the American Medical Association, 288*, 581-588.

Sharan, P., Chaudhary, G., Kavathekar, S. A., & Saxena, S. (1996). Preliminary report of psychiatric disorders in survivors of a severe earthquake. *American Journal of Psychiatry; 153*, 556-558.

Sjöberg, L. (2000). Factors in risk perception. *Risk Analysis, 20*(1), 1-11.

Sjöberg, L. (2004). The perceived risk of terrorism. *SSE/EFL Working paper series in Business Administration* (No 2002:11). Stockholm School of Economics, Stockholm, Sweden.

Slovic, P., Fischoff, B., & Lichtenstein, S. (1979). Rating the risks. *Environment, 21*, 3, 14-20.

Slovic, P., Fischoff, B., & Lichtenstein, S. (1980). Facts and fears: understanding perceived risk. In D. Schwing & R. Albers (Eds.) *Societal risk assessment: how safe is safe enough?* (pp. 181-216). New York: Plenum.

Stein, B. D., Tanielian, T. L., Eisenman, D. P., Keyser, D. J., & Burnam, M. A. (2004). Emotional and behavioral consequences of bioterrorism: planning a public health response. *The Milbank Quarterly, 82*(3), 413-455.

Straus, S. E., Wilson, K., Rambaldini, G., Rath, D., Lin, Y., Gold, W. L., & Kapral, M. K. (2004). Severe acute respiratory syndrome and its impact on professionalism: quantitative study of physicians' behavior during an emerging healthcare crisis. *BMJ, 329*, 83.

Sunstein, C. R. (2003). Terrorism and probability neglect. *Journal of Risk and Uncertainty, 26*, 121-136.

Tam, C. W., Pang, E. P., Lam, L. C., & Chiu, H. F. (2004). Severe acute respiratory syndrome (SARS) in Hong Kong in 2003: stress and psychological impact among frontline healthcare workers. *Psychological Medicine, 34*, 1197-1204.

The New York Times. (1938). Radio listeners in panic, taking war drama as fact. October 31. Retrieved January 12, 2005, from http://members.aol.com/jeff1070/wotw.html.

Udwin, O., Boyle, A., Yule, W., Bolton, D., & O'Ryan, D. (2000). Risk factors for long-term psychological effects of a disaster experienced in adolescence: Predictors of post traumatic stress disorder. *Journal of Child Psychology and Psychiatry, 41*(8), 969-979.

UNDP/UNICEF (2002). The human consequences of the Chernobyl nuclear accident: a strategy for recovery. *A Report Commissioned by UNDP and UNICEF with the support of UN-OCHA and WHO*. Retrieved February 10, 2005, from http://www.reliefweb.int/library/documents/2002/undp_rus_25jan.pdf.

Ursano, R. J., Grieger, T. A., & McCarroll, J. E. (1996). Prevention of posttraumatic stress: Consultation, training, and early treatment. In B. A. Van der Kolk, A.C. McFarlane, & L. Weisaeth (Eds.), *Traumatic stress: The effects of overwhelming experience on mind, body, and society*, 441-462, New York: Guilford Press.

US Centers for Disease Control and Prevention [CDC]. (2003). Severe cute respiratory syndrome. Retrieved January 4, 2004, from http://www.cdc.gov/ncidod/sars

Viscusi, W. K., & Zeckhauser, R. J. (2003). Sacrificing civil liberties to reduce terrorism risks. *Journal of Risk and Uncertainty, 26*, 99-120.

Washington Post. (2005). Bird flu called global human threat. Sec. A16. Retrieved February 26, 2005, from http://www.washingtonpost.com/wp-dyn/articles/A46424-2005Feb23.html.

Wilson, M. (2002). Personal communication. FBI NICS information officer. July 15, 2002.

Chapter IV
Individual Reactions and Psychological Impact

INTRODUCTION

The possible psychosocial consequences associated with a threat or disaster, as discussed in Chapter III, indicate that people's behaviors and/or reactions can indicate whether they are affected and the degree of impact if affected. If affected, possible reactions can range from common responses, such as fear and anxiety, to fatigue, sadness, depression, and stress disorders. Whereas some people experience significant subjective discomfort, others display conspicuous impairment in their day-to-day functioning, such as sleeplessness; still others indicate clear impairment in one or more functional aspects, such as work productivity or the ability to engage in and enjoy leisure activities.

Such disaster/threat-induced reactions may be classified into four categories on the basis of human mental functions (NSW, 2000, p. 28): emotional (e.g., feelings of shock and helplessness, loss of pleasure, sadness), cognitive (e.g., impaired concentration and decision-making ability, disbelief, decreased self-efficacy), physical (e.g., fatigue, exhaustion, startled response, reduced immune response, insomnia, vulnerability to illness), and interpersonal (e.g., social withdrawal, impaired work or school performance, distrust, externalization of vulnerability). If they occur, these effects weaken people's response capabilities during the course of a disaster.

In this chapter, we model how people react to an unexpected disaster or threat and thus quantify the possible psychosocial effects a person may experience. For modeling purposes, we make several simplifying assumptions. First, we assume that people are randomly attacked by the disaster event, as either witnesses or direct victims. That is, given the occurrence of a disaster event in a region or area; those who directly encounter the danger or threat are assumed to be random. Second, each affected person will have a different psychological reaction to the disaster event, in accordance with his or her personal experiences, risk perceptions of the disaster event, and self-immune systems. Third, we assume people are risk neutral and engage in rational conduct.

HOW PEOPLE REACT TO UNEXPECTED THREATS

When determining possible reactions, a person may receive two possible forms of perceived information, in addition to memory information: direct observations about the disaster event and social influence information received at time t. As we defined in Chapter III, social influence information includes information indicated by other people's behavior or reaction, information from news media, and/or information from word-of-mouth social communications.

When a person faces a threat, the perceived information is transmitted to the amygdala and hippocampus through the brain cortex. In addition to setting off a chain reaction and activating the sympathetic nervous system, the amygdala can prompt an immediate reaction, such as fight or flight. This natural role reflects human instinct (an inborn function), which does not require conscious thought processing. Sometimes people follow or rely on their instincts to make quick decisions. When they encounter danger, the emotional reaction is likely driven by the amygdala, so they display a fear instinct. Meanwhile, the adrenal glands produce adrenaline and, through a different pathway, cortisol. The more adrenaline produced, the more anxious the person is, which increases his or her stress level.

In contrast, the hippocampus receives information from the cortex and combines the encountered threat event, such as the source or context, with separate features of past experiences into an integrated memory picture that helps the person make thoughtful decisions. In collaboration with the brain cortex, the advanced-level nervous system performs a conscious thought process with the aid of the hippocampus. If thoughtful decisions and associated response methods can control or handle the threat situation, the person perceives a signal of decreasing risk, which triggers the amygdala to command the adrenal glands to reduce the secreted amount of adrenaline; then, stress levels decrease, and body functions such as heart rate and blood pressure gradually return to normal. In this case, the coalition forces of the brain cortex and the hippocampus surpass the effect of the amygdala. Thus, some people can keep calm and design dealing strategies when they encounter trouble, danger, or an urgent situation, even if they sense fear initially.

Figure 4.1 Generating a response decision

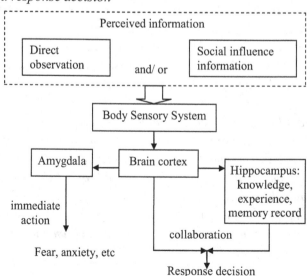

If a thoughtful decision and the associated response methods do not alter the threat situation and the threat still exists, the threat information is continuously perceived together with a signal of situational uncertainty. The amygdala continuously stimulates the sympathetic nervous system and the adrenal glands. More and more adrenaline gets secreted, which then leads to increased anxiety. A "threat still exists" signal suggests that the generated decision has not produced the expected effects and thus that the situation is uncertain. Such uncertainty increases both anxiety and stress. When a person experiences increasing stress, his or her productive thoughts decrease, whereas distracted thoughts increase (Sime, 1997). The continuing activation of the amygdala inhibits the functioning of the coalition force (i.e., collaboration between the brain cortex and the hippocampus). If this situation continues for as much as several days or weeks, the person's ability to make rational decision declines. When stress reaches a certain level, the person may consider only immediate survival goals; thus, the amygdala is playing the dominant role in responding to the threat situation, and these people are more anxious and distressed when facing a disaster event. Because of the accumulative character of psychosocial effects (i.e., prior negative experiences remain in memory in the hippocampus), when facing a new threat, the hippocampus brings them back to influence the decision-making thought process. The past negative impact, together with the new threat signal, strongly stimulates the amygdala and enhances its activity and role. Lonigan and colleagues (1991) find that greater anxiety leads to more PTSD symptomatology in children who have experienced more severe exposures to a disaster event. Therefore, people with prior psychological distress histories suffer a much greater risk of becoming retraumatized by an experience.

Figure 4.1 sketches the internal process of how a response decision gets generated when a person faces a threat. In a normal brain, the roles of the amygdala and the hippocampus are in balance. When people must respond to danger or an emergent situation, factors such as time pressure, the lack of information (e.g., perhaps only direct observation is available), or the influence of others (e.g., seeing or hearing others' actions) all can affect emotion and stress levels, which upset the balance between the amygdala and the hippocampus.

MODELING THE PSYCHOLOGICAL IMPACT

When a person perceives a threat, his or her brain, particularly the cortex, the amygdala, and the hippocampus, biologically and cognitively interpret that threat (see Figure 4-2). This information also gets processed in the limbic system, which manages emotional behavioral responses, such as anger, anxiety, sadness, or fear. Previous post-disaster analyses suggest that affected people may display decreased self-efficacy, reduced working hours, startled responses, or reduced work performance, including burnout and emotional exhaustion. Suppose, for example, a disaster occurs at time π, and people can generate normal productivity before π. After time π, if affected, people's performance on a task may not exhibit the same productivity. Let λ_i be the average frequency of performance error or startled response for person i per unit of time. The possible impact of a disaster on person i's behavior (i.e., Impact$_i$) can be evaluated by examining how often affected person i shows maladaptive coping and reduced work performance. That is,

$$\text{Impact}_i = 1 - e^{-\int_{\pi}^{t} \lambda_i(t)\,dt} \qquad (4\text{-}1)$$

Now we need to find λ_i, which reflects an individual-specific measure corresponding to a specific disaster event. A threat event is not perceived in the same way by all people, therefore, individual's reaction will vary depending on each person's personal experiences, perceptions of risk about the disaster event, and self-immune systems.

Let R_{ij} denote the reaction of person i when exposed to disaster j, where i refers to the ith person exposed to the disaster. Also let pr_{ij} represent person i's perceived risk about disaster j. Perceived risk is a measure of the imminent danger a person feels she is in (Slociv, 1987). In turn, $D_{ij}(t)$ denotes the information set that person i possesses at time t when determining the perceived risk pr_{ij} and the subsequent reaction. Then, person i's expected reaction when facing disaster j is

$$E(R_{ij} \mid D_{ij}(t)) = F_{ij}(D_{ij}(t), PEXP_i)\alpha + \beta \, E(pr_{ij} \mid D_{ij}(t)) + \varepsilon_{ij}, \tag{4-2}$$

where $F_{ij}(D_{ij}(t), PEXP_i)$ contains information about the features of disaster j and the past experience and personal characteristics of person i (i.e., $PEXP_i$) which affect her behavior, ε_{ij} denotes the idiosyncratic shock encountered by person i when evaluating perceived risk about disaster j, and α and β are constants.

The features of a disaster also affect people's behavior or reactions. For example, the characteristics of a bio-terror attack differ from those of a severe weather event such as a tornado. In the former, people in all areas, including those not in the affected site, may worry whether the bio-agent in the attack can spread through air; a tornado event only directly affects those who live in the touchdown area, and people living elsewhere may not sense fear about it.

If there is no disaster and people behave normally, person i exhibits normal behavior or action R_{i0}:

$$R_{i0} = \eta \times PEXP_i + \varepsilon_{i0}, \tag{4-3}$$

where η is a constant. ε_{i0} denotes an unobservable idiosyncrasy person i posses.

Therefore, the difference in person i's behavior or reaction due to disaster j can be captured on average by

$$\lambda_{ij}(t) = F_{ij}[D_{ij}(t), PEXP_i] \, \alpha + \beta \, E(pr_{ij} \mid D_{ij}(t)) \, \varepsilon_{ij} - PEXP_i\eta - \varepsilon_{i0}. \tag{4-4}$$

If we substitute Equation (4-4) into Equation (4-1), we can quantify the individual-level psychological damage that a person may incur at time t when exposed to an unexpected disaster, as follows.

$$\text{Impact}_i = 1 - e^{-\int_\pi^t \{F_{ij}[D_{ij}(t), PEXP_i]\alpha + \beta E(pr_{ij} \mid D_{ij}(t) - PEXP \times \eta + \varepsilon_{ij} - \varepsilon_{i0}\} \, dt} \tag{4-5}$$

If this impact continues, the psychological damage may alter the neurons in a person's hippocampus, resulting in short-term memory impairment (Pawlak & Melchor, 2005). If this impairment occurs without any interruption, the amygdala may not work with the hippocampus properly, and a disconnection from the real world can occur, which prevents the association of flashback memories with real events. In this case, PTSD results.

Because some people are more affected by a disaster event than others, depending on the nature of the event and individual characteristics, and because studies show no single pattern of psychological

Figure 4.2. The formation of individual-level psychological damage

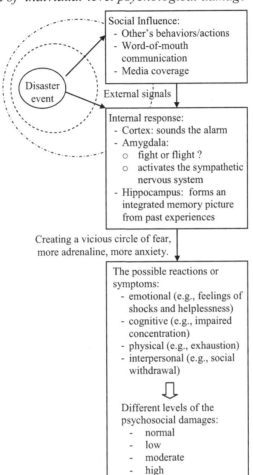

consequences of disasters exists (e.g., Burkle, 1996), many post-disaster analyses adopt a measure to quantify negative psychological impacts into three levels on the basis of their severity: low, moderate, and high (e.g., Norris et al., 2002b; NRC, 2006). Following a similar measurement scale, we also use low, moderate, and high to indicate the level of psychological damages a person experiences at time t. According to this classification, the "high" level indicates that a person may incur a severe impairment that results in long-term distress.

Figure 4.2, a graphic illustration of Equation (4-5), displays how such individual-level psychological damage can be produced.

INFORMATION INFLUENCE

Without observing other people's behavior or communicating with others, person i's information set about disaster j is $D_{ij}(t) = D_{ij}^{individual} = \{$own observations about disaster $j\}$. In this case, person i's behavior is governed by his or her own evaluations only.

Action reflects information. When witnessing other people's behavior, such as purchasing gas masks or stockpiling lots of food and water; learning about such behaviors from the news media; or receiving information through social communication, person *i* may infer the threat on the basis of three pieces of information: own evaluation of disaster *j*, observed actions of others, and word-of-mouth communication. The information set thus is

$$D_{ij}(t) = \{D_{ij}^{\ individual}, [(O_a \cup O_c) - (O_a \cap O_c)]\},$$

where O_a denotes the signals reflected in actions of others, and O_c represents signals from word-of-mouth communication.

Because O_a and O_c may provide information overlap, we can perform the operation $[(O_a \cup O_c) - (O_a \cap O_c)]$ to remove any redundant information. If we let

$$O_u = [(O_a \cup O_c) - (O_a \cap O_c)],$$

then

$$D_{ij}(t) = \{D_{ij}^{\ individual}, O_u\}.$$

When observing what everyone else is doing or if the situation is ambiguous or difficult to assess, person *i* will follow others' actions, even if own information $D_{ij}^{\ individual}$ suggests a different action. The information set in this scenario becomes

$$D_{ij}(t) = \{D_{ij}^{\ individual}, O_u \mid O_u \succ D_{ij}^{\ individual}\},$$

where $O_u \succ D_{ij}^{\ individual}$ indicates that the information reflected in others' actions is more important than own information for making the decision. In this case, actions speak louder than words. An affected

Figure 4.3 Transmission of influence between people

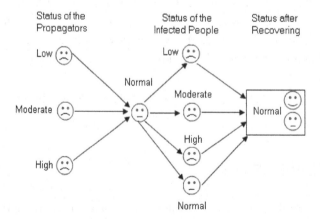

Note: *An unaffected person (i.e., in the normal category in Figure 4.3) can be influenced by people in the propagator group. Their resulting status can be classified as low, moderate, high, or normal on the basis of the level of psychosocial damage the person experiences.*

person highlights his or her risk perceptions of a threat after viewing others' anxiety behavior and therefore becomes more inclined to believe those reactions. The person's reactions in turn increase the risk for others in the society or communication chain, which again triggers more action down the network. Thus, anxiety spreads and becomes social behavior. Massive social imitation can be triggered by the actions of just a few people.

In Figure 4.3, we depict the transmission of influence and people's resulting status. For example, an affected person may influence another normal person, who in turn develops a low, moderate, or high degree of impairment, depending on that person's characteristics and immune system.

REFERENCES

Burkle, F. M. (1996). Acute-phase mental health consequences of disasters: implications for triage and emergency medical services. *Annals of Emergency Medicine, 28,* 119-128.

Lonigan, C. J., Shannon, M. P., Finch, A. J., Daugherty, T. K., & Taylor, C. M. (1991). Children's reactions to a natural disaster: Symptom severity and degree of exposure. *Advances in Behavior Research and Therapy, 13,* 135-154.

National Research Council [NRC], (2006). *Facing hazards and disasters: Understanding human dimensions.* Committee on Disaster Research in the Social Sciences: Future Challenges and Opportunities. Washington DC: National Academies Press.

Norris, F. H., Friedman, M. J., Watson, P. J., Byrne, C. M., Diaz, E., & Kaniasty, K. (2002). 60,000 disaster victims speak. Part I. An empirical review of the empirical literature, 1981-2001. *Psychiatry, 65*(3), 207-239.

Pawlak, R., & Melchor, J. (2005). Long-term stress can impair short-term memory. *Proceedings of the National Academy of Sciences,* December 5.

Slociv, P. (1987). Perception of risk. *Science, 236*(17), 280-285.

Chapter V
Disaster Promulgation and Collective Behaviors

As mentioned previously, the actions or anxiety moods of others directly affect a person's attitude, especially when the situation is ambiguous and difficult for an individual to assess. The observed actions of others may suggest the situation is more severe. Once an observable anxiety with somatic symptoms is initiated, it tends to be imitated by the population and become a social trend. In this chapter, we quantify the disaster induced possible collective anxiety and estimate population level social productivity and response efforts. We then discuss the application of the proposed models in examining the potential psychosocial effects of an infectious disease like SARS.

MATHEMATICAL DESCRIPTION

Let C be the total population size in the targeted area (i.e., country, region, or state). At any time t during the course of the disaster, a person in C may be affected or not. If affected, the psychological damages the person experiences coincide with one of three levels: low, moderate, or high at time t. Therefore, the aggregate behavior of the population at each point in time t can be summarized by a "state" labeled L(t), M(t), H(t), or N(t), where N(t) denotes a state in which people have not been affected or have recovered by time t. That is, at any time t of the disaster, any member of the population C will reside in one of four states: N(t), L(t), M(t), or H(t), depending on his or her degree of exposure (i.e., the value of Impact$_i$ in Equation (4-5)).

Therefore, as time passes, people's status in the population may change from one state to another, on the basis of whether (1) the situation becomes more severe, such that collective social anxiety behavior deteriorates over time if ignored, or (2) the individual human body can make self-adjustments to recover through resilience. Since the duration of a disaster is short compared to the life of an individual, the size of the target population is assumed to be constant and the death toll due to the disaster itself is counted in the severe state H. Because the social influence (i.e. a person in one state may be influenced by another person in the same or other state) has been captured at the individual level in equation (4-5), in the aggregate level model, we assume the rate of change per unit time from one state such as N(t) to another state (e.g. L(t)) is proportional to the number of people in state N(t) at time t times the state transition rate. For example, to model the quantity N($t + \Delta t$), we check the number of people in state N at time t plus those converted to state N(t) over Δt, but minus the number of people who are affected and transferred to another state such as L(t), M(t) or H(t) during the same time interval Δt. Thus

N($t + \Delta t$) = N(t) + [β_ϕ L(t) − ($\gamma_\phi + \gamma_\psi + \gamma_\xi$) N($t$)] Δt.

If we allow the time interval becomes very small, then in the limit the above equation becomes

$$\frac{dN(t)}{dt} = \beta_\varphi L(t) - (\gamma_\varphi + \gamma_\psi + \gamma_\xi) N(t).$$

For practical purposes, we assume that the impact of the disaster takes place immediately and continuously when the disaster event occurs. Thus, the affected population can be modeled as a four-dimensional dynamic system, as shown in Figure 5.1, in which the four states intertwine over time. The arrows in the graph indicate the changing directions of transitions in state.

This leads to the following differential equation system:

$$\frac{dL(t)}{dt} = -(\beta_\varphi + \mu_\psi) L(t) + \beta_\psi M(t) + \gamma_\varphi N(t),$$

$$\frac{dM(t)}{dt} = \mu_\psi L(t) - (\beta_\psi + \mu_\xi) M(t) + \gamma_\psi N(t),$$

$$\frac{dH(t)}{dt} = \mu_\xi M(t) + \gamma_\xi N(t), \text{ and} \qquad\qquad (5\text{-}1)$$

$$\frac{dN(t)}{dt} = \beta_\varphi L(t) - (\gamma_\varphi + \gamma_\psi + \gamma_\xi) N(t),$$

where the initial conditions are $N(0) = C$, $L(0) = 0$, $M(0) = 0$, and $H(0) = 0$ (i.e., $t = 0$); and the equation $N(t) + M(t) + L(t) + H(t) = C$ holds at any time t. The unit for t is any convenient unit of time such as a second, an hour, day, week, and so on. The constants β_ϕ and β_ψ represent the average recovery rates as persons move from low to normal states or recover from moderate to low states, respectively. Similarly,

Figure 5.1. Changing behavior of a population

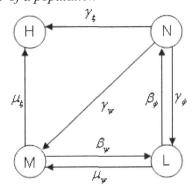

μ_ξ and μ_ψ denote the average deterioration rates as people move from moderate to severe or low to moderate states, respectively. Furthermore, γ_ϕ, γ_ψ, and γ_ξ are the transition rates by which people move from normal to low, moderate, or high states, respectively. Note that γ_ξ denotes the transition rate at which people immediately enter a severe state and incur long-term stress when exposed to the disaster. In line with NRC (2006) and NSW (2000), H(t) represents the average number of people who suffer extreme fear and may have developed more severe levels of distress psychologically at time *t*, whereas L(t) refers to the number of people who show mild distress or anxiety behavior but not clinical somatic symptoms. The moderate level M(t) denotes that the person expresses anxiety behaviors, together with obvious somatic symptoms (i.e., clinically significant morbidity as opposed to mild symptoms in level L(t)).

We solve System (5-1) to obtain quantitative information about the changing behavior of the system and the social effects of psychological damages on the population. Applying the Laplace transformation, we arrive at the following explicit analytical solutions (for a detailed derivation, see Appendix A):

$$N(t) = \frac{u_1 k^2 - v_1 k + w_1}{(g-k)(s-k)} e^{-kt} + \frac{u_1 s^2 - v_1 s + w_1}{(k-s)(g-s)} e^{-st} + \frac{u_1 g^2 - v_1 g + w_1}{(s-g)(k-g)} e^{-gt},$$

$$M(t) = \frac{u_2 k^2 - v_2 k + w_2}{(g-k)(s-k)} e^{-kt} + \frac{u_2 s^2 - v_2 s + w_2}{(k-s)(g-s)} e^{-st} + \frac{u_2 g^2 - v_2 g + w_2}{(s-g)(k-g)} e^{-gt},$$

$$L(t) = \frac{u_3 k^2 - v_3 k + w_3}{(g-k)(s-k)} e^{-kt} + \frac{u_3 s^2 - v_3 s + w_3}{(k-s)(g-s)} e^{-st} + \frac{u_3 g^2 - v_3 g + w_3}{(s-g)(k-g)} e^{-gt}, \qquad (5\text{-}2)$$

and

$$H(t) = \frac{-Qk^3 + u_4 k^2 - v_4 k + w_4}{-k(g-k)(s-k)} e^{-kt} + \frac{-Qs^3 + u_4 s^2 - v_4 s + w_4}{-s(k-s)(g-s)} e^{-st}$$
$$+ \frac{-Qg^3 + u_4 g^2 - v_4 g + w_4}{-g(s-g)(k-g)} e^{-gt} + \frac{w_4}{skg},$$

where $u_1 = N(0)$,

$v_1 = \beta_\phi L(0) + (\beta_\phi + \beta_\psi + \mu_\psi + \mu_\xi) N(0)$,

$w_1 = (\beta_\phi \beta_\psi + \beta_\phi \mu_\xi) L(0) + \beta_\phi \beta_\psi M(0) + (\beta_\phi \beta_\psi + \beta_\phi \mu_\xi + \mu_\xi \mu_\psi) N(0)$,

$u_0 = \gamma_\phi + \gamma_\psi + \gamma_\xi + \beta_\phi + \beta_\psi + \mu_\psi + \mu_\xi$,

$v_0 = \mu_\xi (\gamma_\phi + \gamma_\psi + \gamma_\xi + \beta_\phi + \mu_\psi) + \beta_\phi (\gamma_\xi + \beta_\psi + \gamma_\psi) + (\gamma_\phi + \gamma_\psi + \gamma_\xi)(\beta_\psi + \mu_\psi)$, and

$w_0 = \mu_\xi \mu_\psi (\gamma_\phi + \gamma_\psi + \gamma_\xi) + \beta_\phi (\beta_\psi \gamma_\xi + \mu_\xi \gamma_\xi + \gamma_\psi \mu_\xi)$.

We obtain *k* from the following equation:

$$-k^3 + u_0 k^2 - v_0 k + w_0 = 0, \text{ and} \qquad (5\text{-}3)$$

s can be solved from

$$s^2 - (u_0 - k) s + v_0 - k(u_0 - k) = 0, \qquad (5\text{-}4)$$

$$g = u_0 - k - s, \tag{5-5}$$

here, k, s, and g are eigenvalues of the system (5-1).

In addition, we have

$$u_2 = M(0),$$
$$v_2 = \gamma_\psi N(0) + (\beta_\phi + \mu_\psi + \gamma_\phi + \gamma_\psi + \gamma_\xi) M(0) + \mu_\psi L(0),$$
$$w_2 = (\beta_\phi \gamma_\psi + \gamma_\phi \mu_\psi + \mu_\psi \gamma_\psi + \mu_\psi \gamma_\xi) L(0) + (\gamma_\phi \mu_\psi + \beta_\phi \gamma_\psi + \gamma_\psi \mu_\psi) N(0)$$
$$+ (\gamma_\phi \mu_\psi + \gamma_\psi \beta_\phi + \beta_\phi \gamma_\xi + \gamma_\xi \mu_\psi + \mu_\psi \gamma_\psi) M(0),$$

$$u_3 = L(0),$$
$$v_3 = \gamma_\phi N(0) + \beta_\psi M(0) + (\beta_\psi + \mu_\xi + \gamma_\phi + \gamma_\psi + \gamma_\xi) L(0),$$
$$w_3 = (\gamma_\psi + \gamma_\phi + \gamma_\xi)[(\beta_\psi + \mu_\xi) L(0) + \beta_\psi M(0)] + (\gamma_\phi \beta_\psi + \mu_\xi \gamma_\phi + \beta_\psi \gamma_\psi) N(0),$$
$$Q = H(0),$$
$$u_4 = \gamma_\xi N(0) + \mu_\xi M(0) + (\beta_\psi + \beta_\phi + \mu_\xi + \mu_\psi + \gamma_\phi + \gamma_\psi + \gamma_\xi) H(0),$$

$$v_4 = \mu_\xi (\gamma_\psi + \gamma_\xi)[C - L(0)] + \gamma_\xi \beta_\phi [C - M(0)] + \mu_\xi \mu_\psi [C - N(0)]$$
$$+ \gamma_\xi (\beta_\psi + \mu_\psi)[N(0) + H(0)] + \mu_\xi (\beta_\phi + \gamma_\phi)[M(0) + H(0)]$$
$$+ [\beta_\phi (\gamma_\psi + \beta_\psi) + (\gamma_\phi + \gamma_\psi)(\beta_\psi + \mu_\psi)] H(0),$$

$$w_4 = C[\beta_\phi (\gamma_\psi \mu_\xi + \gamma_\xi \mu_\xi + \gamma_\xi \beta_\psi) + \mu_\psi \mu_\xi (\gamma_\phi + \gamma_\psi + \gamma_\xi)].$$

Equation (5-2) offers a fundamental set of solutions to System (5-1) that measures the average social effects of psychological damages on the population as a result of a disaster.

A POSSIBLE LONG-TERM EFFECT

From Equation (5-2), we find that when $t \to \infty$, $e^{-kt} \to 0$, $e^{-st} \to 0$, and $e^{-gt} \to 0$. Therefore, the following happens when $t \to \infty$:

$$N(t)|_{t \to \infty} \Rightarrow 0, \ L(t)|_{t \to \infty} \Rightarrow 0 \ M(t)|_{t \to \infty} \Rightarrow 0, \text{ and } H(t)|_{t \to \infty} \Rightarrow \frac{w_4}{kgs}.$$

From Equation (5-5), we know that $g = u_0 - k - s$. Therefore, we have

$$kgs = ks(u_0 - k - s) = k[(u_0 - k)s - s^2]. \tag{5-6}$$

Then, from Equation (5-4), we can derive $(u_0 - k)s - s^2 = v_0 - k(u_0 - k)$. When we substitute it into Equation (5-6), we get

$$kgs = k[v_0 - k(u_0 - k)] = kv_0 - u_0k^2 + k^3.$$

Equation (5-3) also indicates that $kv_0 - u_0k^2 + k^3 = w_0$; thus, $kgs = w_0$. When we reexamine w_4, we find that

$$w_4 = C[\beta_\phi(\gamma_\psi\mu_\xi + \gamma_\xi\mu_\xi + \gamma_\xi\beta_\psi) + \mu_\psi\mu_\xi(\gamma_\phi + \gamma_\psi + \gamma_\xi)] = Cw_0.$$

Therefore,

$$H(t)|_{t\to\infty} \Rightarrow \frac{w_4}{kgs} = \frac{Cw_0}{w_0} = C. \tag{5-7}$$

These derivations suggest that when people are exposed to a disaster without any intervention for an extended period, their tolerance of the disaster decreases, and they become psychologically exhausted. That is, when neither resistance nor escape is possible, the human system of self-defense becomes overwhelmed and disorganized. In the long run, disaster events produce profound and lasting changes in people's physical arousal, emotion, cognition, and memory, which result in long-term, severe damages. The Adverse Childhood Experiences study (http://acestudy.org) has examined the health and social impacts of disasters on 18,000 children and finds that negative consequences are far more prevalent than previously recognized and that the impacts are cumulative. Therefore, if left unaddressed, such damage can cause a wide range of health problems (e.g., heart disease, cancer, chronic lung disease, liver disease, skeletal fractures) and social problems such as homelessness and inability to hold a job (Felitti, 2003; Felitti et al., 2004).

MACRO-LEVEL SOCIAL PRODUCTIVITY

Moreover, at any time t during the course of a disaster event, social productivity also decreases. Suppose people in the normal state can produce at a normal level, such that the number of working units before the disaster is C. During the disaster, the number of people in the normal state (i.e., $N(t)$) may change over time because some people may be influenced and psychologically distressed. Thus, the working units available that can produce normal productivity at time t decrease from C to

$$N(t) + A_1L(t) + A_2M(t) + A_3H(t),$$

where A_1, A_2, and A_3 are weight parameters, such that $0 < A_1, A_2,$ and $A_3 < 1$ for the proportions of people in states L, M, and H who can achieve normal productivity, respectively, at time t. People suffering moderate- or high-level damage may not be able to work normally during the disaster, so remaining social productivity at time t during the disaster can be calculated as

$$\text{work forces available} = \frac{(u_1 + Au_3)k^2 - (v_1 + Av_3)k + w_1 + Aw_3}{(g-k)(s-k)}e^{-kt} +$$

$$\frac{(u_1 + Au_3)s^2 - (v_1 + Av_3)s + w_1 + Aw_3}{(k-s)(g-s)}e^{-st} + \frac{(u_1 + Au_3)g^2 - (v_1 + v_3)g + w_1 + Aw_3}{(s-g)(k-g)}e^{-gt}.$$

MEASURING THE EFFICIENCY OF POLICY INTERVENTIONS

Our analysis in previous sections suggests the need for psychosocial interventions that may relieve anxiety and depression. These interventions should be designed to support four overlapping functions: emotional support (e.g., someone to confide in who provides comfort or emotional attachment), instrumental support (e.g., strong services, money), informational support (e.g., advice/guidance, help with problem solving), and companionship support (e.g., feeling connected to others).

If appropriate intervention efforts occur during time $t = \tau_0$, the transition rates γ_ϕ, γ_ψ, and γ_ξ gradually decrease after τ_0, as do the deteriorating rates μ_ξ and μ_ψ. From Equation (5-2), we know that the effects of psychosocial damages at time τ_{0-} can be calculated as $L(\tau_0)$, $M(\tau_0)$, and $H(\tau_0)$. After time τ_0, the influence of the disaster on the public decreases. If we let $\bar{\gamma}(t)$ be the average influence rate of the disaster on the public's mind after time τ_0, the average change of the decrease in $\bar{\gamma}$ per unit of time is proportional to the time spent implementing intervention efforts, the types of intervention efforts (e.g.., policy designs for mitigating the disaster, supporting service), and the transition rates before the intervention efforts (i.e., before time τ_0). Because types of intervention efforts may differ according to policy designs, for simplicity, we use a constant $P > 0$ to represent the average efficiency of the intervention efforts. In turn,

$$\frac{\Delta\bar{\gamma}}{\Delta t} = -P \times t \times \bar{\gamma}.$$

When Δt becomes arbitrarily small, we can solve this equation as

$$\bar{\gamma}(t) = \bar{\gamma}(\tau_0) e^{-p\tau^2/2} \tag{5-8}$$

where τ denotes the duration of policy interventions.

When $t = \tau_0$, $\bar{\gamma}(t) = \bar{\gamma}(\tau_0)$, which is the average influence rate before time τ_0. To get $\bar{\gamma}(\tau_0)$, we may require statistical sample data about the target population. Alternatively, we can calculate it by letting $\bar{\gamma}(\tau_0) = (\gamma_\phi + \gamma_\psi + \gamma_\xi)/3$, with the assumption that γ_ϕ, γ_ψ, and γ_ξ remain unchanged until τ_0, at which time the intervention efforts occur. In section 3.1 we have presented a measurement for the individual-level psychosocial damage (i.e., equation (4')). We can use this measurement to compute an average influence rate in collective level before time τ_0. Suppose out of the population of size C there are n people affected by disaster j before time τ_0. Then the average influence rate of disaster j on the targeted population per unit time before time τ_0 can be obtained using (5-9).

$$\bar{\gamma}(\tau_0) = \frac{\frac{n}{C} \times \frac{\sum_{i=1}^{n} Impact_{ij}}{n}}{\Delta t} = \frac{\sum_{i=1}^{n} Impact_{ij}}{C\Delta t} \tag{5-9}$$

If we rewrite Equation (5-8) and let ε represent a minuscule number, which indicates that the impact rate of the disaster is very small, we get

$$P = \frac{\ln\bar{\gamma}(\tau_0) - \ln\varepsilon}{\tau^2/2} \tag{5-10}$$

Equation (5-10) thus shows the efficiency of policy interventions that may be achieved given a minuscule number ε. For instance, if $\varepsilon = 10^{-3}$, the intervention or policy designed would decrease the influence of the disaster such that only 1 out of 1000 people may develop psychosocial damages, given the uncontrolled incursions of the disaster.

ON TARGETING INTERVENTIONS AND RESOURCE ALLOCATIONS

The individual-level Equation (4-5) discussed in Chapter IV and the population level's four different levels of psychosocial measurements—normal (N), low (L), moderate (M), and high (H)—can be used to suggest appropriate targeting interventions and resource allocations at time *t*. To reduce the probability of people becoming affected and moving from normal to low, moderate, or high states, Equation (4-4) in Chapter IV targeted interventions that reducing people's perceived risk. As illustrated in Figure 4.1 and 4.2, the characteristics of the threat event itself and social influence play important roles in determining perceived risk. Sometimes the uncertainty in the disaster event may increase the level of psychosocial morbidity. When the perceived threat is greater than the tangible exposure (e.g., biological or chemical threat), those who are not in the affected area may still perceive themselves as being at risk and seek medical screening. Understanding the characteristics of a disaster and providing rapid and accurate information to the public thus may reduce uncertainty and avoid unnecessary anxiety.

The analytic solutions to the system (i.e., Equation (5-2)) project the proportion of persons affected in each state during the course of a disaster. That is, the solutions project the range and severity of the expected psychosocial consequences. These numbers indicate that the segments of the affected population (i.e., people in the four states) respond differently because they are affected to different degrees. Thus, these numbers suggest the type of interventions and resources needed in each corresponding state. For example, the value of H(t) suggests the scope and volume of supplies needed at time *t* to care for those who have developed more severe levels of psychological distress. For those people who show anxiety and fear with obvious clinical somatic symptoms, the value of M(t) reflects the required amount of medical care and mental health services.

In next section, we use an example to illustrate the application of our proposed model.

AN EMPIRICAL APPLICATION

The outbreak of SARS in 2003 in multiple countries, especially those in Asia and Canada, caused not only extraordinary public health concerns but also tremendous psychological distress, particularly among health care workers. Several studies have examined the psychological impacts of SARS on health care workers in Hong Kong, Singapore, and Toronto (Bai et al., 2004; HSC, 2006; Maunder et al., 2006; Nickell et al., 2004; Tam et al., 2004) and reveal that health care workers suffer much more psychological distress, including anxiety, fear of contagion, feelings of stigmatization, loneliness, boredom, anger, burnout, emotional exhaustion, and a sense of uncertainty, compared with the general population. To illustrate the proposed model, we use the survey results reported in Maunder and colleagues' (2006, p. 1931) study. In their study, 769 health care workers at 9 Toronto hospitals that treated SARS patients during the 2003 SARS outbreak completed a survey related to several adverse outcomes. The proportion of health care workers who reported more than two negative consequences during the period from 13 to 26 months after the SARS outbreak appears as the scattered dots in Figure 5.2.

Figure 5.2. The prolonged psychosocial effects after the SARS outbreak

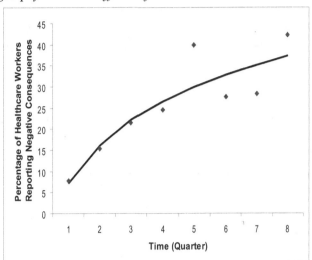

This survey result provides only a summary measure of the negative psychological consequences, whereas our proposed model includes four different levels of psychosocial measurements: normal (N), low (L), moderate (M), and high (H). To make use of the data and capture multiple negative psychosocial effects at the same time, we add L, M, and H in Equation (5-2) together to represent the total number of people who displayed psychological distress. Note that the unit measurement that Maunder and colleagues (2006) use is the percentage of the population instead of the absolute population number. To reflect this characteristic, we also adopt the percentage as a unit measurement.

Using Mathematica 6 (i.e., non-linear fit function) software and applying Equation (5-2) (in particular, L(t) + M(t) + H(t)) to the survey results, we obtain the following formula:

$$\text{Psychosocial effects} = 1 - 0.276e^{-0.52t} - 0.402e^{-0.029t} - 0.384e^{-0.03t}. \tag{5-11}$$

The predicted psychosocial effects obtained using Equation (5-11) appear in Figure 5.2, represented by the bold line. Comparing the predicted psychosocial effects (bold line) to the actual data (scattered dots), we find that the prediction derived from Equation (5-11) fits the observed data very well. Meanwhile, the mean absolute prediction error for the proposal model is 3.83 (percentage), which is much smaller than that (5.40, also percentage) of the benchmark exponential model, which relies on the observed data's trend line using Excel. This result demonstrates the significant effectiveness of the proposal model. As we mentioned previously, the proposed model consists of four equations that quantify different levels of psychosocial effects. If such detailed data are available, similar empirical analyses may be performed.

DISCUSSION

Whether or not SARS outbreaks recur, other new emerging pathogens, such as a pandemic caused by a deadly avian influenza virus (H5N1), offer ongoing threats. Even though disaster-induced negative psychological outcomes take time, the resultant psychosocial effects start immediately after a disaster occurs. For example, widespread emotional reactions such as fear and anxiety are common responses to imminent threats and actual disaster events. These effects have important impacts on the effectiveness of the response efforts used to mitigate disasters and may decrease social productivity.

We introduce differential dynamics to analyze and evaluate both individual-level and population-level psychosocial impacts during a disaster event. Since the duration of a disaster is short compared to the life of an individual, the size of the target population is assumed to remain constant and the death toll due to the disaster itself is counted in the severe state H. Because previous research has found that the impact of disaster-/threat-induced psychological damage is cumulative, additive, and summative, a continuous system approach is used to capture such psychological damage. The resulting equations (4-5) and (5-2) can be applied to different time frames such as hours, several days or weeks without changing any parameters. Our modeling efforts shed greater light on how people respond to a threat and the dynamics of psychological effects.

REFERENCES

Bai, Y., Lin, C. C., Chen, J. Y., Chue, C. M., & Chou, P. (2004). Survey of stress reactions among health care workers involved with the SARS outbreak. *Psychiatry Service, 55*, 1055-1057.

Felitti, V. (2003). The relationship of adverse childhood experiences to adult health status. Presented at the *Snowbird Conference of the Child Trauma Treatment Network*, DVD published by the National Child Traumatic Stress Network. The Intermountain West, September 2003.

Felitti, V., Anda, R., Nordenberg, D., Williamson, D., Spitz, D., Edwards, V., Koss, M., & Marks, J. (2004). Relationship of childhood abuse and household dysfunction to many of the leading causes of death in adults: The adverse childhood experiences study. *American Journal of Preventive Medicine, 14*(4), 245-258.

Homeland Security Council [HSC]. (2006). *National strategy for pandemic influenza: Implementation plan*. Washington DC: US Homeland Security Council.

Maunder, R. G., Lancee, W. J., Balderson, K. E., Bennett, J. P., Borgundvaag, B., Evans, S., & Fernandes, C. M. B. et al. (2006). Long-term psychological and occupational effects of providing hospital healthcare during SARS outbreak. *Emerging Infectious Diseases, 12*(12), 1924-1932.

National Research Council [NRC] (2006). *Facing hazards and disasters: Understanding human dimensions*. Committee on Disaster Research in the Social Sciences: Future Challenges and Opportunities. Washington DC: National Academies Press.

Nickell, L. A., Crighton, E. J., Tracy, C. S., Al Enazy, H., Bolaji, Y., & Hanjrah, S. et al. (2004). Psychosocial effects of SARS on hospital staff: survey of a large tertiary case institution. *Canadian Medical Association Journal, 170*, 793-798.

NSW. (2000). *Disaster mental health response handbook*. Institute of Psychiatry and Center for Mental Health, North Sydney: NSW Health.

Tam, C. W., Pang, E. P., Lam, L. C., & Chiu, H. F. (2004). Severe acute respiratory syndrome (SARS) in Hong Kong in 2003: stress and psychological impact among frontline healthcare workers. *Psychological Medicine, 34*, 1197-1204.

APPENDIX A: A DETAILED SOLUTION DEVELOPMENT

In this appendix, we show how we derive Equation (5-2), the analytical solution to the model system. For easy reference, we use new labels (a1)–(a4) to denote each equation in our model System (5-1). That is,

$$\frac{dL(t)}{dt} = -(\beta_\varphi + \mu_\psi) L(t) + \beta_\psi M(t) + \gamma_\varphi N(t),$$ (a1)

$$\frac{dM(t)}{dt} = \mu_\psi L(t) - (\beta_\psi + \mu_\xi) M(t) + \gamma_\psi N(t),$$ (a2)

$$\frac{dH(t)}{dt} = \mu_\xi M(t) + \gamma_\xi N(t), \text{ and}$$ (a3)

$$\frac{dN(t)}{dt} = \beta_\phi L(t) - (\gamma_\phi + \gamma_\psi + \gamma_\xi) N(t),$$ (a4)

where the initial conditions are as follows: $N(0) = C$, $L(0) = 0$, $M(0) = 0$, and $H(0) = 0$ (i.e., $t = 0$); and the equation $N(t) + M(t) + L(t) + H(t) = C$ holds at any time t. We use Laplace transform technique to solve (a1)–(a4).

Step 1. Transform (a1) – (a4) into four algebraic equations.

Let $a(p) = \textbf{Lap}[L(t)]$, $b(p) = \textbf{Lap}[M(t)]$,
   $c(p) = \textbf{Lap}[H(t)]$,   and $d(p) = \textbf{Lap}[N(t)]$.

Since the Laplace transform of a variable $x(t)$ can be written as:

   $\textbf{Lap}[x(t)] = X(p)$,
   $\textbf{Lap}[\dot{x}(t)] = p \times X(p) - x(0)$,
and
   $\textbf{Lap}[K] = K \times \dfrac{1}{p}$,

on the basis of this formula, we can apply the Laplace transform to (a1)–(a4) and obtain the following four algebraic equations, respectively:

$$a(p)[p + \beta_\phi + \mu_\psi] - \beta_\psi b(p) - \gamma_\phi d(p) = L(0),$$
$$-\mu_\psi a(p) + (p + \beta_\psi + \mu_\xi) b(p) - \gamma_\psi d(p) = M(0),$$
$$-\mu_\xi b(p) + p c(p) - \gamma_\xi d(p) = H(0),$$ (a5)
$$-\beta_\phi a(p) + (p + \gamma_\phi + \gamma_\psi + \gamma_\xi) d(p) = N(0).$$

Rewriting (a5) in a matrix format yields

$$
\begin{bmatrix}
p+\beta_\phi+\mu_\psi & -\beta_\psi & 0 & -\gamma_\phi \\
-\mu_\psi & p+\beta_\psi+\mu_\xi & 0 & -\gamma_\psi \\
0 & -\mu_\xi & p & -\gamma_\xi \\
-\beta_\phi & 0 & 0 & p+\gamma_\phi+\gamma_\psi+\gamma_\xi
\end{bmatrix}
*
\begin{bmatrix}
a(p) \\ b(p) \\ c(p) \\ d(p)
\end{bmatrix}
=
\begin{bmatrix}
L(0) \\ M(0) \\ H(0) \\ N(0)
\end{bmatrix}
\tag{a6}
$$

Step 2. Solve (a6) for $a(p)$, $b(p)$, $c(p)$, and $d(p)$.

Obviously,

$$
\begin{aligned}
a(p) &= \frac{\Delta_a(p)}{\Delta(p)}, \\
b(p) &= \frac{\Delta_b(p)}{\Delta(p)}, \\
c(p) &= \frac{\Delta_c(p)}{\Delta(p)}, \\
d(p) &= \frac{\Delta_d(p)}{\Delta(p)},
\end{aligned}
\tag{a7}
$$

where

$$
\Delta(p) =
\begin{vmatrix}
p+\beta_\phi+\mu_\psi & -\beta_\psi & 0 & -\gamma_\phi \\
-\mu_\psi & p+\beta_\psi+\mu_\xi & 0 & -\gamma_\psi \\
0 & -\mu_\xi & p & -\gamma_\xi \\
-\beta_\phi & 0 & 0 & p+\gamma_\phi+\gamma_\psi+\gamma_\xi
\end{vmatrix},
$$

$$
\Delta_a(p) =
\begin{vmatrix}
L(0) & -\beta_\psi & 0 & -\gamma_\phi \\
M(0) & p+\beta_\psi+\mu_\xi & 0 & -\gamma_\psi \\
H(0) & -\mu_\xi & p & -\gamma_\xi \\
N(0) & 0 & 0 & p+\gamma_\phi+\gamma_\psi+\gamma_\xi
\end{vmatrix},
$$

$$
\Delta_b(p) =
\begin{vmatrix}
p+\beta_\phi+\mu_\psi & L(0) & 0 & -\gamma_\phi \\
-\mu_\psi & M(0) & 0 & -\gamma_\psi \\
0 & H(0) & p & -\gamma_\xi \\
-\beta_\phi & N(0) & 0 & p+\gamma_\phi+\gamma_\psi+\gamma_\xi
\end{vmatrix},
$$

$$\Delta_c(p) = \begin{vmatrix} p + \beta_\phi + \mu_\psi & -\beta_\psi & L(0) & -\gamma_\phi \\ -\mu_\psi & p + \beta_\psi + \mu_\xi & M(0) & -\gamma_\psi \\ 0 & -\mu_\xi & H(0) & -\gamma_\xi \\ -\beta_\phi & 0 & N(0) & p + \gamma_\phi + \gamma_\psi + \gamma_\xi \end{vmatrix},$$

and

$$\Delta_d(p) = \begin{vmatrix} p + \beta_\phi + \mu_\psi & -\beta_\psi & 0 & L(0) \\ -\mu_\psi & p + \beta_\psi + \mu_\xi & 0 & M(0) \\ 0 & -\mu_\xi & p & H(0) \\ -\beta_\phi & 0 & 0 & N(0) \end{vmatrix}.$$

Step 3. Evaluate $\Delta(p)$.

Expanding the matrix $\Delta(p)$, we have

$$\Delta(p) = (-1)^{4+1}(-\beta_\phi) \begin{vmatrix} -\beta_\psi & 0 & -\gamma_\phi \\ p + \beta_\psi + \mu_\xi & 0 & -\gamma_\psi \\ -\mu_\xi & p & -\gamma_\xi \end{vmatrix}$$
$$+ (p + \gamma_\phi + \gamma_\psi + \gamma_\xi) \begin{vmatrix} p + \beta_\phi + \mu_\psi & -\beta_\psi & 0 \\ -\mu_\psi & p + \beta_\psi + \mu_\xi & 0 \\ 0 & -\mu_\xi & p \end{vmatrix}$$

$$= \beta_\phi[-\gamma_\phi(p + \beta_\psi + \mu_\xi)p - (-\beta_\psi)p(-\gamma_\psi)] + (p + \gamma_\phi + \gamma_\psi + \gamma_\xi)$$
$$\times [p(p + \beta_\psi + \mu_\xi)(p + \beta_\phi + \mu_\psi) - p(-\mu_\psi)(-\beta_\psi)]$$

$$= p\{(p + \gamma_\phi + \gamma_\psi + \gamma_\xi)[p(p + \beta_\psi + \mu_\xi) + \mu_\psi p + \mu_\psi \mu_\xi]$$
$$+ \beta_\phi[p(p + \beta_\psi + \mu_\xi + \gamma_\psi + \gamma_\xi) + \gamma_\psi \mu_\xi + \mu_\xi \gamma_\xi + \gamma_\xi \beta_\psi]\}$$

$$= p[p^3 + u_0 p^2 + v_0 p + w_0]. \qquad (a8')$$

Where,

$$u_0 = \gamma_\phi + \gamma_\psi + \gamma_\xi + \beta_\phi + \beta_\psi + \mu_\psi + \mu_\xi,$$

$$v_0 = \mu_\xi(\gamma_\phi + \gamma_\psi + \gamma_\xi + \beta_\phi + \mu_\psi) + \beta_\phi(\gamma_\xi + \beta_\psi + \gamma_\psi) + (\gamma_\phi + \gamma_\psi + \gamma_\xi)(\beta_\psi + \mu_\psi),$$
$$w_0 = \mu_\xi \mu_\psi(\gamma_\phi + \gamma_\psi + \gamma_\xi) + \beta_\phi(\beta_\psi \gamma_\xi + \mu_\xi \gamma_\xi + \gamma_\psi \mu_\xi).$$

Rewriting (a8'), we obtain

$$\Delta(p) = p[p^3 + u_0 p^2 + v_0 p + w_0]$$
$$= p(p + k)(p + s)(p + g), \qquad (a8)$$

where k, s, and g are the three roots of the equation $p^3 + u_0 p^2 + v_0 p + w_0 = 0$.

Step 4. Solve $\Delta_d(p)$ for $N(t)$.

$$\Delta_d(p) = \beta_\phi \begin{vmatrix} -\beta_\psi & 0 & L(0) \\ p+\beta_\psi+\mu_\xi & 0 & M(0) \\ -\mu_\xi & p & H(0) \end{vmatrix} + N(0) \begin{vmatrix} p+\beta_\phi+\mu_\psi & -\beta_\psi & 0 \\ -\mu_\psi & p+\beta_\psi+\mu_\xi & 0 \\ 0 & -\mu_\xi & p \end{vmatrix}$$

$$= \beta_\phi [p\beta_\psi M(0) + L(0)p(\mu_\xi + p + \beta_\psi)]$$
$$+ N(0)[(p+\beta_\phi+\mu_\xi)(p+\beta_\psi+\mu_\psi)p - (-\beta_\psi)(-\mu_\psi)p)]$$

$$= p\{ p^2 N(0) + p[\beta_\phi L(0) + (\beta_\phi + \mu_\psi + \beta_\psi + \mu_\xi)N(0)]$$
$$+ L(0)(\beta_\phi \beta_\psi + \mu_\xi \beta_\phi) + M(0)\beta_\psi \beta_\phi$$
$$+ N(0)(\beta_\phi \beta_\psi + \mu_\xi \beta_\phi + \mu_\psi \gamma_\psi)\}$$

(a9)

$$= p(u_1 p^2 + v_1 p + w_1),$$

where $u_1 = N(0)$,

$$v_1 = \beta_\phi L(0) + (\beta_\phi + \beta_\psi + \mu_\psi + \mu_\xi)N(0),$$
$$w_1 = (\beta_\phi \beta_\psi + \beta_\phi \mu_\xi)L(0) + \beta_\phi \beta_\psi M(0) + (\beta_\phi \beta_\psi + \beta_\phi \mu_\xi + \mu_\xi \mu_\psi)N(0).$$

Substituting (a8) and (a9) into (a7) yields

$$d(p) = \frac{\Delta_d(p)}{\Delta(p)}$$
$$= \frac{p(u_1 p^2 + v_1 p + w_1)}{p(p+k)(p+s)(p+g)}$$

(a10)

$$= \frac{X_1}{p-(-k)} + \frac{Y_1}{p-(-s)} + \frac{Z_1}{p-(-g)}.$$

Solving for (a10), we have

$$X_1 = \frac{u_1 k^2 - v_1 k + w_1}{(g-k)(s-k)},$$
$$Y_1 = \frac{u_1 s^2 - v_1 s + w_1}{(k-s)(g-s)},$$

and

$$Z_1 = \frac{u_1 g^2 - v_1 g + w_1}{(k-g)(s-g)}.$$

After we take the inverse Laplace transform of equation (a10), the solution is

$$N(t) = Lap^{-1}[d(p)]$$

$$= Lap^{-1}(\frac{X_1}{p-(-k)}) + Lap^{-1}(\frac{Y_1}{p-(-s)}) + Lap^{-1}(\frac{Z_1}{p-(-g)})$$

$$= X_1 e^{-kt} + Y_1 e^{-st} + Z_1 e^{-gt}.$$

Step 5. Solve $\Delta_b(p)$ for $M(t)$.

$$\Delta_b(p) = (-1)^{4+1}(-\beta_\phi) \begin{vmatrix} L(0) & 0 & -\gamma_\phi \\ M(0) & 0 & -\gamma_\psi \\ H(0) & p & -\gamma_\xi \end{vmatrix} + N(0) \begin{vmatrix} p+\beta_\phi+\mu_\psi & 0 & -\gamma_\phi \\ -\mu_\psi & 0 & -\gamma_\psi \\ 0 & p & -\gamma_\xi \end{vmatrix}$$

$$+ (p+\gamma_\phi+\gamma_\psi+\gamma_\xi) \begin{vmatrix} p+\beta_\phi+\mu_\psi & L(0) & 0 \\ -\mu_\psi & M(0) & 0 \\ 0 & H(0) & p \end{vmatrix}$$

$$= \beta_\phi[p(-\gamma_\phi)M(0)-L(0)p(-\gamma_\psi)] + N(0)[\gamma_\phi\mu_\psi p + (p+\beta_\phi+\mu_\psi)\gamma_\psi p]$$

$$+ (p+\gamma_\phi+\gamma_\psi+\gamma_\xi)[(p+\beta_\phi+\mu_\psi)M(0)p - p(-\mu_\psi)L(0)]$$

$$= p[(\beta_\phi\gamma_\psi L(0)-\beta_\phi\gamma_\phi M(0))$$

$$+ (\gamma_\phi\mu_\psi N(0)+\beta_\phi\gamma_\psi N(0)+\mu_\psi\gamma_\psi N(0)+p\gamma_\psi N(0))+p^2 M(0)$$

$$+ p(\beta_\phi M(0)+\mu_\psi M(0)+\mu_\psi L(0)+\gamma_\psi M(0)+\gamma_\phi L(0)+\gamma_\xi L(0)$$

$$+ (\gamma_\phi\beta_\phi+\gamma_\phi\mu_\psi)M(0)+(\gamma_\xi+\gamma_\psi)(\beta_\phi+\mu_\psi)M(0)+\gamma_\phi\mu_\psi L(0)$$

$$+ (\gamma_\psi+\gamma_\xi)L(0)\mu_\psi]$$

$$= \quad p[u_2 p^2 + v_2 p + w_2], \tag{a11}$$

where, $u_2 = M(0)$,

$v_2 = \gamma_\psi N(0)+(\beta_\phi+\mu_\psi+\gamma_\phi+\gamma_\psi+\gamma_\xi)M(0)+\mu_\psi L(0)$, and

$w_2 = (\beta_\phi\gamma_\psi+\gamma_\phi\mu_\psi+\mu_\psi\gamma_\psi+\mu_\psi\gamma_\xi)L(0)+(\gamma_\phi\mu_\psi+\beta_\phi\gamma_\psi+\gamma_\psi\mu_\psi)N(0)$
$\qquad + (\gamma_\phi\mu_\psi+\gamma_\psi\beta_\phi+\beta_\phi\gamma_\xi+\gamma_\xi\mu_\psi+\mu_\psi\gamma_\psi)M(0)$.

Substituting (a8) and (a11) into (a7) yields

$$b(p) = \frac{\Delta_b(p)}{\Delta(p)}$$

$$= \frac{p(u_2 p^2 + v_2 p + w_2)}{p(p+k)(p+s)(p+g)}$$

$$= \frac{X_2}{p-(-k)} + \frac{Y_2}{p-(-s)} + \frac{Z_2}{p-(-g)}. \tag{a12}$$

Solving for (a12), we have

$$X_2 = \frac{u_2 k^2 - v_2 k + w_2}{(g-k)(s-k)},$$

$$Y_2 = \frac{u_2 s^2 - v_2 s + w_2}{(k-s)(g-s)},$$

and

$$Z_2 = \frac{u_2 g^2 - v_2 g + w_2}{(k-g)(s-g)}.$$

After we take the inverse Laplace transform of (a12), we get

$$M(t) = Lap^{-1}[b(p)]$$

$$= Lap^{-1}\left(\frac{X_2}{p-(-k)}\right) + Lap^{-1}\left(\frac{Y_2}{p-(-s)}\right) + Lap^{-1}\left(\frac{Z_2}{p-(-g)}\right)$$

$$= X_2 e^{-kt} + Y_2 e^{-st} + Z_2 e^{-gt}.$$

Step 6. Solve $\Delta_a(p)$ for $L(t)$.

$$\Delta_a(p) = -N(0) \begin{vmatrix} -\beta_\psi & 0 & -\gamma_\phi \\ p+\beta_\psi+\mu_\xi & 0 & -\gamma_\psi \\ -\mu_\xi & p & -\gamma_\xi \end{vmatrix} + (p+\gamma_\phi+\gamma_\psi+\gamma_\xi) \begin{vmatrix} L(0) & -\beta_\psi & 0 \\ M(0) & p+\beta_\psi+\mu_\xi & 0 \\ H(0) & -\mu_\xi & p \end{vmatrix}$$

$$= -N(0)[-\gamma_\phi(p+\beta_\psi+\mu_\xi)p - (-\beta_\psi)p(-\gamma_\psi)]$$
$$+ (p+\gamma_\phi+\gamma_\psi+\gamma_\xi)[L(0)p(p+\beta_\psi+\mu_\xi) - (-\beta_\psi)M(0)p]$$

$$= p\{ p\gamma_\phi N(0) + N(0)[\gamma_\phi\beta_\psi + \gamma_\phi\mu_\xi + \beta_\psi\gamma_\psi]$$
$$+ (p+\gamma_\phi+\gamma_\psi+\gamma_\xi)[L(0)p + L(0)(\beta_\psi+\mu_\xi) + \beta_\psi M(0)]\}$$

$$= p\{ p^2 L(0) + p[\gamma_\phi N(0) + \beta_\psi M(0) + (\gamma_\phi+\gamma_\psi+\gamma_\xi+\beta_\psi+\mu_\xi)L(0)]$$
$$+ N(0)[\gamma_\phi(\beta_\psi+\mu_\xi) + \beta_\psi\gamma_\psi]$$
$$+ (\gamma_\phi+\gamma_\psi+\gamma_\xi)[L(0)(\beta_\psi+\mu_\xi) + M(0)\beta_\psi]\}$$

$$= p[u_3 p^2 + v_3 p + w_3],$$

where $u_3 = L(0)$,

$v3 = \gamma_\phi N(0) + $ by $M(0) + \beta_\psi + \mu_\xi + \gamma_\phi + \gamma_\psi + \gamma_\xi) L(0),$

and

$$w_3 = (\gamma_\psi + \gamma_\phi + \gamma_\xi)\,[(\beta_\psi + \mu_\xi)\,L(0) + \beta_\psi M(0)] + (\gamma_\phi \beta_\psi + \mu_\xi \gamma_\phi + \beta_\psi \gamma_\psi)\,N(0).$$

Substituting (a8) and (a13) back into (a7), we get

$$a(p) = \frac{\Delta_a(p)}{\Delta(p)}$$
$$= \frac{p(u_3 p^2 + v_3 p + w_3)}{p(p+k)(p+s)(p+g)}$$
$$= \frac{X_3}{p-(-k)} + \frac{Y_3}{p-(-s)} + \frac{Z_3}{p-(-g)}\ . \tag{a14}$$

Solving for (a14) then yields

$$X_3 = \frac{u_3 k^2 - v_3 k + w3}{(g-k)(s-k)},$$

$$Y_3 = \frac{u_3 s^2 - v_3 s + w3}{(k-s)(g-s)},$$

and

$$Z_3 = \frac{u_3 g^2 - v_3 g + w3}{(k-g)(s-g)}\ .$$

After taking the inverse Laplace transform of equation (a14), we obtain

$$L(t) = Lap^{-1}[a(p)]$$
$$= Lap^{-1}\left(\frac{X_3}{p-(-k)}\right) + Lap^{-1}\left(\frac{Y_3}{p-(-s)}\right) + Lap^{-1}\left(\frac{Z_3}{p-(-g)}\right)$$
$$= X_3\, e^{-kt} + Y_3\, e^{-st} + Z_3\, e^{-gt}.$$

Step 7. Solve $\Delta_c(p)$ for $H(t)$.

$$\Delta_c(p) = \gamma_\phi \begin{vmatrix} -\mu_\psi & p+\beta_\psi+\mu_\xi & M(0) \\ 0 & -\mu_\xi & H(0) \\ -\beta_\phi & 0 & N(0) \end{vmatrix} - \gamma_\psi \begin{vmatrix} p+\beta_\phi+\mu_\psi & -\beta_\psi & L(0) \\ 0 & -\mu_\xi & H(0) \\ -\beta_\phi & 0 & N(0) \end{vmatrix}$$

$$+\ \gamma_\xi \begin{vmatrix} p+\beta_\phi+\mu_\psi & -\beta_\psi & L(0) \\ -\mu_\psi & p+\beta_\psi+\mu_\xi & M(0) \\ -\beta_\phi & 0 & N(0) \end{vmatrix}$$

$$+\ (p+\gamma_\phi+\gamma_\psi+\gamma_\xi) \begin{vmatrix} p+\beta_\phi+\mu_\psi & -\beta_\psi & L(0) \\ -\mu_\psi & p+\beta_\psi+\mu_\xi & M(0) \\ 0 & -\mu_\xi & H(0) \end{vmatrix}$$

$$= p\left[(-\beta_\phi)\gamma_\phi H(0)\right] + \beta_\phi\gamma_\phi\left[-H(0)(\beta_\psi + \mu_\xi) - \mu_\xi M(0)\right] + \gamma_\phi\mu_\psi\mu_\xi N(0)$$
$$+ p(\gamma_\psi\mu_\xi N(0) + (\beta_\phi + \mu_\psi)\mu_\xi\gamma_\psi N(0) + \gamma_\psi\mu_\xi\beta_\phi L(0) - \gamma_\psi\beta_\psi\beta_\phi H(0)$$
$$+ p^2\gamma_\xi N(0) + p\left[\gamma_\xi\beta_\phi(N(0) + L(0)) + (\mu_\psi + \beta_\psi + \mu_\xi)\gamma_\xi N(0)\right]$$
$$+ \gamma_\xi N(0)(\beta_\phi\beta_\psi + \beta_\phi\mu_\xi + \mu_\xi\mu_\psi) + \gamma_\xi\beta_\phi\beta_\psi(M(0) + L(0)) + \gamma_\xi L(0)\beta_\phi\mu_\xi$$
$$+ (p + \gamma_\phi + \gamma_\psi + \gamma_\xi)\{(p + \beta_\phi + \mu_\psi)(p + \beta_\psi + \mu_\xi)H(0) + (-\mu_\psi)(-\mu_\xi)L(0)$$
$$- (p + \beta_\phi + \mu_\psi)M(0)(-\mu_\xi) - H(0)(-\mu_\psi)(-\beta_\psi)\}$$

$$= p^3 H(0) + p^2[\gamma_\xi N(0) + \mu_\xi M(0) + H(0)(\mu_\psi + \beta_\psi + \beta_\phi + \mu_\xi + \gamma_\xi + \gamma_\phi + \gamma_\psi)]$$
$$+ p\{(\gamma_\psi + \gamma_\xi)\mu_\xi[C - L(0)] + \gamma_\xi\beta_\phi[C - M(0)] + \mu_\psi\mu_\xi[C - N(0)]$$
$$+ \gamma_\xi(\mu_\psi + \beta_\psi)[N(0) + H(0)] + \mu_\xi(\beta_\phi + \gamma_\phi)[M(0) + H(0)]$$
$$+ H(0)[\beta_\phi(\gamma_\psi + \beta_\psi) + (\mu_\psi + \beta_\psi)(\gamma_\psi + \gamma_\phi)]\}$$
$$+ [N(0) + L(0) + M(0) + H(0)] \times$$
$$[\beta_\phi(\gamma_\psi\mu_\xi + \mu_\xi\gamma_\xi + \gamma_\xi\beta_\psi) + \mu_\xi\mu_\psi(\gamma_\phi + \gamma_\psi + \gamma_\xi)]$$

$$= Q p^3 + u_4 p^2 + v_4 p + w_4,$$

where $Q = H(0)$,

$$u_4 = \gamma_\xi N(0) + \mu_\xi M(0) + (\beta_\psi + \beta_\phi + \mu_\xi + \mu_\psi + \gamma_\phi + \gamma_\psi + \gamma_\xi) H(0),$$
$$v_4 = \mu_\xi(\gamma_\psi + \gamma_\xi)[C - L(0)] + \gamma_\xi\beta_\phi[C - M(0)] + \mu_\xi\mu_\psi[C - N(0)]$$
$$+ \gamma_\xi(\beta_\psi + \mu_\psi)[N(0) + H(0)] + \mu_\xi(\beta_\phi + \gamma_\phi)[M(0) + H(0)]$$
$$+ [\beta_\phi(\gamma_\psi + \beta_\psi) + (\gamma_\phi + \gamma_\psi)(\beta_\psi + \mu_\psi)]H(0),$$
$$w_4 = C[\beta_\phi(\gamma_\psi\mu_\xi + \gamma_\xi\mu_\xi + \gamma_\xi\beta_\psi) + \mu_\psi\mu_\xi(\gamma_\phi + \gamma_\psi + \gamma_\xi)].$$

Substituting (a8) and (a15) back into (a7), we get

$$c(p) = \frac{\Delta_c(p)}{\Delta(p)}$$
$$= \frac{Q p^3 + u_4 p^2 + v_4 p + w_4}{p(p+k)(p+s)(p+g)}$$
$$= \frac{l}{p} + \frac{X_4}{p-(-k)} + \frac{Y_4}{p-(-s)} + \frac{Z_4}{p-(-g)}. \tag{a16}$$

Then, by expanding (a16), we can get the following four algebraic equations:

$$Q = l + X_4 + Y_4 + Z_4,$$
$$u_4 = -l(s + k + g) - X_4(s + g) - Y_4(k + g) - Z_4(s + k),$$
$$v_4 = l(sk + kg + gs) + X_4 sg + Y_4 kg + Z_4 sk,$$

and

$$w_4 = -lskg.$$

Solving these four equations yields

$$X_4 = \frac{-Qk^3 + u_4 k^2 - v_4 k + w_4}{-k(g-k)(s-k)},$$

$$Y_4 = \frac{-Qs^3 + u_4 s^2 - v_4 s + w_4}{-s(k-s)(g-s)},$$

$$Z_4 = \frac{-Qg^3 + u_4 g^2 - v_4 g + w_4}{-g(k-g)(s-g)},$$

and

$$l = \frac{w_4}{kgs}.$$

After taking the inverse Laplace transform of equation (a16), we realize

$$H(t) = Lap^{-1}[c(p)]$$

$$= Lap^{-1} \left(\frac{l}{p} + \frac{X_4}{p-(-k)} + \frac{Y_4}{p-(-s)} + \frac{Z_4}{p-(-g)} \right)$$

$$= l + X_4 \, e^{-kt} + Y_4 \, e^{-st} + Z_4 \, e^{-gt}.$$

Section II
Improving Response Capability to Counter the Threat

Unit III
Forming Situation Awareness for First Decisions and Lifesaving

As defined by the White House (HSC, 2007), homeland security is the concerted effort to prevent attacks, reduce vulnerability to terrorism, and minimize the damages and recover from attacks that do occur. Part of the "minimize the damage" component entails the need for effective responses to damages or catastrophes.

In this unit, we explore how an effective response to any sudden and unexpected emergency might be generated to protect the public. When responding to an unexpected incident, according to past experience, the first necessary task demands securing the area and ascertaining the nature and severity of the threat. Therefore, responders must already know of the occurrence of the threat, enabling them to implement their reactions immediately. In reality however, if an unexpected incident occurs suddenly, responders may not be immediately aware of its occurrence. In some cases, awareness may be quick, such as in the case of an explosion, but in other times, it may take longer. For example, awareness of the September 11 tragedy (see Table 7.1) occurred only when authorities realized something was wrong with the aircraft. The time of awareness of the hijackings ranged from 9 minutes (for flight AA11) to 30 minutes (for flight AA77) after the actual hijackings—relatively fast responses. Because flight attendants, passengers, and air traffic controllers can detect and inform people of the occurrence of a hijacking event, event awareness occurs sooner. However, if an incident involves a covert release of a biological agent or radiological materials, it might not be recognized for several days, until the people exposed develop symptoms and seek treatment in hospitals.

Therefore, a time delay may exist between the time of the attack and the time when the responders realize it. One of the most serious considerations by emergency planners must be how to realize quickly the occurrence of a sudden unexpected attack and thereby start a response immediately. In Chapter VI, we explore when it is possible to recognize that an event has occurred and how to ascertain the nature and severity of the event.

Because a reaction to any unexpected incident initiates only after awareness of its occurrence, in most cases, there is no time to think of a detailed strategic plan or analyze the state of the situation and the magnitude of the hazards involved, which already exist, before taking action. Sometimes, responders may not even have enough time to take action. For example, on September 11, responders had only 8–30 minutes after they knew of the hijacking to take action (see Table 7.1). The urgent circumstances and time pressure indicate that generating an effective response is not an easy task.

A response usually involves *at least* two different levels of responders: incident commanders and frontline responders. The incident commander issues, often a mayor, city manager, chairperson of a city council, or director of an emergency operations center (EOC), commands and determines directions for the response in the event of an incident. This incident commander normally must make many decisions immediately to minimize damages, yet it remains very common to find ineffective and unclear directions about how to respond after many disasters. In the aftermath of Hurricane Katrina, responders had confusion, a lack of response, and mass chaos and violence to contend with (Walters & Kettl, 2005). Some actually refer to Hurricane Katrina as a man-made disaster because of the poorly constructed levees and lack of government responsiveness (UAS Today, 2006). As Senator David Vitter (R-La.) remarked, "this disaster was not out of the blue or unforeseeable. It was not only predictable, it was actually predicted. That what made the failures in response—at the local, state, and federal level—all the more outrageous" (Vitter, 2006). Indeed, incident commanders preferably generate quick and effective first decisions, which can lead to achievable responses. Therefore, in Chapter VII, we discuss how to generate effective initial decisions, even with limited information and under time pressures.

Frontline responders normally include personnel on the scene of an incident, or first responders, such as law enforcement, firefighters, emergency medical services, and so forth. These people execute response strategies and perform tasks associated with such strategies. Usually, when a disaster occurs, the response activities or tasks take place at the incident site or somewhere near it, though some disasters, such as infectious disease outbreaks or biological attacks, may move the battleground to hospitals or other sites distant from the event source because of the delayed awareness. Therefore, response activities can be roughly classified into two branches, depending on the location of the battle. One branch refers to activities implemented at the site of the incident, which we label onsite response, including pre-hospital rescue. The other branch refers to hospital responses. Therefore, in this context, we consider two classes of the first responders: firefighters and hospital staff.

When a disaster is related to nuclear or radiological material, radiation contamination is easy to detect with relatively inexpensive equipment. Such detectors could confirm a radioactive release. However, quickly identifying a release of toxic chemicals or recognizing an infectious disease outbreak is very difficult. Therefore, in Chapter VIII, we introduce a computer-support chemical substance discovery system—like a portable, digitized fire chief—that can assist firefighters in identifying agents on the basis of only limited or observed symptoms and thereby generate an incident-specific response operation under time pressures. In Chapter IX, we present a hospital emergency support system that integrates existing health care routine functions within a real-time data analysis and thus suggests early alerts for a potential disease outbreak, regardless of whether it is natural or man-made. In addition, if an incident occurs, the exposed or injured people rapidly seek care, which means they may not wait to find facilities designed by existing response plans. Thus, every health care facility must be able to organize an effective response quickly; speed is critical in life saving. A means to employ existing health care capacities quickly to generate a "dual-use" response infrastructure therefore becomes an urgent issue, because many of the capabilities required to respond to a large-scale chemical or biological attack also are required to respond to naturally occurring disease outbreaks. So, the systems introduced in Chapter VIII and IX address specific issues, such as what fire chiefs or hospital managers must do to control the situations they face. What are the most important tasks? Which task should be performed first, and which can be processed simultaneously?

Then in Chapter X, we consider ways to channel evacuees quickly during an emergency situation. Although incident commanders and others assume that people will act rationally—hear a warning, realize the danger based on the warning, and leave when told to do so—more often, people do not do as emergency commanders expect. In an emergency, urgency creates a sense of uncertainty and forces people to act to escape from the danger. Congestion normally occurs. We propose a mathematical model with algorithms to help incident commanders organize at-risk populations and evacuate them from potentially dangerous environments to safer areas during an emergency. Specifically, we present a computer support system, the *Emergency Evacuation Command System*, with a simulation. Compared with two benchmark cases (i.e., random self-evacuation and herding behavior), we show that the proposed method can rescue people at risk and move them to safe area in a much shorter time and without congestion.

In summary, the following are the key elements of capability-based effective response:

- Realizing the occurrence of an attack and gaining situation awareness.
- Generating effective initial decisions and managing emergency functions, even with limited information and under time pressure.
- Identifying chemical terrorism to generate an incident-specific response operation
- Providing hospital emergency support in response to bio terrorism or infectious disease.
- Organizing at-risk populations to safer areas during an emergency.

The next chapters examine these issues one by one.

REFERENCES

USA Today (May 23, 2006). Editorial: In Katrina disaster, human error claimed heavy toll. Retrieved May 24, 2006, from http://www.usatoday.com/news/opinion/editorials/2006-05-23-our-view x.htm.

U.S. Homeland Security Council [HSC] (2007), *National Strategy for Homeland Security*. Washington DC: Homeland Security Council.

Vitter, D. (March 2, 2006). *Vitter statement on Katrina Video*. Retrieved March 10, 2006, from http://vitter.senate.gov/?module=pressroom/pressitem&ID=0a46a873-6bed-486d-8f77-eadc3f36c7b4.

Walters, J., & Kettl, D. (2005). The Katrina breakdown—coordination and communication problems between levels of government must be addressed before the next disaster strikes. *Governing*, December. Retrieved March 2, 2006, from http://www.governing.com/articles/12disast.htm.

Chapter VI
Situation Awareness through Feature Recognition

INTRODUCTION

To help establish response plans for protecting U.S. homeland security, a standardized set of scenarios that can function as a "common operating picture" has been developed under the leadership of the U.S. Homeland Security Council (HSC) and Department of Homeland Security (DHS), according to The New York Times (Lipton, 2005). The 15 developed scenarios help identify critical capabilities and procedures for response, define operational parameters for layer response capabilities, establish a foundation for resource decisions, and pave the way to identify needed technology enhancements. To ensure that emergency planning is adequate, each scenario generally reflects suspected terrorist capabilities and known tradecraft. Of the 15 scenarios, 12 refer to human-made intentional terror attacks, and 3 pertain to catastrophic natural disasters (i.e., influenza pandemic, magnitude 7.2 earthquake in a major city, and slow-moving category 5 hurricane hitting a major East Coast city). Of the 12 human-made terror attacks, 8 are biological or chemical strikes, including the release of a Sarin nerve agent in an office building, spraying aerosolized anthrax over five cities in two weeks, and spreading pneumonic plague in the bathrooms of an airport, sports arena, and train station. Two scenarios involve the use of nuclear and radiological dispersion devices in a large metropolitan area or regionally significant cities, and one suggests an explosion using improvised explosive devices. The scenarios also include a cyber attack that affects several parts of the nation's finance infrastructure. Biologically or chemically related threats clearly have prompted heightened concern; an attack involving biological or chemical contagious pathogens, if it were to occur, would cause tremendous damage to the public.

A great deal of discussion and research surrounds these 15 scenarios. Some researchers use them as platforms and suggest a variety of response strategies (e.g., U.S. General Accounting Office [GAO], 2007; Relman & Olson, 2001); others consider them the worst-case scenarios and conduct risk assessments to evaluate their probability of occurrence to suggest resource allocations. Several researchers further argue that the threats of terrorist attacks involving chemical, biological, radiological, or nuclear materials (CBRN) may have a low probability in reality for various reasons, including the difficulty terrorists have obtaining some of required components of nuclear materials or highly infective strains of biological and chemical agents, as well as the significant technical and operational challenges to making chemical or biological agents of sufficient quality and quantity to kill or injure a large number of people (GAO, 2000; Powers & Ban, 2004). Such threat risk assessments can be described using the following equation:

Intentions + Capabilities => Probable Threat Risk.

The threat risk thus is based on the motivation and capability of the perpetrators to carry out such attacks. The September 11 event demonstrated terrorists' intentions to cause maximum damage. Therefore, the level of potential threat risk relies on the magnitude of the capabilities, such as acquisition of materials and technical competency, that terrorists possess to carry out an attack. If the level of potential threat risk is obtained, this value can be interpreted using the following classification scheme (GAO, 1997):

- **Frequent:** (Indicating) an unexpected event is likely to occur frequently.
- **Probable:** An unexpected event will occur several times.
- **Occasional:** An unexpected event is likely to occur sometime.
- **Remote:** An unexpected event is unlikely but possible to occur.
- **Improbable:** An unexpected event is very much unlikely to occur.

CIA Director George Tenet testified before the U.S. Congress that terrorists currently rely on conventional explosives, but several groups (e.g., al-Qaida, the most familiar example) seek chemical, biologi-

Figure 6.1. Steps for terrorists to conduct chemical and biological terrorism and obstacles to overcome (Source: GAO, 2000)

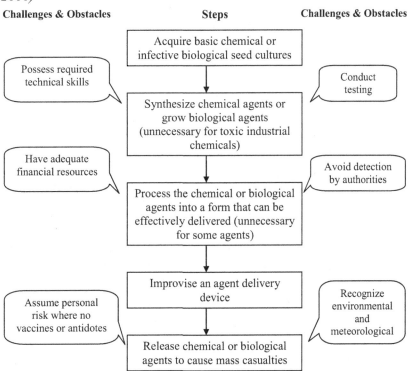

cal, and radiological strike capacity (Hoffman, 2002). This strand of terrorism is no longer a question of will but a matter of means and opportunity—the capabilities and considerations required to pursue the means and execution of a terrorist attack. Figure 6.1 shows the obstacles that terrorists may face in conducting chemical and biological terrorism.

Consider smallpox as an example. Smallpox is a highly contagious disease, and unprotected populations have little or no immunity against it. However, a terror attack using smallpox has a very low probability of occurrence, because terrorists face difficulties passing through the first stage of Figure 6.1, that is, getting the smallpox virus. Smallpox as a naturally occurring disease has been eradicated, and the virus that causes smallpox is secured at only two high-security laboratories: one in Atlanta at the Centers for Disease Control and Prevention(CDC), United States, and the other at Vector laboratories in Siberia, Russia. Therefore, mass destruction using smallpox is not the most likely contingency (Powers & Ban, 2004).

Smallpox may be an extreme case however, and other types of viruses and infective agents exist (CDC, 2006). Recently, an increasing concern is the possibility of using the influenza virus as an agent for bioterrorism, which arises in response to recent bird flu outbreaks around the world that have devastated poultry flocks. The influenza virus is readily available, and human populations lack immunological protection against such a virus should it mutates to become easily transmittable among humans, because existing antiviral drugs would not afford any protection (HSC, 2006; Krug, 2003; Madjid et al, 2003; Zamiska, 2005). Although making and releasing such lethal and highly noxious biological or chemical agents, as well as operating radioactive materials, requires specialized knowledge, the rapid development in commercial biotechnology and genetic engineering and fast knowledge dissemination through the Internet may lower such technical bars.

Research indicates that terrorists exploit easily obtained or commonly used materials that are less technically challenging to achieve their threat goals. For example, stealing materials is one obvious way, especially for radioactive materials or industrial chemicals. On May 2002, ten tons of sodium cyanide was stolen during a truck hijacking in Mexico. Weeks later, only one fifth of the cyanide had been recovered, and the hijackers had not been found (Keim, 2006). Research also finds that "purchase" may be another easiest way to acquire those agents. The World Directory of Collections of Cultures lists 453 repositories in 67 nations that supply biological agents, with 57 stocking *Bacillus anthracis* and 18 *Yersinia pertis* (Osterholm, 1999). In 1998, reporters from the *London Sunday Times* posing as businessmen, were allegedly able to obtain anthrax and plague cultures for £600 pounds from an Indonesian research institute (Leppard, et al, 1998).

In addition, to overcome some technical challenges, terrorists use the ready availability of high-speed Internet access to acquire technical operation skills. For example, some web sites provide detailed instructional documents and videos explain how to make rockets, improvised devices, and even crude chemical weapons (Kohlmann, 2006). According to the Global Terror Alert Web site (http://www. globalterroralert.com/), some people deliberately provide information on the Internet about how to use discarded household smoke detectors to make a nuclear warhead, eliminating the need to look for expensive materials. Although smoke detectors are important home safety devices, which many families have installed as alarm systems for protections, one particular type, the ionization-type detector, contains a small quantity of radioactive americium-241, a source of alpha radiation, according to the fact sheet published by the U.S. Environmental Protecting Agency (EPA, 2005b). Few people are aware of this fact. Americium-241 has a half-life of approximately 432 years, so at the end of the 10–20 years of functional life of a smoke detector, americium-241 retains essentially all its original energy. If homeowners are unaware of the long-lasting nature of americium-241 and discard their used smoke detectors into garbage cans, others with ill intent could easily find the discarded detectors in any garbage pile at local dumps. Although the amount of americium-241 in a smoke detector is a very small, if someone intentionally collected them, a threat exists. London's dirty bomb plot is just such an example. According to London *Time* (2004), in August 2004, British authorities broke up a cell of suspected Islamic terrorists who were trying to construct a crude radiological dirty bomb to attack London and "blow up high-rise buildings housing multinational companies" and "the Heathrow Express—a rail line between the airport and London," as well as an unspecified synagogue by driving bomb-laden cars into these target areas. The arrests turned up a cache of household smoke detectors, which the British authorities suspect they wanted to cannibalize for their minute quantities of americium-241.

Some officials believe it unlikely that enough americium could be harvested from smoke detectors to create a device potent enough to inflict radiation sickness, let alone kill people. But others argue that spewing even a small amount of radioactive material into a crowded stadium or subway station could trigger sensitive radiation sensors, incite panic, and cause long-lasting contamination (*London Time*, 2004).

In contrast with the low probability of large-scale incidents involving CBRN, because of the technical and operational difficulties summarized in Figure 6.1, the number of small- or middle-scale incidents, including intentionally using toxic chemicals or highly infective biological agents as weapons or tools of fear against a civilian population, are more plentiful (Gurr & Cole, 2002). According to the Swedish Defence Research Agency's FOI NBC database (Heurgren-Carlstrom & Malmberg, 2003; Melin, 2002), approximately 16,000 different types of terror incidents occurred between 1960 and 2002. As shown in Figure 6.2, most incidents involve explosives, accounting for approximately 80 percent of the total. Biological and chemical incidents constitute 2.4 and 5.8 percent, respectively. Other incidents, such as hijacking, kidnapping, hostage, and attacks with radiological or nuclear materials, account for about 11 percent of the total. These data suggest that explosions, radiological/nuclear deterrents, and chemical and biological terrorism remain four major forms of terrorist attacks. Explosion may be the easiest, in that it requires fewer technical skills compared with the other three types. In addition, these data indicate that the occurrence rate for biological and chemical terrorism seems much higher than that for radiological or nuclear incidents.

If we only consider chemical attacks, almost 920 incidents occurred during the period, 41 percent of which resulted in physical casualties, whereas 24 percent caused no casualties because either the dispersion methods were inefficient or the terrorists chose low-toxic chemicals. The rest of the incidents

Figure 6.2. Forms of terrorist attacks (1960–April 2002)

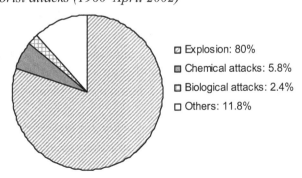

☑ Explosion: 80%

■ Chemical attacks: 5.8%

☐ Biological attacks: 2.4%

☐ Others: 11.8%

Figure 6.3. Classification of chemical incidents: Threatening and physical damages (1960–April, 2002)

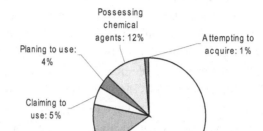

involve "threatening to use," "claiming to use," "possessing," and "attempting to acquire" chemical agents. Figure 6.3 details this classification of chemical attacks. As we discussed in Chapter III, the effect of an incident involves a dual role: causing directly visible physical damages and indirectly threatening people's mindsets. In this summary, it appears 35 percent of incidents attempted to cause a threat.

Whether a large-scale event with low probability of occurrence or a small-scale attack of high frequency, the only acceptable result for populations is non-occurrence. Regardless of their forms or scales, these different types of attacks share two common features: (1) sudden occurrence with surprise and (2) targeting civilians with a threatening purpose. The second feature seems obvious: Any attack on civilian populations causes either direct physical casualties or indirect psychosocial damages, and sometimes both. Past disaster events suggest that almost all terrorist attacks occur suddenly at different times and in different areas, which could create significant response difficulties.

If an unexpected attack occurs suddenly, the event does not automatically indicate that responders are immediately aware of the occurrence. For example, if an attack releases a radiological material or biological agent, it must be unexpected and have occurred suddenly and covertly, or a deterrent action would have been taken in advance to prevent it had authorities had intelligence about it in advance. Furthermore, the occurrence might not be recognized for several days until people exposed develop symptoms and seek treatment in hospitals. If a cluster of cases is small or singular, it may not even attract attention. Alternatively, if the symptoms are common and look like a natural disease, it may not prompt an investigation. Therefore, a time delay may exist between the time of the attack and the time the responders realize it. In this context, we term this delay the "time lag of event awareness." If the released agent can cause a communicable disease, during that time lag period, the resulting communicable disease could spread to many people who were not initially exposed.

Hence, if an unexpected incident occurs suddenly, this time lag of event awareness must be short enough that appropriate response actions can be taken immediately to control the incident situation and save lives. Otherwise, once authorities realize that an attack has occurred, casualties may have occurred, which would leave no time for detailed and carefully planning or assessment of possible countermeasures.

The ability to detect the occurrence of an attack quickly is a critical factor for generating an effective response to any unexpected emergency situation. Existing research focuses on different response preparations, assuming that both the occurrence of an incident and the type of the incident are known. In reality, however, unless the incident generates obvious signs, such as an explosion accompanied by audible sounds and a visible blast, or eyewitnesses on the scene directly experience the event, awareness comes only some time later when signs or symptoms suggest what might have happened.

In this chapter, we attempt to explore the question of when it is possible to realize an event has occurred and how to ascertain the nature and severity of the event. On the basis of DHS's classification of 15 planning scenarios and the data suggested in Figure 6.2, we consider emergencies caused by five types of incidents: explosives, chemical, biological, radiological, and nuclear (denoted ECBRN). We examine the characteristics of these five types of incidents and identify possible markers that might improve awareness. Because the timeframe for response is also critical to whether control is successful, we examine the dynamics and timeline for each type of incident and suggest ways to help recognize or detect and thus reduce the time delay of awareness.

ECBRN EMERGENCY: CHARACTERISTICS AND FEATURE EXTRACTION

Explosives Incident

As Figure 6.2 suggests, among all known terrorist attacks, explosion remains the most common form used by terrorists. Between 2001 and 2003, more than 500 international terrorist bombings have occurred, resulting in more than 4,600 deaths (DOS, 2002, 2003, 2004). In 2005 alone, 758 worldwide terrorist events occurred, of which 399 were bombings (TRC, 2005). After the attacks on the World Trade Center and the Pentagon in 2001, worrying about the use of commercial airplanes as explosives became more widespread. In addition to increasing ground security checks in airports, including systematic detection of checked and carried baggage, several thousands U.S. Federal Air Marshals fly on scores of domestic and international flights each day to guard the flights and search the aircrafts' lavatories and other spaces for bomb-making components. According to *London Time* (2006), liquid explosives may provide terrorists with a secret weapon, because they are easily concealed in many items found in most travelers' hand luggage, such as perfume, hair gel, deodorant, medicine, drinks, toothpaste, lotions, and so on, and are extremely difficult to detect (i.e., metal detectors cannot sense them).

Characteristics. Through a sudden energy release, an explosion can result in direct and immediate damage to a target. People in the blast zone would be killed or injured by the blast. If the explosion involves radioactive materials or biological agents, people onsite might be contaminated by those materials. Explosions are easy to make and demand fewer technological skills; they also rely on easy to obtain materials and are easy to operate. The degree of damage caused by explosives depends on the type and amount of explosive material used, the size and number of the buildings in the area attacked, and the ballistics at detonation.

Timeline of activation. The detonation of explosives is instantaneous, usually less than a minute, after the combustible materials are ignited. High-order explosives cause reactions that can accelerate at speed of greater than 1000m/s. A visible effect occurs immediately, which offers no chance for warning during the occurrence. Therefore, an effective detection system is necessary to avoid such damages.

Type of delivery. Bombing is a common delivery type used by terrorists, including car bombing, suicide bombing, mail bombing, and so forth. The September 11 attacks on the World Trade Center and the Pentagon suggest that airplanes also can be used as explosive devices by terrorists.

Clear/visible signs on site. Because an explosion involves a sudden increase in volume and extreme release of energy, usually with the generation of high temperatures and a shock wave, it often offers two obvious signs during its occurrence: visible damage and an audible blast. In most situations, black smoke from the explosion site is visible, and a sudden sound can be heard.

Time lag of event awareness. People's attention gets captured immediately when they hear the sound of an explosion. Thus, there is almost no time lag for awareness.

Affected area. If the explosion does not involve radioactive materials or chemical or contagious biological agents, the affected area will be the incident site, that is, the area where the explosion took place. Otherwise, the affected areas would be more geographically dispersed, including areas that the radioactive or chemical cloud/stream passes through or those affected by air contaminated by the biological agent or radiological materials.

First responders. In most situation, local firefighters, police, and emergency medical service personnel are the first responders.

Detection/deterrence. Because of the direct and immediate effects, detection in the pre-event stage is absolutely necessary. Many detection approaches exist, including hand checks, bomb dogs, and machines. Specially trained bomb dogs are trained to help detect explosives using their noses, which are very sensitive to scents. The dogs indicate a "hit" by taking an action they are trained to provide, generally a passive response. Although effective, their usefulness becomes degraded as a dog becomes tired. New technologies may provide explosive detection systems, such as a X-ray–like screening systems for checking baggage, bottled liquid scanners to differentiate liquid explosives from common, benign liquids, and so forth.

Chemical Incidents

Chemical incidents entail the release of toxic chemicals in the form of vapors, aerosols (suspension of microscopic droplets), liquids, or solids (absorbed powder) that have hazardous effects on people, animals, or plants. The most notorious case of a lethal chemical attack is the use by Aum Shinrikyo in 1995 of Sarin gas in the Tokyo subway. Various industry incidents also involve the release of industrial chemicals such as acid, ammonia, chlorine, or phosgene. According to the U.S. Hazardous Substances Emergency Events Surveillance (HSEES) system, 1,080 events involved the release of chemicals during 1999–2004 in United States. The most common substances released were sulfuric acid, sodium hydroxide, and hydrochloric acid. The HSEES system collects and analyzes data pertaining to public health consequences (e.g., morbidity, mortality, evacuations) associated with the release of hazardous substances in facilities or during transportation (ATSDR, 2001). The most recent chemical incident, on January 6, 2005, involved two freight trains that collided in Graniteville, South Carolina, releasing an estimated 11,500 gallons of chlorine gas, which caused nine deaths and sent at least 529 persons in search of medical treatment for possible chlorine exposure (EPA, 2005a; South Carolina Emergency Management Division, 2005)

Characteristics. The key characteristic of a chemical attack pertains to its fast action once released. A chemical attack can be very harmful depending on the location, population affected, weather conditions, material deployed, and disposal techniques. Although the length and time scales are limited, because dangerous concentrations of chemical agents quickly are diluted through diffusion and degradation by ultraviolet radiation, the damage range is very wide, and the resulting frightening images can cause severe psychosocial effects on the population.

Historical records suggest that many chemical incidents use materials widely found in industry, such as chlorine, ammonia, or benzene. These industry agents have dual applications, being important in industrial processes as well as potential weapons. They are easy to acquire with limited control. Others employ agents developed by military organizations for use in warfare, such as nerve agents (e.g., Sarin, VX), mustard gasses (e.g., sulfur, nitrogen), and pulmonary agents (e.g., phosgene). Thus, it may be relatively easier for terrorists to acquire such materials compared with nuclear, radiological, or biological weapons.

Timeline of activation. Release acts very quickly (often within a few seconds or minutes), though some clinical somatic symptoms can take longer to become manifest if concentrations are low. People have very little time to react to an attack unless they are warned in advance that their food or water is contaminated or that a lethal, and silent, aerosol cloud is headed their way, which is unlikely.

Type of attack. Chemical agents can be released by a variety of methods, including throwing the chemical out of a bottle or a jar, causing injections through syringes, rubbing it into doorknobs, pouring it into wells, mixing it directly into food or beverages, spraying from weapons or vehicles, or exploding as bombs.

Clear/visible sign on site. If a chemical release occurs, the possible routes of exposure include inhalation or contact by eyes and skin. The immediate symptoms may appear within minutes or hours, but the actual clinical syndromes vary depending on the type of agent, the amount and concentration of the chemical, and the route of exposure. When the released chemical is concentrated, immediate symptoms likely appear, such as colored residue, dead foliage, pungent odors, or dead insect or animal life. Table 6.1 categorizes common chemical agents by their routes of exposure, possible clinical signs and symptoms, and how long a noticeable sign persists for each category.

Basic classes of chemical agents that could be used in a terrorist attack include blood agents (e.g., hydrogen cyanide, cyanogen chloride), blister agents (e.g., mustard gas, lewisite), nerve agents (e.g., Sarin, tabun), and pulmonary agents (e.g., chlorine, phosgene) (CDC, 2000). Blood agents interfere with cellular respiration, such that their inhalation causes no immediate symptoms, but symptoms emerge 2–24 hours after exposure as a result of massive hemolysis. Blister agents, the most commonly used chemical warfare agents during World War I, cause severe chemical burns to the skin and lungs. The most likely routes of exposure are inhalation, dermal contact, and ocular contact. Its possible effects may occur immediately (for phosgene oxime or lewisite) or be delayed 2–24 hours (mustards). Following exposure, the most commonly encountered clinical effects include skin erythema and blistering, respiratory distress such as cough and dyspnea, ocular damage such as burns, and nausea and vomiting. Pulmonary agents damage lung tissue. The clinical symptom may be delayed 1–48 hours.

Time lag of event awareness. An occurrence would be realized when exposed people develop symptoms related to a chemical release. However, early detection of a chemical attack is not easy, because most agents do not display biological markers, which increases the challenge of developing a laboratory test, and many symptoms relate to respiratory, eye, or skin irritations, which can be similar to those caused by a natural accident or disease.

Affected area. When released in the air, some agents can be broken down by compounds, but they also may persist in the air for several days before doing so. Therefore, the affected area may not be concentrated but instead be geographically dispersed according to the wind direction.

First responders. Local firefighters, police, and emergency medical service professionals are the first responders. However, physicians and poison control centers may be the first to recognize an illness, treat patients, and implement the appropriate emergency response to a chemical release or incident.

Biological Attack

A biological attack describes the deliberate release of biological agents, such as viruses, bacteria, or other germs, to cause illness or death in people, animals, or plants. These biological agents actually are

Table 6.1. Categories of hazardous chemicals, effects, and timeline

Category	Route of Exposure	Immediate Symptoms	When to Appear (noticeable sign)	Biological Marker for Exposure
Blister agents • Lewsite • Nitrogen and sulfur mustards • Phosgene oxime	Eyes, skin, and inhalation.	Nasal irritation, sore throat, cough, shortness of breath, chest tightness	Immediately or in 2–12 hours	Yes for sulfur mustard. No for others.
Blood agents • Arsine • Sodium monfluoroancetate • Hydrogen cyanide • Cyanide • Carbon monoxide	Eye, skin, inhalation, or ingestion	Fatigue, headache, rapid breathing, dizziness, weakness, headache, nausea vomiting, abdominal pain	Several minutes to 24 hours after exposure depending on concentration	No for arsine and sodium monofluoroacetate Yes for cyanide
Caustic Agents • Hydrofluoric acid • Phosphoric acid • Sulfuric acid	Inhalation or direct injury to tissue upon exposure (e.g., skin, eyes, and mucus membranes)	Severe pain at the exposure may be the only symptom. Upper or lower respiratory irritation possible	May not appear until 12–24 hours after exposure	No
Nerve agents • Tabun • Sarin • Soman • VX • GF	Multiple routes of exposure. Mainly through inhalation.	Tightness of the chest, runny nose, nausea, abdominal cramps, diarrhea and blurred vision, diaphoresis	Immediately if concentration is high. The onset of mild to moderate effects may be delayed for 18 hours.	Can be detected in urine
Pulmonary agents • Phosgene • Chlorine • Ammonia • Methyl bromide	Inhalation. nose, throat	Respiratory irritation, eye redness, nose and throat irritation, cough.	Onset of symptoms might be delayed 1–48 hours if concentration is not high. Obvious clinical symptoms delayed up to 4–5 days.	No

airborne particles floating in the air or sticking to the surfaces of contacted materials, such as the human body, clothes, and so on. They infect through one or more of the following exposure mechanisms, depending on the type of agent:

- Inhalation with infection through respiratory mucosa or lung tissues.
- Ingestion.
- Contact with the mucous membranes of the eye or nasal tissues.
- Penetration of the skin through open cuts, even very small cuts and abrasions of which people might be unaware.

Incidents involving biological agents have become more frequent in recent decades. In 1984, devotees of Bhagwan Shree Rajneesh infected 751 people in Oregon with Salmonella typhimurium by intentionally contaminating local self-service salad bars. On August 28, 1996, 12 laboratory workers in Dallas, Texas, fell ill as a result of eating muffins and doughnuts in their cafeteria, which had been intentionally contaminated with Shigella dysenteriae type 2 (a type of bacteria which causes diarrhea) by Diane Thompson, a disaffected worker. Thompson is believed to have gained access to the Shigella dysenteriae type 2 from the culture collection of the hospital where she worked. An epidemiological study of the case supports the theory of intentional contamination. The most recent threat, the anthrax event, occurred in October–November 2001 and involved the deliberate delivery of anthrax spores to the public in a relatively unsophisticated way—through the U.S. postal system.

If another anthrax event were to occur, the prevention of deaths would probably depend on heightened surveillance and rapid diagnostics to identify an attack and prompt prophylaxis with antibiotics and vaccination. According to projections about the potential consequences of a bioterrorism attack and the actuality of the immense impact of the small-scale anthrax incident in 2001, the need for bioterrorism preparedness has become a national priority and a moral imperative.

Characteristics. Biological attacks exhibit the following obvious key characteristics: First, they require covert delivery, and the delayed nature of the effect makes it difficult to discover and trace their origin. Because of the agent's incubation period, perpetrators might be gone before anyone knows an attack has occurred. Second, if an agent is dispersed in the air, it can be carried by the wind and potentially land anywhere, which increases its destructive potential (some agents are contagious and can survive in the environment for a long time, causing further risk of exposure). If a concentrated biological agent were released in large enough quantities and efficiently, its impact could be catastrophic. One report even suggests that well-dispersed anthrax in ideal weather conditions could inflict 20 percent more casualties than a 12.5 kiloton nuclear bomb (Cordesman, 2000), and other research suggests that 110 kg of anthrax could inflict as much damage on a densely populated metropolis as a 1 megaton hydrogen bomb (O'Toole, 2000). Third, in addition to causing physical casualties, biological attacks have huge psychosocial impacts because of people's fears about being infected. Even a minor biological attack could have a disproportionate impact.

On the basis of how easily they can be spread and the severity of illness or death they can cause, biological agents can be classified into three categories: highest (A), moderate (B), and emerging (C) agents, as shown in Table 6.2 (CDC, 2006b). Category A agents spread easily and can be transmitted from person to person with high death rates, making them the highest risk. Category B agents are moderately easy to disseminate but threaten low mortality rates because they are not transmissible among persons.

Table 6.2. Risk classifications of biological agents

Characters	Category A Agents	Category B Agents	Category C (Emerging) Agents
Spread	Easily	Moderate	Easily
Human transmission	Yes	No	Yes
Illness rate	High	Moderate	High
Death rate	High	Low	High
Risk	Highest	Moderate	Unknown

Category C agents refer to those emerging infectious disease, such as the Nipah virus, that could be engineered for mass dissemination in the future because of their availability, ease of production, and potential for high morbidity and mortality.

Agents in Category A, once released, require special action to ensure public health preparedness and may cause public panic and social disruption. These agents include anthrax, plague, smallpox, botulism, tularemia, filoviruses (e.g., Ebola hemorrhagic fever, Marburg hemorrhagic fever), arenaviruses, Argentine hemorrhagic fever, and related viruses.

Timeline of activation. Biological weapons act very quickly and often complete their actions within a short time. However, the effects cannot be seen immediately onsite. Each agent has its own timeline, depending on its clinical and epidemological characteristics.

Type of delivery. Common delivery methods including spreading through the air, water, or food. Some agents can spread from person to person, such as smallpox or the plague. Some devices used for intentional biological terrorism also may have the capacity to disseminate lager quantities of biological material in aerosol form.

Clear/visible sign on site. No immediate sign appears onsite. The occurrence of symptoms caused by many pathogens and toxins emerge hours or even days after an exposure.

Time lag of event awareness. The possible consequences might not be realized for several days to weeks after the attack. The occurrence will be realized only after those exposed develop symptoms, report to health care facilities, and are diagnosed with the disease caused by the biological release. Thus, there is a delayed time of awareness.

Affected area. Released biological agents often float in the air and move with winds, which spread the agents from the epicenter of the attack to other, geographically dispersed areas. The movement of infected persons, especially in a busy metropolitan setting or through transportation systems, sometimes can enlarge the areas affected, resulting in an increasing number of victims.

First responders. In a bioterrorist attack, physicians and health care professionals represent the frontline workers. They play critical roles in recognizing and defining the scope of the disease zone and therefore must be familiar with the features of biological agents, the symptoms associated with their use, and differences from naturally occurring disease. In addition, infection-control professionals can help confirm changing patterns or clusters in a hospital or a community that might otherwise go unrecognized.

Radiological Event

Radioactive attacks entail the deliberate use of different types of radioactive materials to harm people and animals or contaminate food and water supplies. Radiation can affect the human body in various ways, ranging from mild effects, such as skin reddening, to serious effects such as cancer and death, depending on the amount of radiation absorbed by the body, the type of radiation, the route of exposure, and the length of time a person was exposed. Exposure to very large doses of radiation may cause death within a few days or months. Exposure to lower doses may lead to an increased risk of developing cancer or other adverse health effects later in life.

Characteristics. The key feature of a radiological attack is its delayed and prolonged effect, in addition to the injuries and damages caused by the explosion. The direct number of casualties may not be substantially greater than those from a conventional explosion, yet the long-term casualties, mostly as a result of radiation-induced cancer, can be substantial. Thus, in addition to physical damage, a radiological attack often causes terror and panic among the population.

Timeline of activation. The dispersal of radiological material is quick. If it is released by explosives, such as bombs, much of the material scatters with the smoke cloud and then gets deposited in the ground within several hours of the explosion as the cloud passes overhead.

Type of delivery. Possible terrorist events could involve introducing radioactive material into food or water supplies; using explosives to scatter radioactive materials, as in the case of dirty bombs; bombing or destroying a nuclear facility; or exploding a small nuclear device.

Clear/visible sign on site. Because radiological materials are not recognizable by human senses, because they are colorless and odorless, a covert release of radioactive materials offers no immediately visible sign, unless unreasonable symptoms such as skin reddening appear among many affected people. The adverse health effects of exposure may not appear for many years. If the radioactive materials are dispersed using conventional explosives, the injury and property damage caused by the explosion can be seen immediately, which informs the public that an explosion has occurred.

Time lag of event awareness. If an incident uses conventional explosives, knowledge that the explosion has taken place is immediate. However, it could take hours or more to detect radiation. People within the area affected will not know that radiation is present immediately after the explosion. If the radioactive material is released covertly, authorities will not know it until the people exposed become ill. Overall, there is a delayed appearance of symptoms in radiological incidents.

Affected area. With conventional explosives, the area affected by a radiological attack could be several blocks. Specialized equipment can determine the size of the affected area and whether the level of radioactivity poses an immediate or long-term health threat. Winds may spread radiation, so the affected area may be very large.

First responders. Local firefighters and police are the first responders if the attack uses conventional explosives. For a covert release, health care professionals may be the first to realize and treat patients with related symptoms.

Detection. Radioactive material can be detected and/or cached in the pre-event stage. However, once an attack occurs, the detection of contamination and type of radioactive material requires complex instruments and can take a long time if a radiation monitoring system is not installed. It would be hard to assess exactly where and when the radioactivity has returned to safe levels.

Nuclear Event

The power generated by a nuclear detonation is huge and terrible: a powerful blast with high-energy radiation released from the nuclear reaction, a strong bright light, widespread physical destruction, searing heat, and the unique mushroom cloud. As evidenced by the atomic bombs dropped in Japan in 1945, the consequences are horrific.

There is no record of nuclear attack by terrorists in recent years, though in the aftermath of September 11, heightened concerns have centered around terrorists trying to smuggle nuclear or radiological materials into the United States. These materials could produce either an improvised nuclear device or a radiological dispersal device, known as a dirty bomb. An improvised nuclear device is a crude nuclear bomb that, if it succeeds, could achieve yields in the 10–20 kiloton range, equivalent to 10,000–20,000 tons of TNT. A 20-kiloton yield matches the yield of the bomb that destroyed Nagasaki and could devastate the heart of a medium-sized U.S. city, resulting in thousands of casualties and radiation contamination over a wider area (GAO, 2007).

Characteristics. Huge damage potential and immediate effects are the key characteristics of a nuclear attack. A nuclear denotation not only damages buildings but also interferes with electronic equipment. A ground burst will produce a larger footprint on the ground around the highly radioactive fallout cloud, extending possibly tens of miles. If it occurs without warning, people inside the blast zone become contaminated with radioactive material and could be injured by an explosion, which suggests both immediate and long-term effects such as cancer. People who receive a large dose might develop acute radiation syndrome, and people in the surrounding area likely are exposed or contaminated.

Timeline of activation. The immediate effects of nuclear denotation are quick. Activation starts immediately after the detonator is ignited, followed by a blast and a rising mushroom cloud. In the first 48 hours after the blast, radioactivity in the fallout is extremely high.

Type of delivery. The delivery approaches include explosives with nuclear materials, nuclear weapons, missiles, trucks, or ships.

Clear/visible sign onsite. Several signs appear immediately: a strong bright flash with searing heat and a unique mushroom cloud. An electromagnetic pulse could damage electronic devices within or near the area of the detonation.

Time lag of event awareness. Because a huge blast sound and a visible mushroom cloud accompany nuclear detonation, people's attention is captured immediately, which prompts investigation.

Affected area. The affected area is wide and large. After a nuclear explosion, radioactive fallout extends over a large region, far from the point of blast zone, and potentially increases people's risk of developing cancer over time.

First responders. In most situations, the first responders are local firefighters, police, and emergency medical service professionals.

Summary

Our analysis suggests that when an incident relates to an explosion, it often generates clear signs of the event occurrence, such as visible smoke or audible explosions, which prompt investigations to explore the cause. Therefore, explosion-related incidents such as conventional bombings, including dirty bombs that disperse radioactive material, radiological events with explosives, or nuclear incidents, will be realized soon after their occurrence. However, realizing a biological or radiological incident that does not include an explosion may take a long time because no immediate impact is visible. If attacks involving an explosion may be called overt attacks, biological or radiological attacks are covert. A covert release of toxic chemicals might cause immediate impacts (e.g., symptoms appearing in a few seconds) or delayed effects (e.g., several hours), depending on the type of chemical agents. Figure 6.4 shows comparison among types of attacks in terms of their frequency of occurrences, killing capacities, and ease of procurement.

In addition to the direct injuries caused by an explosion, most symptoms caused by chemical, biological, radiological, or nuclear attacks involve respiratory irritation, eye and/or skin irritation, nausea, and vomiting. Illnesses resulting from these symptoms can be classified into three forms: cutaneous, inhalational, and gastrointestinal. Cutaneous illness consists of skin lesions evolving from papules, through a vesicular stage, to a depressed black eschar, edema, erythema, or necrosis without ulceration. Inhalational illness begins with a brief prodrome, resembling a "nonspecific febrile" illness, that rapidly progresses to a fulminant illness with signs of sepsis and/or respiratory failure, often with radiographic evidence of mediastinal widening. Finally, gastrointestinal illness is characterized by severe abdominal pain, usually accompanied by bloody vomiting or diarrhea, followed by fever and signs of septicemia.

These three forms of illness also may be caused by natural diseases though. Thus, familiarity with the general characteristics of ECBRN incidents and recognition of epidemilogic clues and syndromic presentations of biological or chemical agent exposures could improve the recognition of such attacks and may reduce morbidity and mortality. Table 6.3 summarizes the specific characteristics of ECBRN incidents. Whether the attack is a hoax, a small food-borne outbreak, a lethal aerosol cloud moving silently through a city at night, or the introduction of contagious disease, frontline responders who

Figure 6.4. Comparison among types of weapons

Frequency of occurrences:	Explosion >> Chemical >> Biological >> Radiological > Nuclear
Killing capacity:	Radiological ≈ Explosion < Chemical <<< Biological ≈ Nuclear
Easy of procurement:	Explosion ≈ Radiological >>> Chemical ≈ Biological >>> Nuclear
Disaster Promulgation:	Explosion ≈ Radiological < Chemical <<< Biological ≈ Nuclear

Table 6.3. ECBRN incident characterization

	Explosives	Biological	Chemical	Radiological	Nuclear
When effects appear	Immediate	Delayed (days to weeks)	Minutes to hours	Immediate for explosion, delayed for radiation.	Immediate for explosion, delayed for radiation
Route of exposure	Direct damage	Inhalation, skin and eye contact	Inhalation eyes and skin	Radiation	Direct damage and radiation
Knowledge of attack scope	Well understood	Scope unknown	Scope unknown	Scope unknown	Scope unknown
Release site	Specific	Unknown	Unknown	Specific	Specific
Distribution of affected area	The damage site	Geographically dispersed	Downwind to point of release	The damage site	Geographically dispersed
Signs of awareness	Hear explosions	Symptoms among some people or animals	Symptoms among some people or animals.	1. Hear explosions 2. Symptoms among some people or animals.	1. Hear explosions 2. Symptoms among some people or animals.
Decontamination of victims and environments	Conventional: no Dirty bomb: yes	Yes	Yes	Yes	Yes
Psychosocial impact	Moderate	High	High	High	High
First responders	Police, firefighter, EMS	Health care providers	EMS, police, firefighter	Police, firefighter, EMS	Police, firefighter, EMS

understands the threat agent characteristics and diagnostic and treatment options will have the greatest success in terms of limiting the impact of the attack.

REDUCING TIME LAG: FROM PASSIVE RESPONSE TO PROACTIVE RESPONSE

Clinic symptoms caused by the covert release of hazardous biological agents or radiological material without an explosion usually appear some time after the exposure (see Table 6.4). For a biological attack, the symptoms might be similar to those caused by common diseases. Thus, when victims visit hospitals, health care professionals cannot immediately diagnose whether the symptoms are caused by a biological incident or a natural disease. For example, in 1978, the assassination of Bulgarian defector Georgi Markov involved a Ricin pellet. Some say the Ricin-laced pellet was fired or injected from an umbrella tip as Markov waited at a bus stop; other accounts suggest the assailant used a syringe to inject the poison into Markov's leg as he bent down to pick up an umbrella he had been carrying. In any case, he experienced a sudden stinging pain in the back of his right lag. By evening, Markov had developed a high fever and died three days later. Because the poison Ricin mimicked symptoms of a natural disease, doctors spent several weeks conducting research and experiments before they finally could prove that Markov was killed by Ricin.

Unless authorities receive intelligence in advance, event awareness relies on whether the incident produces obvious signs. Figure 6.5(a) sketches sample timelines for event awareness and detection. For

Table 6.4. ECBRN Incidents: Signs and time lag of awareness

Type of Attack	Noticeable Signs During Occurrence	When Signs Occur	Time Lag of Awareness
Conventional explosives	Yes	Immediately	No
Unconventional explosives (radioactive or biological materials)	Yes	1. Damage caused by an explosion appears immediately. 2. Symptoms caused by the involved materials may appear sometime later.	1. No 2. Yes—time to determine whether radioactive materials or biological agents are involved.
Chemical	No	Vary, depends on when symptoms develop.	Vary, depends on type of symptoms.
Biological	No	Vary, depends on when symptoms develop.	Yes.
Radiological using explosives	Yes	1. Symptoms caused by explosion: immediately 2. Delayed for radiation	1. No for explosion. 2. Yes for radiation
Radiological (covert)	No	Later	Yes
Nuclear	Yes	Later	No

example, suppose that a release or incident occurs at time t_0; the event occurrence is known at t_0 if an explosion accompanies the release. However, if the release involves biological agents or radiological materials, the outbreak of symptoms caused by the release might appear at time t_1, which involves a delay between exposure and the onset of illness. The delayed time of awareness thus is $t_1 - t_0$. By t_2, as patients continue to visit health care facilities, the definitive diagnosis gets confirmed and reported to public health agencies, prompting widespread response. In the meantime, more people could be affected during $t_2 - t_0$. Figure 6.5(b) suggests an approximately seven-day delay between the exposure and response actions to a covert biological release.

Because chemical, biological, and radiological incidents exhibit a delayed time of awareness, we discuss them in turn to identify the potential markers and indicators that might help reduce the time lag, as well as possible proactive and protective responses.

Biological Incident: Markers for Awareness

A covert biological attack may be recognized only during the course of the epidemic, such as because of a sudden increase in the number of people visiting health care facilities. To determine when and where such sudden increases occur, weekly surveillance data get analyzed to detect any signals that may indicate an outbreak or release that should prompt an investigation. Specifically, respiratory, gastrointestinal, rash, neurologic, and sepsis syndromes are monitored consistently (Begier et al., 2003; DOD, 2008). To monitor influenza-related activity in the United States, the U.S. CDC (2006a) collects weekly influenza surveillance data, starting on Sunday and ending on Saturday of each week. Each participant summarizes weekly data and submits them to the CDC by Tuesday afternoon of the following week. The report includes the number of consultations with patients complaining of influenza-like illness (ILI)

Figure 6.5. Timeline of event awareness and detection of release

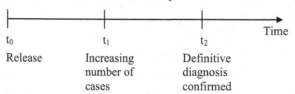

(a) Timelines for event awareness and detection

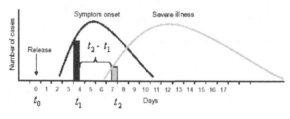

(b) Awareness for a biological attack

symptoms, categorized by age groups and total number of consultations. The ILI symptoms consist of fever (i.e., temperature of ≥ 100°F [37.8°C]), cough, and/or a sore throat in the absence of a known cause other than influenza. The CDC then compiles and analyzes these data and posts a report containing epidemic curves on its Web site (http://www.cdc.gov/flu/weekly/fluactivity.htm) each Friday.

According to this data collection timeframe, if a typical person visits a health care facility complaining of fever and throat pain (symptoms that might appear to be an ordinary cold) on Monday, the information gets be reported the next day as a cold. People may view it as just the flu—a temporary annoyance. But if this typical person actually is infected by influenza A, from Wednesday until the following Tuesday, as the disease progresses, the person likely becomes infectious to other people. The following Tuesday may be the earliest time that the CDC knows about the case. Therefore, acknowledging an event can require a delay of seven days later or longer. During the anthrax scare, for example, a primary concern was distinguishing anthrax infections from "just the flu."

Newly infected people usually pass through a latent and then an infectious state, after which they recover with immunity or die (Longini et al., 2005). The incubation period equals the time period during which people who are infected develop influenza symptoms, if they develop symptoms at all. However, some people who are infected do not develop influenza symptoms because they have self-immunity; if such a person does not show any symptoms, we cannot know whether he or she has been infected. The lack of symptoms does not mean the infected person is not contagious, nor is there any evidence that infected people in their latent state are not contagious. Therefore, we must consider the following notations:

We define one generation as secondary infectious cases resulting from upstream parental primary cases. If person A infects person B, then person B is the first generation of person A. If person B infects person C, then person C is the first generation of person B but the second generation of person A.

x_0 denotes the number of initial primary cases (zero or parental generation).

τ is the average interval from the infection of one individual to the infection of their contacts. It measures average generation time. The unit is a day.

y is the time interval between the moment a newly infected person becomes infectious until he or she recovers with immunity or dies. It measures the average infective period an infected person exhibits. The unit is a day.

R refers to the basic reproduction number, which measures the average number of secondary infections caused by a single, typical infectious person in an entire susceptible population.

Therefore, we have the following heuristic rules:

A disease spreads if $R \geq 1$;
Chains of transmission die out if $R < 1$.

There is no single value for R, though the values for most epidemic diseases range from 1.1 to 2.4, depending on attack rates (Ferguson et al., 2005; Longini et al., 2005). Using this basic transmission reproduction number, we can derive a formula to count the accumulated number of illnesses caused by a typical infectious person, given the assumption that authorities do not know of the event occurrence in advance so that no prevention, such as isolation, occurs during the first seven days.

When the number of initial infectious persons is x_0, labeled $X(0) = x_0$, then
the total number of infected people after the first generation with respect to x_0 would be

$$X(1) = x_0 + R\, x_0 = x_0(1 + R)^1;$$

the total number of infected people after the second generation is

$$X(2) = x_0(1 + R)^2;$$

the total number of infected people after the third generation equals

$$X(3) = x_0(1 + R)^3; \text{ and thus,}$$

the total number of infected people after the ith generation would be

$$X(i) = x_0(1 + R)^i.$$

For x_0, because its infective period is y days, after which the person either recovers or dies, and because each infected person caused by x_0 takes another τ days to become contagious and infect others, $\frac{y}{\tau}$ is the maximum possible generations during the infective period of x_0.

If $i = \frac{y}{\tau}$, when producing the $(i + 1)^{th}$ generation, the initial infectious person x_0 moves out of the circulation cycle and no longer is a contagious source, because that person has either recovered with immunity or died. Thus, the total number of ill people after the $(i + 1)^{th}$ generation is

$$X(i+1) = [X(i) - X(0)] (1 + R)$$
$$= x_0 (1+R)^{i+1} [1 - \frac{1}{(1+R)^i}]; \qquad \text{when } i > \frac{y}{\tau}.$$

When the disease spreads to produce the $(i + 2)^{th}$ generation, members of the first generation, $X(1)$, have either recovered with immunity or died, moving them away from the source. The accumulated number of illnesses would then be

$$X(i+2) = [X(i+1) - X(1)] (1 + R).$$

This procedure continues until we arrive at the following general formula to quantify the accumulated number of illnesses caused by the initial primary infectious individuals x_0:

$$X(n) = x_0 (1+R)^n, \text{ for } n = 0, 1, 2, .., \frac{y}{\tau},$$
$$X(n+1) = [X(n) - X(n - \frac{y}{\tau})] \times (1+R)], \text{ when } n > \frac{y}{\tau}, \tag{6-1}$$

where n denotes the number of generations.

Regarding the generation time τ, if the infected people do not show symptoms, it will be difficult to identify whether they have been infected. Therefore, some research uses the incubation period as the generation time, or 1.9 days on average (Longini et al., 2005), whereas others use an estimated value of 2.6 days (Ferguson et al., 2005). Generally, τ ranges from 1 to 4 days (Elveback et al., 1976). If we let τ equal 1.9 days and $x_0 = 1$ person, Figure 6.6 shows the resulting simulation of an influenza strain, introduced by a single random infective case, when $R = 0.9$ and $R = 1.5$, respectively.

As we show in Figure 6.6(a), the disease stops spreading if the reproduction number of transmissibility R is 0.9. However, if R is 1.5 (greater than 1), the number of newly infected persons increases dramatically after one week (see Figure 6.6(b)). In our simulation, without intervention, the number of infected people caused by a single primary case increases to several hundreds within two weeks. By that time, it would be very difficult to control the spread of the disease. Hence, some research suggests that if a pandemic were to occur, the epidemic could rapidly transform from predominantly local to country-wide between 60 and 90 days (Longini et al., 2005).

By varying the value of R, we can obtain the number of new increments per day after the infection (see Figure 6.7). When R increases, they increase from tens to hundreds, suggesting an increased virus attack rate. Thus, reducing R is very important, and three possible methods are available. First, reducing social contacts among the population can reduce the infection rate. Second, infected persons must be isolated. Third, authorities can reduce the susceptibility of uninfected persons with vaccination or antiviral prophylaxis. However, these three approaches often are implemented only after the realization of a disease attack, and any response plan still relies on the ability of local health officials across the region to spot the disease and report it quickly. Recognition of the potential attack at an early stage thus remains critical.

Because of the similarity between early symptoms of influenza and other biological and chemical agents (see Tables 6.1 and 6.3) and the prolonged and variable incubation period of most biological agents,

Figure 6.6. Number of Illnesses by Days with No Intervention

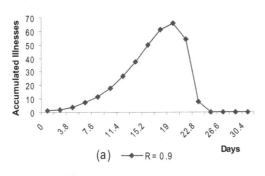

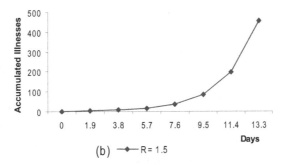

investigation usually starts several days after the receipt of a report of a cluster of illnesses that suggests an intentional release of a biological agent; an emergency command center then is set up in response to the attack. Physicians and public health care workers must understand the differences in symptoms and signs to help accelerate detection and diagnosis. Because many biological agents produce nonspecific symptoms, they may be very difficult to diagnose if physicians are not focused on the possibility of an intentional attack. Using epidemic characteristics may help arrive at a correct diagnostic direction. Table 6.5 displays some possible epidemiological clues that suggest a covert biological release.

Figure 6.7. New increments per days with various R

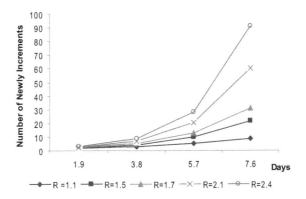

An unusually high number of samples, particularly from the same biologic medium, such as blood and stool cultures, may represent an alert of an outbreak. However, for some agents, even a single case should arouse suspicion. For example, a single case of smallpox certainly suggests an intentional release. After discovering an outbreak, it is necessary to estimate an epidemic curve on the basis of the number of cases during the time period $(t_2 - t_1)$, as in Figure 6.5(b). An epidemic curve for a disease outbreak caused by an intentional attack likely will differ from a curve for a naturally occurring outbreak. For example, agents disseminated through aerosol exposure likely produce a compressed epidemic curve (Franz et al., 1997). Patterns displayed by the epidemic curve also might help identify whether a disease can be transmitted through human contact. Agents with high person-to-person transmissibility may cause numerous disease spikes.

In addition, illness patterns may provide useful clues to indicate an unusual infectious disease outbreak associated with the intentional release of a biological agent. Table 6.6 lists some obvious patterns that can help this recognition. For example, Venezuelan equine encephalitis virus is endemic to South America, Trinidad, Central America, Mexico, and Florida, so if a case or outbreak appears in Europe, it should arouse suspicion and prompt an investigation (Army, 1998). If multiple urban office workers present tularemia symptoms and have not been exposed to animals or animal products, it may suggest an intentional release.

For rapid identification, a Laboratory Response Network for Bioterrorism (LRN) has been established that links state and local public health laboratories with advanced capacity laboratories, including clinical, military, veterinary, agricultural, water, and food-testing facilities.

To realize early detection goals, various ongoing activities attempt to improve surveillance and response, ranging from enhancing communications (among state, local, and public care providers) to installing special surveillance systems, including active surveillance for shifts in the number of hospital admissions, emergency department visits, or occurrence of specific syndromes. However, what we need most is a pre-event alert system that can detect a lethal agent in the air or at least the initial case of an

Table 6.5. Possible epidemiologic clues: Covert biological release

Rank	Epidemiologic Clues
1	An unusual increase in the number of patients seeking care for illness that are unlikely caused by seasonal diseases. An epidemic curve may exhibit a sharp early peak rather than a more prolonged pattern, especially for disease agents that do not involve person-to-person spread and produce acute disease.
2	Patients presenting with clinical signs and symptoms that suggest an infectious disease outbreak.
3	Unexplained illness cases and deaths in an area.
4	Symptoms in an area in the absence of the usual host risk factor. For example, monkeypox and Ebola hemorrhagic fever would not be expected to appear in patients in the United States in the absence of contact with primates or travel to specific areas in Africa.
5	Massive numbers of cases with nontraditional modes of transmission.
6	A single case of smallpox.
7	A syndrome, such as a constellation of clinical signs and symptoms in patients, suggesting a disease associated commonly with a known chemical exposure. For example, neurologic signs or pinpoint pupils in the eyes of patients with a gastroenteritis-like syndrome or acidosis in patients with altered mental states.
8	Unexplained death of plants, fish, or animals, both domestic and wild.
9	Patients exhibit drug resistance.

Table 6.6. Indicators suggesting an intentional biological release

Rank	Indicators
1	An unusual temporal or geographic clustering of illness, such as persons who attended the same public event.
2	More than two patients presenting with unexplained febrile illnesses associated with sepsis, pneumonia, respiratory failure, or rash or a botulism-like syndrome with flaccid muscle paralysis, especially if occurring in otherwise healthy persons.
3	An unusual age distribution for common diseases. For example, an increase in what appears to be a chickenpox-like illnesses among adult patients, which might be smallpox.
4	A large number of cases of acute flaccid paralysis with prominent bulbar palsies, suggestive of a release of *botulinum toxin*.
5	An unusual outbreak in a geographic area where such disease is unlikely to occur naturally. For example, Venezuelan equine encephalitis virus is endemic to South America, Trinidad, Central America, Mexico, and Florida, but any case or outbreak in Europe should arouse suspicion (Army, 1998).
6	A non-session epidemic in an area where the natural environmental conditions do not favor disease transmission. For example, mosquito-borne viral encephalitides in the United States tends to occur in summer or early fall, so a cluster of cases during late winter might be suspicious.
7	Cases of diseases in the absence of the usual host risk factors, such as tularemia in urban office workers with no exposure to animals or animal products.
8	Unexplained death of plants, fish, or animals, both domestic and wild.
9	Ill people found along a specific wind direction.

attack, which may signal a new outbreak or release. Biosensor technology might be used to achieve such goals (Chaubey & Malhotra, 2002), because biosensors can contain an immobilized biological active compound, such as an RNA aptamer, that specifically interacts with a target it senses. This interaction results in a physical-chemical change in the immobilized biological active compound that gets rapidly converted into an electronic output signal to alert the public. Undoubtedly, the development of such biosensors should be accelerated.

Monitoring Chemical Hazardous Substances

A state-based surveillance system for monitoring the acute releases of hazardous substances (i.e., Hazardous Substances Emergency Events Surveillance [HSEES]) has been developed by Agency for Toxic Substances and Disease Registry (ATSDR) of the U.S. Department of Health and Human Services. The system collects and analyzes information about (1) sudden uncontrolled or illegal release of one or more hazardous substances that require cleanup or neutralization according to federal, state, or local law in United States, and (2) threatened releases that result in public health actions such as evacuation. According to ATSDR, a substance is considered hazardous if it might reasonably be expected to cause adverse health outcomes. At present, 15 states participate in HSEES and provide information about the releases, such as the time of the event, event type (fixed-facility or transportation-related), event description (substances involved, substance name, geographical location, place where the event occurred), persons affected (e.g., age, sex, type, and extent of injures; distance from spill; population groups such as general public, responder, student), and the public health action taken (e.g., information about decontaminations, orders to evacuate or shelter-in-place).

To achieve the monitoring function of the system, each state possesses a tool to submit a notification of a reportable event. Once the acute release of a hazardous substance has been reported to the state health department, the state submits the event information to the system within 48 hours. From this point of view, the HSEES system actually provides an event record system rather than a pre-event monitoring system that can alert the public ahead of time.

As we discussed previously, most incidents are unforeseeable. If September 11 had been foreseen, it would have been prevented. Likewise, chemical terrorism is a covert event, so the presence of ill persons might be the first sign of exposure. However, recognizing the covert release of a chemical agent is not easy because symptoms developed after exposure often mimic those of common natural diseases. Moreover, immediate symptoms of certain chemical exposures might be nonexistent or mild, even though the exposure may be causing long-term health effects, such as neuro-cognitive impairments or cancer. A mixed clinical presentation also is possible, such that persons exposed to two or more agents might have symptoms that do not suggest any one chemical agent. Thus, early recognition largely depends on whether public health care providers are alert to and familiar with the signs and symptoms that indicate exposure to chemical agents, as well as how soon these signs and symptoms can be confirmed.

Table 6.7 provides some additional epidemiologic clues and pattern of illness that suggest the covert release of a chemical agent. Some indicators or markers, such as temporal and regional increases in hospitalizations, sudden increases in case frequency or severity, and characteristic symptom complexes, may arouse suspicious and prompt investigations (CDC, 2003). For example, an epidemic disease caused by a chemical attack usually occurs suddenly, and the number of illnesses reaches a peak within a short period of time, such as several hours or days.

Monitoring Radiological or Nuclear Material

Even if effective responses start immediately after the occurrence of an incident, its impact may already have occurred. To avoid such an impact, the best method is to prevent the event. Various protection efforts and detectors offer a means for early discovery of a potential attack. To respond to potential nuclear and radiological threats, for example, an elite team of federal scientists, unknown to most Americans, uses radiation detectors to scan cities for signs of weapons approximately every three days (*Los Angeles*

Table 6.7. Possible epidemiologic clues: Covert chemical release

Rank	Epidemiologic Clues
1	An unusual increase in the number of patients seeking care for illnesses that are unlikely caused by seasonal diseases. An epidemic disease caused by a chemical attack usually occurs suddenly, and the number of illnesses will reach its peak within a short period of time, such as several hours.
2	Clusters of illness in persons who have common characteristics.
3	Unexplained deaths among young or healthy persons.
4	Emission of unexplained odors by patients.
5	A syndrome such as a constellation of clinical signs and symptoms in patients, suggesting a disease associated commonly with a known chemical exposure. For example, neurologic signs or pinpoint pupils in the eyes of patients with a gastroenteritis-like syndrome or acidosis in patients with altered mental states.
6	Rapid onset of symptoms after exposure to a potentially contaminated medium, such as paresthesias, and vomiting within minutes of eating a meal.
7	Unexplained death of plants, fish, or animals, both domestic and wild.

Times, 2008). The team members blend into crowds at major sporting events, wearing backpacks containing instruments that can identify plutonium or highly enriched uranium. If a device were located, the teams would rush to the scene and defuse it immediately. In addition, scientists have created a system of nuclear forensics that tracks nuclear materials to their country of origin through scientific analysis and thus can quickly identify the source of a nuclear attack or attempted attack. For example, if a bomb detonates, by analyzing the fallout, the system can identify the terrorists and their state sponsors.

To detect radiological and nuclear threats quickly, aerial background radiation surveys of U.S. cities levels appear necessary (GAO, 2007). These surveys record the location of radiation sources and contain maps showing existing or baseline radiation levels within U.S. cities. Helicopters or planes equipped with radiation detectors fly over an area and collect information about background radiation sources, such as rock quarries, granite found in buildings, statues in a city, or medical isotopes used at hospitals. Any change between the measured and the baseline radiation levels suggests a new radiation source that might prompt investigation. For example, a survey of the New York City metro area has identified more than 80 radiological sources that require further investigation to determine their risk. While investigating the 80 locations, the New York City police department found an old industrial site contaminated with radium—a radiological material linked to diseases such as bone cancer. They used the survey information to close that area and protect the public better.

Figure 6.8. Ways irradiation enters human bodies from environmental radiation materials

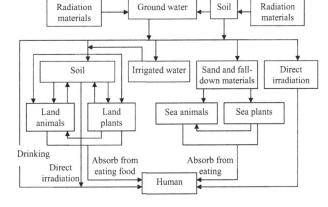

Radiation materials usually enter the environment through air and water. As it progresses through different media, such as air, groundwater, underground water, food made of animal meat, milk, and plants, the radiation material eventually enters human bodies. Figure 6.8 displays how radiation materials from the environment can irradiate humans.

The baseline information surveys also can be used to assess contamination levels after a radiological attack to assist cleanup efforts.

SUMMARY

Quickly realizing the occurrence of a surprise attack and then identifying the type of attack—a conventional explosion, a dirty bomb, a biological/chemical agent release, a natural disease—and its severity are critical steps for first responders that enables them to provide an effective response. We examine the characteristics of ECBRN incidents case by case, focusing particularly on identifying the visible signs and their timelines, in an attempt to increase event awareness. An explosion provides an obvious sign to prompt an investigation, but otherwise, realizing an event occurrence often is delayed. To increase awareness of the symptoms of biological or chemical agent and reduce time lags, we explore several epidemiologic clues and identify markers/indicators for early recognition. However, it should be emphasized that the presentation of patients following the release of a chemical agent, would be differ substantially from those exposed to a biological agent. The former may present as a discrete event, but the latter may probably present as an increasing number of presentations to health care facilities, often with non-specific "flu-like symptoms" over a periods of days or weeks.

Obviously, no attack represents the best outcome, and to achieve this goal, we suggest several ongoing efforts related to surveillance systems that enable protection and the early discovery of threats. Because a reaction to any unexpected event starts after awareness of its occurrence, in most cases, there is no time to think of a detailed strategic plan or analyze the state of the situation and the magnitude of hazards, which already exist, before taking action. This set of urgent circumstances and time pressures indicates that response teams must be ready and initiate their action immediately. Most initial decisions about emergency phase protective actions should be well known by the incident commanders. Because such initial decisions are critical for controlling the situation, they must occur prior to an attack or be generated immediately and codified in incident commanders' or first responders' operational procedures. In Chapter VII, we discuss in detail how to generate effective initial decisions, even with limited information and under time pressure.

REFERENCES

Begier, E. M., Sockwell, D., Branch, L. M., et al (2003). The national capitol region's emergency department syndromic surveillance system: do chief complaint and discharge diagnosis yield different results? *Emerging Infect Disease*, *9*, 393-396.

Chaubey, A., & Malhotra, B. D. (2002). Mediated biosensors. *Biosense and Bioelectronics*, *17*, 441-456.

Cordesman, A. (2000). *The risks and effects of indirect, covert, terrorist and extremist attacks with weapons of mass destruction.* September. Washington DC: Center for Strategic and International Studies (CSIS).

Elveback, L. R. & et al. (1976). An influenza simulation model for immunization studies. *American Journal of Epidemiology, 103,* 152-165.

Ferguson, N. M., Cummings, D. A. T., Cauchemez, A., et al. (2005). Strategies for containing an emerging influenza pandemic in southeast Asia. *Nature,* August, 1-7.

Franz, D. R., Jahrling, P. B., Friedlander, A. M., et al. (1997). Clinical recognition and management of patients exposed to biological warfare agents. *Journal of American Medical Association, 278,* 399-411.

Gurr, N., & Cole, B. (2002). *The new face of terrorism: Threats from weapons of mass destruction.* London: Tauris Publishers.

Heurgren-Carlstrom, G., & Malmberg, E. (2003). Online information resources of toxicology in Sweden. *Toxicology, 190*(1-2), 63-73.

Hoffman, F. (2002). A member of the Hart-Rudman Commission, *Intellibridge report.*

Keim, M. E. (2006). Terrorism involving cyanide: the prospect of improving preparedness in the prehospital setting. *Prehospital and Disaster Medicine, 21*(2), s56-s60.

Kohlmann, E. (2006). The real online terrorist threat. *Foreign Affairs, 85*(5), 115-120.

Krug, R. M. (2003). The potential use of influenza virus as an agent for bioterrorism. *Antiviral Research, 57,* 147-150.

Leppard, D., Hastins, C., & Berry, J. (1998). Killer germs on sale for just 600 pounds. *The London Sunday Times,* p8, November 22, 1998.

Lipton, E. (2005). U.S. report lists possibilities for terrorist attacks and likely toll, *The New York Times.* Retrieved March 17, 2005, from http://www.nytimes.com/2005/03/16/politics/16home.htm

London Time (2004). London's dirty-bomb plot, October 11, 2004. Retrieved February 11, 2008, from http://www.time.com/time/magazine/article/0,9171,995357,00.html.

London Time (2006). Why liquid explosives may be terror's secret weapon, August 10, 2006. Retrieved February 11, 2008, from http://www.time.com/time/nation/article/0,8599,1225032,00.html.

Longini, I. M., Nizam, A., Xu, S. F., et al. (2005). Containing pandemic influenza at the source. *Science, 309,* 1083-1087.

Los Angeles Times (2008). How the U.S. seeks to avert nuclear terror. Retrieved January 6, 2008, from http://www.latimes.com/news/printedition/front/la-na-nuke6jan06,1,6779317.story?ctrack=5&cset=true

Madjid, M, Lillibridge, S. Mirhaji, P., & Casscells, W. (2003). Influenza as a bioweapon, *Journal of the Royal Society of Medicine, 96,* 345-346.

Melin, L. (2002). Terrorist profiles: An analysis based on 920 chemical incidents. *The ASA Newsletter, 91*, 2-4. Applied Science and Analysis, Inc.

Osterholm, M. T., (1999). The medical impact of a bioterrorism attack. *Postgraduate Medicine, 106*, 121-124.

O'Toole, T. (2000). *Biological weapons: National security threat & public health emergency.* Washington DC: Center for Strategic and International Studies (CSIS).

Powers, M. J., & Ban, J. (2004). *Bioterrorism: Threats and preparedness.* Retrieved January 12, 2005, from http://www.nae.edu/nae/bridgecom.nsf/weblinks/CGOZ-58NLKB?OpenDocument.

Relman, D. A., & Olson, J. E. (2001). Bioterrorism preparedness: What practitioners need to know. *Infectious Medicine, 18*(11), 497-515.

South Carolina Emergency Management Division (2005). *Graniteville train accident situation reports.* Retrieved December 10, 2005, from http://www.scemd.org.

Terrorism Research Center [TRC] (2005). *News release.* Retrieved December 10, 2005, from http://www. Terrorism.com.

U.S. Agency for Toxic Substances and Disease Registry [ATSDR] (2001). *Hazardous Substances Emergency Events Surveillance System biennial report, 1999–2000.* Atlanta, GA: US Department of Health and Human Services, Agency for Toxic Substances and Disease Registry.

U.S. Army Medial Research Institute for Infectious Diseases [Army] (1998). *Medial Management of Biological Casualties Handbook.* 3rd ed. Fort Detrick, Frederick, MD: USAMRIID.

U.S. Centers for Disease Control and Prevention [CDC] (2006a). *Fact sheet: Overview of influenza surveillance in the Untied States.* Retrieved December 4, 2007, from http://www.cdc.gov/flu/.

U.S. Centers for Disease Control and Prevention [CDC] (2006b). *Bioterrorism overview.* Retrieved December 4, 2007, from http://www.bt.cdc.gov/bioterrorism/.

U.S. Centers for Disease Control and Prevention [CDC] (2003). Recognition of illness associated with exposure to chemical agents–United States, *MMWR, 52*, 938-940.

U.S. Centers for Disease Control and Prevention [CDC] (2000). Biological and chemical terrorism: strategic plan for preparedness and response, *MMWR, 49*, 1-14.

U.S. Department of Defense [DOD] (2008). *Electronic surveillance system for the early notification of community-based epidemics (ESSENCE).* Retrieved January 10, 2008, from http://www.geis.ha.osd. mil/geis/surveillanceactivities/essence/essence.asp.

U.S. Department of State [DOS] (2002). *Patterns of global terrorism 2001.* Retrieved December 12, 2007, from http://www.state.gov/documents/organization/10319.pdf.

U.S. Department of State [DOS] (2003). *Patterns of global terrorism 2002.* Retrieved December 12, 2007, from http://www.state.gov/documents/organization/20177.pdf.

U.S. Department of State [DOS] (2004). *Patterns of global terrorism 2003.* Retrieved December 12, 2007, from http://www.state.gov/documents/organization/31912.pdf.

U.S. Environmental Protection Agency [EPA] (2005a). *Norfolk Southern Graniteville derailment*. Washington, DC: Environmental Protection Agency.

U.S. Environmental Protection Agency [EPA] (2005b). *Smoke detectors and radiation*. Retrieved January 11, 2005, from www.epa.gov/radiation/sources/smoke_alarm.htm.

U.S. General Accounting Office [GAO] (1997). *Combating terrorism: threat and risk assessments can help priorities and target program investments*. Retrieved April 5, 2006, from http://www.gao.gov/docsearch/repandtest.html/GAO-NSIAD-98-74.pdf

U.S. General Accounting Office [GAO] (2000). *Combating terrorism: Linking threats to strategies and resources*. July 26, 2000. Retrieved April 5, 2006, from http://www.gao.gov/docsearch/repandtest.html/GAO-T-NSIAD-00-218.pdf.

U.S. General Accounting Office [GAO] (2007). *Combating nuclear terrorism: Federal efforts to respond to nuclear and radiological threats and to protect key emergency response facilities could be strengthened*. November 15, 2007. Retrieved December 22, 2007, from http://www.gao.gov/docsearch/repandtest.html/GAO-08-285T.pdf.

U.S. Homeland Security Council [HSC] (2006). *National strategy for pandemic influenza: Implementation plan*. Retrieved August, 2006, from http://www.whitehouse.gov/homeland/pandemic-influenza-implementation.html.

Zamiska, N. (2005). Asian countries gear up to tackle bird-flu threat. *The Wall Street Journal,* October 3, 2005. Retrieved October 3, 2005, from http://online.wsj.com/article/SB112829683236458056.html/.

APPENDIX

Further Information about ECBRN can be accessed from the following Web sites:

1. Association for Professionals in Infection Control and Epidemiology: http://www.apic.org/html/resc/biomain.html
2. CDC bioterrorism homepages: http://www.bt.cdc.gov/
3. The Johns Hopkins University Center for Civilian Biodefense Studies: http://www.hopkins-biodefense.org/
4. The World Health Organization: http://www.who.international/

Chapter VII
Incident Commander:
Toward Effective First Decisions

FACTORS AFFECTING FIRST DECISIONS

In natural or human-induced emergencies, decisions made during the very first minutes and hours are critical to successful damage control, the prevention of casualties and structural losses, and ultimately the overall resolution of the disaster (Asaeda, 2002; Aylwin et al., 2006). In the Three Mile Island nuclear accident, for example, the response efforts in the early stages included a serious mistake; as many investigations have noted, without this mistake, Three Mile Island would have been limited to a relatively insignificant incident (The President's Commission Report, 1980). However, the initial information in emergency situations often is unclear and limited, which can lead to different interpretations of the problem. During the first few minutes of the Three Mile Island nuclear accident, more than 100 alarms went off, and there was no system for suppressing the unimportant signals so that operators could concentrate on the significant ones. That is, the information was not presented in a clear or sufficiently understandable manner. Although warnings displayed the pressure and temperature within the reactor coolant system, there was no direct indication that the combination of pressure and temperature would mean that the cooling water was turning into steam. Rather than adding cooling water then, the operators (or those who supervised them) turned off the pumps—a seriously poor decision. Obviously, understanding differences makes a difference. Different response methods may result in different resolutions, and a deficient response may increase losses.

Keinan and colleagues (1987) find that deficient decision making results mainly from a person's failure to undertake a systematic consideration of all relevant decision alternatives. In emergency situations however, decision makers usually do not have enough time to take all alternatives into systematic consideration when making the first decisions in the very first minutes. During the events of September 11, for instance, after realizing the potential hijacking, command center supervisors had little time to take action. According to the 9/11 Commission Report (2004), the time interval from the awareness of the hijacking to the first flight crash was approximately 8–30 minutes (see Table 7.1). Given such time constraints, it is almost impossible for commanders to conduct systematic analyses and carefully consider all alternatives. Therefore, such a theoretical decision-making approach is useful only in ideal situations that include absolutely no time constraints.

Table 7.1. Timeline of the U.S. September 11, 2001, event

Takeoff (EST, a.m.)	Likely Takeover	Crash Time	Event	Control Center Awareness	Elapsed Time (crash – awareness)
7:59	8:14	8:46:40	Flight AA 11 (Boston to Los Angeles) crashes into North tower of World Trade Center (WTC) in New York .	8:25 (Boston center aware of hijacking)	21 minutes
8:14	8:42–8:46	9:03:11	Flight UA 175 (Boston to Los Angeles) crashes into South tower of WTC.	8:55 (New York center suspects hijacking)	8 minutes
8:20	8:51–8:54	9:37:46	Flight AA 77 (Washington, D.C. to Los Angeles) crashes into the Pentagon.	9:25 (Herndon command center)	12 minutes
8:42	9:28	10:03:11	Flight UA 93 (Newark to San Francisco) crashes in field in Shanksville, PA	9:34 (Herndon command center	30 minutes

Source: The 9/11 Commission Report (2004).

One goal of decision making is to turn chaos or disorder into an orderly and normal response. Specifically, decision making during emergency response situations must (1) attempt to minimize the consequence of the disaster/incident as much as possible and (2) make use of the best abilities from among limited available resources. The associated response actions determined by decisions thus must prioritize according to their importance and urgency.

All responses to an emergency can be classified into two categories. In the first category, when responders are aware of the occurrence of an incident, the event itself has already ended (e.g., an explosion) and may have resulted in causalities. Thus, much of the response attention priority focuses on assessing the site impact and conducting search and rescue operations, including pre- and in-hospital medical treatment for affected people, distribution of relief supplies, logistics, tracing victims and aiding family reunification, psychological counseling, or monitoring secondary threats. In the second category, responders are aware of the occurrence, but the event itself has not yet ended. Thus, the priority becomes preventing the continuing development of the event, in addition to rescue and emergency service efforts. For example, on 9/11, Boston, New York, and Herndon center controllers realized the occurrence of possible hijackings approximately 25–65 minutes after the flights took off from the airports and before they crashed into the World Trade Center (WTC), the Pentagon, and a field in Shanksville, Pennsylvania, respectively. After recognizing the possible hijackings, the controllers' priority became how to handle the hijacking event. Each command center immediately implemented an existing protocol, which included clearing the airspace, monitoring and tracking the flights, assigning military escort aircraft to follow the flights, and reporting anything unusual. This protocol presumes that (1) the hijacked aircraft are readily identifiable and will not attempt to disappear; (2) there is sufficient time to address the problem through the appropriate FAA and NORAD chains of command; and (3) the hijacking will take a traditional form and not be a suicide hijacking designed to convert the aircraft into guided missiles. This existing protocol, in place on 9/11, clearly was unsuited in every respect for what was about to happen (9/11 Commission Report, 2004): The tragedies were not averted, and crashes occurred. At that point, the priority moved to activating rescue and emergency service actions immediately.

Obviously then, first decisions are critical and determine the direction of response efforts. If they are wrong though, unthinkable consequences result. A small mistake may cause big trouble. During the rescue and emergency services operations for the World Trade Center, the decision about where to locate the emergency management command post represented an illustrative case. The building that housed the command center of New York's Office of Emergency Management had caught fire and been evacuated, then collapsed (McCarthy, 2001). The scenario reflects an old saying: "Haste makes waste."

Conventional wisdom implies that the best decisions are rational ones, based on logical and factual information. So what factors cause a person to make good decisions during an emergency? Is the first decision an optimal one or just a satisfactory solution? An interaction of these two (i.e., optimal and satisfactory solutions) affects human decision making, but we do not know the exact nature of this interaction. Therefore, we first examine existing decision-making theories in this chapter, then explore useful rules for generating first decisions. Because of time pressures, limited information, and uncertainty, which are inherent in dealing with an urgent situation, the decision-making process becomes even more complex. To assist incident commanders in generating effective first decisions, we present a unified incident command support system that can address both categories of responses: those to an emergency event that already has ended, and those to events still ongoing.

EXISITING DECISION-MAKING THEORIES

To model individual decision making and its possible outcomes, two approaches are available. One follows the utility maximization principle, which postulates that a decision maker can capture adequate or complete information about the targeted situation and thereby forecast the profit-maximizing or utility-maximizing choice (Sargent, 1993). Such models are referred to as contemporary optimization models or classical decision-making models. In contrast, behavioral scientists appeal to empirical observations of how people "actually" behave (Simon, 1977).

Classical decision-making models follow the theory of rational expectations, which implicitly assumes that the targeted object environment is completely known; decision makers have a full understanding of how the state will change, as well as the probability distribution of outcomes to expect in all states. This assumption in turn implies that such an understanding is common knowledge, so the estimates of what others intend to do feature no diversity of opinions. In reality, however, possible outcomes include probabilities that are unknown or "unmeasurable," especially in an emergency situation. In the 9/11 hijackings, the hijackers did not take expected or traditional actions; instead, they turned the aircraft into guided missiles.

Rational expectation theory also postulates that change in the future is already knowable and foreseeable in the present and that the possible states of a given future date are all known already, such that a calculable probability, conditional on the present state, can reveal of each future state's occurrence. If an incident commander follows this theory to make decisions, he or she must know all possible outcomes across their probability distributions, and either there is no change in the world (which the commander can describe with his or her models) or whatever change occurs can be incorporated into the model in a fully predetermined way. However, when responding to any unexpected emergency, it is impossible to know everything about the situation or changes to that situation in advance. Therefore, it is inappropriate to use this theory in a setting in which information is limited and unclear and time is urgent.

Another approach to decision making addresses empirical observations and decision makers' past experiences and accrued knowledge. Decision makers usually select an experience that has worked before in similar situations instead of engaging in detailed calculations and comparisons of the expected utilities of each decision choice.

If a situation is one that decision makers have never experienced, a problem arises. They must either come up with a new strategy to handle the situation or select an experience they believe is similar to the current situation. When it is difficult to make a choice, decision makers usually stick to what they have experienced. Responders and incident commanders during both the Three Mile Island accident and the 9/11 event actually faced such a case. According to the President's Commission Report (1980) on Three Mile Island nuclear accident, the control room crew later described the accident as a combination of events they had never experienced, whether while operating the plant or during their training. The 9/11 Commission Report (2004, p. 45) similarly states that

the details of what happened on the morning of September 11 are complex, but they play out a simple theme. NORAD and the FAA were unprepared for the type of attacks launched against the United States on September 11, 2001. They struggled, under difficulty circumstances, to improvise a homeland defense against an unprecedented challenge they had never before encountered and had never trained to meet.

Responders thus need to adapt themselves to changing circumstances and come up with new strategies accordingly.

RULES FOR GENERATING FIRST DECISIONS

The post-incident analyses of major incidents, such as the 9/11 event in 2001 and the London bombings in 2005, suggest that first decisions should lead to the proper direction to influence the outcomes of the incidents (Asaeda, 2002; Aylwin et al., 2006). Today's threats may not match yesterday's preparation, so in responding to an unexpected emergency, regardless of its type, the means to generate effective first decisions becomes very important.

We consider two categories of responses: one in which the emergency event already has ended, and another in which the incident is ongoing. For the former, by the time commanders know the incident has occurred, casualties likely have resulted. The response focus therefore centers on rescue and emergency services, including humanitarian relief aid. No time remains to evaluate possible countermeasures. The first decisions pertain to how to generate a rescue response quickly. For the latter type, in contrast, the event still continues. For example, a large-scale radiological or nuclear incident may evolve over many hours or days before the radioactivity or toxic chemicals actually get released. Thus, generating an effective strategy to prevent the continuing development of the incident and control the situation during the first several hours is most critical.

Speed is key, and the first 24 hours represent the acute phase for both situations; this period determines whether a successful control and rescue can occur. We divide this acute phase into four stages: immediate response (hours 0–2), intermediate response (hours 2–12), follow-up response (hours 12–24), and extended response (after 24 hours). Table 7.2 presents the response priorities for incident commander, discussed in detail next.

Each response level consists of mission lists; a mission is defined as an assignment with a purpose that consists of operations. An operation is an action that supports a mission and consists of tasks. In turn, a task is a discrete event/action based on technical and standard operating procedures, executed to accomplish a mission or operation.

These mission lists reflect decisions made during each stage, with a set of clear priorities based on the following heuristic rules:

[R1] In any situation, saving lives is the top priority.

[R2] Any operation must be applicable and produce some desirable effects in terms of rescuing people at risk or mitigating a disaster.

[R3] Any operation, when implemented, should not cause more damage.

[R4] Coordination has higher priority than conflict in task execution.

[R5] If an operation or task is critical in disaster control, implement it regardless of the costs.

[R6] Those actions that may result in irreversible consequences should be performed first.

When facing a sudden event, people need to turn their attention away from what they are currently doing to the event itself. Usually they do not have time to think of a response carefully, which creates the need to have priorities included in response strategies that can guide an incident commander's decisions.

The four-stage response lists, integrated into a Computer-Supported Incident Commander System, appear when the system is activated in response to the declaration of an incident. If necessary, the system also can communicate with other connected systems, such as the Hospital Emergency Support System (introduced in Chapter IX) and the Emergency Evacuation Command System (introduced in Chapter X), to provide updated information.

INCIDENT COMMAND SUPPORT SYSTEM

The declaration of an incident triggers the system, which activates the mission list in the immediate response stage. These mission lists provide step-by-step response procedures that guide incident commanders to organize their response and thereby control the situation.

Immediate Response Stage (Hours 0–2)

Response activities listed in the immediate response stage identify which actions should be performed first, as well as who the key responders are. As shown in Table 7.3, an incident commander needs to acquire and assess information, develop a course of action, and issue directions. These capabilities represent key elements of an effective response to any emergency situation. Thus, the system first suggests

Table 7.2. Four stages of priority responses for incident commanders

1.	Immediate response stage (hours 0–2)
2.	Intermediate response stage (hours 2–12)
3.	Follow-up response stage (hours 12–24)
4.	Extended response stage (hours 24+)

that the incident commander initiate a situation awareness operation. The execution of this operation provides basic information about the incident, such as the location of the incident site, the type of incident (though it may not be clear at the onset what has caused the incident), whether hazards are present, the potential for a secondary attack targeting first responders, and the potential impact areas.

The type of incident helps determine the right response strategies and personnel (see Table 7.4). For an unknown type of an incident (i.e., unsure whether toxic chemical, radiological, or nuclear material has been released), the HazMat response support system will be activated. Meanwhile, the checking key personnel module is executed. This module contacts personnel with emergency response roles and responsibilities, such as emergency response coordinators, fire chiefs, law enforcement officers, environmental health specialists, safety and health specialists, epidemiologists, medical officers, mental and behavioral health personnel, public information officers, and technical, logistical, and other support personnel.

When an emergency occurs, ambulance services traditionally take control of transport and communications, while firefighters assess the safety of the scene, coordinate and perform decontamination, and make the situation safe to rescue patients. The police meanwhile secure the perimeter and perform traffic and crowd control. We assume the incident situation is unlike the routine conditions envisioned for an archetypal hazardous materials emergency involving radioactive materials, such as a vehicular accident. Rather, the situation might involve an extreme emergency with mass casualties. Therefore, leadership must be established immediately after the occurrence becomes known. Leadership includes command posts for on-site response, site safety control, emergency services, epidemiology services if disease-related, community services, communication, liaisons, logistics, finance administration, decontamination sites, and sheltering services.

Table 7.3. Immediate response stage: Response activities

1. Situation assessment (for awareness and public safety concerns).
    • Determine event time, place, and witnesses.
    • Establish communication with the first responders on the scene.
    • Determine which geographical area(s) has been or may be adversely impacted.
    • Identify and establish incident perimeter and zone, and monitor any changes in site situation; activate an operation for immediate scene reports.
    • Determine how many people are threatened, affected, exposed, injured, or dead.
    • Identify whether critical infrastructures have been affected, such as electrical power, water supplies, sanitation, telecommunications, or transportation.
    • Identify exposure pathways.
    • Consider how current and forecasted weather conditions might affect the situation.

2. Activate emergency operation facilities. Contact key response personnel. For an unknown type of incident (e.g., unsure whether toxic chemical, radiological, or nuclear material used), initiate HazMat response support system.

3. Check whether medical and healthcare facilities have been affected.
    • If no, activate the hospital emergency support system
    • If yes, determine how they have been affected. Activate an operation for interregional collaboration.

4. Identify whether escape routes are open and accessible.
    • If yes, activate the evacuation command system and sheltering services.
    • If no, activate an operation for emergency transportation services.

5. Activate an operation for search and rescue, and dispatch rescue forces. 6. Activate an operation to collect information about people with special needs who are at risk. 7. Activate supply facility, ground support, and food and water supplies. 8. Communicate to the public and direct media inquires to public information officers. 9. Estimate responding capabilities and availability. Prioritize them according to limited resources and personnel. 10. Send requests to state and federal authorities to declare a state of emergency.

Table 7.4. Decision rules

1.	If dealing with a radiation emergency (e.g., nuclear incident, explosion with a radioactive element), evaluate the direction that the radioactive plume is moving and implement public notification.
2.	If it is a chemical incident, activate the digital fire chief support system.
3.	If it involves a biological agent or disease outbreak, activate the hospital emergency support system.

Because collecting the right information is very important to ensure proper response judgments, one of key components of this stage is identifying and establishing the incident perimeter and zone, as well as monitoring any changes in the site situation.

Upon arrival at the scene, first responders should identify points of refuge and potential escape routes, using the following four steps to prioritize the initial scene surveillance.

1. Ensure continuous awareness of potential hazards.
2. Establish back-up system for communications.
3. Designate at least two escape routes.
4. Consider an appropriate distance to a safety zone, which should be located upwind.

If an incident involves a chemical attack, the spread of any vapor depends on prevailing weather conditions. With wind speeds of less than 1 meter per second, the vapor hazard area extends to a radius of 550 meters, outside of which toxic concentration is negligible. With wind speeds of greater than 1 meter per second, the hazard area extends as a cone from the liquid hazard area, extending 550 m with an opening angle of 20° (Laurent et al., 1999). A digital fire chief support system can help first responders identify the type of chemical agent involved and thereby generate agent-specific response and rescue plans (discussed in detail in Chapter VIII).

If an incident involves the use of radioactive material, the protocol for the response will be displayed to first responders, who must enter the contaminated area to rescue victims and protect critical infrastructure. Meanwhile, after a release of radioactive materials, local authorities must monitor the levels of radiation and determine the protective actions to take. If a radiation emergency involves large amounts of radioactive materials, these authorities must determine if an area evacuation is needed. If so, they implement evacuation actions.

Table 7.5 illustrates the content of a public notice. Actions to suggest that the public should take are listed in Table 7.6.

If regional medical and health facilities are not affected, the commander should activate an hospital emergency support system (discussed in Chapter IX); otherwise, an operation for interregional collaboration is executed, which calls for collaboration among system partners—EMS, hospitals, community

Table 7.5. Public notification

1. Type of emergency, such as radiation emergency.
2. Area in danger of exposure to the radioactive plume.
3. Direction in which people should travel to avoid the radioactive plume.
4. Ways to cover skin, nose, and mouth.

Table 7.6. Public response actions

For the public
1. If at the exposure site, follow action "On-Site Response."
2. If near a contaminated area, listen to public notice.
3. Check if actions "Evacuation" or "Seeking and Taking Shelter" are required.
4. Follow appropriate directions.

(a) Rules for the public

Action: On-Site Response
1. Leave the area where the chemical has been released.
2. Remove clothing as quickly as possible.
3. Rapidly wash your entire body with water.
4. If wearing contacts, remove them after washing your hands and place them with the contaminated clothing. If wearing eyeglasses, wash them with soap and water.
5. Dispose of the contaminated clothing in a sealed bag.
6. Get medical care as quickly as possible.

(b) Rules for On-Site Response

Action: Evacuation
1. Determine evacuation direction and routes.
2. Follow specific plans for people who cannot or do not drive.
3. Take a flashlight, portable radio, batteries, first-aid kit, supply of sealed food and water, hand-operated can opener, essential medicines, and cash and credit cards.
4. Bring any medicines that you are taking and clothes.

(c) Rules for Evacuation

Action: Seeking and Taking Shelter:
1. Determine where the shelter is located.
2. Go to a room in the middle of your home or workplace, or go to the basement.
3. Close and lock all doors and windows.
4. Turn off fans and air conditioners and close fireplace dampers.
5. Turn off air heating units that bring air in from the outside.
6. Keep radio tuned to the emergency response channel or local news channel to find out what else you need to do.

(d) Rules for Seeking and Taking Shelter

and migrant health centers, rural health centers, tribal health clinics, outpatient facilities, poison control centers, military and veteran health care facilities, and other health care provider organizations in the region—and incorporates the full spectrum of patient care into the overall response to an all-hazard emergency situation. In the United States, disaster medical assistance teams, known as National Medical Response Teams, have been developed for responses to CBRN incidents (GAO, 1997; McCarthy, 2001; Maniscalco et al., 1998). These teams consist of 54 personnel members, including 28 medical responders, and are extensively trained in HazMat management. They can deploy within four hours of an incident and are entirely self-sufficient, except for water. They can decontaminate 200–300 ambulatory patients per hour, as well as 30–60 non-ambulatory patients. The teams carry enough antidotes for a nerve agent attack to treat 3,000–5,000 patients per day.

Interoperability between the pre-hospital and hospital command structures is a significant challenge, manifested not only in the technical aspect of radio interoperability but also in the interdisciplinary aspect of communications plans. We incorporate the digital fire chief support system, the hospital emergency support system, and the emergency evacuation command system into this unified incident command system to ensure field response commanders (fire chiefs), EMS staff, and health care professionals can work together and communicate with one another.

Meanwhile, rescue and emergency services operations must be executed, including the following:

1. If evacuation is required, an evacuation command system will help organize the evacuation (described in Chapter X).
2. Activate a procedure by which schools and childcare centers notify parents, arrange care for children whose parents cannot reach them, and render first aid.
3. Communicate to the public, and direct media inquires to public information officers.

The last operation represents a very important component during emergency responses. According to media reports (Media, 2006) pertaining to the emergency phone calls during the 9/11 attacks, the communication confusion on that day made people anxious and scared. People living close to the accident site worried about their safety, asking questions such as "What should we do? Do you think it's safe that we stay, or do you think we should go somewhere else?" Therefore, clear and updated information must be released to the public at all times.

Intermediate Response Stage (Hours 2–12)

Once operations in the immediate response stage have been initiated during the first 0–2 hours after an incident, the incident commander must ensure these operations actually have been implemented. Because the on-site situation continuously changes, the system checks operations and provides incident commanders with updated information. Thus, the system keeps track of each action and reminds the incident commanders to gather this updated information. Additional operation models also are activated in the intermediate response stage (see Table 7.7). Thirteen response activities need to be performed during 2–12 hours after the occurrence of an incident.

The system first sends a request to check the current progress of the on-site situation. On the basis of the updated information, the system helps the incident commander assess the resource needs and acquire them as necessary. The checking and monitoring processes continue periodically to ensure their availability. Effective allocation and monitoring of resources and assets should be sustainable for at least 24 hours before counting on the arrival of further supplies.

Table 7.7. Intermediate response stage (hours 2–12): Response activities

1. Communicate with on-site responder to assess the situation and gain updated information.
2. Ensure the hospital incident command system is operational.
3. Ensure the evacuation command system is operational.
4. Ensure supply facility, ground support, and food and water supplies are in service.
5. Ensure emergency transportation services, including sheltering, are operational.
6. Ensure interregional collaboration is working.
7. Ensure that people with special needs are being addressed.
8. Ensure that the risk communication messages are updated.
9. Request updated information from the HazMat response support system.
10. Request updated information from the hospital emergency support system.
11. Request updated information from the emergency evacuation command system if an evacuation has been ordered.
12. Check and review resources needed and acquire them to ensure their availability.
13. Prepare for state and federal on-site assistance.

The system next sends requests for updated information from the hospital emergency command system. The updated information includes concurrent, real-time data about direct physical damages (i.e., current number of people injured without being hospitalized, hospitalized, or dead; property damages), treatment, and in-hospital care, which provide the basis for decisions regarding medical care and other relief services. If an incident involves the release of a biological agent, the estimated illness rate and estimated number of required vaccine packages with anti-virus drugs also must be determined. Meanwhile, the system sends a request to check the current updated information from the HazMat response support system.

If a state emergency has been declared, the commander should prepare for state and federal on-site assistance to integrate these personnel into the local established response structure. Such personnel might include technical experts and emergency response coordinators, staff from the Centers for Disease Control and Prevention (CDC), Strategic National Stockpile (SNS) personnel, environmental response teams (ERTs), federal radiological (FRMAC) personnel, National Disaster Medical System (NDMS) teams (i.e., Disaster Medical Assistance Teams, National Medial Response Teams, Disaster Mortuary Operational Response Teams, National Pharmacy Response Teams, National Nurse Response Teams), and Veterans Health Administration (VHA) emergency medical response teams.

Follow-Up Response Stage (Hours 12–24)

Response activities during hours 12–24 are listed in Table 7.8. In addition to repeatedly checking for any updates, during this period, operations for providing mental and behavioral health/social services and transitioning to extended operations are initiated. Frontline responders may have worked for 12–24 hours already, so different shifts may need to be scheduled. Depending on the type of incident, a corresponding environmental hazard identification needs to be conducted. Information from the dynamic model of psychosocial effect, discussed in Chapter V, can help evaluate possible impacts.

Extended Response Stage (Hours 24+)

During this last stage, the system continues checking operations conducted in the previous stages and provides updated information to incident commanders. Because the emergency response already has lasted for at least 24 hours, the operation to assess community needs to be activated. These assess-

Table 7.8. Follow-up response Stage (hours 12–24): Response activities

1. Continue recheck operations listed in the Intermediate Response stage.
2. Initiate an operation to provide mental and behavioral health/social services.
3. Initiate an operation for transitioning into extended operations.
4. If the event is a biological, chemical release, or infectious disease outbreak,
• Activate epidemiological services and contamination control.
• Assess health and medical needs.
• Update public health information.
• Ensure food and water safety.
5. If the event involves radiological or nuclear material,
• Active an operation for conducting environmental hazard identification.
• Undertake contamination control.
• Ensure food and water safety.
6. Initiate an operation for wastewater and solid-waste disposal.
7. Initiate an operation for animal rescue/control/shelters if needed.

Table 7.9. Extended response stage (hours 24+): Response activities

1.	Continue to recheck operations listed in the Follow-Up Response stage.
2.	Initiate an operation to conduct community needs assessment.

ments include the total population affected, number of displaced, number of deaths, number of houses damaged, number of temporary camps needed and their locations, and number of persons hospitalized. Such assessments then can be used to set priorities and direct public health interventions in the weeks following the event.

DISCUSSION AND CONCLUSIONS

When an unexpected incident occurs suddenly, decision making during the early stages is very difficult because of the uncertainty and limited information inherent to such calamities. Rational expectation theory requires decision makers to understand the target situation fully and consider all possibilities, but this approach may not be suitable in urgent situations in which time is critical and the situation is unclear. Behavioral decision-making theory calls for direct observations, using previous experience. However, if decision makers face a completely new situation, such experience may not be useful. Decision makers therefore need to adapt to changing circumstances and come up with new strategies accordingly. We propose guidelines to help incident commander generate strategies, represented by a sequence of response activities or missions based on importance and priorities. Because incident commanders may confront a variety of issues, we present a unified incident command and decision support system with capabilities that enable incident commanders to capture important incident-related information, analyze captured information, more effectively disseminate critical information to emergency responders, present decision guidance options to responders, efficiently coordinate emergency responders' efforts, and store incident-related information for analysis. The system also provides situation awareness for individual emergency responders and hence increases the overall success potential of the missions.

REFERENCES

Asaeda, G. (2002). The day that the START triage system came to a STOP: observations from the World Trade Center Disaster. *Academic Emergency Medicine, 9*(3), 255-256.

Aylwin, C. J., Konig, T. C., Brenan, N. W., & et al. (2006). Reduction in critical mortality in mass casualty incidents: analysis of triage, surge, and resource use after the London bombings on July 7, 2005. *Lancet, 368*(9554), 2219-2225.

Keinan, G., Friedland, N., & Ben-Porath, Y. (1987). Decision-making under stress: scanning of alternatives under physical threat. *Acta Psychologica, 64*, 219-228. North Holland: Elsevier Science Publishers.

Laurent, J. F., Richter, F., & Michel, A. (1999). Management of victims of urban chemical attacks: the French approach. *Resuscitation, 42*, 141-149.

Maniscalco, P. M., Christen, H. T., Rubin, D. L., & Kim, P. (1998). Terrorism. Part I: calibrating your risks and response. *Journal of Emerging Medical Service, 23*, 38-51.

McCarthy, M. (2001). Attacks provide the first major test of USA's national antiterrorist medical response plans. *Lancet, 358*, 941.

Media (2006). *New 9/11 tapes show communication confusion.* Retrieved August 17, 2006, from http://www.msnbc.msn.com/id/14375089/page/2/

Sargent, T. J. (1993). *Bounded Rationality in Macroeconomics*, Oxford: Oxford University Press.

Simon, H. A. (1997). *Models of Bounded Rationality: Empirical Grounded Economic Reason*, Cambridge, MA: The MIT Press.

The President's Commission Report (1980). *The Accident at Three Mile Island*, Authorized Edition. Retrieved August 17, 2007, from http://www.pddoc.com/tmi2/kemeny/

The 9/11 Commission Report (2004). *Final Report of the National Commission on Terrorist Attacks upon the United States.* Authorized Edition, New York: W.W. Norton & Company.

U.S. General Accounting Office [GAO] (1997). *Combating terrorism: threat and risk assessments can help priorities and target program investments.* Retrieved April 5, 2006, from http://www.gao.gov/docsearch/repandtest.html/GAO-NSIAD-98-74.pdf

Chapter VIII
Countering Chemical Terrorism:
A Digitized Fire Chief Supporting System for Rapid Onsite Responding to HazMat Emergencies

INTRODUCTION

An industrialized society makes widespread use of toxic chemicals, transported daily in large amounts on the roads or by rail. Approximately 800,000 shipments of hazardous substances, including chemical and petroleum products, travel daily throughout the United States by ground, rail, air, water, and pipeline (DOT, 1998). Although nearly all of these materials safely reach their destinations, many are explosive, flammable, toxic, and corrosive and can be extremely dangerous if released improperly. These materials frequently are transported over, through, and under areas that are densely populated or populated by schools, hospitals, or nursing homes, where the consequences of an acute release could result in environmental damage, severe injury, or death (DOT, 1999; AAR, 2004).

According to the U.S. Hazardous Substances Emergency Events Surveillance (HSEES) system, 643 incidents involving chemicals in the highest-ranked group—designated as those that are easy to obtain, travel far by air if released, are highly toxic, and could be used as weapons—occurred in 15 U.S. states between October 2006 and February 2007. These 643 chemical incidents affected 225 victims (who could be associated with more than one chemical) and resulted in 1,200 persons being evacuated. Table 8.1 displays the disposition of most affected people.

For an industrial chemical incident, the type of chemical agent involved (if released) is normally known during the occurrence. On the basis of the agent's characteristics and possible poisonous effects, an event-based, specific response and associated medical rescue procedure can be generated and implemented to handle and control the situation. When an unexpected chemical attack suddenly occurs

Table 8.1. Treatment location

Treated on scene using first aid	*97*
Treated at hospital (not admitted)	*59*
Treated at hospital (admitted)	*12*
Observation at hospital with no treatment	*3*
Seen by private physician within 24 hours	*7*
Injury reported by officials	*2*

Note that half the victims were treated at the incident sites, suggesting that onsite pre-hospital rescue is crucial to responses to such emergency situations.

however, because responders do not know the type of agent used in advance, the onsite response plan may be general, regardless of the type of incident. For example, a common response involves rushing assistance to the nearest patient/affected people in need. Although this response may be appropriate in the controlled environment of a disaster, it is of little use in the unclear situation that results from the release of a toxic chemical, because responders may become victims themselves, which would increase the burden on rescue efforts.

Air provides not only the basic elements needed for human survival but also a medium through which toxic materials can be propagated and transmitted. Because air is everywhere, unobservable and uncatchable, people exposed may not sense any difference if a salient, colorless, and tasteless toxic chemical floats in the air. Once they reach this recognition, they likely already have been poisoned. In addition, some toxic chemicals, such as cyanide or hydrogen cyanide gas, act very quickly and can knock down people within several seconds at high concentrations. Therefore, if first responders can quickly identify or recognize the agent involved, an agent-specific response procedure would be more effective than a general response plan. According to a report by Trust for America's Health (TFAH, 2007), most routine response forces, including firefighters, police, and EMS, lack sufficient capabilities to identify or recognize chemical terrorism.

In this chapter, we explore an idea of using direct field observations from the incident scene as a means to identify a potentially dangerous chemical substance. As we show in Figure 6-1, different toxic chemical substances have their own unique physical properties and can cause different health impacts, though some initial symptoms and signs appear similar. For example, if a person is exposed through eye contact, he or she will suffer eye irritation, regardless of the type of agent. However, symptom observation data, together with a chemical substance's unique physical characteristics, may indicate whether the symptoms are by a specific agent with particular likelihood.

To implement this idea, we propose a computer-supported chemical discovery system, similar to a potable digitized fire chief. In an event of a chemical, radiological, or nuclear (CRN) incident, fire-fighters appear on the front line, so the proposed system focuses on helping onsite fire chiefs use their direct scene observations to identify the agent and generate a quick, incident-specific response operation. Without detailed laboratory and animal testing, response commanders lack the basic information needed to make correct judgments and wise decisions. Yet most laboratory testing requires special equipment and a recent sample (i.e., taken within two hours of the exposure). Few fire departments or doctors' offices have such special equipment, and a covert release prevents the collection of samples quickly enough. Moreover, many chemical agents do not generate biological markers in the human body (i.e., indicators that signal agents or substances in biologic systems or samples, such as body fluids), limiting the effectiveness of simple or quick diagnostic tests, which means that more complex testing procedures are required and may take a longer time. For example, the most frequently used biomarker of hydrogen sulfide exposure is urinary thiosulfate levels, but thiosulfate is not specific to hydrogen sulfide metabolism, because the ingestion of food or water with high sulfur content also can increase urinary thiosulfate concentrations (Milby & Baselt, 1999). That is, a quantitative relationship between hydrogen sulfide exposure and urinary thiosulfate levels has not been established, so for such chemical poisoning, urine and blood sample tests cannot distinguish exposure to different chemicals. Furthermore, no blood tests or other diagnostics can return results within the time required for effective intervention (Baskin et al., 1992; Isom & Johnson, 1987). In response, we attempt to generate a simple method for quick identification and response.

Recognizing the type of agent involved has clear implications for both rescue actions and pre-hospital treatment, because it indicates the appropriately specific plan and decontamination steps. In designing the proposed system, in addition to focusing on agent recognition, we also attempt to address the following questions: What does fire chief need to do to control the situation? What are the most important tasks? Which task should be performed first, and which can be processed simultaneously? How should responders perform those tasks?

Many of the capabilities required to respond to an unexpected explosion or chemical, biological, radiological, and nuclear (ECBRN) attack are also needed during responses to industry accidents. The proposed system therefore offers a "dual-use" response that may improve local firefighters' ability to respond to all hazards.

This chapter is organized as follows: We first describe the system components, knowledge representation, working procedure, and underlying design philosophy of our proposed system. We then use a simulation to test the proposed system if a fire chief were to organize a response to an unexpected chemical incident. We conclude with some further extensions of this research.

SYSTEM ARCHITECTURE AND WORKING PROCEDURE

System Structure

The proposed system consists of one working platform and three operators, namely, problem-posters, decision-analysts, and action-proposers (see Figure 8.1). The working platform provides a space for data sharing among the three operators, who each carry out problem-solving processes and suggest response actions to the fire chief at different stages during the course of the incident response. Specifically,

- *Problem-posters* ask or propose new problem(s) or subproblem(s) on the working platform, on which the *decision-analysts* then can focus their attention and work.
- *Decision-analysts* are expert doers, each of whom has specific knowledge about some type of hazard materials. When a doer decides to focus on a particular problem or task, he or she conducts analyses and solves the problem.
- *Action-proposers* suggest or generate response actions or strategies to the fire chief on the basis of results posted by the *decision-analysts*.

Figure 8.1. Digitized fire chief: System architecture

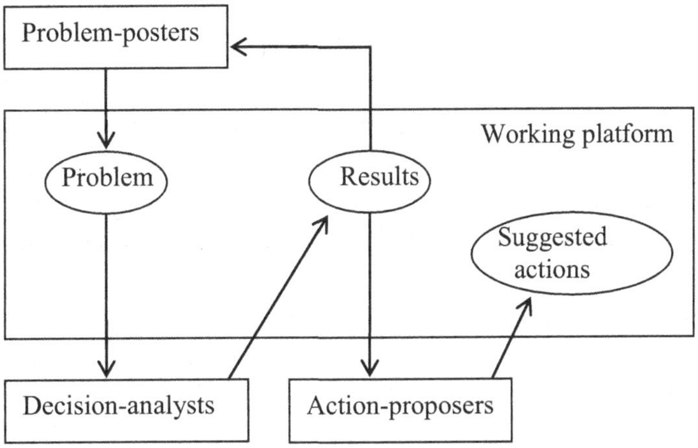

The system initiates when the fire chief specifies a possible incident type, including fire, explosion, traffic accident, or other. This selection triggers *problem-posters* to ask questions of the fire chief and post problem(s) on the working platform. As we discussed in Chapter VI, the first responders may not know the type of incident immediately when an unexpected incident occurs, unless either of the following two conditions is satisfied:

1. The incident itself exhibits obvious/noticeable sign(s) manifesting its type, such as a fire, an explosion, or a traffic accident.
2. The responders have intelligence or information regarding the incident.

Initially the fire chief relies on only the direct observations and facts from an incident scene to reason about the type of an incident and may select from the four incident types (i.e., fire, explosion, traffic accident, or other) during the initial stage. As more information gets added and the analyses delve deeper, the system helps the fire chief determine the agent involved and designate specific actions.

After the fire chief selects the type of incident, the *problem-posters* request inputs about site or scene information, such as whether a smell exists on the scene (i.e., perception of odor), if people are affected, the physical appearance of the victims (e.g., skin rash), and whether people are losing consciousness. These inputs and the results generated by the system represent data elements that get displayed on the working platform. The experimentation, hypotheses, and processes used by the *decision-analysts* also provide data elements.

Representation of Data

Data elements in the system appear as attribute–value pairs. We consider six types of data elements: *observation, substance, hypothesis, response strategy/action, experimental operation*, and *process*.

Observation. Observation elements describe physical signs and features displayed by victims or noticeable sign(s) reflected by the event scene or possible released material(s). These features include the severity, speed of impact, nature of exposure, route of exposure, presence of smoke, effects on surroundings (e.g., dead animals, human casualties), and evidence of exposure to other chemicals. Specifically, the system uses the following notations:

- Some substances act quickly and are easily absorbed through skin contact; others cannot be absorbed through skin. We use Time Effect (TE_i for $i = 1, 2, ..., I$) to denote the speed of reaction, such that TE_1 = immediate, TE_2 = rapid, TE_3 = moderate, and TE_4 = slow.
- Observations about the physical appearance of a possible released material (if observable) are denoted PS_i for $i = 1, 2, ..., I$, where PS_i represents the attribute name of the physical state of a substance, and i is the number of possible appearances that the substance can exhibit. Thus, this data element can indicate PS_1 = gas, PS_2 = liquid, PS_3 = solid, or PS_4 = other (e.g., quantum state). If the physical appearance of a substance is not liquid, then the system sets PS_2 as $\overline{PS_2}$, which indicates it does not display a liquid state.
- Observations about the color appearance of a substance (if observable) are denoted CA_j for $j = 1, 2, ..., J$, where CA_j is the attribute name and J is the number of colors. For example, CA_1 = colorless or clear, CA_2 = white, CA_3 = yellow, CA_4 = pale blue, and so forth. If a color exists, the system sets CA_1 to $\overline{CA_1}$.
- Observations about the perception of odors in the scene (if perceptible) are denoted PO_i for $i = 1, 2, ..., I$, such that PO_1 = tasteless, PO_2 = bitter almond odor, PO_3 = slightly fruity odor, PO_4 = a camphor-like odor, PO_5 = rotten egg odor, and so forth. If there is a smell, the system sets PO_1 to $\overline{PO_1}$.
- Observations about the number of victims (if any) are denoted as NV.
- Observations about the route of exposure for affected people on the site are denoted RE_j for $j = 1, 2, ..., J$, where RE_1 = through breath (i.e., inhalation), RE_2 = skin contact, RE_3 = eye contact, and RE_4 = other.
- Observations about direct damage sign(s) displayed by victims include
  - The location of observable damage on the body, denoted LB_i for $i = 1, 2, ..., I$, such that LB_1 = skin, LB_2 = eyes, LB_3 = head, LB_4 = limbs, and LB_5 = other.
  - Diaphoresis, such that $OD = 1$ when diaphoresis is observed, and $OD = 0$ otherwise.
  - Color of skin rashes or burns, denoted ASC_i for $i = 1, 2, ..., I$, where ASC_1 = bright red, ASC_2 = cherry-red, ASC_3 = cyanosis, and ASC_4 = other.
  - Nasal symptoms, denoted NT_i for $i = 1, 2, ..., I$, such that NT_1 = cough, NT_2 = sore throat, NT_3 = runny nose, NT_4 = vomiting, and NT_5 = other.
  - Eye irritation, denoted ED_i for $i = 1, 2, ..., I$, where ED_1 = normal pupils, ED_2 = dilated pupils, ED_3 = shrunken pupils, ED_4 = dazzle, ED_5 = blur, ED_6 = lost sight or delayed visual recall, ED_7 = double vision, ED_8 = burn, ED_9 = pain inside and tearing easily, and ED_{10} = other.
  - Nervous system, denoted NS_i for $i = 1, 2, ..., I$, where NS_1 = unconsciousness, NS_2 = fatigue, NS_3 = convulsions, NS_4 = impaired verbal and visual recall, NS_5 = stiff neck, NS_6 = swollen face, NS_7 = vertigo, NS_8 = paralyzed body (right or left side, arm, or leg), NS_9 = progression of symptoms to unconsciousness, and so forth.
  - Cardiac symptoms, such as blood pressure, for which CS_i for $i = 1, 2, ..., I$ indicates CS_1 = bradycardia, CS_2 = irregular heartbeat, CS_3 = shortness of breath or respiratory arrest, CS_4 = dyspnea, CS_5 = apnea, CS_6 = chest pain or discomfort, CS_7 = hypertension, and CS_8 = transient hyperpnea.
  - Mortality sign(s) denoted as MS_i for $i = 1, 2, ..., I$, where MS_1 = sudden death, MS_2 = death within several minutes, and so forth.

Substance. Substance provides information about a given substance, such as hydrogen sulfide. As an attribute, it includes the name of the substance, its chemical formula, some physical properties (e.g., boiling point), and its associated acute, subacute, and chronic health effects. Substance elements represent the specific domain knowledge of the *decision-analysts*.

Hypothesis. A hypothesis describes how a recognized phenomenon might have taken place in the form of frames (Minsky, 1975). A frame is a relational data structure, analogous to an application form, with many blanks or slots to be filled that take values according to what the frame represents. For example, a frame that represents a "person" would have some slots for a body, head, arms, and legs. A frame (or several frames) then may be translated into a production rule. For example, if an observation with inputs <1>, <2>, ..., <i> must provide output that matches subject knowledge about substance X, it can be hypothesized that a class of substances contains X that may be related to the phenomenon.

Response strategy/action. A response strategy/action is a description that the system supports with regard to situation control, based on the available information about the situation.

Experimental operation. An experimental operation describes the logical operation or chemical reaction performed by the *decision-analysts*. Each experimental operation consists of inputs, conditions for conducting it, outputs, name, and a flag indicating whether the operation is complete.

Process. A process describes the entire solution development procedure, which each doer undertakes for a specific task. Thus, it consists of the following attributes: doer's name, inputs, outputs, experimental operations used, and a flag indicating process completion. In the event of an attack, the resulting tasks each have an accompanying process. The length of the process depends on the types of task, its difficulties, and the capabilities of the *decision-analysts*.

Representation of the Working Platform

The working platform consists of four levels: data, agenda, result formation, and goal.

Data level. This level contains information about an incident or a disaster; thus, the observation elements reside at this level.

Agenda level. The *problem-posters* post new problem(s) or subproblem(s) to this level, which therefore contains the problem or task list the system must solve. This level also prepares and performs data abstraction from the data level.

Result formation level. The results reported by each doer among the *decision-analysts* appear in this level; in turn, *action-proposers* use these results to generate suggestions and recommended response strategies.

Goal level. Finally, the goal level stores suggestions, solutions, or recommended response actions for display to the fire chief.

The working platform thus reflects the evolution of the problem-solving and decision-making processes. It is updated by all three operators.

Representation of Operators

Operators' knowledge appears as a set of production rules (for production system details, see Newell & Simon, 1972). Each rule contains one or more conditions that describe the hypotheses or specify the patterns that may occur in the data. Each rule also contains a set of actions that are responsible for formulating hypotheses, carrying out experimental and logical operations on the data, and planning new experiments or other tasks. We discuss each operator in detail.

Problem-posters. The problem-posters serve as an interface by working with both the fire chief, to ask for inputs, and the working platform, to choose or post new problems. Specifically, the heuristic working principles for *problem-posters* are as follows:

[PP1] If there is no problem on the working platform, ask for input from the fire chief.

[PP2] If a process is incomplete, according to the flag, make the process a task and add it to the agenda so that other doers may address it.

[PP3] If the outcome of an experiment is inconsistent with the observation data, make the study of this puzzling phenomenon a task and add it to the agenda on the working platform.

[PP4] If the outcome of an experiment violates the hypothesis, make the study of this puzzling phenomenon a task and add it to the agenda.

[PP5] If a task failure is posted, add this task to the agenda again so that other doers may address it.

[PP6] If an implied task failure is posted, add this task to the agenda again.

Decision-analysts. Among this set of expert doers, the objective is to contribute knowledge that will lead to a solution to a problem or task. Thus, each doer is modeled as an independent, goal-directed problem solver and assumed to have some specific domain knowledge that enables the doer to formulate a hypothesis based on the observation data, perform experiment(s) to test the hypothesis, and provide recommendations using only expertise in a timely manner. To ensure execution, each doer encompasses both knowledge and inference mechanisms that can make use of knowledge. Therefore, in the proposed system, each doer comprises two components: header and analyzer.

The header of a doer resides at the agenda level of the working platform as a means to declare expertise. The header chooses which problem the doer should work on next from the problem agenda on the working platform. Along with a doer name, the header includes attribute slots that represent conditions and expertise. One of attribute slots is the action slot, which stores the doer's reference to the body, that is, the analyzer. The assumption slot indicates the condition that must be matched before the analyzer can be activated. Attribute slots can consist of various data types, such as numerical, logical, or symbolic.

We present in Figure 8.2 a simplified version of the LISP code, which defines the structure of a doer's header. The bold lines, beginning with a semicolon, are comments about the LISP code. The slot (Function) describes this doer's expertise, whereas the slot (Parameters) refers to variables, assumptions, or conditions that the doer requires to execute a task. The slot (Paths) indicates where the header will be stored as it is created. Finally, the slot (Result Status) reveals whether the doer has completed a task successfully, according to the following four options: success, failure, implied failure, and implied success.

- Success is the number of experiments or facts that verify a hypothesis, or the generation of a solution to the task.
- Failure is the number of experiments that deny a hypothesis or the lack of analytic methods to carry out the process.
- Implied failure is the number of efforts expended without proving the hypothesis (or generating a response strategy), which indicates the hypothesis may be false.
- Implied success occurs when many facts suggest a positive indication, but not conclusively, such that the hypothesis may be true.

Figure 8.2. Simplified LISP code for defining the header of a doer

```
(define-unit-class Headers}()
;; indicates a doer name
(Name)
;; function/expertise description
(Function: enumerated : any)
;; Assumption/condition under which the doer can be activated
(Parameters: P_1, P_2, ...., P_n)
;; where the Headers will be stored.
(paths '(working platform agenda-level))
;; Activate analyzer to run when the conditions are satisfied.
(creation-event-functions analyzer)
;; Possible status of a result after implementation
(Result Status:  Success, Failure, Implied-failure, Implied-success)
```

The initial attribute values of the result status are set to 0 before performing any task or solving any problem, but they get updated with progress, according to a simple rule: If a fact indicates that a hypothesis is probably false, the implied failure slot increases by 1. We discuss this updating process in more detail subsequently.

The analyzer, in contrast, represents the doer's subject matter knowledge and domain-specific heuristics about some chemical substances, their properties, and the associated general health effects. Depending on the type of tasks, some doers may use their existing knowledge to suggest response actions, whereas others may need to formulate a hypothesis and plan an experiment before providing a solution. For example, suppose a chemical container catches fire and the fire chief has decided to enter the site area to rescue injured victims. Once the fire chief specifies the type of an incident as "fire" in the system, this information activates doers with subject matter knowledge related to fire. Without knowing the size of the affected area, a typical doer provides two suggestions to the fire chief as a reminder: "If there is no knowledge of the size of the initial chemical source, establish a high zone at a 500-meter (about 1000 yards) radius in all directions from ground zero" (Harper et al., 2007; Laurent et al., 1999) and "Check for secondary explosive devices that might hinder the initial response." Other reminders about how to protect onsite responders also will be displayed to the fire chief. Depending on the type of hazardous materials, release methods, and potential for airborne concentration, the U.S. National Institute for Occupational Safety and Health (NIOSH) recommends protective respirators and clothing for use in different situations (http://www.niosh.org). Such rules for protecting frontline responders remain embedded within the system and display for the fire chief in different situations.

Protection rules suggest actions for protecting frontline responders. In particular:

[PR-0] Wear personal protective clothing, such as gloves and booties, in response to an emergency. Use half-masks or full facepiece air-purifying respiratory with particulate filter efficiencies ranging from N95 for hazards such as pulmonary tuberculosis to P100 for hazard such as hantavirus as a minimum level of protection. (This is a general rule.)

[PR-1] If entering a hot zone or dealing with contaminated causalities, and if the level of risk for hazards and airborne concentration are either unknown or expected to be high, use a fully encapsulated suit with a self-contained breathing apparatus (SCBA) during emergency responses.

[PR-2] If any of the following conditions are satisfied or the event is uncontrolled, use a NIOSH-approved, pressure-demand SCBA in conjunction with a fully encapsulated protective suit in response to a suspected incident:

- *Unknown* type(s) of airborne agent(s).
- Unknown dissemination method.
- Dissemination via an aerosol device is still occurring or has stopped but there is *no* information about dissemination duration.
- *No* information about the exposure concentration.

[PR-3] If the situation can be defined to indicate that the suspected biological or chemical aerosol is no longer being generated, wear SCBA and chemical protective suit or charcoal suit.

[PR-4] If the level of risk is known and no aerosol device was used to create high airborne concentrations, use powered air-purifying respirator (PAPR) and chemical protective suit.

[PR-5] If dissemination was by a letter or package that can be easily bagged, use powered air-purifying respirator (PAPR) and chemical protective suit.

[PR-6] If no hazard is presented or detected, wear work clothes (uniforms).

[PR-7] If responders are near the warm zone, wear work clothes (uniforms).

[PR-8] Dispose of contaminated clothes in a sealed bag. Responders should shower using copious quantities of soap and water.

[PR-9] Use soap and water and 0.5% hypochlorite solution to decontaminate contaminated equipment.

In this analyzer sector, a hot zone is the area immediately surrounding a hazardous material incident, whereas a warm zone is the area surrounding the hot zone, where personnel and equipment decontamination and support for the hot zone take place. A cold zone contains the command post and other support functions and does not require any personal protective clothing (PPC) other than that appropriate for normal patient care.

When trying to determine if a chemical substance X may be involved, doers need to work with the observation data to formulate a hypothesis and plan experiment(s) to test the hypothesis. For example, if some affected people mention that they smelled the odor of rotten eggs in the air initially but the smell later disappeared, such observational information activates the doer to establish an expectation for a possible hypothesis. One such expectation might indicate, "[H1] If given observation with inputs <1>, <2>, …, <i> is to have output that matches subject matter knowledge about substance X, then hypothesize that there is a class of substances containing X that may be related to the phenomenon." A corresponding experimental operation attempts to verify this hypothesis, with two heuristic rules: "[E1] If your expectation is to study the relation of a related fact with X to a phenomenon, then study the phenomenon with X as a reactant" and "[E2] If you are studying a phenomenon with X as a reactant, then carry out experimental operation on X under various conditions."

Now consider applying rules [H1], [E1], and [E2] to our hypothetical case. A witness initially smelled the odor of rotten egg, which may suggest a colorless gas in air that causes such a perception. Smelling rotten egg is a phenomenon characteristic of some chemical substances, and sensing the odor initially but then losing the scent is another phenomenon. The observation data—namely, gas, colorless, odor, and time interval—provide heuristics for a system search. These heuristics should match some subject matter knowledge about a substance; for example, hydrogen sulfide becomes a potential candidate substance, because it is colorless gas with a characteristic odor of rotten eggs, and people usually can smell it at low concentrations. However, at high concentrations, they might lose their ability to smell it, which is part of what makes hydrogen sulfide very dangerous.

Applying heuristic [E2], a doer with subject matter knowledge about hydrogen sulfide compares observation data about the signs displayed by affected people with the possible health effects of substance X and plans some experimental operations. In a logical operation, the doer translates some observation data attributes into a logic expression, whereas in a chemical operation, the doer undertakes a chemical reaction between two substances. Through feature extraction from the observation data set, several logic expressions can be formulated to suggest data patterns to compare with or against the properties of substances in the system to determine if they match. Some logic expressions can be simple, such as $(RE_1 \cap NT_1) = ?$, which evaluates whether exposed people display cough symptoms. However, other expressions are complex, such as $[(RE_3 \cap ED_9) \cup (RE_1 \cap NT_1) \cup \overline{LB_1}]$, which indicates "people who have been exposed indicate pain inside their eyes and tearing easily, cough, but no obvious signs on their skin." The chemical operation then determines, for example, "is a substance X soluble in water, or does it react with acid?" Because many materials used in chemical reactions cannot be obtained at the incident scene, chemical papers impregnated with various chemicals, such as sodium hydroxide, calcium hydroxide, acids, lead, or caustic substances, provide the tools for testing. The system asks the user for the result of the reactions; that is, the outcomes of the chemical reactions are supplied interactively by the user. However, the system also lists information about the types of additional tests that the hospital should conduct when it receives the victims transferred there.

Results from these experimental operations must be compared with subject matter knowledge about the substances. The findings could change, verify, or falsify the proposed hypotheses. For example, if a new hypothesis were needed, it might state, "[H2] If the preferred hypothesis studies the relation of a known fact with X to a phenomenon and if the conducted experimental operations and the given phenomenon both produce the same output or patterns, create a new hypothesis and add it to the hypothesis set: There is evidence for a hypothesis that substance X is involved and caused this phenomenon."

Each time a hypothesis is modified, verified, or created through the process of experimental operations, the attribute values of the result status for a doer who performs such processes gets updated. Each doer thus uses the following rules to update the corresponding result status when focusing on a specific task:

[Update-RS1] If there is a hypothesis that a substance X may be related to a phenomenon in certain conditions and a negative result emerges from experimental operations, the failure slot increases by 1.

[Update-RS2] If no response action can be generated regarding a specific task, the failure slot increases by 1.

[Update-RS3] If there is a hypothesis that a substance X may be related to a phenomenon in certain conditions and there is a positive result from experimental operations, the success slot increases by 1.

[Update-RS4] If a solution step is found for a specific task, the success slot increases by 1.

[Update-RS5] If there is a hypothesis that a substance X produces this outcome and the experimental operations show that the observations match most of attributes of X, the implied success increases by 1; otherwise, the implied failure slot increases by 1.

[Update-RS6] If there are many facts or observations that indicate a hypothesis is true, the implied success slot increases by 1.

When a doer posts a hypothesis/strategy or a solution step on the working platform after completing a specific task, the associated value of the result status also gets posted, which provides a heuristic for the *action-proposers* to make a choice.

Action-proposers. On the basis of the results posted by the *decision-analysts*, the *action-proposers* choose or generate response action(s), represented by a set of rules. The heuristics that guide action-proposers are as follows:

[AP1] Take into consideration all strategies on the working platform.

[AP2] Other things being equal, prefer a strategy whose result status has a higher value in the success slot.

[AP3] Other things being equal, prefer the strategy that can be carried out quickly.

[AP4] If a hypothesis suggests substance X is involved, generate the associated action steps for substance X.

[AP5] If a hypothesis suggests substance X is likely involved (i.e., implied success value), generate associated action steps for substance X and mark a notice to engage in further laboratory testing for affected people.

[AP6] If there are no other criteria applicable, make a random choice.

[AP7] If a process is incomplete, according to its flag, eliminate it, and mark its associated task incomplete.

Decision-analysts thus are multiple doers with subject matter knowledge who collaborate to discover a potential data pattern exhibited by a target chemical substance when the fire chief inputs onsite observations into the system. These doers contribute their knowledge during the course of the discovery process. Then, when a specific data pattern results from the associated hypothesis that indicates the most likely involved substance, they generate a corresponding real-time, specific response plan for this substance and recommend it to the fire chief. For example, if the system infers that the incident likely involves the release of hydrogen sulfide, in addition to producing a general procedure of onsite prehospital treatment, the system specifies the particular properties that require attention when dealing with hydrogen sulfide to remind the firefighters.

Some of these precautions, excerpted from a specific plan for hydrogen sulfide, where [AP-Substance-number] refers to a special recommendation regarding a specific chemical agent and [AP-R-number] indicates a general action step, appear next.

[AP-Substance-1] If the substance is released as a gas, it will remain in the atmosphere for an average of 18 hours. Check weather conditions for wind direction to determine a place with fresh air and when to evacuate affected people.

[AP-R-4] If victims can walk, lead them to the decontamination zone. Use backboards for victims who are unable to walk. Perform symptom checks and simultaneously execute decontamination procedures.

[AP-R-6] Transfer victims immediately to the support zone, and implement cardiac monitoring.

[AP-Substance-2] Avoid mouth-to-mouth resuscitation and instead administer high-flow oxygen, airway management, and ventilatory support to persons who report serious headache or lose consciousness.

[AP-R-7] If ventilators are unavailable, use an endotracheal tube to ventilate the patient manually.

[AP-Substance-3] Apply advanced cardiac life (ACLS) measures for dysrhythmias.

[AP-Substance-4] Administer hydrogen sulfide antidotes as soon as possible, being careful not to create toxic methemoglobinemia.

KNOWLEDGE AND UNDERLYING PHILOSOPHY PRINCIPLES

The old saying, "two heads are better than one," acknowledges that one person's knowledge is always limited. Similarly, Laotse, an ancient Chinese philosopher, noted "If three of us are working together, there will surely be a teacher for me." When responding to a HazMat incident with an unknown situation, multiple experts with different specific domain knowledge must collaborate to generate strategies rather than just relying on a person's individual knowledge or thoughts. Based on this philosophy, we implement a machinery-based multi-doer system in designing our *decision-analysts*.

Each doer's specific knowledge about a substance is coded in the production rules and based on education materials, published online by the Agency for Toxic Substances and Disease Registry, U.S. Department of Health and Human Services (http://www.atsdr.cdc.gov). Thus, whether a hypothesis or not, each solution or response strategy that can be generated depends on the working ability of each doer, particularly the core component analyzer, and the collaboration mechanism among these analyzers. In the proposed system, the analyzer design is based on findings from extensive empirical research in scientific discovery and creative thinking (e.g., Ding, 2002; Klahr & Dubar, 1988, Langley et al., 1987), particularly the dual-space model of the process of scientific discovery proposed by Klahr and Dunbar (1988), as shown in Figure 8.3. The dual-space model posits that scientific discovery entails a process of searching in two related spaces: a hypothesis space and an experiment space. Therefore, each analyzer searches in both spaces. The hypothesis space consists of the subject matter knowledge, knowledge about the logical process, knowledge about previous experiments, and hypotheses generated during the task-solving process. The possible experimental operations and outcomes define the experiment space, and consist of performing experiments. The outcome of the experimental operations modifies or generates the hypotheses.

When an analyzer is activated by the header (residing at the agenda level), with a focus on a specific task, that analyzer may provide an answer without carrying out experimental operations or may need

Figure 8.3. A dual-space model of scientific discovery

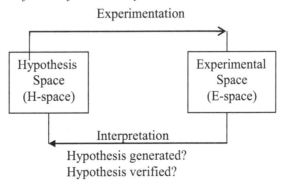

to carry out experiments. Figure 8.4 illustrates a general task-solving procedure for an analyzer if experimental operations are needed. With observations as inputs, "generating an experiment" represents a process of discovering possible data patterns in the observations though an experimental operation. This process comprises four steps: analyzing the observation data and planning an experimental operation, executing the experiment, capturing outcomes, and interpreting the experimental outcomes. In Figure 8.4, we use four branches connected by a curved line to represent these steps, which are executed in order from left to right. This notation also applies to Figure 8.5. For example, if bright red skin is observed on some victims, and some victims display dilated pupils, the analyzer sets $LB_1 = 1$ $ASC_1 =$ 1, and $ED_2 = 1$, then plans experimental operations, such as "Check if $(RE_3 \cap ED_2)$ and $(RE_2 \cap ASC_1 \cap PO_2)$ hold simultaneously." An experiment can be either a logical operation or a chemical reaction. In our design, the analyzer usually starts by finding logical operations to derive the initial data pattern from the observation and generate corresponding hypotheses. In a continuous hypothesis-refining and -updating process, the initial data pattern gets modified. A hypothesis with higher values in the success slot requires further verification through chemical reactions. The analyzer also uses existing domain knowledge to evaluate the experimental outcomes. When the results cannot be explained or a puzzling phenomenon occurs, a new hypothesis may need to be generated (see Figure 8.5).

The "testing a hypothesis" step involves performing experimental operations to uncover any evidence that contradicts a hypothesis. Four basic steps appear: planning an experimental operation, making a prediction, carrying out the experiment, and checking if the outcomes support the hypothesis. If supported, the analyzer updates its result status and the summary information about the target substance. If the experiment does not support the hypothesis, the analyzer must update the hypothesis space and study one of the remaining hypotheses.

Figure 8.4. Analyzer: General working procedure

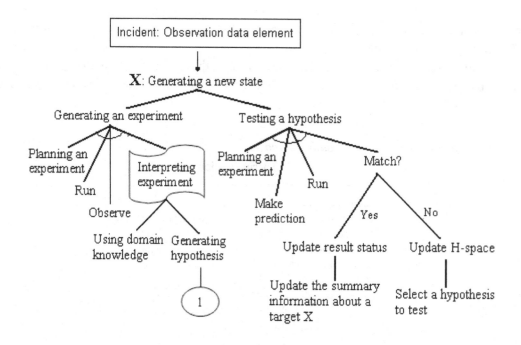

Figure 8.5. Creating a new hypothesis

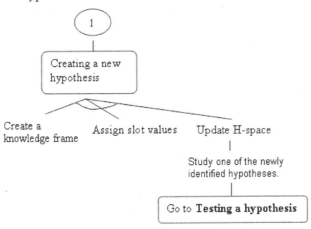

APPLICATION SIMULATION

When a substance is released, either by accident such as a leak at an industrial plant or by a terrorist attack, it enters the environment. The release does not always lead to exposure, unless people accidentally come into contact with the substance. Such contact may occur by breathing air, eating contaminated food, drinking contaminated water, or skin contact.

To determine if the proposed system can use the symptoms observed to produce a data pattern that indicates the involvement of a specific substance, we conduct a simulation in which we provide three different onsite symptom descriptions to the system, one by one. We then present the system's response.

The three test examples are hydrogen cyanide, hydrogen sulphide, and hydrogen fluoride, all of which are common industrial materials used in manufacturing (e.g., hydrogen cyanide helps produce synthetic fibers, plastics, or dyes; hydrogen fluoride is used in the process of making refrigerants; hydrogen sulphide is associated with paper operations and coke oven plants) and can be obtained easily from industrial sites. They do not require specialized skills or knowledge for effective use, and they can cause massive physical and psychological damages. More important, no simple test, such as blood tests or other diagnostics, can return results within the time required for effective intervention (Baskin & Brewer, 2004; ATSDR, 2006). Rather, such incidents require specific resources or equipment for laboratory testing, and most responders lack such specialized testing equipment. Therefore, the chances of responding effectively to such an attack generally are low today.

Before describing our simulation, we first briefly introduce the basic characteristics of these three substances. Hydrogen cyanide appears as a colorless or blue liquid at room temperature but rapidly becomes a gas that can produce death in minutes if inhaled. Exposure by any route may cause systemic effects. Generally, the more serious the exposure, the more severe the symptoms. Breathing small amounts of hydrogen cyanide may cause headache, dizziness, nausea, and vomiting; however, after a serious exposure, the victim may suffer brain or heart damage (Way, 1984). Blood and urine analyses and other tests can indicate whether the brain or heart has been injured, but they are not useful for identifying the cause of the injury (Baskin & Brewer, 2004).

Hydrogen sulphide is a poisonous, colorless gas with a characteristic odor of rotten eggs. The general population can be minimally exposed from accidental or deliberate releases of emissions from pulp and paper mills, natural gas drilling and refining operations, and areas of high geothermal activity such as hot springs. Exposure to low concentrations of hydrogen sulfide may cause irritation to the eyes, nose, or throat, and brief exposures to high concentrations can cause a loss of consciousness. Despite the recovery from this unconsciousness, many victims report permanent or persistent neurological effects, including headaches, poor concentration ability and attention spans, impaired short-term memory, and impaired motor function. Scientists have little information about what happens when people are exposed to hydrogen sulfide through the skin (ATSDR, 2006). The most frequently used biomarker of hydrogen sulfide exposure is urinary thiosulfate levels, though a quantitative relationship between exposure levels and urinary thiosulfate levels has not been established.

Hydrogen fluoride is highly corrosive, and its primary effects include tissue damage resulting from direct contact. Acute inhalation exposure can result in irritation, inflammation, bronchiolar ulceration, pulmonary hemorrhage and edema, and death. The general population typically is exposed to very low levels of gaseous fluoride, primarily as hydrogen fluoride in the United States and Canada, with levels ranging from 0.01 to 1.65 $\mu g/m^3$. The dissolved form is called hydrofluoric acid. Direct contact with hydrogen fluoride/hydrofluoric acid in the eyes or on the skin can produce burns. In addition, exposure can result in skeletal and cardiac effects. No well-documented information suggests biomarkers of the effects of fluoride, though some studies indicate that cellular changes occur after fluoride exposure (ATSDR, 2006).

Release of Hydrogen Cyanide

In our first hypothetical scenario, the true chemical agent released is hydrogen cyanide. We examine if the system can derive the proper judgment, given the various symptoms observed. The system's output is labeled with [system] and displayed in italics, while user's input is labeled with [user] and displayed in normal font in the subsequent discussion.

[system]	*Do you see a fire?*
[user]	No.
[system]	*Do you see smoke?*
[user]	No.
[system]	*Is there an explosion?*
[user]	No.
[system]	*Are there any victims?*
[user]	Yes.
[system]	*Do you see anyone coughing or vomiting?*
[user]	Yes.
[system]	*Do you see anyone who was knocked down?*
[user]	Yes.
[system]	*Do you see anyone showing distress in their breathing?*
[user]	Yes.
[system]	*Check if victims had eaten something before feeling uncomfortable?*
[user]	No.

[system]	*Is there any suspicions suggesting a cause?*
[user]	No.
[system]	*[AP-R-1] Establish a high zone boundary at a 500 m (or about 1000 yards) radius in all directions from ground zero.*
[system]	*[AP-R-2] Check wind direction, and establish support zone along upwind side.*
[system]	*[AP-R-3] Establish decontamination zone.*
[system]	*[PR-2] Use a NIOSH-approved, pressure-demand SCBA in conjunction with fully encapsulated protective suit to respond to the suspected incident.*
[system]	*[AP-R-4] If victims can walk, lead them to the decontamination zone. Use backboards for victims who are unable to walk. Perform symptom checking simultaneously with decontamination procedures.*
[system]	*[AP-R-5] Administer of 100% oxygen to victims who lose consciousness.*
[system]	*Where are the observed damages? choose any that apply:* • *skin* • *eyes* • *head* • *limbs* • *other*
[user]	Skin
[system]	*Color of skin rash? choose any that apply:* • *bright red* • *cherry-red* • *cyanosis* • *other*
[user]	Cyanosis
[system]	*Check the size of the pupils, and choose any that apply:* • *normal* • *dilated* • *shrunken*
[user]	Dilated
[system]	*[AP-R-6] Transfer victim immediately to the support zone, and implement cardiac monitoring.*
[system]	*Do victims display transient hyperpnea or hypertension?*
[user]	Yes.
[system]	*Are bradycardia accompanied by hypertension?*
[user]	Yes.
[system]	*Ask people affected if they smelled anything when they started to feel uncomfortable* • *yes* • *no* • *both*
[user]	Both
[system]	*Smell odor, choose any applied:* • *tasteless* • *almond odor* • *slightly fruity odor* • *camphor-like* • *rotten egg* • *other*
[user]	Tasteless and almond
[system]	*$[RE_2 \cap (LB_1 \cap ASC_1)] = true$*
[system]	*$[PS_1 \cap CA_1 \cap (PO_1 \cup PO_2)] = true$*
[system]	*Very likely $RE_1 = true$, suggesting exposure through inhalation.*
[system]	*There is a chance that the substance belongs to a class of cyanide.*
[system]	*Are bradycardia accompanied and followed by hypertension?*
[user]	Yes.
[system]	*Do victims demonstrate diaphoresis?*
[user]	Yes.

[system] $[(OD = 1) \cap ED_2] = true$
[system] $[CS_7 \cup NT_1 \cup NS_1] = true$

The data pattern generated thus is

[system] $[PS_1 \cap CA_1 \cap (PO_1 \cup PO_2)] \cap \{RE_1 \cup [RE_2 \cap (LB_1 \cap ASC_1)] \cup [(OD = 1) \cap ED_2]\} \cap$
$CS_7 \cup NT_1 \cup NS_1$
[system]   *Very likely the substance is HCN.*
[system]   [AP-HCN-1] *If eye irritated, use plain water or saline for 5 minutes.*
[system]   [AP-HCN-2] *Administer cyanide antidotes (sodium nitrite and sodium thiosulfate).*
[system]   [AP-HCN-3] *If the victim has not responded to oxygen, infuse sodium nitrite intrave-*
nously as soon as possible. The usual adult dose is 10 mL of a 3% solution (300 mg)
*infused over **absolutely no less than 5 minutes**; the average pediatric dose is 0.12 to*
0.33 mL/kg body weight up to 10 mL, infused as above.
[system]   [AP-HCN-4] *Monitor blood pressure during sodium nitrite administration, and slow*
the rate of infusion if hypotension develops.
[system]   [AP-R-8] *Transfer victims to hospital based on severity.*
[system]   [AP-HCN-5] *Victims who have direct skin or eye contact should be observed in the*
Emergency Department for at least 4 to 6 hours.

The system correctly identifies the true released chemical substance as hydrogen cyanide. After experiments begin to indicate that the substance has specific effects, such as the perception of smell and skin colorations, the system entertains hypotheses regarding the meaning of these effects. A class of substances related to cyanide is one such possibility. To test this hypothesis, however, the system asks for more information related to cyanide poison and plans more experimental operations to compare the observed information against the hypothesis. Finally, the system generates a data pattern that represents the characteristics of the target substance based on the observed symptoms. Meanwhile, it also suggests agent-specific response actions.

Similarly, we conduct simulations for two additional substances: hydrogen sulphide and hydrogen fluoride. The system provides the same level of success of correctly identifying the true substance used. As two more examples, we provide the corresponding data patterns for hydrogen sulphide and hydrogen fluoride here:

Hydrogen sulphide: $(PS_1 \cap CA_1 \cap PO_5) \cap$
$\{[(RE_1 \cap (NT_2 \cap NT_1)) \cup (RE_2 \cap TE_4) \cup (RE_1 \cap TE_2) \cup (RE_3 \cap ED_4)] \cap$
$[(NS_1 \cup CS_4 \cup CS_6 \cup NS_7) \cup (RE_1 \cap RE_2 \cap RE_3)] \cup MS_2\}$

Further tests for hydrogen sulphide contamination, as suggested by the system, include spraying water into the air and observing if vapor evaporates from the water, then using paper impregnated with sodium hydroxide (NaOH) to catch the air and determine if there is any change. A change confirms that the released substance is hydrogen sulphide.

Hydrogen fluoride: $[(CA_1 \cap PS_1) \cup PS_2] \cap \{[RE_2 \cap (TE_2 \cap ASC_1)] \cup [RE_1 \cap (NT_1 \cup NT_2 \cup NT_3 \cup CS_3 \cup NT_4)]\} \cap (RE_3 \cap ED_8)$.

The substance-specific suggestions in this scenario include thorough irrigation with cold water or saline to limit absorption through exposed skin and eyes; washing the affected skin with an alkaline soap and water; and applying calcium gluconate paste, magnesium oxide paste, or iced solutions of quaternary ammonium compounds to the exposed skin.

The simulation results reveal that our proposed system can generate data patterns from limited observed symptoms and accurately identify different kinds of substances by incorporating each substance's characteristics. Such data patterns can be refined and further used as a quick screening tool to identify hazardous agent involvement in future incidents.

DISCUSSION AND CONCLUSIONS

If a fire chief cannot identify quickly whether a toxic chemical is involved in an incident, casualties may begin to occur. However, the vast number of toxic chemicals each has its own unique characteristics and health effects. It is difficult for an onsite commander or first responders to know all of these toxic chemicals and come up with an agent-specific response plan quickly, especially in a rapidly progressing incident. The system proposed here serves as a quick decision support assistant that can help the fire chief or first responders take effective rescue steps in response to a HazMat event. In an emergency situation, people often are unsure what actions to take; for example, according to media reports about September 11 (Media, 2006), tapes feature a fire official describing the near chaos inside the World Trade Center, and communication became increasingly difficult as firefighters tried to reach people trapped in a devastating blaze that raged high overhead. With the proposed system on hand, however, the fire chief or first responders on the scene could interact with the system and receive instant rescue guidelines. Because speed is critical to save lives, such a system might dramatically increase firefighters' capability in response to chemical incidents.

At the current stage, we assume that a hazardous material release contains only a single chemical agent/component. In reality though, affected people might be exposed to multiple agents or components. Further extensions of this system therefore will investigate ways to identify many different chemical substances involved at the same time—a very difficult task. Some researchers recently have proposed using ultra-fast lasers to measure the breath exhaled by affected people to detect if they have been exposed to specific materials. This idea mirrors the concept of a breathalyzer, which provides instant analysis of alcohol levels in the blood from a sample of breath given by a person, such as a driver suspected of driving under the influence. Some diseases and conditions cause small changes to the breath, and people's exposure to a chemical or biological agent similarly may create health effects that alter people's breath. By analyzing breath, we might be able to detect chemical components in a hazardous material incident as well.

REFERENCES

Agency for Toxic Substances and Disease Registry [ATSDR] (2006). *Educational material—toxicological profile guidelines.* U.S. Department of Health and Human Services. Retrieved January 12, 2007, from http://www.atsdr.cdc.gov

Association of American Railroads [AAR] (2004). *Railroads: the safe way to move.* Washington, DC: Association of American Railroads. Retrieved December 12, 2004, from http://www.aar.org/pubcommon/documents/policy/safe_way_to_move.pdf.

Baskin, S. I., & Brewer, T. G. (2004). Cyanide poisoning. In *Textbook of Military Medicine: Medical Aspects of Chemical and Biological Warfare*, Chapter 10. Retrieved January 12, 2005, from http://www.vnh.org/MedAspChemBioWar/chapters/chapter_10.htm.

Baskin, S. I., Horowitz, A. M., & Nealley, E. W. (1992). The antidotal action of sodium nitrite and sodium thiosulfate against cyanide poisoning. *Journal of Clinical Pharmacology, 32*, 368-375.

Ding, W. (2002). *A Study of Collaborative Scientific Discovery.* Unpublished doctoral dissertation, Carnegie Mellon University, USA.

Harper, F. T., Musolino, S. V., & Wente, W. (2007). Realistic radiological dispersal device hazard boundaries and ramifications for early consequence management decisions. *Health Physics, 93*(1), 1-16.

Isom, G. E., & Johnson, J. D. (1987). Sulfur donor in cyanide intoxication. In Ballantyne, B. M., & Marrs, T. C. (Eds.), *Clinical and experimental toxicology of cyanides* (pp. 413-426). Bristol: Wright.

Klahr, D., & Dunbar, K. (1988). Dual space search during scientific reasoning. *Cognitive Science, 12*, 1-48.

Langley, P., Simon, H.A., Bradshaw, G.L., & Zytkow, J.M. (1987). *Scientific Discovery.* Cambridge, MA: MIT Press.

Laurent, J. F., Richter, F., & Michel, A. (1999). Management of victims of urban chemical attacks: the French approach. *Resuscitation, 42*, 141-149.

Media (2006). The new tapes reveal communication confusion. August 16, 2006.

Milby, T. H. & Baselt, R. C. (1999). Hydrogen sulfide poisoning: clarification of some controversial issues. *American Journal of Industry Medicine, 35*, 192-195.

Minsky, M. L. (1975). A Framework for Representing Knowledge. In P. H. Winston (ed.), *The Psychology of Computer Vision.* New York: McGraw-Hill.

Newell, A., & Herbert A. S. (1972). *Human problem solving.* Englewood Cliffs, NJ: Prentice Hall.

Trust for America's Health [TFAH] (2007). Ready or not? 2007. Retrieved December 12, 2007, from http://healthamericans.org/reports/bioterro07/.

U.S. Department of Transportation [DOT] (1998). *Hazardous materials shipments.* Washington, DC: U.S. Department of Transportation. Retrieved May 15, 2003, from http://hazmat.dot.gov/pubs/hms/hmship.pdf.

U.S. Department of Transportation [DOT] (1999). *Biennial report on hazardous materials transportation, calendar years 1996–1997.* Washington, DC: U.S. Department of Transportation. Retrieved May 15, 2003, from http://hazmat.dot.gov/pubs/biennial/96_97biennial.rpt.pdf.

Way, J. L. (1984). Cyanide intoxication and its mechanism of antagonism. *Annual Review of Pharmacology Toxicology, 24,* 451-481.

Chapter IX

A Hospital Emergency Support System for Real Time Surveillance Modeling and Effective Response

INTRODUCTION

Before 2001, public health departments, including hospitals, rarely played a role in disaster planning, though they functioned in critical roles for victim treatment and recovery. Their roles in disaster response usually initiated after a disaster event had occurred. But the potential for chemical or biological terrorism has pushed them to become frontline responders, as well as critical and central players in most state and local emergency planning teams. According to U.S. General Accounting Office [GAO] (2003), increasing expectations demand that public health agencies at all levels in the United States develop their capacities to respond to incidents of terrorism and other disasters (Bashir et al., 2003). For healthcare facilities, hospital emergency response plans rely on their emergency departments' response. That is, the emergency department must determine the magnitude of the event and initiate the appropriate institutional response, including decisions to declare an institutional disaster or institutional lock-down and determinations of whether victim decontamination is needed. From this point of view, the extent of the response depends on the capability of each emergency department. At present, however, even without a terrorism incident, emergency departments are crowded, and patients might wait up to a full day to receive treatment (Brownstein, 2007; U.S. National Center for Injury Prevention and Control [NCIPC], 2007). According to a Harvard Medical School survey, the number of ER visits rose from 93.4 million in 1994 to 110.2 million in 2004. A patient has a one in four chance of waiting for more than 50 minutes because of overcrowding in the emergency department, and wait times appear likely to keep increasing (Reuters, 2008). This widespread problem logically will negatively influence their ability to respond to high-consequence chemical, biological, radiological, or nuclear (CBRN) attacks or natural disasters. Should a huge influx of patients arrive due to an unexpected disaster event, the current crowding situation of most emergency departments implies that real emergencies may be lost in the shuffle without an organized response (Conte, 2005 Morse, 2002).

Because a variety of challenges, such as organizational, logistical, and patient-care related issues, arises when dealing with an unexpected disaster event, units other than the emergency department within a healthcare facility or hospital may also need to engage in response processes. One of the most important challenges is determining how to increase facilities' ability to generate and organize a response rapidly (NCIPC, 2007). Effective preparedness and response demand an established functional leadership structure with clear organizational responsibilities, which knows what actions need to be implemented and how to handle clinical management during a disaster. Should an incident occur, those exposed or injured rapidly seek care and may not do so at the facilities designed by existing response plans. Thus, every healthcare facility must be able to organize a response quickly; speed is critical to save lives. The best means to employ existing health care capacities and generate a "dual-use" response infrastructure therefore becomes an urgent issue, because many of the capabilities required for responding to a large-scale chemical or biological attack are also required for responses to naturally occurring disease outbreaks. Furthermore, in a fast-paced disaster such as an explosion, there is little time for meetings or discussion about the appropriate use of different support functions and personnel.

In this chapter, we present a framework for a hospital emergency support system that helps hospital managers generate a dual-use response infrastructure based on existing hospital facilities. Ideally, healthcare routine functions and hospital emergency response functions work together as an integrated system that exploits existing resources effectively and efficiently. We consider two situations. In the first, healthcare professionals detect an event, such as influenza pandemic, that triggers an emergent response. In the second, a passive reaction creates a sudden surge of calls for an immediate response. For example, if an incident such as a bombing occurs, hospitals near the scene may expect to receive a large influx (or surge) of victims. In the 2004 Madrid bombings, for instance, the hospital closest to the scene received 272 patients in less than three hours. For the former situation, we consider how hospital routine care functions might be integrated to provide health surveillance for early disease detection. For the latter, we explore how overcrowding might be reduced through effective organization. In either situation, the proposed framework offers step-by-step assistance to hospital administrators, which may help bring some order to the chaos, improve response times, and save lives.

To provide early detection of events such as influenza, real-time data collection is critical. For example, to monitor influenza-related activity in the United States, a health surveillance system requires each participant to submit the number of consultations with patients complaining of influenza-like illness (ILI) symptoms, categorized by age group and total number of consultations. These data then help determine if there exists any unusual pattern that might suggest a possible disease outbreak. As we discussed in Chapter VI, such patient data analysis usually starts one week after the data are received, which means that detections of unusual patterns refer to the previous week, and there is a seven-day delay period. Such a data collection and analysis approach creates no real concerns when time is not critical, but for a disease response, particularly for infectious diseases, time is crucial, because many people may become infected during the delay period. Therefore, public health officials require a real-time data analysis that uses concurrent rather than previous data. In our proposed framework, we introduce a Web-based module for data collection and real-time analysis.

This chapter is organized as follows: We first review some existing clinical support systems, then discuss how hospital routine care functions might be captured using a patient care system. Next, we discuss how a real-time data analysis could be conducted to suggest an early alert of a potential disease outbreak. A proposed hospital emergency support system shows how clinical management issues involved in emergency response can be handled. We conclude with a discussion and future implications.

BRIEF LITERATURE REVIEW

The development of computer-based clinical decision support systems started in the early 1970s. Since then, such applications have appeared in various healthcare efforts, especially related to disease diagnostics (Perreault et al. 1999). For example, De Dombal's 1972 system was designed to support the diagnosis of acute abdominal pain and the need for surgery; in 1974, the rule-based INTERNIST-I system attempted to diagnose complex problems in general internal medicine; and 1976's MYCIN, another rule-based system, provided help in diagnosing and recommending treatments for certain blood infections. Most current clinical systems provide decision support for some particular diagnostic or therapeutic tasks, such as interpreting pulmonary function tests, analyzing electrocardiograms, or managing the use of anti-infective agents. However, they rarely apply as a form of emergency decision support for responding to CBRN incidents, those that involve the release of biological, chemical, radiological or nuclear materials (Coiera, 2003; Gaynor et al., 2005; Michalowski et al., 2003).

In a disaster response situation, tracking patient movement is a critical function for any mass casualty. A successful computer system must be able to track patients from the disaster scene to the hospital and across the facility network, including transfers to other facilities. However, current systems involving emergency services, hospitals, and health departments lack this ability because each party uses separate data management systems that are not compatible (NCIPC, 2007). To overcome this barrier, we present a Web-based patient care system that can be shared by the various parties in a disaster response. Its functions continue tracking each patient's situation and treatment, identify their supply consumption, and monitor bed use. Furthermore, the system incorporates real-time patient data analyses to enable dynamic decision support.

HOSPITAL DAILY ROUTINE CARE

A typical health care center/hospital consists of a group of medical doctors and nurses, receptionists, pharmacists, lab technicians, and radiologists. When patients arrive to see doctors, they usually check in with the receptionist, who registers new patients. Nurses then prescreen the patients prior to the doctor's examination. The nurse likely conducts some basic diagnoses, such as checking patients' temperature, blood pressure, heart rate, height, and weight. The physician then examines patients and may refer them to a radiologist for X-rays or to the laboratory for additional tests. At the end of the encounter, the physician may prescribe some medication or suggest further treatments. Patients then return to the receptionist to schedule follow-up appointments if necessary and pay for the visit.

Such daily routine care functions, as performed in any health care facility, can be described or captured by a patient care system (PCS), as shown in Figure 9.1. The proposed PCS entails a Web-based digital health records system with two primary roles. First, on the hospital or clinic side, the system enables the automation of the clinical workflow process, captures medical data in a standard format, and makes data collection, comparison, and use across different health care units quick and efficient. The type of information stored in the system includes patients' medical ailments, the list of drugs taken, and tests prescribed. Second, on the patient side, the PCS gives patients more control over their personal healthcare, particularly when they change health insurers or doctors. Patients can view the details of visits for different health problems in a report format, including the date of each clinic visit, the doctor's diagnosis, the name of the examining doctor, a list of tests prescribed, test results, drug history, personal

Figure 9.1. Proposed patient care system: Interface

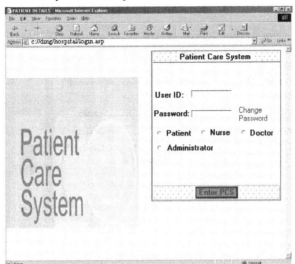

information (e.g., name, age, gender, health insurer, insurance plan), and payment account information. Thus, an online PCS ensures the availability of the right information at the right place at the right time, which is particularly important during an emergency.

The PCS also contains the following components:

Authentication. Patients and staff working in a health care facility, such as receptionists, nurses, and physicians, are users who have access to the system. Each user owns a unique user ID and a password for access to the system. The authentication system provides access to data on the basis of each user's access level. For example, a receptionist would not be able to access a patient's diagnostic record except when registering a patient. A nurse would not be able to prescribe drugs or tests for a patient. Every time a user accesses the system, his or her navigation path across different components of the system gets recorded to avoid any unauthorized activities.

User registration. All new patients must be registered in the system and assigned a unique identification number, referred to as a medical record number (MR number). During the registration process, the patient's demographic, contact, and health insurance information gets collected (see Figure 9.2a). After check-in, a nurse likely conducts some basic examination of the patient, such as checking blood pressure, temperature, weight, height, and so on. This information then gets entered into the system, as shown in Figure 9.2b.

Encounter function. An encounter refers to a patient's one-to-one interaction with a doctor, defined as the first time the patient meets the doctor. Therefore, after a patient visits a doctor for the first time and receives an encounter number, each subsequent time the patient visits the same doctor, even with a different ailment, the same number applies. If a patient sees another doctor, a new encounter number tracks that appointment. The system therefore helps keep track of encounters, which can assist physicians in gaining an insight into the patient's previous ailments and responses to treatments. Patients also know

Figure 9.2(a). Nurse window: Register new patient

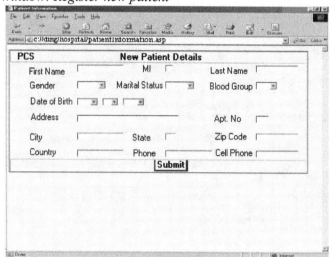

how many doctors they have met, because each has a different encounter number. In addition, a patient may visit the same doctor for different ailments, and each ailment may need more than one visit. Thus, each encounter can have many complaints/ailments, and each ailment may require many visits in the system. Each separate ailment/complaint of a patient receives a unique complaint ID. Patients visiting for different ailments get assigned different complaint IDs.

Visit tracking function. This function keeps track of patient visits for a particular encounter. As mentioned in the previous section, each time a patient visits a doctor, the system notes an encounter and a visit.

Figure 9.2(b). Nurse window: Patient visit details screen

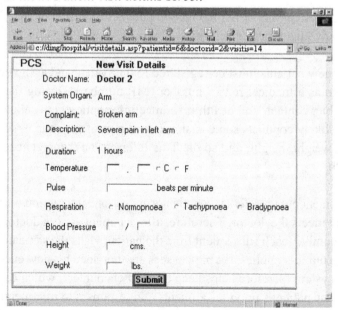

Treatment tracking function. This function monitors all treatments of a patient for all encounters. Treatment information includes medication prescriptions from each visit, medical tests conducted or prescribed, and diagnostic records from each visit. When different parties, such as EMS staff, firefighters, and hospital physicians, use the system during an emergency situation, this function is especially useful. A doctor can use the system to record diagnosis details (Figure 9.3a), prescribe medications if necessary (Figure 9.3b), and issue some tests (Figure 9.3c). Prescription reminders also might be sent to patients if they fail to undertake a prescribed test.

Report. Patients and doctors can view different reports about patients' medical and examination history. For example, by checking the encounter list, a patient can view the diagnosis reports issued by each doctor (see Figure 9.4a).

Figure 9.4b shows a summary report of a patient's last visit information when the patient chooses encounter number 19 with Doctor 2.

Figure 9.3(a). Doctor window: Diagnosis details screen

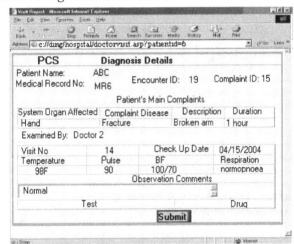

Figure 9.3(b). Doctor window: Drug prescription screen

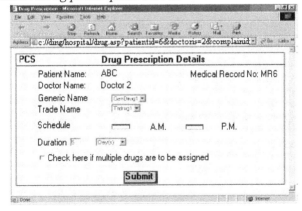

Figure 9.3(c). Doctor window: Test prescription screen

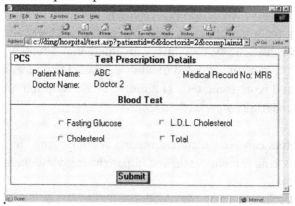

Figure 9.4(a). Patient window: Medical history tracking

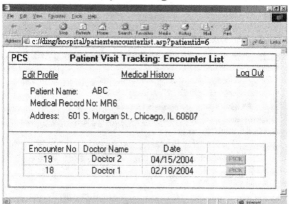

Figure 9.4(b). Patient Window: Patient Record Information

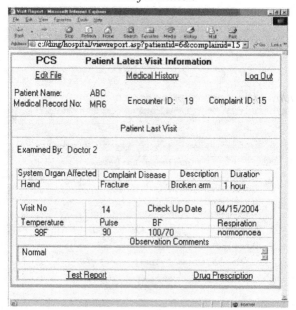

If the patient wants to see a test result during that visit, he or she can click the "Test Report" link, which produces the clinical laboratory report window screen, as in Figure 9.4c. The report lists the type of tests undertaken by the patient, the date it was conducted, who prescribed that test, the test results, and comments about each result.

EMERGENCY DEPARTMENT: DAILY ROUTINE OPERATION

If a patient is brought to the emergency department, the clinical working procedure follows a similar process pattern but includes one additional step, namely, checking the patient's condition. A direct visit to the ER may indicate an urgent situation, so during check-in, the patient's sickness condition must be determined and an ER doctor called upon immediately if the patient is in serious or critical condition. Figure 9.5 displays the ER workflow in a hypothetical case in which a person has been shot. The clinical process flow starts at label ①.

Emergency departments usually are subdivided into separate areas to serve patients better, such as pediatric, chest pain, fast track for monitoring injuries and illnesses, trauma centers for severely injured patients, and observation units for patients who do not require hospital admission but need prolonged treatment or many diagnostic tests. On the basis of patients' symptoms and severity, the doctor on duty performs physical examinations and medical treatment.

Figure 9.4(c). Patient window: Viewing test report

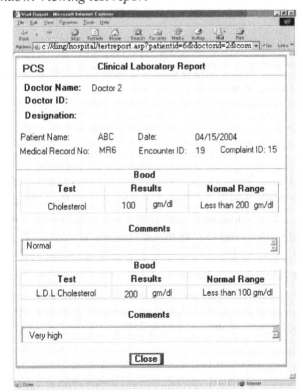

Figure 9.5. Processing flow in ER

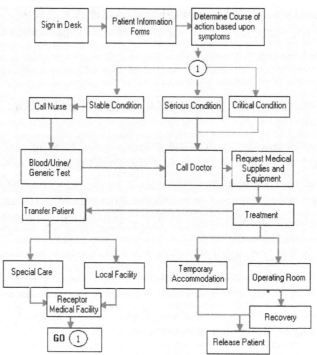

REALIZING AN EMERGENCY FOR QUICK RESPONSE

If an incident, such as a bombing, occurs, the event sign can immediately signal the type of health care necessary to treat victims. However, quickly recognizing a potential outbreak of communicable diseases, whether natural or human made, is not easy.

Because the proposed PCS keeps track of daily patient numbers and sickness symptoms, these data can depict the number of patients who complain of influenza-like illness (ILI) symptoms per day or concurrently. A real-time percentage of visits for ILI or acute respiratory illnesses can be displayed graphically along time zones. For instance, developed from records from a community hospital in the Midwestern United States, Figure 9.6 shows the percentage of patients complaining of ILI-like symptoms out of total patient visits between January 1, 2008, and March 2, 2008. During January 2008, the percentage of patients with ILI-like symptoms first slightly decreased from 0.348% on January 1 to 0.316% on January 14, then gradually increased to 0.488% on January 31. Compared with the January data, the percentage of patients with ILI-like illness increased to 0.49 on February 1 and 0.61 on February 15, 2008. By comparing these percentage rates with an estimated local baseline number, any fluctuation change can be observed concurrently. The baseline number equals the mean percentage of patient visits for ILI during non-influenza days for the previous three seasons, plus two standard deviations. The U.S. Centers for Disease Control (CDC, 2008) provides weekly baselines for the 2007–08 influenza season in different regions (see Table 9.1).

Tracking daily changes in ILI-like illness percentages can reveal when unusual or surprise activity occurs, which may prompt an early alert. According to the CDC (2008), normal (i.e., no influenza activ-

Figure 9.6 Example: Trend of percentage of patient visits for ILI-like illness

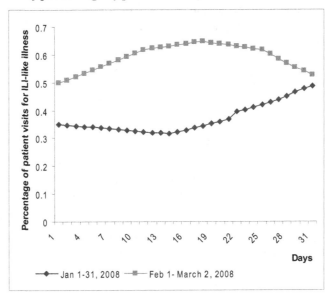

ity) occurs when the level of ILI-like illness percentages are below the local baseline. But if the illness percentage is greater than the local baseline for several days, though less than a week, can we necessarily infer that an influenza-type disease outbreak is occurring? Because the CDC uses weekly data, results published in the current week describe what had happened in the previous week, which represents a passive prediction of influenza activities. The proposed PCS instead provides real-time daily data and thus may offer, through its daily trend of illness percentages, an indicator for early warnings.

Surveillance Module

In Chapter VI, we derived a general formula (equation 6-1) to quantify the accumulated number of illnesses caused by the initial primary infectious individuals x_0. We rewrite this formula as follows:

$$X(n) = x_0 (1 + R)^n \text{ for } n = 0, 1, 2, ..., \frac{y}{\tau},$$

$$X(n + 1) = [X(n) - X(n - \frac{y}{\tau})] \times (1 + R)], \text{ when } n > \frac{y}{\tau}, \tag{6-1}$$

where n denotes the number of generations. One generation is defined as secondary infectious cases resulting from upstream parental primary cases. *R* refers to the basic reproduction number; *y* measures the average infective period an infected person exhibits, with a day as the unit; and τ is the average interval from the infection of one individual to the infection of his or her contacts, which generally ranges from 1 to 4 days (Elveback et al., 1976).

A disease spreads if $R \geq 1$; the chains of transmission die out if $R < 1$. For a pandemic influenza such as 1918 Spanish flu or the 1968–69 influenza A (H3N2) pandemic in the United States, the average value for *y* is 3–7 days or approximately 3τ (τ = 1.9 days).

Infectious diseases in their early stages follow a natural transmission pattern, because people are unaware of the occurrence and no intervention occurs. Therefore, the first component of equation (6-1) offers early discovery of a potential disease outbreak. That is, R can be solved as

$$R = \sqrt[n]{\frac{X(n)}{x_0}} - 1 \text{ for } n = 0, 1, 2, ..., \frac{y}{\tau}. \tag{9-1}$$

If $y = 6$ and $\tau = 2$ days, equation (9-1) indicates three consecutive Rs, from which we can reason the likelihood of a disease spreading. For example, when observing that the daily trend is greater than the local baseline on day t and continues for several days, we can use patient illness numbers on day t as x_0 and assume they represent the primary case. The accumulated number of illness on day $(t + 2)$, day $(t + 4)$, and day $(t + 6)$ then can be obtained from the daily data. That is, we can obtain $X(t+2)$, $X(t+4)$, and $X(t+6)$ from the real-time daily data. If the average of these Rs is less than 1, there is no disease outbreak; otherwise, health care authorities need to be alerted, and further tests need to be initiated for confirmation.

If all hospitals in a region share the PCS, daily data can capture all patients in that region, which enables users to capture the reproduction generations based on x_0, unless some victims travel to another region during the period. Therefore, equation (9-1) provides useful supplemental evidence to help identify an occurrence of a disease when the daily trend of the illness percentage is greater than the local baseline. Note that equation (9-1) can be used only in a situation in which a disease is in its early stage

Table 9.1. Weekly baselines for 2007–08 influenza season in United States

Region Areas (United States)	Baselines for Weekly Data
New England: Connecticut, Maine, Massachusetts, New Hampshire, Vermont, Rhode Island.	1.4%
Mid-Atlantic: New Jersey, New York City, Pennsylvania, Upstate New York.	3.1%
East North Central: Illinois, Indiana, Michigan, Ohio, Wisconsin.	1.9%
West North Central: Iowa, Kansas, Minnesota, Missouri, Nebraska, North Dakota, South Dakota.	1.5%
South Atlantic: Delaware, Florida, Georgia, Maryland, North Carolina, South Carolina, Virginia, Washington, D.C., West Virginia.	2.1%
East South Central: Alabama, Kentucky, Mississippi, Tennessee.	2.4%
West South Central: Arkansas, Louisiana, Oklahoma, Texas.	4.3%
Mountain: Arizona, Colorado, Idaho, Montana, Nevada, New Mexico, Utah, Wyoming.	1.6%
Pacific: Alaska, California, Hawaii, Oregon, Washington.	3.1%

Source: CDC (2008)

and no intervention has taken place. If people recognize the occurrence and control procedures, the disease transmission pattern will change, resulting in decreased illness numbers.

Differential dynamics also can analyze whether an outbreak might happen, based on daily patient numbers. Suppose that $i(t)$ denotes the number of patients in the target area at time t and that $s(t)$ is the number of susceptible individuals in a targeted area at time t. The unit of time is a day. The size of the susceptible population in a target area may change because of travelers and newborn babies; therefore, the variation rate of the susceptible population is assumed to be δ, where $\delta \geq 0$. When an infected person enters a community of susceptible individuals, he or she may convey the infection to the unaffected. Each infected person then runs through the course of his or her illness and finally is either recovered or dead. Assume the average infective rate from the affected to the unaffected by contact is a per unit of time, the average recovery rate from sickness to health is b per unit of time, and the average death rate is c per unit of time in the targeted area. Thus, we derive the following equations:

$$\frac{di(t)}{dt} = ais - (b+c)i \text{, and} \tag{9-2}$$

$$\frac{ds(t)}{dt} = -ais - \gamma i^2 s + \eta i + \delta \text{,} \tag{9-3}$$

where a, b, c, γ, and $\eta \in (0, 1)$ are constant. Furthermore, ais indicates patient increment speed because of contact infection; $(b+c)i$ reflects the changes in the number of persons who are recovered or dead; $-\gamma i^2 s$ is the decrement of the possible number of people infected when a health intervention occurs, such that parameter γ denotes the degree of health intervention, such as vaccines, antiviral medication, or isolation; and ηi denotes that more infected individuals in the targeted area means more susceptible people will being affected.

Setting the right-hand sides of equations (9-2) and (9-3) to 0 yields

$$ais - (b+c)i = 0 \text{, and} \tag{9-4}$$

$$-ais - \gamma i^2 s + \eta i + \delta = 0. \tag{9-5}$$

Solving equation (9-4) for critical points, we find that $i = 0$, or $s = \frac{(b+c)}{a}$. In this scenario, $i = 0$ indicates that nobody gets sick, so no disease occurs. Therefore, we only examine what happens to the susceptible population when s is near the critical point $\frac{(b+c)}{a}$. We find one critical point in the i–s plane:

$$(i_0, s_0) = [\frac{a(\eta - b - c) + \sqrt{a^2(\eta - b - c)^2 + 4a(b+c)\gamma\delta}}{2(b+c)\gamma}, \frac{(b+c)}{a}].$$

When s falls in the area in which $s > \dfrac{(b+c)}{a}$, the trajectories $i(t)$ increase when t increases, indicating that the number of patients increases with time. When s falls in the area in which $s < \dfrac{(b+c)}{a}$, the number of patients decreases when time t increases, indicating the disease may be treated effectively. Therefore, $s = \dfrac{(b+c)}{a}$ is a threshold value, above which, even if there are few patients, the disease can spread quickly and result in an outbreak. However, if the size of the susceptible population in the targeted area is below the threshold, even if many patients exist, the disease can be controlled.

Using daily data from the patient care system, we can calculate parameters a, b, and c using the following equations:

$$a = \frac{\text{the number of people who is diagnosed as patients per day}}{\text{the size of the susceptible population}}, \tag{9-6}$$

$$b = \frac{\text{the number of recovered per day}}{\text{the total numbebr of patients on the same day}}, \text{ and} \tag{9-7}$$

$$c = \frac{\text{the death toll per day}}{\text{the total numbebr of patients on the same day}}. \tag{9-8}$$

Equations (9-6), (9-7), and (9-8) provide daily values for a, b and c, which in turn indicate their probability distributions for estimating their average values. The average values can be used to compute threshold values to determine if the disease can become epidemic.

We can also find out the quantitative solution of the system (9-2) and (9-3).

Substituting $s = \dfrac{(b+c)}{a}$ into equation (9-5), we have

$$-ai\frac{(b+c)}{a} - \gamma i^2 \frac{(b+c)}{a} + \eta i + \delta = 0.$$

Solving for i, we get

$$i = \frac{a(\eta - b - c) \pm \sqrt{a^2(\eta - b - c)^2 + 4a(b+c)\gamma\delta}}{2(b+c)\gamma} \tag{9-9}$$

Because $i > 0$, we use the "+" sign when determining a feasible solution for i. Then, let $x = i - i_0$, and $y = s - s_0$. In turn,

$$\frac{dx}{dt} = \frac{\partial x}{\partial i} \cdot \frac{di}{dt} = \frac{\partial}{\partial i}[i - i_0] \cdot \frac{di}{dt}$$
$$= ais - (b+c)i,$$

and

$$\frac{dy}{dt} = \frac{\partial y}{\partial s} \cdot \frac{ds}{dt} = \frac{\partial}{\partial s}[s - s_0] \cdot \frac{ds}{dt}$$
$$= -ais - \gamma\, i^2 s + \eta i + \delta$$

Substituting $s = y + s_0$, $i = x + i_0$, and $s_0 = \dfrac{(b+c)}{a}$ into the above equations, we get

$$\frac{dx}{dt} = a(x + i_0)(y + s_0) - (b + c)(x + i_0) \qquad (9\text{-}10)$$
$$= ai_0 y + axy,$$

and

$$\frac{dy}{dt} = -a(x + i_0)(y + s_0) - (y + s_0)\gamma\,(x + i_0)^2 + \eta(x + i_0) + \delta$$
$$= (-as_0 - 2\gamma\, i_0 s_0 + \eta)x - (ai_0 + \gamma\, i_0^2)y - (a + 2\gamma\, i_0)xy - \gamma\, s_0 x^2 - \gamma\, x^2 y. \qquad (9\text{-}11)$$

Notice that equations (9-10) and (9-11) are nonlinear, the approximate linear system for equations (9-10) and (9-11) can then be written as

$$\frac{dx}{dt} = ai_0 y, \text{ and} \qquad (9\text{-}12)$$

$$\frac{dy}{dt} = (-as_0 - 2\gamma\, i_0 s_0 + \eta)x - (ai_0 + \gamma\, i_0^2)y. \qquad (9\text{-}13)$$

The eigenfunction for equations (9-12) and (9-13) is

$$\begin{bmatrix} \dfrac{dx}{dt} \\ \dfrac{dy}{dt} \end{bmatrix} - \begin{bmatrix} \lambda & 0 \\ 0 & \lambda \end{bmatrix} \cdot \begin{bmatrix} x \\ y \end{bmatrix} = 0.$$

That is,

$$\begin{bmatrix} 0 - \lambda & ai_0 \\ (-as_0 - 2\gamma\, i_0 s_0 + \eta) & -(ai_0 + \gamma\, i_0^2) - \lambda \end{bmatrix} \cdot \begin{bmatrix} x \\ y \end{bmatrix} = 0.$$

Rewritting it yields

$$\lambda^2 + (ai_0 + \gamma i_0^2)\lambda - ai_0\,(\eta - as_0 - 2\gamma i_0 s_0) = 0. \qquad (9\text{-}14)$$

Solving for equation (9-11), we have

$$\lambda_{1,2} = \frac{1}{2}[-(ai_0 + \gamma\, i_0^2) \pm \sqrt{(ai_0 + \gamma\, i_0^2)^2 + 4ai_0(\eta - as_0 - 2\gamma\, i_0 s_0)}\,].$$

(9-15)

The general solution to the linear approximated system of the original equations (9-2) and (9-3) is

$$\begin{bmatrix} i(t) \\ s(t) \end{bmatrix} = \begin{bmatrix} m_1 \\ m_2 \end{bmatrix} e^{\lambda_1 t} + \begin{bmatrix} n_1 \\ n_2 \end{bmatrix} e^{\lambda_2 t} + \begin{bmatrix} i_0 \\ s_0 \end{bmatrix},$$

(9-16)

where m_1, m_2, n_1, n_2 are constants.

This solution shows the variant in the number of patients and susceptible individuals over time in the target area.

HOSPITAL EMERGENCY SUPPORT SYSTEM

Should an incident occur, such that a hospital is in an emergency response situation, hospital administrators may face many critical issues simultaneously. Because leadership is a key element of an effective response and there is little time for meetings or discussion about appropriate steps or how to use existing functions and personnel, we present a hospital emergency support system (HESS) to assist administrators in generating step-by-step actions focused on critical areas. The procedure for HESS is depicted in Figure 9.7. Triggers of HESS might include the identification of a potential disease outbreak or the occurrence of CBRN incidents. The system user is the hospital manager, who likely assumes responsibility as the institutional commander and must make decisions and organize responses during a hospital emergency.

Current planning and preparation activities assume that care providers who function prior to hospital entry will be dispatched in a coordinated fashion, arrive on the scene to triage patients, and transport them to appropriate facilities, thereby preventing any component of the response system from being overwhelmed. In many disasters, however, victims may arrive at hospitals by means other than EMS, bypassing all triage and decontamination measures at the scene (Auf der Heide, 2006). This arrival situation has clear implications for hospitals in terms of the organization of mass victims, as well as exposure of the hospital and its staff to potential contamination. In the absence of EMS transport, patients likely go to the nearest hospital, which may rapidly become overwhelmed. Thus, hospitals need to implement a safety procedure to decontaminate patients before they may enter the building to avoid the potential contamination of health care facilities, exposure of staff, and serious compromise to the response. For example, in the Tokyo Sarin incident, patients were not decontaminated prior to hospital entry, which resulted in 13 of 15 doctors working in the Keio University Hospital Emergency Department simultaneously developing symptoms, of whom 6 required atropine and 1 received pralidoxime (Okumera et al., 1998).

The type of incident determines the strategies for handling the incoming patient flows. The procedure used to handle a disease outbreak (whether biological incident or naturally occurring outbreak) differs from that for a chemical incident. For the former, isolation may be needed, whereas the latter likely requires a decontamination procedure before medical treatment. Therefore, the proposed HESS asks whether the emergency is caused by an infectious disease. If an incident involves a biological agent or natural disease outbreak, patient process module I gets implemented, together with the model that checks on "isolation capacity" and "special care facilities." For an incident other than a disease outbreak, patient process module II gets implemented as actions begin to prepare a "decontamination area." Regardless of the type of incidents, the system executes some checking modules simultaneously, which we describe in detail next.

Patient process module I: Anyone arriving at the hospital must pass through a screening room to determine if isolation is needed.

Check hospital isolation capacity: The model determines if isolation rooms are ready. To be prepared, these isolation rooms must include negative pressure areas to manage airborne diseases, air-filtered quarantine areas, and general "decontamination" areas with showers and floor drains connected to a sanitary sewage system adjacent to the hospital's emergency entrance.

Figure 9.7. Hospital emergency support system framework

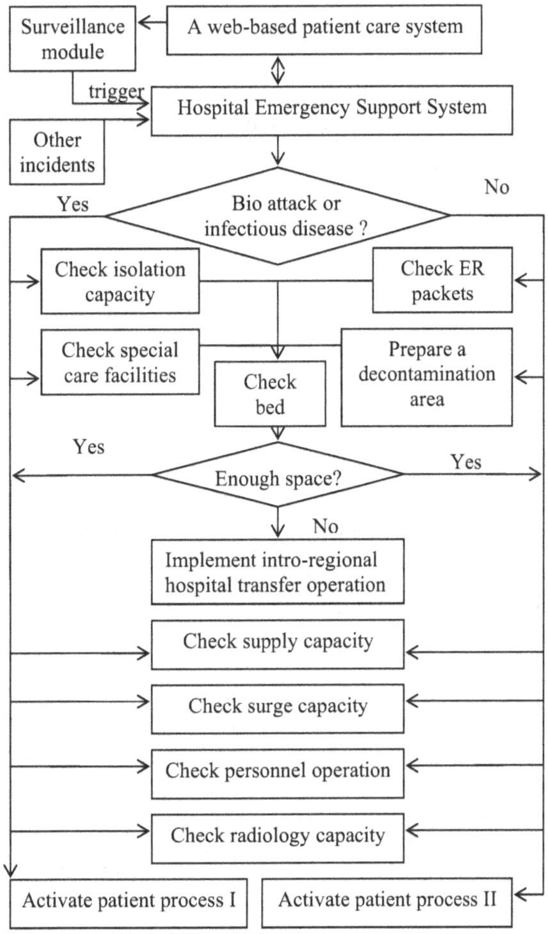

Figure 9.8. Patient process module I: Flow chart

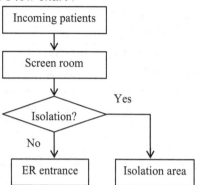

Patient process module II: All incoming patients enter the decontamination area; those patients already decontaminated by EMS and who have no skin or eye irritation can be transferred immediately to the ER or critical care area. Patients who need further medical assessment or treatment enter the ER, where they are registered by the patient care system (PCS). Patients who are not in need of medical attention in the short term should be directed to a separate holding area that should be well lit, shielded from the weather, distant from the ER entrance to reduce congestion, and upwind or protected from the decontamination facility.

Patient Care System: All patients get registered in the PCS to ensure unified data management. The facility helps document patients' information in one place and keeps track of all patients. The collated information also can be used to determine the number of medical supplies needed, such as beds or special medications. Furthermore, EMS can use the system to determine how to dispatch patients to avoid unnecessary overcrowding for some hospitals.

Check ER packets: This module determines if packets for patients are ready. After patients are directed to the ER entrance, each patient receives a packet with disaster bands, manual charting forms, and manual lab or radiology order forms.

Check special care facilities: Special care facilities include filtration, ventilators, and personal protective equipment (e.g., N-95 or other tight-fitting masks). For example, if many patients with severe respiratory problems associated with anthrax or botulism were to arrive at a hospital, a comparable number of ventilators would be required to treat them. If ventilators were unavailable to treat all patients in need, at least skilled personnel could know that they would need to use endotracheal tubes to ventilate patients manually.

Check radiology capacity: This module verifies the availability of necessary radiology equipment and radiologists and ensures adequate portable equipment is available. Operational radiology support for the initial treatments and ongoing care should be maintained for up to 72 hours after an incident. When disaster patients arrive, a radiology ultrasound technician should be available in the ER to enable an immediate exam. When an incident involves an explosion, some necessary imaging equipment, such as computed tomography (CT), magnetic resonance imaging (MRI), ultrasound, and digital imaging, also should be ready.

Check surgical capacity: This module checks the availability of mobilized or fixed operating rooms and related equipment for life- and limb-saving surgical care. At least one or more surgeons, anesthesiologists, and critical care specialists should be in the hospital or available immediately after an incident. If surgical capacity is insufficient, the module also checks alternate offsite surgical capacity, such as the Red Cross, local schools, churches, armories, and so forth, to incorporate these facilities outside of the hospital and increase surgical capacity. The module then displays these options to hospital administrators.

Check beds and ER room capacity: This module gets implemented to evacuate all but the sickest patients from the ER to other wards and thereby clear the ER for attack victims. If space still is not sufficient, it creates additional capacity in non-intensive care rooms concentrated in specific wards or floors. To free more beds, hospitals should cancel elective surgeries and admissions, open traditionally non-patient hospital areas for patient care, and begin early discharges for inpatients as appropriate. If still not enough space is available, the system suggests implementing intra-region hospital operations.

Intro-regional hospital operation: This module checks for possibility of rural to urban and urban to rural patient flow, possible transportation routes, and their availability and geographic limitations. It also maintains active contact with facilities and organizations outside of the hospital that might accept temporary patient overflows. The receptor medical facility that receives patients also confronts issues, such as how to triage the large number of incoming patients, whether to seek assistance from other departments, and when to alert other departments or request additional resources.

Check supply operation: The model determines the hospital inventory of pharmaceutical supplies, such as antibiotics, antidotes, and vaccines in dosages. This check also includes the blood supply, because large amounts of blood would be needed if many victims were seriously injured. In the event of a disaster, the American Association of Blood Banks (AABB) International Task Force will inform the public if blood donations are needed and tell them when and where to donate.

Check personnel operation: The system's database contains hospital personnel's specialized areas, such as emergency medicine, trauma surgery, burn surgery, pediatrics, otolaryngology, intensive care medicine, radiology, and laboratory medicine. When a large-scale incident occurs, demand for critical care services provided by existing critical care practitioners increases. To increase capabilities, a two-tiered model should be implemented.

The two-tiered staffing model pairs non-critical care physicians and nurses with critical care counterparts. Research reveals that a critical care physician can supervise up to four non-critical care physicians, who can each manage up to six critically ill patients. This research also indicates that a critical care nurse can supervise up to three non-critical care nurses, each of whom can care for up to two patients (Rubinson et al., 2005). According to this model, a hospital's critical care staff can be multiplied, such that one critical care physician can oversee the care of up to 24 critically ill patients, and one critical care nurse can oversee the care of up to 6 critically ill patients.

Check volunteers: The module can identify volunteers and additional specialties, display their contact information and type, and generate the number and type of clinical volunteers needed.

Check morgue capacity: This module gets activated when the situation involves highly contagious biological agents or other weapons of mass destruction. It checks hospital or regional capabilities for the disposition of human remains. Proper records are marked in the PCS.

A CBRN attack also can create a significant psychosocial effect on the public, causing people with little or no evidence of clinical illness to worry that they may have been exposed and go to hospitals for screening. Furthermore, hospital staff may fear for their personal safety or that of their family. Therefore, in addition to organizing response actions in an orderly and timely manner, hospital administrators will need to address mental health issues that may affect their staff, manage appropriate communications with the public, and work with and respond to the media.

The use of an appropriate computer support system does not guarantee a successful response, but without one, failure is almost certain (NCIPC, 2007).

DISCUSSION AND CONCLUSIONS

Current approaches to preparing for responses to terrorist attacks at health care facilities attempt to educate health care providers proactively about the clinical management of casualties caused by explosives, biological, chemical, radiological and nuclear (ECBRN) incidents. Such education is expensive. Even if health care providers initially receive training to care for these ECBRN-related injuries, unless such incidents become a more frequent and unfortunate reality, the education must be repeated regularly to ensure current knowledge and clinical competency. Moreover, every hospital has some capability, but the clinical and administrative capabilities of each vary widely. Within each hospital, the leadership and managerial capabilities represent key elements in an effective response. Should an incident occur, hospital administrators must consider many issues simultaneously, such as medical responses (e.g., clearing beds to accommodate incoming victims, determining alternative care sites), ensuring control of hospital grounds such as facility security and traffic, personnel issues to establish constant coverage (e.g., balancing between the individual needs of staff and the organization as a whole to ensure adequate coverage for short- and long-term medical responses), coordinating logistics and supplies to ensure sufficient medical supplies, and so on. Because there is little time to engage in meetings and discussion about which response actions are most appropriate and to assist hospital administrators in quickly organizing a response in a timely and orderly manner, in this chapter, we present a hospital emergency support system (HESS) that uses hospital routine daily care functions to form an integrated system that recommends the best use of existing resources in responses.

Because effective emergency responses also require coordination between on-scene EMS services and available community resources, to prevent overloading specific facilities, we also introduce a Web-based patient care system (PCS). When it encounters an emergency, both EMS and local hospitals can share the PCS to keep track of patients' movements and avoid overload situations.

In addition, the PCS provides real-time patient data for surveillance analysis. The surveillance model we present uses daily data for early disease detection. Thus, the proposed integrated framework might greatly improve the capacity of local public health agencies to respond to all hazards.

Web-Based Systems, Security, and Privacy

A Web-based PCS is not new, but the idea has been slow to catch on because there have been few incentives for health care facilities and doctors to automate health records or patients to put all their personal information together in one place.

Security and privacy are crucial features of systems that maintain critical patient information. Providing an authentication screen for every person who tries to access the systems can help ensure security. As mentioned previously, the PCS encompasses three key users, namely, physicians, nurses, and patients. Physicians must not only complete a log-in procedure but also submit to verification that they are still employees of the hospital and a privilege access, such that physicians may view or access only the records of patients who are undergoing or have undergone treatment with them.

The user level for nurses enables them to enter patients into the system, in addition to performing administrative tasks. Similar to the physician authentication process, the PCS provides a verification to check if the nurse who wants to access the system is a current hospital employee. Finally, only registered patients can access the system to view their own personal health records.

The system also can support the use of volunteers to help with patient registration during a disaster emergency. Volunteers must be verified according to specific credentials before using the system. Furthermore, patients who arrive through EMS service would be entered into the system by EMS staff members.

Hospital Security

In our assessment of using the proposed system, we assume that the hospital itself is safe. However, what if the hospital is attacked in a bombing incident? Who will deliver emergency services to victims? The hospital must have certain safeguards to protect itself when responding to any such incident.

The Use of Mobile Devices in Emergency Room

With the development of information technology, the advance environment in which critical care retrieval teams and ambulance crews function is becoming increasingly sophisticated, with electronic medical devices in close proximity to high-powered radios, global positioning satellite (GPS) tracking systems, radio telemetry, and mobile phone technology. However, in emergency departments of hospitals, concerns about possible electromagnetic interference with medical electronics by active mobile phones and the consequent safety of patients who depend on these electronic equipments prevents such uses. After testing more than 220 electronic medical devices in a hospital environment, researchers discovered a safe operating distance between electronic medical devices and potable digital devices, such as phones, namely, more than 1 meter (Fung et al., 2002; Irnich & Tobisch, 1999). This finding may enable the use of low-powered portable hospital emergency support systems, clinical information systems, and some other monitoring devices in emergency departments. Because the extent of electromagnetic interference created depends on the type of mobile devices used, an appropriate collaboration between manufacturers of electronic medical equipment and those of digital phones, as well as systematical biomedical testing, may be required.

REFERENCES

Auf der Heide, E. (2006). The importance of evidence-based disaster planning. *Annals of Emergency Medicine, 47*(1), 34-49.

Bashir, Z., Lafronza, V., Fraser, M. R., et al. (2003). Local and state collaboration for effective preparedness planning. *Journal of Public Health Management Practice, 9*(5), 344-351.

Brownstein, J. (2007). ER wait time problems widespread. ABC News Medical Unit. June 28, 2007.

Coiera, E. (2003). *The Guide to Health Informatics* (2nd Edition). Arnold: London.

Conte, C. (2005). Are we ready yet? *Outlook*, October, A2-A6.

Elveback, L. R. & et al. (1976). An influenza simulation model for immunization studies. *American Journal of Epidemiology, 103*, 152-165.

Fung, H. T., Kam, C. W., & Yau, H. H. (2002). A follow up study of electromagnetic interference of cellular phones on electronic media equipment in the emergency department. *Emergency Medicine, 14*, 315-319.

Gaynor, M., Seltzer, M., Moulton, S., & Freedman, J. (2005). A dynamic, data-driven, decision support system for emergency medical services. *Lecture Notes in Computer Science, 3515*, 703-711.

Irnich, W. E., & Tobisch, R. (1999). Mobile phones in hospitals. *Biomedical Instrument and Technology*, Jan/Feb, 28-34.

Michalowski, J. J., Rubin, S., Slowinski, R., & Wilk, S. (2003). Mobile clinical support system for pediatric emergencies. *Decision Support Systems, 36*, 161-176.

Morse, A. (2002). Bioterrorism preparedness for local health departments. *Journal of Community Health and Nurse, 19*(4), 203-211.

Okumera, T., Suzuki, K., Fukuda, A., & et al. (1998). The Tokyo subway Sarin attack: Disaster management. Part 2: Hospital response. *Academy of Emergency Field, 5*, 618-624.

Perreault, L., & Metzger, J. (1999) A pragmatic framework for understanding clinical decision support. *Journal of Healthcare Information Management, 13*(2), 5-21.

Reuters (2008). ER waits dangerously long in U.S.. Retrieved January 16, 2008 from http://content. healthaffairs.org/cgi/content/abstract/hlthaff.27.2.w84/

Rubinson, L., Nuzzo, J. B., Talmor, D. S., & et al. (2005). Augmentation of hospital critical care capacity after attacks or epidemics: recommendations of the working group on emergency mass critical care. *Critical Care Medicine, 33*(10), Supplements.

U.S. General Accounting Office [GAO] (2003). Hospital Preparedness. Retrieved December 18, 2007 from http://www.gao.gov/cgi-bin/getrpt?GAO-03-924.

U.S. Center of Disease Control and Prevention [CDC] (2008). Overview of influenza surveillance in the United States. Retrieved March 10, 2008, from http://www.cdc.gov/flu/weekly/fluactivity.htm.

U.S. National Center for Injury Prevention and Control [NCIPC] (2007). In a moment's notice: surge capacity for terrorist bombings. Atlanta (GA): U.S. Centers for Disease Control and Prevention.

Chapter X
Quickly Channeling Crowd Population in Emergency:
An Emergency Evacuation Command System

INTRODUCTION

Evacuation remains one of the main public protection strategies in response to a man-made or natural incident when people are at risk. In most cases when an evacuation is required, it indicates the presence of danger and urgency. By instinct, people affected act to escape from the danger; thus, two typical phenomena often occur during an evacuation: competitive behavior and herding behavior (Festinger, 1954).

If people perceive a threat and are trapped at an incident site, they try to get out as soon as possible. Usually, they look for exit signs or evacuation routes that can lead them to a safer place and proceed to the nearest one. For people near the exit or route entrance, moving toward the exit or entering the evacuation route may be the only likely escape choice. Thus, two forms of competitive behavior may exist simultaneously: the effort to pass through the exit (or enter the route) as quickly as possible, and the effort among those at risk to run toward the exits. Such behavior may cause congestion at the exits or entrance points, even to the point that people may crush one another. The India stampede event on January 26, 2005, is just such a tragedy. According to media reports (BBC, 2005; CNN, 2005), a screaming crowd fled down narrow walkways chaotically when fires broke out, causing many people to be crushed and resulting in 250 deaths.

Another well-known phenomenon in emergencies is herding behavior. When faced with uncertainty or lacking sufficient information about the situation, people tend to follow others. In an emergency situation, people trapped at the incident site may not know the location of evacuation routes or which route will lead them to a safer place. If everybody else moves toward certain directions, individuals may not undertake detailed decision making but rather just follow the others. Thus, a mass of people moving toward the exits in the same directions form. Unconsciously, the people involved create a new emergent norm that guides their behavior. Herding behavior sometimes can facilitate safe evacuations, when the people at risk form an orderly movement to avoid a stampede. However, if those in the rear push forward, injuries from falling and crushing likely will occur.

In other cases, people receive injuries because of the behaviors of the crowd during the evacuation rather than the actual cause of the emergency. Because evacuation is a form of collective behavior, reducing the occurrence of crowd stampeding, and congestion represents a major issue for those who must organize an effective evacuation. In addition, factors such as the number of available evacuation routes and the capacity of each route affect a successful evacuation. In this chapter, we present a model of evacuation that helps both evacuees and evacuation commanders achieve a quick and safe evacuation plan, should an emergency situation occur. We implement the model as a computerized emergency evacuation command system (EECS).

The EECS guidance system adopts everyday methods of direction, such as traffic signs guiding traffic flow, directional markers pointing people to the right store inside a huge mall, or descriptive signs helping patrons find a specific aisle in a grocery store. The system also takes dual roles. First, it informs all people at risk about the location of the nearby evacuation routes, the condition of each route, and where to leave safely without congestion. On the basis of this information, people in the affected area can make quick decisions to follow the least congested route and escape from the affected area safely.

Second, it helps evacuation commanders determine (1) the time required to evacuate people at risk safely; (2) the routes to use for the evacuation (inbound or outbound traffic), according to their geographic characteristics; (3) the capacity of each evacuation route, given its constraints; and (4) the number of people or rescue materials that should be assigned to each route to avoid overload and congestion. Depending on the characteristics of the incident site, the proposed model can generate an evacuation strategy that allows for safe evacuations of a big crowd in the least time and without congestion. By simulating human movement, the system also can display this information graphically, updated within very short time periods to reflect the current situation of each route.

Because evacuation may be necessary in any place—a high-rise building, a social gathering place (e.g., sport field, lecture hall, subway station, shopping mall), a city, or a region—and because the characteristics of evacuation sites determine human walking behavior, we consider three types of cases. First, an evacuation may occur in a place in which stairways are not used as evacuation routes, such that people may crowd in a non-compartment open area, with single or multiple routes leading away from the affected site. Second, an evacuation may happen underground, such as in a subway station. In this case, people must go up to the ground level using stairways. Third, an evacuation could happen in a high-rise building, for which stairways are the primary evacuation routes. We model human moving behavior and discuss how to generate a strategy that can quickly channel the crowd safely during an emergency in each case.

In the remainder of this chapter, we briefly review existing research on evacuation, and discuss some of its important factors. We next discuss evacuations in three cases: non–high-rise site, one-story building, and high-rise site. In each case, we consider the geographic characteristics of the evacuation site and model people's moving behavior using models that calculate the minimum time required for safe and complete evacuation. To help evacuation commanders organize a quick and successful evacuation during an emergency, we present our computerized emergency evacuation command system (EECS), which indicates the evacuation routes from the affected area, displays alternative routes, and manages congested rotes. To verify the proposed evacuating method, we conduct a simulation in which we compare EECS with two benchmark cases:, random self-evacuation and herding behavior.

The results demonstrate that the proposed methods can rescue people at risk in a much shorter time and without congestion.

BRIEF LITERATURE REVIEW ON EVACUATION

Research on evacuation consists roughly of two major groups with distinct objectives, namely, disaster management and safety engineering. In the disaster management area, most evacuation research focuses on exploring why some people take actions to evacuate but others do not when an evacuation is declared. These studies investigate the characteristics of those who evacuate and those who do not to understand how people make evacuation decisions (Baker, 1979, 1991; Cross, 1979; Drabek, 1999; Fischer et al., 1995; Regnier, 2008).

Safety engineering literature, in contrast, centers on egress designs and walking infrastructures in places of public assembly. Using controlled experiments, researchers in this group investigate human walking behavior in general environment (e.g., commercial areas, shopping areas, sport stadiums, high-rise buildings) to determine the relationship between density and velocity and thereby support the design of better walking infrastructures (Daeemen & Hoogendoorn, 2003; Fruin, 1971; Fujiyama & Tyler, 2004; Hankin & Wright, 1958; Lam et al., 1979; Lam & Cheung, 2000; Navin & Wheeler, 1969; O'Flaherty & Parkinson; Pushkarev & Zupan, 1975). Within this research stream, a variety of computer simulation systems help clarify occupant behavior, determine the location and appropriate number of elevators or stairs in a specific building, and facilitate building code design (Averill et al., 2005; Klote et al., 1992; Kuligowski, 2003; Musse et al., 1998; Proulx, 2001).

When examining building evacuations, most simulation models describe each room or exit-door as a node. Thus, a building is represented as a connected network, in which a link between two nodes indicates a path that connects two rooms. Evacuation in turn is modeled as how people find the shortest path that connects their current node to the safe node. They start from their current location (node) and search for a shortest path; when they find a path that they believe to be the shortest, they proceed to that path and follow it to the exit, unless it becomes blocked by the incident (e.g., fire), in which case they move out of the path and find a location that enables them to repeat the same procedure. This approach can have a local optimal solution but not a global one, because people are not finding the truly shortest path out of the building. This approach also wastes time, because people must figure out the relatively shortest path from their current location node and make sure that path is not blocked in advance. Because an effective response requires getting people out of the building as soon as possible, people inside may not have enough time to search for the shortest path from their present location.

Therefore, in this chapter we investigate how to help evacuation commanders organize a quick and safe evacuation based on geographic information about the evacuation routes. Because uncertainty and urgency cause anxiety, which may affect people's behavior, our modeling efforts provide concurrent information to evacuees during an emergency and guide them to a safer place in the least time and without congestion.

GENERAL CONSIDERATIONS

In this context, we define an evacuation route as an exit path that can lead to a safe place, away from the affected area. When an emergency evacuation is in place, time is critical, especially in a building evacuation, because the building may collapse. Two factors may affect the time required for an effective evacuation: the characteristics of the affected area, and the number of evacuees and their walking speed.

Characteristics of the Affected Area

Numerous incident reports (e.g., 2003 nightclub incident in Chicago, 2003 Rhode Island nightclub fire) suggest that the characteristics of the affected area influence the outcome of an evacuation. These characteristics may include the number of available evacuation routes, their capacities (i.e., possibly overcrowded), the condition of entry points to each route (i.e., possibly a narrow or small entrance), the atmosphere of the situation (e.g., if people are upset or scared), and so on.

Evacuation commanders may be uncertain about the characteristics of an affected site, which prevents them from taking these elements into account and planning accordingly.

Walking Speed

When people walk, their bodies require space for movement, and the required walkway width theoretically depends on walking speed. People also need more space in a longitudinal direction when their walking speed increases. Empirical studies (Weidmann, 1993) show that the relationship between the space used and speed is given by the following:

$$DimSpace(V) = DimSpace_{Jam} - 0.52D\ln(1 - \frac{V}{V_f}),$$

(10-1)

where V is the walking speed, V_f is the average free walking speed in a normal situation, and $V_f \approx 1.34$ meter/per second. In addition, $DimSpace (V)$ denotes the space required for body movement with walking speed V. Usually, $DimSpace$ equals the longitudinal spatial use a multiplied by the lateral spatial use b. $DimArea_{Jam}$ is the smallest area space in which walking is impossible, such that $DimSpace_{Jam} \approx$ 0.19 $meter^2$. Finally, D is the density of a stream of people.

While walking, people intuitively use subconscious processes to scan the infrastructure or obstructions in their path (Goffman, 1971). Thus, people expect others to be cooperative rather than obstructive in their walking. In an emergency situation however, this cooperative behavior may be disrupted, because the mental pressure to increase speed rises as people try to get out as soon as possible. People increase their velocity at the beginning of the emergency, because they hope to move out as fast as possible, which then increases density and perhaps restricts people in their freedom of movement. With increasing velocity, more and more people become jammed, due to the limited available moving space, such that bodily contact with others likely cannot be avoided. With growing density, the desired velocity declines rapidly and may even decrease close to zero, as when congestion occurs. When the density continues to increases after this point, the situation might become very dangerous, because people may fall over by pushing against one another.

In addition, research into pedestrian movement finds that flows of pedestrians walking in the same direction tend to form streams or lanes with uniform movement directions (Isobe et al., 2004; Older, 1968; Toshiyuki, 1993; Yamori, 2001). That is, when moving to the same direction, each person follows the person in front of him or her to avoid a collision. We use these empirical findings about people's movement to calculate the maximum capacity of each evacuation route without creating congestion.

EVACUATION FROM A NON–HIGH-RISE SITE

A non–high-rise site refers to an area such as a mall, sports field, lecture hall, or city. Assume an emergency evacuation is required, and the affected site has N evacuation routes connecting the site to a safe area, such that the length of each route is L_i (where $i = 1, 2, ..., N$) and the width of each route is denoted W_i. Also suppose that the number of people trapped is Q. The dimensional area that each person requires for movement is $a \times b$, where a, or longitudinal spatial use, refers to the forward distance that a person requires to move forward and b, or the lateral spatial use, is the horizontal distance required to walk. For simplicity, we assume that each person uses the same space when moving through evacuation routes, though we can easily relax this assumption without changing the main results of the model.

The affected site may have many different evacuation routes, some of which may be full and others of which may be empty. To make use of each route's capacity and avoid overcrowding, we attempt to organize an evacuation that allocates people trapped to different routes, such that the total time used to evacuate all people safely out of the affected site is minimal.

Let Q_i be the number of people in the same stream at the entrance to route i. The maximum number of people that can walk together to enter the entrance simultaneously can be calculated as

$$B_i = W_i/b \qquad \text{(for } i = 1, 2, ..., N),\tag{10-2}$$

and the length of the stream will be

$$L(Q_i) = \frac{Q_i}{B_i} \times a \quad \text{(for } i = 1, 2, ..., N),\tag{10-3}$$

so that the maximum space each person has is equal to his or her required space for movement. We now examine the time required to evacuate all people Q by considering two situations: the affected area has only one evacuation route or the area has multiple routes.

Situation 1: One Route

If people are organized to enter the evacuation route continuously, they can form a stream in which several people walk in the same row during the evacuation. In this stream, each person follows the person in front to avoid collisions. To prevent crushing, they must maintain the same or similar walking speed. Otherwise, if some increase their speed suddenly, their social distance declines, resulting in reduced space for walking. In turn, the internal friction force among neighbors will decrease their speed unless they push forward. The total time required from the first person (or row) entering the route until the last batch of people in the same row exiting the path is

$$T = \frac{\text{Total length of the stream before entering the route } L(Q) + \text{the length of the route}}{\text{The walking speed of the stream}}$$

$$= \frac{\frac{Q}{B} \times a + L}{V} = \frac{abQ/W + L}{V}.$$

Therefore,

$$T = \begin{cases} 0, & when\ Q = 0; \\ \dfrac{abQ/W_i + L_i}{V}, & when\ Q \neq 0, i = 1. \end{cases}$$

(10-4)

where V can be obtained using Equation (10-1).

When $i > 1$, the problem becomes how to arrange Q into different routes. Because the length of each route may differ, the number of people entering different routes also may be unique. For example, a short route may contain more people than a long route, because people may believe using the shorter route will get them out faster. However, this belief may not be true if the route is overcrowded which slows speeds. Our strategy allows people to enter each evacuation route in a steady stream, without stopping or congestion, to achieve a situation in which all routes are occupied without being idle, and there is no congestion inside each route. In doing so, we can realize that (1) the evacuation time for each route is the same, and (2) the evacuation time is minimal. To achieve these goals, people must be organized in an orderly manner. Subsequently, we derive an algorithm that exhibits this idea.

Situation 2: Multiple Routes

Assume there are N routes. To determine how many people should be allocated and queue in each route, we sort all routes by ascending order on the basis of their lengths. Figure 10.1 displays such a queuing strategy, where Q_i is the number of people in the stream queuing outside route i, and $0 < L_1 \leq L_2 \leq L_3 \leq \ldots \leq L_n$.

Suppose the number of people Q_1 outside route 1 can be divided into n sections, such that the following settings are satisfied:

The length of section 1 is $L_2 - L_1$,
The length of section 2 is $L_3 - L_2$,
…, and
The length of section n − 1 is $L_n - L_{n-1}$.
The length of section n is ΔL.

Note that ΔL is the length of the stream queuing outside route n. Given such settings, Q_1 can be obtained by calculating

$$Q_1 = q_{1,n} + q_{1,n-1} + \ldots + q_{1,2} + q_{1,1},$$

where $q_{1,1}$ represents the number of people queuing in section 1 at route 1, and $q_{1,n}$ is the number of people queuing in section n at route 1. In addition, W_1 is the width of route 1.

Similarly,

$$Q_2 = q_{2,n-1} + q_{2,n-2} + \ldots + q_{2,2} + q_{2,1},$$

...,

$$Q_{n-1} = q_{n-1,2} + q_{n-1,1}, \text{ and}$$
$$Q_n = q_{n,1}. \tag{10-5}$$

Through addition, we have

$$
\begin{aligned}
Q &= Q_1 + Q_2 + \ldots + Q_{n-1} + Q_n \\
&= q_n + q_{n-1} + \ldots + q_2 + q_1,
\end{aligned} \tag{10-6}
$$

where $q_n = q_{1,n} + q_{2,n-1} + \ldots + q_{n-1,2} + q_{n,1}$,

$$q_{n-1} = q_{1,n-1} + q_{2,n-2} + \ldots + q_{n-1,1},$$
$$q_2 = q_{1,2} + q_{2,1}, \text{ and}$$
$$q_1 = q_{1,1}.$$

Figure 10.1. Determining queuing length for each route

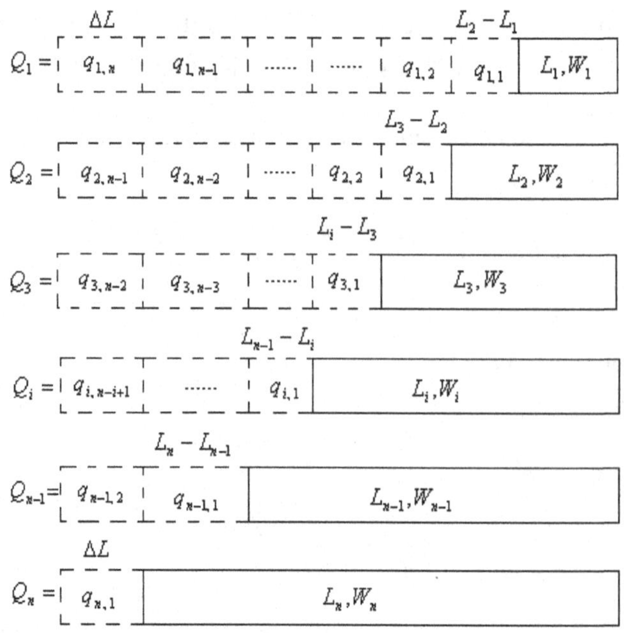

Now we need to determine $q_1, q_2, \ldots, q_{n-1}$, and q_n.

Because $q_{1,1} = (L_2 - L_1) \times B_1 / a = \dfrac{L_2 - L_1}{ab} W_1$, we have

$$q_1 = \frac{L_2 - L_1}{ab} W_1. \tag{10-7}$$

Similarly, we can obtain

$$q_2 = q_{1,2} + q_{2,1} = \frac{L_3 - L_2}{ab} (W_1 + W_2), \tag{10-8}$$

$$q_i = \frac{L_{i+1} - L_i}{ab} (W_1 + W_2 + \ldots + W_i), \text{ and}$$

$$q_n = \frac{\Delta L}{ab} (W_1 + W_2 + \ldots + W_n). \tag{10-9}$$

Suppose that the time required for the last person to get out of the route n is T; then

$$TV = \Delta L + L_n.$$

Substitute this value into Equation (10-9), and we obtain

$$q_n = \frac{\displaystyle\sum_{i=1}^{n} W_i}{ab} (TV - L_n). \tag{10-10}$$

When we substitute Equations (10-7), (10-8), and (10-10) into Equation (10-6), we get

$$Q = \frac{\displaystyle\sum_{i=1}^{n} W_i}{ab} (TV - L_n) + \frac{1}{ab} \left[L_n \sum_{i=1}^{n-1} W_i - \sum_{i=1}^{n-1} W_i L_i \right]. \tag{10-11}$$

Solving this equation, we obtain the total evacuation time T,

$$T = \frac{1}{V \displaystyle\sum_{i=1}^{n} W_i} \left[abQ + \sum_{i=1}^{n} W_i L_i \right]. \tag{10-12}$$

To determine $Q_1, Q_2, \ldots, Q_n$, we need to substitute Equations (10-7)–(10-11) into Equation (10-5), respectively. Then the number of people that should be allocated to route n is

$$Q_n = q_{n,1} = \frac{W_n}{ab} \Delta L,$$

where $\Delta L = \dfrac{abQ - \sum\limits_{i=1}^{n} W_i (L_n - L_i)}{\sum\limits_{i=1}^{n} W_i}.$ (10-13)

Similarly, the number of people that should be allocated to each of routes from 1 to $n-1$ can be calculated as follows:

$$Q_1 = \frac{W_1}{ab} [\,\Delta L + L_n - L_1\,],$$

$$Q_2 = \frac{W_2}{ab} [\,\Delta L + L_n - L_2\,],$$

$$\ldots,$$ (10-14)

$$Q_{n-1} = \frac{W_{n-1}}{ab} [\,\Delta L + L_n - L_{n-1}\,], \text{ and}$$

$$Q_n = \frac{W_n}{ab} \Delta L$$

Thus, Equation (10-14) indicates how to arrange people into different evacuation routes ($Q_1, Q_2, ..., Q_n$) to achieve a minimal escape time T, given the total number of people trapped in the affected area.

EVACTION FROM A ONE-STORY BUILDING

We define a one-story building as a site with one floor above and one floor below the ground. In this case, people inside the building are crowed into two different areas: the underground and the first floor. During an evacuation, people underground need to go up one floor, using stairways, while people on the first floor need to go down one floor to the ground level. These two streams of people can use stairways simultaneously without waiting for each other's movement because, in reality, the people underground will head to the ground floor directly and not move up to the first floor, and the people on the first floor similarly do not descend to the underground floor. Therefore, when computing the minimal time to evacuate all people from the building, we can treat these two streams of flow as two independent movements and calculate their evacuation times separately, using the maximum of the two. Hence, the algorithm to calculate time is similar to the one we introduced in the previous section.

When using stairways as evacuation routes, the walking speed may decrease compared with that on flat terrain because of the slope of stairs, which influences people's movement and lowers the density. The steeper the stars, the slower the speed. Suppose the building has (1) I routes connecting the first floor to the ground, (2) J routes from underground to the ground floor, and (3) K exits on the ground level. The length of each route is L_i, and the width of each is W_i (where $i = 1, 2, ..., I + J$). Also suppose that the width of each exit on the ground floor is W_k (where $k = 1, 2, ..., K$).

Using Equation (10-12), we can calculate the time required for people moving from the first floor to the ground level (T_{first}), as well as from underground to the ground floor (T_{Base}), as follows:

$$T_{first} = \frac{1}{V_{down} \sum_{i=1}^{I} W_i} [ab\,Q_{first} + \sum_{i=1}^{I} W_i L_i] \text{ and,} \tag{10-15}$$

$$T_{Base} = \frac{1}{V_{up} \sum_{i=1}^{J} W_i} [ab\,Q_{Base} + \sum_{i=1}^{J} W_i L_i], \tag{10-16}$$

where Q_{first} and Q_{Base} are the number of people trapped on the first floor and underground, respectively; and V_{up} and V_{down} represent walking speeds for people to travel upstairs and downstairs, respectively. According to Predtechenskii & Milinskii's (1978) empirical formula, V_{down} = 1.21V, and V_{up} = **0.8**V.

When these two streams of people meet on the ground floor, they may form several queues leading to the exits to get out of the building safely. Suppose the velocity for the movement along the horizontal paths through openings is V; then, the time (T_{queue}) for the last person in the queue to travel out the exit is

$$T_{queue} = \frac{ab(Q_{first} + Q_{Base})}{V \sum_{k=1}^{K} W_k}.$$

The number or people in each queue can be calculated using Equations (10-13) and (10-14), and the total evacuation time for a one-story building is given by

$$T = \text{Maximum}(T_{first}, T_{Base}) + T_{queue}. \tag{10-17}$$

HIGH-RISE BUILDING EVACUATION

Throughout most of the world, buildings post signs next to elevators that indicate they should not be used in emergency evacuations during fire. Instead, stairways are recommended as evacuation routes if an evacuation is initiated.

Consider a high-rise building with J floors, and the total number of people trapped inside the building is Q. In an emergency situation, people on each floor use the evacuation stairs simultaneously, though usually there are several such staircases connecting from the top floor to the ground exits. People on each floor must move to the entrance of the stairway, where they should automatically form rows/lines and walk down the stairs row by row. From this point of view, people on each floor should line up at the entrance to the stairs, similar to the lines people form before cashers' stands in a shopping scenario. In our model, we use the term "a stream of people" to represent the situation in which people line up at the stair entrance and form lines or rows in stairway.

We let Q_j ($j = 1, 2, …, J$) be the number of people trapped on the jth floor of the building and $L(Q_j)$ be the length of the stream of people lined up at the stair entrance on the jth floor. If the floor-to-floor height is H, and the slope of the stairway (stair gradient) is 32° (common in most buildings), the length of the stairs between any two adjacent floors is L_{stair} = H/Sin32°. It is reasonable to assume that this length is constant within whole building. To analyze people's movement and time used to get out of the building, we begin from the top floor and examine the movement walking down the stairways, passing through each floor's entrance, and walking toward the ground exits.

To simplify, we consider a building with one evacuation stairway connecting from the top floor to the ground exit. If the building has a multiple evacuation stairways, the same calculation procedure can be applied easily to each route. However, people on each floor likely choose the entrance randomly before entering the stairway. The total evacuation time will be the maximum of all the streams. Our goal is to identify the time required to evaluate people in an organized way, which means people line up at the entrance on each floor to enter the stairway and avoid any congestion at the stair entrance.

Model Formulation

Situation 1.

If the length of the stream of people lined up at the stair entrance on each floor is less than the length of the stairway between two adjacent floors — that is, if $L(Q_j) \le L_{stair}$ for every floor ($j = 1, 2, …, J$) — then all people can walk into the stairway without waiting. If so, the evacuation time will be the time that the last occupant on the top floor (i.e., the Jth floor) takes to travel along the stairway to the ground exit. That is,

$$T = [L(Q_J) + \sum_{j=1}^{J} L_{stair}]/V_{down},$$
(10-18)

where $L(Q_j) = \dfrac{abQ_J}{W_J}$, and W_J is the width of the stair entrance on the Jth floor. Furthermore, a and b represent each person's body dimension needed to walk.

Situation 2.

If situation 1 is not true, people on each floor must wait at the entrance to the stairway, because the stairway is fully occupied. That is, people from the $(j-1)^{th}$ floor may need to wait at the entrance when the first row of the stream from the jth floor has arrived at the $(j-1)^{th}$ floor.

Suppose that on the highest J^{th} floor, the time for the last row of the stream walking to the entrance of the stairway is $t(L(Q_j))$, and the time each row takes to travel along the stairway between two adjacent floors is $t(L_{stair})$. The time used for the last row of the stream of people from the Jth floor traveling along the stairway to arrive at the $(J-1)^{th}$ floor then is

$$t^*_J = t(L(Q_j)) + t(L_{stair}) = t(L(Q^*_j)) + t(L_{stair}),$$
(10-19)

where $L(Q^*_j)$ is the length of the stream from the Jth floor.

Note that on the highest floor, no people come from other floors to join the stream, so $L(Q_j^*) = L(Q_j)$. However, on all other floors, the people from the floors above join them at the stairway entrance. For example, on the $(J-1)^{th}$ floor, the stream may consist of people from the Jth floor and those originally from the $(J-1)^{th}$ floor. Therefore, the number of people in the stream during the movement through each floor may change, such that $L(Q_j^*) \neq L(Q_j)$, when j $\neq$ J (for j = 1, 2, ..., J).

Meanwhile, we have examined the situation on the $(J-1)^{th}$ floor during the time period t_J^*, but suppose that the time for the last row of the stream Q_{J-1} (i.e., people originally from the $(J-1)^{th}$ floor) to move to the entrance of the stairway is t_{J-1}' (i.e., $t_{J-1}' = L(Q_{J-1})/V$, where V equals people's walking speed on the horizontal paths). We thus compare t_J^* and t_{J-1}' to determine the location of the stream from the Jth floor.

If $t_{J-1}' \leq t_J^*$, then

Q_{J-1} (i.e., people originally on the $(J-1)^{th}$ floor) already is in the stairway when the last row of the stream from the Jth floor arrives on the $(J-1)^{th}$ floor. Hence, the stream from the top floor lines up at the end of Q_{J-1}. Together, the joined length, denoted as $L(Q_{J-1}^*)$, will be

$$L(Q_{J-1}^*) = L(Q_J^*) - (t_J^* - t_{J-1}') \times V. \tag{10-20}$$

Otherwise, during period t_J^*, the $(J-1)^{th}$ floor still contains people waiting to enter the stairway. Thus, the length of remaining people, lined up at the entrance on the $(J-1)^{th}$ floor, will be

$$\Delta l = (t_{J-1}' - t_J^*) \times V.$$

When the stream of people from the Jth floor (i.e., Q_J) arrives at the $(J-1)^{th}$ floor, they join the remaining queue and may take turns to enter the stairway. In this case, the total length of the new stream on the $(J-1)^{th}$ floor changes to

$$\begin{aligned} L(Q_{J-1}^*) &= L(Q_J^*) + \Delta l \\ &= L(Q_J^*) + (t_{J-1}' - t_J^*) \times V. \end{aligned} \tag{10-21}$$

Obviously, Equations (10-20) and (10-21) are the same, and in either of these situations, the length of the new stream on the $(J-1)^{th}$ floor is given by

$$L(Q_{J-1}^*) = L(Q_J^*) + (t_{J-1}' - t_J^*) \times V. \tag{10-22}$$

At this moment, all people on the Jth floor have moved to the $(J-1)^{th}$ floor, and the $(J-1)^{th}$ floor becomes the highest floor with people at risk.

Following Equation (10-19), the time for the last row of this new stream from the current $(J-1)^{th}$ floor to travel along the stairs and arrive at the entrance of the $(J-2)^{th}$ floor can be calculated as

$$t_{J-1}^* = t(L(Q_{J-1}^*)) + t(L_{stair}). \tag{10-23}$$

As we mentioned previously, people on each floor use the evacuation stairs simultaneously, so during time period t_J^* when people from the Jth floor move to the $(J-1)^{th}$ floor, we also must examine what has happened on the $(J-2)^{th}$ floor.

Let t'_{J-2} denote the time required for the last row of Q_{J-2} on the $(J-2)^{th}$ floor to pass through the entrance and walk into the stairway, where $t'_{J-2} = L(Q_{J-2})/V$. If $t'_{J-2} \leq t^*_J$, then all Q_{J-2} already walk into the stairway, and no people are lined up at the entrance on the $(J-2)^{th}$ floor. Otherwise, some people have moved into the stairway, while others still wait to enter. The length of the remaining stream is $(t'_{J-2} - t^*_J) \times V$.

Meanwhile, some people from the $(J-1)^{th}$ floor may arrive at the $(J-2)^{th}$ floor and join the stream. The resulting stream may contain people from three floors: the Jth, the $(J-1)^{th}$, and the $(J-2)^{th}$. After time t^*_J, the length of the new stream on the $(J-2)^{th}$ floor is

$$D^{J-2}_{t^*_J} = I(t'_{J-2} - t^*_J) \times [(t'_{J-2} - t^*_J) \times V + Max(t^*_J \times V_{down} - L_{stair}, 0)], \qquad (10\text{-}24)$$

where $I(t'_{J-2} - t^*_J)$ is an indicator function, and $I(t'_{J-2} - t^*_J) = \begin{cases} 1, & if\ t'_{J-2} - t^*_J > 0 \\ 0, & if\ t'_{J-2} - t^*_J \leq 0 \end{cases}$.

Then, $Max(t^*_J \times V_{down} - L, 0)$ returns the current position of the first row of Q^*_{J-1}.

After $(t^*_J + t^*_{J-1})$, all people on the $(J-1)^{th}$ floor have moved to the $(J-2)^{th}$ floor. Thus, the $(J-2)^{th}$ floor becomes the highest floor with people at risk. Following Equation (10-19), the length of the new stream queuing up on the $(J-2)^{th}$ floor is

$$L(Q^*_{J-2}) = L(Q^*_{J-1}) + (\Delta T - t^*_{J-1}) \times V,$$

where $\Delta T = D^{J-2}_{t^*_J}/V$. The time for the last row of Q^*_{J-2} to walk through the stairway and arrive on the $(J-3)^{th}$ floor is given by

$$t^*_{J-2} = t\ (L(Q^*_{J-2})) + t(L_{stair}). \qquad (10\text{-}25)$$

Following steps similar to those we discuss for Equation (10-24), after $(t^*_J + t^*_{J-1})$, the length of a stream on the $(J-3)^{th}$ floor will be

$$D^{J-3}_{(t^*_J + t^*_{J-1})} = I(t'_{J-3} - (t^*_J + t^*_{J-1})) \times \{[t'_{J-3} - (t^*_J + t^*_{J-1})] \times V + Max[(t^*_J + t^*_{J-1}) \times V_{down} - L_{stair}, 0]\},$$

where $t'_{J-3} = L(Q_{J-3})/V$ denotes the time required for the last row of Q_{J-3} on the $(J-3)^{th}$ floor to pass through the entrance to the stairs, and

$$I(t'_{J-3} - (t^*_J + t^*_{J-1})) = \begin{cases} 1, & if\ t'_{J-3} - (t^*_J + t^*_{J-1}) > 0 \\ 0, & if\ t'_{J-3} - (t^*_J + t^*_{J-1}) \leq 0 \end{cases}.$$

After $(t^*_J + t^*_{J-1} + t^*_{J-2})$, some people from the $(J-2)^{th}$ floor may join Q_{J-3} on the $(J-3)^{th}$ floor, so the length of the people queuing on the $(J-3)^{th}$ floor becomes

$$L(Q^*_{J-3}) = L(Q^*_{J-2}) + (\Delta T - t^*_{J-2}) \times V,$$

where $\Delta T = D^{J-3}_{(t^*_J+t^*_{J-1})}/V$. For this new stream of people Q^*_{J-3}, the time required for the last row to walk down the stairway and arrive on the $(J-4)^{th}$ floor equals

$$t^*_{J-3} = t\,(L(Q^*_{J-3})) + t(L_{stair}).\qquad(10\text{-}26)$$

This procedure continues, such that after any time $\alpha = \sum\limits_{k=0}^{n-2} t^*_{J-k}$, people have arrived at the nth floor, and the length of people lined up at the stairway entrance of the $[J-(n-1)]^{th}$ floor will be

$$D^{J-(n-1)}_{\alpha} = I(t'_{J-(n-1)} - \alpha)\times[\,(t'_{J-(n-1)}-\alpha)\times V + Max(\alpha\times V_{down} - L_{stair},\,0)],$$

where $t'_{J-(n-1)} = L(Q_{J-(n-1)})/V$ stands for the time required for the last row of $Q_{J-(n-1)}$ on the $[J-(n-1)]^{th}$ floor to move to the entrance of the stairs, and

$$I(t'_{J-(n-1)} - \alpha) = \begin{cases} 1, & if\ t'_{J-(n-1)} -\alpha >0 \\ 0, & if\ t'_{J-(n-1)} -\alpha \leq 0 \end{cases}.$$

After time $(\alpha + t^*_{J-(n-2)})$, the $[J-(n-1)]^{th}$ floor becomes the current highest floor with people at risk, and the length of people queuing on this floor is

$$L(Q^*_{J-(n-1)}) = L(Q^*_{J-(n-2)})+(\Delta T - t^*_{J-(n-2)}) \times V,$$

where $\Delta T = D^{J-(n-1)}_{\alpha}/V$ is the time for the last row of $D^{J-(n-1)}_{\alpha}$ on the $[J-(n-1)]^{th}$ floor to walk to the entrance of the stairs. Then, the time required for all people $Q^*_{J-(n-1)}$ on the $[J-(n-1)]^{th}$ floor to move to the $(J-n)^{th}$ floor is

$$t^*_{J-(n-1)} = t\,(L(Q^*_{J-(n-1)})) + t(L_{stair}).\qquad(10\text{-}27)$$

Adding Equations (10-19), (10-23), (10-25), (10-26), and (10-27) together, we can obtain the total evacuation time required for the entire population in a building with J floors to move to the nth floor as

$$T = t^*_J + t^*_{J-1} + t^*_{J-2} + \ldots + t^*_{J-(n-1)} = \sum\limits_{k=0}^{n-1} t^*_{J-k}.\qquad(10\text{-}28)$$

If we extend Equation (10-28), the total evacuation time required to evacuate all people safely from a building with J floors to the ground will be

$$T = t^*_J + t^*_{J-1} + t^*_{J-2} + \ldots + t^*_{J-(n-1)} + \ldots+ t^*_1 = \sum\limits_{k=0}^{J-1} t^*_{J-k}.\qquad(10\text{-}29)$$

This calculation procedure involves several iterations. We have developed a computer system to implement the proposed evacuation model procedure, and in the next two sections, we introduce this system and present the simulation results.

EMERGENCY EVACUATION COMMAND SYSTEM

A Hypothetical Emergency Situation

Assume an emergency situation in which an underground railway station catches fire and a train is forced to stop operating. People in the station and inside the train must be evacuated. Now suppose the station has three exit paths, and there are approximately 500 people inside the station, including those who are waiting for the train and those inside the train.

Problems

When facing this emergency situation, the evacuation commander must develop a rescue and evacuation plan. The available information probably includes the location of the site, the characteristics of the site (e.g., number of exit paths), and the estimated number of people who need to be evacuated. However, the commander may not know the exact status inside the site, how many people have escaped from the site safely, and the time needed to evacuate all people through the exit paths.

People trapped at the site want to get out as soon as possible, so they look for exit signs and proceed to the nearest one. They likely do not know how many exit paths are available or how far those paths are from their current locations. Suppose a person has located a nearby exit but that exit is crowded. This person might wait or search for other exits, without any clue about whether the other exits are similarly crowded. In either case, the person lacks current information about the other exits. Moreover, if this person enters an exit path, he or she may not know how much time will be needed to escape from the site. Thus, the information perceived by people at risk is inadequate.

The Emergency Evacuation Command System (EECS)

An Emergency Evacuation Command System (EECS) can provide information to both the evacuation commander and all the people who need to be evacuated. Using the models we have discussed in the previous sections, the system calculates (1) the total time needed to evacuate people safely from the site; (2) the capacity of each path, given the constraints of each exit; and (3) the number of people queuing outside the paths, walking in the paths, and escaping from the place safely.

The system takes dual roles. The results of its calculation may be displayed through message boards located in every route (i.e., each route's entry points or inside the route), mobile devices, or Web browsers. The information also can be refreshed within a short amount of time to reflect the current situation of each route. On the basis of this information, people at the evacuation site can make quick decisions to follow the least jammed route and escape safely from the site.

Decision makers (i.e., emergency management and communication officers) also can use this system to provide directions to citizens, police/hospitals/firefighters, and traffic observers, which enables more effective and efficient communication among people and with regard to the resources involved in the evacuation process. The system can assist both building and city/region evacuations. For a city/region evacuation, the system (1) provides evacuation routes from the affected area, (2) displays route characteristics, (3) identifies access routes for emergency response units, and (4) manages congested routes to estimate the time required to rescue all people from the site to nearby parking lots or entries to expressways through usable streets.

Before we introduce the structure of the system, we first explain how the system works in the scenario we have just described.

How the System Works

When an evacuation commander runs the system, the first thing he or she must do is to determine the type of an evacuation: building (including subways) or region/city (see Figure 10.2). The right-hand side of Figure 10.2 displays the evacuation simulation and configuration. When the commander clicks on the building evacuation, he or she may use a feature called "Select Building to Announce" to indicate the affected site (see Figure 10.3), then enter the approximate number of people to be evacuated (see Figure 10.4). The EECS works within just a few seconds and produces results and graphical information.

Figure 10.2. System interface

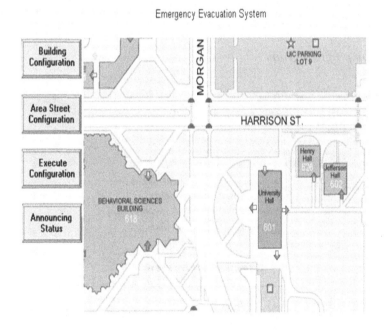

Figure 10.3. Select a building

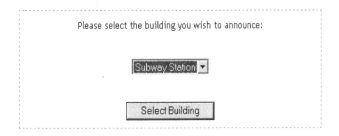

Figure 10.4. Announce the evacuation

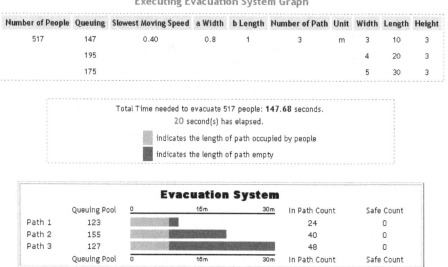

Select a building to announce

Building	a Width	b Length	Number of Path	Unit	Width	Length	Height
Subway Station	0.8	1	3	m	3	10	3
					4	20	3
					5	30	3

Please enter the following information:

number of people in **Subway Station**: [   ]

[Announce Evacuation]

Figure 10.5. Evacuation progress graph

Executing Evacuation System Graph

Number of People	Queuing	Slowest Moving Speed	a Width	b Length	Number of Path	Unit	Width	Length	Height
517	147	0.40	0.8	1	3	m	3	10	3
	195						4	20	3
	175						5	30	3

Total Time needed to evacuate 517 people: **147.68** seconds.

20 second(s) has elapsed.

▨ indicates the length of path occupied by people

▨ indicates the length of path empty

Evacuation System

	Queuing Pool	0 15m 30m	In Path Count	Safe Count
Path 1	123		24	0
Path 2	155		40	0
Path 3	127		48	0
	Queuing Pool	0 15m 30m	In Path Count	Safe Count

The system displays how fast people may be evacuated through which evacuation routes. A dynamic graphical bar with current result information also appears to both the public and the evacuation commander. The information displayed includes not only the building's configuration, such as how many paths can be used as evacuation routes and the length and width of each path, but also the minimum time needed, people's movement in each evacuation route, the number of people queuing outside each route, those walking inside each route, and those escaping from the site (see Figure 10.5).

The simulated human movement information gets updated quickly to reflect the current situation of each route. For example, suppose the population inside the subway station consists of 517 people, and three routes are available for evacuation. The length and width of each route differ. By calculation, the system suggests that the minimum time required to evacuate all people safely through three routes without any congestion is 147.68 seconds, and the maximum capacity for the three evacuation routes is 147, 195, and 175 people, respectively. If the number of people in each route exceeds the threshold (i.e., maximum capacity), the route will become crowded and congestion will result. In this situation, the time needed to evacuate all people will exceed the minimum time requirement. Such visual, dynamic information should help the evacuation commander manage the evacuation effectively.

We describe the system components and their functions in detail next.

System Components and Functions

The system consists of two major parts: general usage and administrative usage (see Figure 10.6). General usage mainly includes specifying the evacuation site, checking its current configuration, and making evacuation announcements. In the system, the site configuration describes the site's geographic information, such as the number of evacuation routes, the status of these routes, and the length, width, and height of each route. The administrative usage part enables a system administrator to add, update, or delete a configuration of a specific building or a region. We explain each function in more detail.

Figure 10.6. System administration interface

Evacuation System Administration Interface

Function	Description
General Usage:	
Select a building to announce	Select a building to announce.
Display current configuration	Display current configuration being use.
Display all configuration	Display all configuration in the system.
Execute current configuration	Executing current configuration -show total time, number of queue, all calculation.
Show graph (Progress)	Display simulation graph of evacuation system.
Administrative Usage:	
Input data into database	Input configuration of the system into the database.
Edit paths for a configuration	Edit/insert path(s) for existing or new configuration.
Configuration enabler	Enable current configuration.
Delete a configuration	Delete a configuration from the database.

Figure 10.7. Input configuration main page

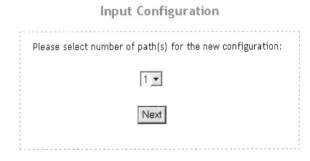

Input Configuration

Please select number of path(s) for the new configuration:

1 ▾

Next

Figure 10.8. Input new configuration

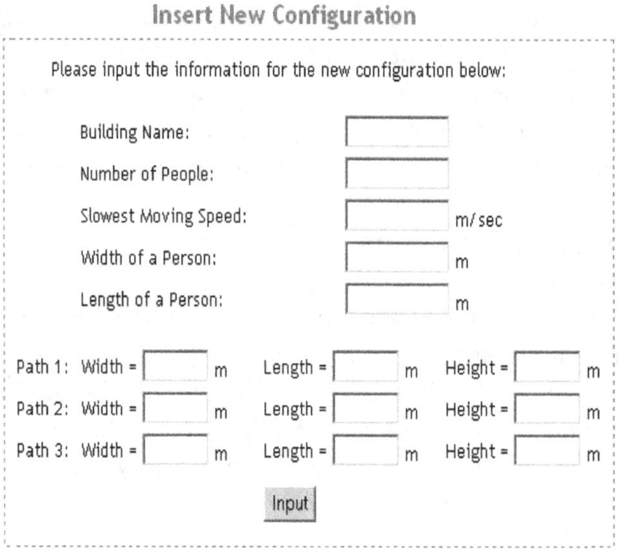

Insert New Configuration

Please input the information for the new configuration below:

Building Name:

Number of People:

Slowest Moving Speed: m/sec

Width of a Person: m

Length of a Person: m

Path 1: Width = m Length = m Height = m

Path 2: Width = m Length = m Height = m

Path 3: Width = m Length = m Height = m

Input

Input Data into Database Function. The system contains a list of buildings and sites, but when a new building or an evacuation site must be added, this function allows an administrator to input a new configuration.

When inputting a new configuration and paths into the database (see Figures 10.7 and 10.8), the administrator may choose how many paths are needed for the new configuration, and then the input

Figure 10.9. Edit and insert current configuration main page

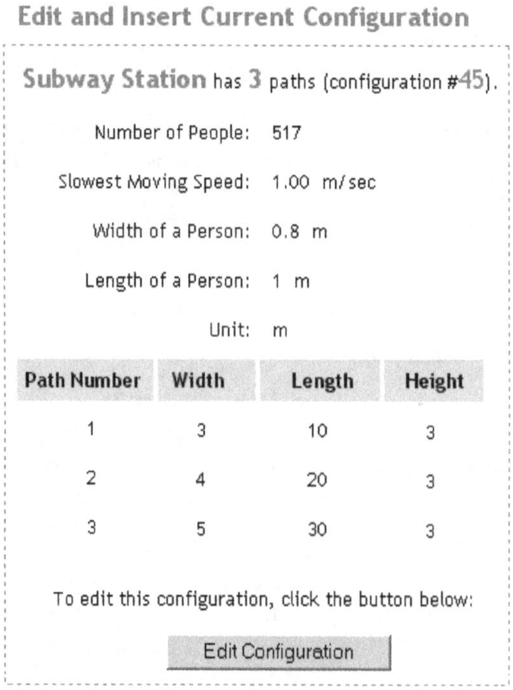

Edit and Insert Current Configuration

Subway Station has **3** paths (configuration #45).

Number of People: 517

Slowest Moving Speed: 1.00 m/sec

Width of a Person: 0.8 m

Length of a Person: 1 m

Unit: m

Path Number	Width	Length	Height
1	3	10	3
2	4	20	3
3	5	30	3

To edit this configuration, click the button below:

Edit Configuration

Figure 10.10. Edit current configuration

Edit and Insert Current Configuration

Please input new value on the fields you are modifying then press the submit button below

Building Name: Subway Station

Number of People: 517

Slowest Moving Speed: 1   m/sec

Width of a Person: 0.8   m

Length of a Person: 1   m

Unit: m

Path 1: Width = 3   m   Length = 10   m   Height = 3   m

Path 2: Width = 4   m   Length = 20   m   Height = 3   m

Path 3: Width = 5   m   Length = 30   m   Height = 3   m

Modify

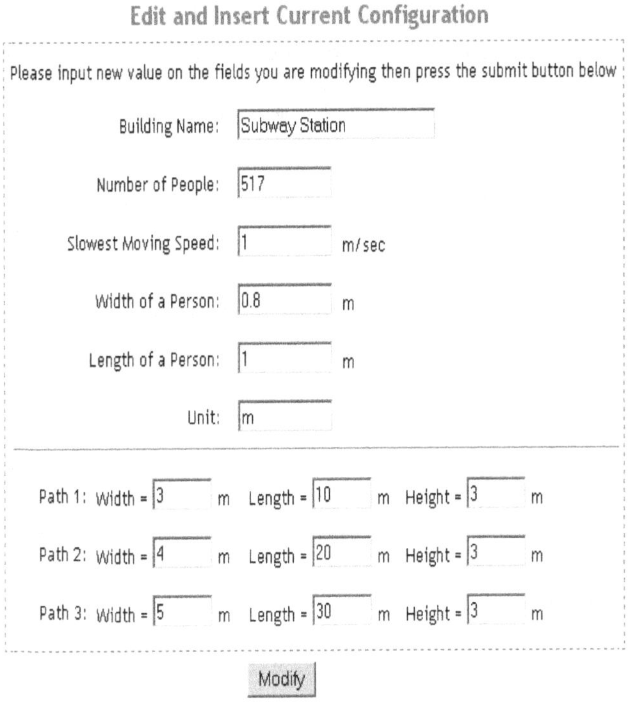

Figure 10.11. Insert new evacuation route

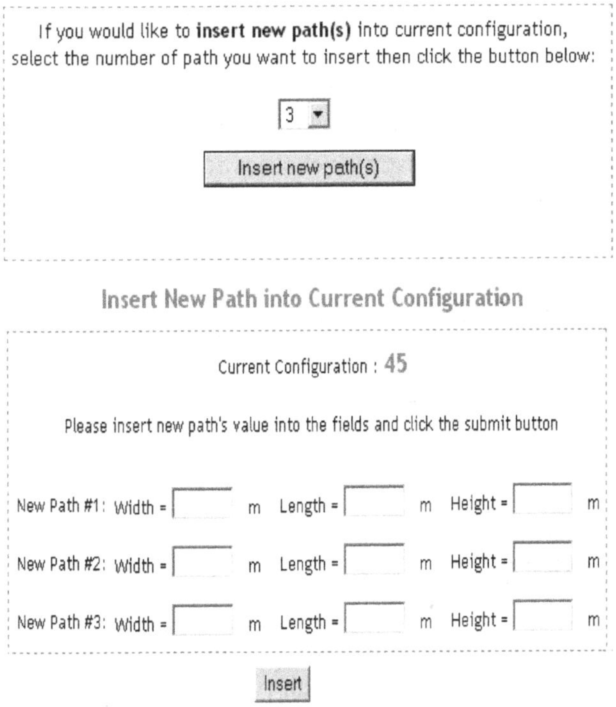

If you would like to **insert new path(s)** into current configuration, select the number of path you want to insert then click the button below:

3 ▼

Insert new path(s)

Insert New Path into Current Configuration

Current Configuration : 45

Please insert new path's value into the fields and click the submit button

New Path #1: Width =   m   Length =   m   Height =   m

New Path #2: Width =   m   Length =   m   Height =   m

New Path #3: Width =   m   Length =   m   Height =   m

Insert

Figure 10.12. Configuration enable function

Enable a Configuration

Please use the radio button on the right side to choose a configuration which you want to enable.

Config #	Num of People	a Width	b Length	Num of Path	Config Use	Unit	Building	Width	Length	Height	Enable Config
1	200	0.7	0.7	3	False	m	LCC	4	2	2	◯ Enable
								4	6	2	
								6	8	2	
2	100	1.5	1.2	2	False	m	CCC	2	6	2	◯ Enable
								4	8	2	
3	1	0.3	1.7	1	False	m	UH	1	23	3	◯ Enable
4	517	0.8	1	3	True	m	Subway Station	3	10	3	◯ Enable
								4	20	3	
								5	30	3	
5	22	1	1	2	False	m	BH	1	1	1	◯ Enable
								2	2	1	

configuration page displays the number of path chosen from the previous page. Note that some slots are optional, such as those for moving speed and body dimension. During the evacuation, the system computes the moving speed on the basis of the number of people inside the building.

Edit Paths for a Configuration Function. With this function, the administrator can edit existing paths or insert a new path. If the administrator chooses to add new paths, he or she can define how many; for example, in the subway station scenario, the system administrator may use this function to check the current configuration and make modifications if an existing path becomes inaccessible as an evacuation route. Figures 10.9, 10.10, and 10.11 illustrate this function.

Configuration Enable Function. Within this function, the administrator can choose to activate one existing configuration from among all current configurations (see Figure 10.12).

Delete Configuration Function. Using this function, the administrator can choose to delete an existing configuration from all current configurations available (see Figure 10.13). If the current configuration is being used, that particular configuration cannot be deleted.

SYSTEM PERFORMANCE

To gauge the performance of this system and verify whether the proposed evacuation method ensures the least time during an evacuation, compared with two other benchmark methods, we conduct two simulation tests.

Figure 10.13. Configuration delete function

Delete a Configuration

Config #	Num of People	a Width	b Length	Num of Path	Config Use	Unit	Building	Width	Length	Height	Delete Config
1	200	0.7	0.7	3	False	m	LCC	4	2	2	⃝Delete
								4	6	2	
								6	8	2	
2	100	1.5	1.2	2	False	m	CCC	2	6	2	⃝Delete
								4	8	2	
3	1	0.3	1.7	1	False	m	UH	1	23	3	⃝Delete
4	517	0.8	1	3	True	m	Subway Station	3	10	3	Delete
								4	20	3	
								5	30	3	
5	22	1	1	2	False	m	BH	1	1	1	⃝Delete
								2	2	1	
6	1000	0.5	0.5	1	False	m	LC E	2	10	2	⃝Delete

To avoid congestion and crushing, the proposed method advocates that evacuees should be organized in an orderly manner during an emergency evacuation. To make use of all available routes, regardless of their lengths, the system guides evacuees to different routes to ensure their evacuation time will be the same and minimal, regardless of the route lengths. However, in reality, people may enter each route randomly (i.e., random choice) or simply follow others (i.e., herding behavior).

Therefore, we first compare the proposed method with these two benchmark cases, then explore competitive behavior by conducting sensitivity analyses of the body dimension space required for the movement.

Simulation Comparison

Suppose an emergency evacuation is announced for a place with four evacuation routes. For simplicity, we number these routes 1, 2, 3, and 4. Assume the widths of these routes are the same, 3 meters, but the lengths are 20 meters (route 1), 12 meters (route 2), 24 meters (route 3), and 15 meters (route 4). We also assume that the total number of people trapped in the affected area is 500. Using EECS, we simulate evacuation progress, the status/usage of each evacuation route, and the total time to evacuate all 500 people safely.

Algorithms used to generate the evacuees' random choice behavior and herding behavior appear in Tables 10.1 and 10.2, respectively; we then implement these two algorithms in our EECS system. We first run the system with the proposed method and display the final results in Figure 10.14. The total time needed to evacuate the 500 people using the four routes is 793.57 seconds. We then use EECS to

Table 10.1. Algorithm for random choice behavior

PROCEDURE (**random choice** of routes for each individual)
1. Generate random variable from uniform distribution between 0 and 1.
2. Determine the route choice on the basis of the value of the random variable and the equal probability of selecting any route.
3. Compute the evacuation time to evacuate the people assigned to each route safely.
4. Determine the final evacuation time to evacuate all the people affected from the route-specific evacuation times.

simulate people's random choice behavior and herding behavior and present the simulation results in Figures 10.15 and 10.16, respectively. When the 500 people randomly choose evacuation routes during the evacuation, the total time to evacuate all of them is 1,168.028 seconds, whereas with herding behavior, it is 1,831.12 seconds.

Obviously, the proposed method incurs a much shorter time for evacuation compared with the two other benchmark cases. Herding behavior requires the most time—almost twice as long as that used with

Table 10.2 Algorithm for herding behavior

PROCEDURE (route selection with **herding** probability p for each individual)
1. Compute the popularity of each route (i.e., current number of people selecting each route)
2. Generate random variable from uniform distribution between 0 and 1.
3. If the value of the random variable is less than the herding probability p, choose the most popular route with most people (if there are more than one most popular routes, they are chosen with equal probability). Otherwise, use the algorithm of random choice of routes to select route.
4. Update the popularity of each route.
5. Compute the evacuation time to evacuate the people assigned to each route safely.
6. Determine the final evacuation time to evacuate all the people affected from the route-specific evacuation times.

Figure 10.14 Evacuation based on proposed method: A simulation

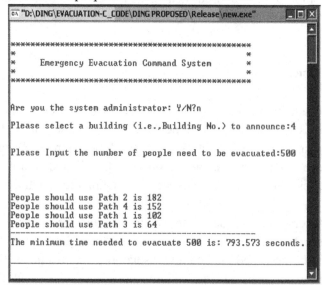

Figure 10.15. Evacuation based on herding behavior: A simulation

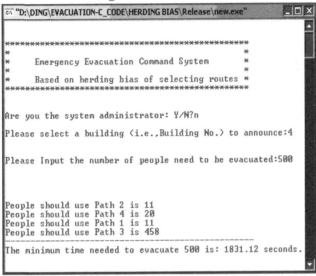

Figure 10.16. Evacuation based on random choice: A simulation

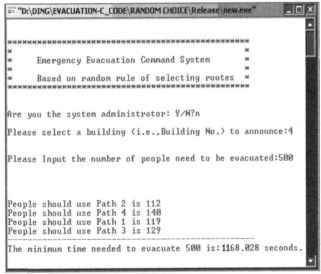

the proposed method. Herding implies that some routes become crowded or congested with people, even though other routes contain few people. In the case of random choice behavior, people evenly choose among the four evacuation routes.

Figure 10.17 shows the number of people evacuated by time using the proposed method, random choice, and herding; again, the proposed method creates a more effective evacuation than the two benchmarked models.

Figure 10.17. Number of people evacuated by time

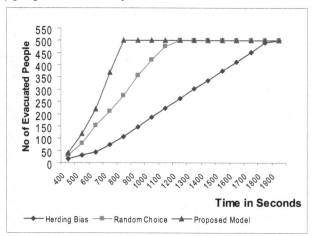

Sensitivity Analysis

As we noted previously, when evacuees increase their walking speed and push forward, their distance to the persons in front of them decreases, resulting in a reduced body dimension space (i.e., values of a and b in our model). We therefore conduct a sensitivity analysis to determine how sensitive both a (forward distance use) and b (horizontal distance use) are to changes in the total evacuation time.

From Equation (10-1), we know that the smallest area space, in which walking is impossible, is approximately 0.19 meter^2. In our simulation, we assume each person requires a space of 0.25 meter^2 to walk, which yields $a = 0.5$ meters and $b = 0.5$ meters. Using these as the current values, we explore the extent of variation in the total evacuation time when a (or b) increases or decreases (by 10%, 20%, and so forth) but everything else remains constant.

Figures 10.18 and 10.19 display the results on an x-axis that represents the amount of variation in the forward (horizontal) distance and a y-axis that indicates the change in total evacuation time to evacuate all 500 people through four evacuation routes, according to the proposed method, the random choice,

Figure 10.18. Impact of forward distance on evacuation time

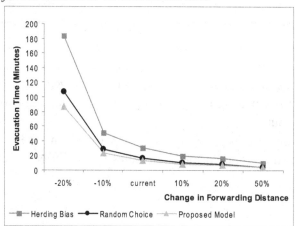

Figure 10.19. Impact of horizontal distance on evacuation time

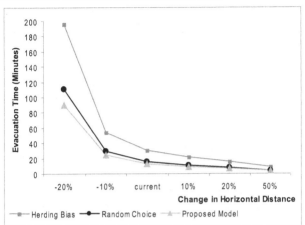

and herding. Increasing the forward (horizontal) distance suggests that evacuees have more space area for their movement, which should increase their walking speed and decrease total evacuation time. Compared with the two benchmark models, the time used in the proposed method is always least. In contrast, decreasing the forward (horizontal) distance restricts people's freedom of movement, decreases their walking speed, and increases the time needed for the evacuation. Again, compared with the two benchmark models, the evacuation time with the proposed method remains the least. In the meantime, the lower the forward (horizontal) distance, the more obvious is the advantage of using the proposed method to evacuate people at risk safely in the shortest time. This demonstration confirms that the proposed method performs better than the two benchmark models in terms of effective evacuation.

DISCUSSION AND CONCLUSIONS

In this chapter, we propose a method that can generate an evacuation strategy to evacuate people using the least time. In exploring different types of evacuation sites (i.e., high-rise buildings, non–high-rise places), we model people's different movement types and compute the total evacuation time, given the constraints of the evacuation routes. Organizing an evacuation using the proposed method can avoid congestion and require the least time compared with a random choice of evacuation routes or following others blindly (i.e., herding behavior).

The proposed method, as implemented in a computer support system called the emergency evacuation command system (EECS), can be used both online and offline. The information required by the system is minimal, and the time required to perform the calculations is very short. Thus, within a very short period of time, like seconds, the system can produce results and corresponding graphical information. If evacuation commanders themselves happen to be inside an evacuation site and are uncertain about the situation, they can use mobile devices, such as cell phones or PADs, to connect to EECS and make decisions or provide directions accordingly.

Because the system easily incorporates geographic information (e.g., area maps) when calculating the capacity of each evacuation route, it also provides benefits not only for simulating evacuation from individual buildings but also for city or regional emergency management.

REFERENCES

ASME (1987). American standard safety code for elevators, escalators, dumbwaiters and moving walks, A17.1, *American Society of Mechanical Engineers*, New York.

Averill, J., Mileti, D., Peacock, R., et al., (2005), *Occupant behavior, egress, and emergency communications* (Tech. Rep. No.1-7). Maryland, United States: National Institute of Standards and Technology, September 2005.

Baker, E. I. (1979). Predicting response to hurricane warnings: a reanalysis of data from four studies. *Mass Emergencies, 4*, 9-24.

Baker, E. I. (1991). Evacuation behavior in hurricanes. *International Journal of Mass Emergencies and Disasters, 9*(2), 287-310.

BBC (2005). Police deny stampede 'inaction'. Retrieved August 8, 2007, from http://news.bbc.co.uk/go/pr/fr/-/2/hi/south_asia/4211839.stm.

CNN (2005). Anger over India stampede deaths. Retrieved August 8, 2007, from http://edition.cnn.com/2005/WORLD/asiapcf/01/26/india.stampede.ap/index.html

Cross, J. (1979, April). *The association between previous residence and hurricane hazard perception and adjustments.* Paper presented at the 75th Annual Meeting of the Association of American Geographers, Philadelphia, PA.

Daeemen, W., & Hoogendoor, S. P. (2003). Controlled experiments to derive walking behavior. *European Journal of transport and Infrastructure Research, 3*(1), 39-59.

Drabek, T. E. (1999). Shall we leave? A study on family reactions when disaster strikes. *Emergency Management Review, 1*, 25-29.

Festinger, L. (1954). A theory of social comparison processes. *Human Relations.* 117-140.

Fischer, H. W., Stine, G. F., Stoker, B. L., Trowbridge, M. L., & Drain, E. M. (1995). Evacuation behavior: why do some evacuate, while others do not? A case study of the Ephrata Pennsylvania (USA) evacuation. *Disaster Prevention and Management, 4*(4), 30-36.

Fruin, J. J. (1971). *Pedestrian planning and design.* Metropolitan Association of Urban Designers and Environmental Planners, New York, USA.

Fujiyama T., & Tyler, N. (2004, January). Pedestrian speeds on stairs–an initial step for a simulation model. In *Proceedings of the 36th Universities' Transport Studies Group Conference*, Newcastle upon Tyne, UK.

Goffman, E. (1971). *Relations in public: microstudies in the public order.* New York: Basic Books.

Hankin, B. D., & Wright, R. A. (1958). Passenger flow in subway. *Operational Research Quarterly, 9*, 81.

Isobe, M., Adachi, T, & Nagatani, T. (2004). Experiment and simulation of pedestrian counter flow. *Physica, A*(336), 638-650.

Klote, H.H., Alvord, D.M., Levin, B.M., & Groner, N. E. (1992). Feasibility and design considerations of emergency evacuation by elevators (Tech. Rep. No. 4870). Maryland, United States: National Institute of Standards and Technology.

Kuligowski, E. (2003, May). Elevators for occupant evacuation and fire department access. In *Proceedings of the CIB-CTBUH International Conference on Tall Buildings*, 8-10, Malaysia.

Lam, W. H. K., & Cheung, C. Y. (2000). Pedestrian speed/flow relationships for walking facilities in Hong Kong. *Journal of transportation Engineering*. ASCE, *126*(4), 343-349.

Lam, W. H. K., Morrall, J. F., & Ho, H. (1979). Pedestrian flow characteristics in Hong Kong. *Transportation Research Record, 1487*, 56-62.

Musse, S., Babski, C., Capin, T., & Thalmann, D. (1998), Crowd modeling in collaborative virtual environments, In *Proceedings of ACM Virtual Reality Software Technology.* 115-123. Taiwan.

Navin, F. P. D., & Wheeler, R. J. (1969). Pedestrian flow characteristics. *Traffic Engineering,* June, 30-36.

O'Flaherty, C. A., & Parkinson, M. H. (1972). Movement in a city centre footway. *Traffic Engineering and Control,* February, *434.*

Older, S. J. (1968). Movement of pedestrians on footways in shopping streets. *Traffic Engineering and Control, 10*(4), 160-163.

Predtechenskii, V. M., & Milinskii, A. I. (1978). *Planning for foot traffic flow in buildings.* New Delhi: Amerind Publishing Company, Inc .

Proulx, G. (2001), As of year 2000, what do we know about occupant behavior in fire? *The Technical Basis for Performance Based Fire Regulations*, United Engineering Foundation Conference, 127-129, San Diego, January 7-11, 2001.

Pushkarev, B., & Zupan, J. M. (1975). *Urban space for pedestrians.* Cambridge, MA: The MIT Press.

Regnier, E. (2008), Public evacuation decisions and hurricane track uncertainty. *Management Science, 54*(1), 16-28.

Toshiyuki, A. (1993). Prediction system of passenger flow. In R. A. Smith & J. F. Dickie (Eds.), *Engineering for crowd safety* (pp. 249-258). Amsterdam: Elsevier.

Weidmann, U. (1993). *Transport technik der fussgaener.* ETH, Schriftenreihe Ivt-Berchte, 90, Zuerich (In German).

Yamori, K. (2001). Going with the flow: micro-macro dynamics in the macrobehavioral patterns of pedestrian crowds. *Psychological Review, 105*(3), 530-557.

Unit IV
Enhancing the Resilience of Critical Infrastructure:
Border Patrol, Cyber Security and Financial Stability

Since an incident area could be in cyber domain, financial zone, or other areas where critical assets are critical for national security, economic stability, and public safety, in this fourth unit, we focus on three major areas: border patrol, cyber security, and financial sustainability. Protecting critical infrastructure components, such as securing energy networks, gas pipelines, reservoirs, or the coastline, require an effective and efficient inspection and patrol system. Using border patrol as an example, in Chapter XI we consider the design of an effective and efficient inspection and patrol system that can help avoid an emergency similar to Northeast Blackout of 2003. In particular, we formulate a model of the relationships among the effectiveness of border patrols, the number of guards, and the rate at which the border becomes out of control. Because available personnel are always limited, we examine how to determine the minimum required patrol teams or additional forces that can ensure control of the border; we also address ways to keep patrol teams that neglect their duties to an acceptable level. The model further enables us to analyze the impact of resource expenditures on patrol effectiveness to help authorities involved in budget decision making strategically plan the needed total or additional forces and still make pursuit and patrol both effective and efficient.

Terrorists also seek sanctuary in the cyber domain, particularly the Internet, because of its geographically unbounded and largely unconstrained space, and use it to create and disseminate propaganda, recruit new members, raise funds, and plan operations. The Internet thus has become a training ground on which terrorists acquire instruction, once possible only through physical training camps, and a weapon to generate cyber fear.

In Chapter XII, we examine the role of the Internet as a battlefield and analyze the course of war in cyberspace. We model the Internet structure, identify its inherent vulnerabilities, and suggest response methods. The inherent vulnerability of the Internet infrastructure permits malicious activities to flourish and perpetrators to remain anonymous. Therefore, we propose that the Internet should have the ability to implement self-awareness mechanisms that sense and identify harmful contents exhibited in various computer codes.

Finally, we turn our attention to the financial zone to explore ways to maintain financial stability, a key component of homeland security. In Chapter XIII, we explore how to use an individual firm's data to provide early warnings of financial distress and thus avoid collapse. Specifically, we assert that simple models using limited information can capture the essential dynamics of an individual firm's credit risk.

Chapter XI
Security Inspection Model of Critical Infrastructure

INTRODUCTION

This chapter presents an approach that can be used to assist in border patrol and security management. On August 12, 2005, New Mexico governor Bill Richardson announced a state of emergency in four counties along the New Mexico-Mexico border in response to the booming smuggling of drugs and illegal immigrants, kidnapping, murder, and destruction of property and livestock (CNN, 2005). Three days later, Arizona governor Janet Napolitano issued a similar declaration (Media, 2005). Both states immediately released emergency funds to help patrol their borders by hiring additional law enforcement officers and paying them overtime. In addition to building fences along the US-Mexico border (Media, 2006) and drawing attention to the political issues involved, such as immigration law, these two announcements indicate the urgency and importance of planning and implementing an effective border patrol.

The border patrol, an important component of the nation's security system, requires daily, around the clock operation and is frequently overt while illegal border-crossings and other criminal events are covert. When an illegal crossing is discovered, a decision must be made immediately whether to track the illegal crossers, to continue patrolling the rest of the assigned areas, or to attempt to do both together. This decision is based largely on whether the unit of border agents itself, or the border patrol station to which it belongs, has an adequate number of guards at the time of the incident. With sufficient forces, both pursuing and patrolling can be handled immediately. Otherwise, a dilemma arises as either the assigned area of the border is left unguarded (i.e., out of control) if the choice is to track the illegal crossers only, or if the decision is to continue patrolling without interruption the team neglects its duty. The border counties mentioned in the two announcements have expressed a desire to expand the number of patrol agents on the border in addition to needing different detection devices. For example, one proposal from Arizona Senator Jon Kyl in a bill is to authorize 10,000 new Border Patrol agents (Carroll & Gonzalez, 2005). On May 15, 2006, President George W. Bush announced sending 6,000 National Guard troops to help secure the southern border (CNN, 2006).

According to the Department of Homeland Security's report on border and transportation security (DHS Portfolios, 2005), the U.S. has over 95,000 miles of coastline, and over 7.5 thousand miles of border spanning Canada and Mexico. Over 500 million people enter the United States each year by crossing the borders, passing through the ports, or arriving on overseas airlines. Although it is difficult to know the exact annual number of illegal crossings along the whole border, the following figures indicate the situation is very serious. From October 1, 2004 (i.e., the start of the federal fiscal year) to August 16, 2005, the U.S. Border Patrol in the Yuma and Tucson sectors reported more than 510,000 arrests, an average of about 1,616 a day, roughly on par with last fiscal year (Carroll & Gonzalez, 2005). Given such a long border with booming illegal crossers, the number of agents required to prevent or reduce the increasing illegal entries to the U.S. with limited resources has become a critical issue. Moreover, it is uncertain whether some specific proposed number of new forces discussed in the media can achieve the reduction of illegal border crossings.

In this chapter, we propose an approach to tackle this problem[1]. Using classical mathematics, we build a model to capture the relationships between the effects of border patrol, the number of guards, and the rate of the border being "out of control" or the patrol teams "neglecting their duty". Doing so allows us to analyze the impact of resource expenditure on patrol effectiveness in order to help strategically plan the needed total or additional forces, and make pursuit and patrol both effective and efficient. Due to the covert nature of illegal border crossing, the number of illegal crossings is modeled as a stochastic process in a defined area of patrol and a given time period. We assume that the expected illegal crossings through the border can be prevented by pursuit and patrol. Then we calculate the expected inspection load of the border patrol team using the duties of searching for illegal crossers or continuing its patrol to complete the inspection of the assigned section of the border during the same time period. Then, the probability of the occurrence of either the section being "out of control" or the team "neglecting its duty" is computed and the minimum number of required border patrol teams is derived.

To illustrate the model, we apply it to an example of protecting important infrastructure such as securing an 890-mile long high voltage energy network. The result shows that by increasing the number of inspection workers by only four members, the rate of failure to secure the network will be reduced from one in ten thousand to one in a million given uncontrolled incursions.

The illustration demonstrates the high effectiveness of our proposed approach. Moreover, the model is simple and easy to use. It can be applied to different areas without being constrained by their geographic conditions. Most importantly, the model, as a decision aid, has a wide variety of potential applications such as protecting critical infrastructure (e.g. energy networks, gas pipelines, reservoirs, etc.) and securing the coastline. Planning and organizing an effective and efficient inspection system is necessary and important. The proposed method can help authorities involved in budget decision-making analyze how enforcement forces impact patrol effectiveness. That is, given a desired patrol effect such as an accepted minuscule level of the rate of the border being out of control or the patrol teams neglecting their duties, the model shows the minimum required enforcement forces for budgeting.

For convenience, we have transformed the results of the calculations into a table which shows the different expected inspection loads (e.g., patrolling miles or duration) associated with the number of required patrol teams, and the effectiveness achieved. Using the table, users can determine the required number of teams immediately by plugging the inspection load and desired patrol effectiveness.

The remainder of this chapter is organized as follows. In next section, Model Formulation, we describe the model formulation and analyze the impact of resource expenditure on patrol effectiveness to derive the minimum number of required border patrol teams. We then use an example of protecting important infrastructure to illustrate how to use the proposed model. We give a processing algorithm that implements the proposed approach step by step and offer some discussions of managerial implications in last section.

MODEL FORMULATION

Estimate the Number of Illegal Border-Crossings that Occur Stochastically During an r Time Period

Due to the covert nature of illegal border crossing, the number of illegal crossings is modeled as a stochastic process in a defined area of patrol and a given time period. Suppose a county's border can be divided into m patrol sections and r is referred to as the duty time of a border patrol team. The unit for r can be an hour or a day. The patrol teams work in shifts and change after every r. Let q_J be the expected number of illegal border-crossings occurring in section J of the border in an r time period. Then the expected number of illegal border-crossings occurring on the whole border of the county during an r time period is $\sum_{J=1}^{m} q_J$. If q is the average number of times illegal border-crossings occur in each section of border during an r time period, we can get $\sum_{J=1}^{m} q_J = mq$. The probability of s out of m sections that have illegal border-crossings occurring during an r time period can be calculated as follows:

$$Q(s) = C_s^m [q^s p^{m-s}] = \frac{m!}{s!(m-s)!} [q^s p^{m-s}],$$ (11-1)

where, $p = 1 - q$ and $s = 0, 1, 2, ..., m$.

To simplify, we let $x = mq$, which gives $q = \frac{x}{m}$ and $p = 1 - \frac{x}{m}$. Substituting them into equation (11-1) yields

$$Q(s) = \frac{m(m-1)(m-2)\cdots(m-s+1)}{s!} [\frac{x}{m}]^s \times [1 - \frac{x}{m}]^{m-s}$$

$$= \frac{x^s}{s!} [\frac{m}{m} \times \frac{(m-1)}{m} \times \cdots \cdots \times \frac{(m-s+1)}{m}] \times [1 - \frac{x}{m}]^{m-s}.$$

To solve the equation, we can take the limit to $Q(s)$ when m becomes larger and larger ($m \to \infty$). That is,

$$Q(s) = \frac{x^s}{s!} \lim_{m\to\infty} [1 \times (1 - \frac{1}{m}) \times (1 - \frac{2}{m}) \times \cdots \times (1 - \frac{s-1}{m})] \times \lim_{m\to\infty} (1 - \frac{x}{m})^m \times \lim_{m\to\infty} (1 - \frac{x}{m})^{-s}$$

$$= \frac{x^s}{s!} [1] \times [e^{-x}] \times [1].$$

Putting $x = mq$ back, we have

$$Q(s) = \frac{(mq)^s}{s! e^{mq}}.$$ (11-2)

Here, when $s = 0$, $Q(0) = \frac{(mq)^0}{0! e^{mq}}$ measures the probability of no section having illegal crossings occur during an r time period;

When $s = 1$, $Q(1) = \dfrac{(mq)^1}{1!\,e^{mq}}$ is the probability of one section having illegal crossings through the border during an r time period;

When $s = 2$, $Q(2) = \dfrac{(mq)^2}{2!\,e^{mq}}$ is the probability of two sections having illegal border-crossings during an r time period;

......

When $s = m$, $Q(m) = \dfrac{(mq)^m}{m!\,e^{mq}}$ measures the probability of m sections having illegal border-crossings occur during an r time period.

Next we need to link this with desired patrol effectiveness to determine the number of required patrol teams.

DETERMINING BORDER PATROL TEAMS

To prevent illegal crossers and secure the border, authorities usually implement routine border patrol operations. Each county has border patrol teams to inspect the sections for which they are responsible.

On patrol duty, if a patrol team discovers illegal crossers at some point in its assigned section, two things can happen. One is that the patrol team stops patrolling and begins to track and capture the illegal crossers. The other is that the patrol team continues patrolling to complete their section. If the patrol team itself has an adequate number of guards, these two things can be handled simultaneously and immediately. That is, part of the team will track the illegal crossers immediately while the rest continue their patrol duty. If this is the case, we say the section is manageable and is "under control." If the patrol team does not have sufficient forces to split, the team is in a dilemma. If the team goes to track the illegal crossers immediately, then the team's section will be left unguarded as there will be no patrolling during the rest of the r time period. A separate illegal crossing may happen during this period. If this occurs, we say this section of the border is "out of control."

On the other hand, if the team continues its patrol duty without tracking down the illegal crossers and capturing them, then the event of the illegal crossing succeeds. We define this situation as the patrol team "neglects its duty." To deal with the dilemma and avoid the situation of either "out of control" or "neglect of duty", the patrol team usually calls the county's border patrol station for reinforcement if the team itself does not have sufficient forces to split. If the border patrol station is able to send the additional reinforcement, then the dilemma disappears and both tracking the illegal crossers and patrolling assigned section can be handled in parallel. However, if the border patrol station does not have additional forces for reinforcement at that time, the dilemma still exists. The situation of either the section being "out of control" or the team "neglecting its duty" will occur. Suppose that the expected illegal crossings through the border can be prevented by pursuit and patrol. Then a higher rate of the patrol teams failing to pursuit and patrol implies a higher "success" rate of illegal crossings. Since the available personnel is always limited, the question of interest here is how many reinforcement teams should be planned in order to minimize the required total or additional patrol forces and keep the rate of both "out of control" and "neglect of duty" incidents in each assigned section during an r time period to below an acceptable minuscule level such as one in a million.

Consider an assigned section J. Suppose there are y_J occurrences of illegal crossings in section J during an r time period. Let n_J denote the number of patrol teams that are available to perform patrol duty and provide reinforcement during the r period. Obviously, when $y_J \le n_J$, the border patrol station has enough agents to handle both routine patrolling and capturing the illegal crossers near the border when illegal crossings occur at different points in section J. That is, section J is manageable and "under control".

Now, suppose section J can be divided into j key points at which illegal crossings are most likely to occur based on border's geographic conditions. If q_J is the average number of times illegal border-crossings occur in any one key point in an r time period from past history, then jq_J implies the number of times that the patrol team is most likely to handle illegal crossing events when patrolling section J in this r period. Following the idea exhibited in equation (11-2), we can compute the probability of y_J occurrences of illegal crossings occurring in section J in an r period. That is

$$Q(y_J) = \frac{(jq_J)^{y_J}}{y_J! \, e^{jq_J}}.$$

Hence the probability of the "under control" situation occurring on section J during an r period is

$$Q_{under-control}(y_J \le n_J) = \sum_{y_J=0}^{n_J} \frac{(jq_J)^{y_J}}{y_J! \, e^{jq_J}}. \tag{11-3}$$

Where, n_J is the number of available patrol teams on section J.

When the number of illegal crossings, y_J, exceeds the number of available patrol teams n_J, the dilemma arises due to inadequate staffing to both track down the illegal crossers and perform patrol duty together. We use the term "neglect-inspection" to represent a situation of either the section being "out of control" or the team neglecting its duty. The probability of the occurrence of "neglect-inspection" can be calculated as follows.

$$
\begin{aligned}
Q_{neglect-inspection}(y_J > n_J) &= 1 - \sum_{y_J=0}^{n_J} \frac{(jq_J)^{y_J}}{y_J! \, e^{jq_J}} = \sum_{y_J=0}^{\infty} \frac{(jq_J)^{y_J}}{y_J! \, e^{jq_J}} - \sum_{y_J=0}^{n_J} \frac{(jq_J)^{y_J}}{y_J! \, e^{jq_J}} \\
&= \sum_{y_J=n_J+1}^{\infty} \frac{(jq_J)^{y_J}}{y_J! \, e^{jq_J}}.
\end{aligned}
\tag{11-4}
$$

As we mentioned earlier, a higher rate of the patrol teams being able to prevent (pursuit and patrol) implies a lower "success" rate of illegal crossings through the border. So, we need to reduce $Q_{neglect-inspection}(y_J > n_J)$ to an acceptable minuscule level because the available personnel are always limited.

Because illegal border crossings are covert and the patrol teams do not know when illegal crossing will occur in their assigned responsible sections in advance (unless they have intelligence), the border enforcement forces in all sections usually do their best in patrolling to reduce $Q_{neglect-inspection}(y_J > n_J)$. Hence, we constrain $Q_{neglect-inspection}(y_J > n_J)$ such that it falls below the authorities' acceptable miniscule threshold value, ε_J. For example, if $\varepsilon_J = 0.000001$, it says the rate of the patrol teams failure to patrol and pursue the illegal crossers is one in a million in section J. Solving $\displaystyle\sum_{y_J=n_J+1}^{\infty}\frac{(jq_J)^{y_J}}{y_J!e^{jq_J}}\leq\varepsilon_J$ for each given acceptable value ε_J, we can get a corresponding n_J, the minimum number of patrol teams required for section J.

Each county can set up its own acceptable rate of "neglect-inspection" for each individual section of responsibility based on its border's geographic conditions. Hence, for a county with m responsible sections, the minimum number of patrol teams the county should plan to have (e.g., N) in order to maintain its expected rate of "neglect-inspection" is

$$\text{Minimize } N = \sum_{J=1}^{m} n_J ,$$

$$\text{subject to } \sum_{y_J=n_J+1}^{\infty}\frac{(jq_J)^{y_J}}{y_J!e^{jq_J}} \leq \varepsilon_J . \tag{11-5}$$

Note that equation (11-5) is computationally tedious even for relatively small values of j in each assigned section. As j or J gets larger, it becomes almost impossible without the help of a computer. For convenience, we have written a computer program to solve equation (11-5). The results of the calculations are listed in table 1 which shows different values of N given different ε_J for each individual section J. Using the table, users can determine the required number of teams immediately by plugging the inspection load and a desired threshold.

When m represents the total number of patrol sections along the whole national border, N in equation (11-5) will be the minimum number of patrol teams required for securing the whole border. The authorities can also use equation (11-5) to calculate the number of additional forces required for the border patrol if the authorities choose to decrease the expected rate of "neglect-inspection."

For example, suppose there are currently n_J patrol teams in section J of the border during an r-hour period patrolling, and that the "neglect-inspection" rate is ε_J. If the authorities want to decrease the "neglect-inspection" rate, say, by a factor of 100, then how many additional patrol teams are required?

According to equation (11-4) we have

$$\sum_{y_J=n_J+1}^{\infty}\frac{(jq_J)^{y_J}}{y_J!e^{jq_J}} = \varepsilon_J . \tag{11-6}$$

If the "neglect-inspection" rate is decreased by 100 times, assuming the required number of additional patrol groups is Δn_J, then we can also have

$$\sum_{y_J=\Delta n_J+n_J+1}^{\infty}\frac{(jq_J)^{y_J}}{y_J!e^{jq_J}} = 0.01\varepsilon_J . \tag{11-7}$$

Using table 1, we can find the corresponding minimum value for the sum of Δn_J and n_J given a value of $0.01\,\varepsilon_J$. After that, it is easy to get Δn_J.

We now use an example to illustrate how to use equation (11-5) and table 1. Due to the lack of behavioral data on border patrol, we use an example of protecting important infrastructures such as a high voltage energy network.

AN EXAMPLE OF PROTECTING CRITICAL INFRASTRUCTURE

An electric power company provides electric service to an area in Mid-West United States. The company owns an 890-mile long, high voltage energy network with 422 transformers/substations. Due to natural damage such as high wind, ice, and light etc, power outages can happen. Past history shows that the average failure rate for the power lines and substations is 0.004 per year. To maintain the reliability of the electric service, discover possible power symptoms in early stage, and nip them in the bud, the company needs to conduct constant preventive checks for inspecting electric power problems. When conducting a routine preventive check, electricians are assigned to form a number of inspection groups to check the whole network and 422 transformers/substations.

Suppose that each inspection group consists of two electricians and is required to perform a certain inspection load, such as inspecting ten miles' high voltage lines or two transformers/substations per patrol duty day. Electric power problems do not only occur on the day of the routine check (sometimes the equipment and network are in normal working condition at the time when electricians perform the routine check). After that a problem may occur due to natural damage or man-made damage. If this situation happens, we say a disrepair event occurs. Since the problems caused by either nature or man-made cannot be known in advance, the company's goal is to decrease such disrepair events in order to reduce the rate of failure to secure the whole network given uncontrolled incursions.

Suppose the company wants to maintain a disrepair rate of less than a fraction of 10,000 that is, $\varepsilon \le$ 0.0001. Then the question is, how many inspection groups are needed in each routine check in order to maintain the reliability of the 890 miles of power lines and keep 422 transformers/substations running at normal operation status?

We can use equation (11-4) to find the number of required inspection groups. Since the power network is 890 miles long and the number of transformers and substations is 422, we can compute the total inspection load performed in each routine check. That is,

$$j = \frac{890}{10} + \frac{422}{2} = 300 \text{ inspection units.}$$

Thus, we have $jq = 300*0.004 = 1.2$, indicating the number of times that electricians are most likely to repair/handle power problems during the routine check.

Given the conditions of $q = 0.004$ and $\varepsilon \le 0.0001$, we need to solve the following to get n, the minimum number of inspection groups.

$$\text{Min.} \sum_{y=n+1}^{\infty} \frac{(1.2)^y}{y!e^{1.2}} \le 0.0001.$$

As we mentioned earlier, computing the left-hand side of the above inequality is difficult. We can use table 1 to get n. Checking the column marked 1.2 in table 1, we can find the table value, ε, the nearest small one that is less than 0.0001. Then, the corresponding value in the row marked "No. of Teams" is our n, the required number of groups. For example, in our case, $\sum_{y=n+1}^{\infty} \frac{(1.2)^y}{y!e^{1.2}}$ is equal to 0.000251 when $n = 6$ under the column marked 1.2. Obviously the condition that the value should be less than 0.0001 is not satisfied. Then go to next line, when $n = 7$, we find $\sum_{y=n+1}^{\infty} \frac{(1.2)^y}{y!e^{1.2}}$ equals 0.000037 which is less than 0.0001. Therefore, the company needs 7 inspection groups (i.e., 7* 2=14 workers) to maintain a disrepair rate of less than a fraction of 10,000.

Now, if the company plans to increase the efficiency of routine inspections by reducing the disrepair rate from one in 10,000 to one in a million, we can compute the number of the additional groups of inspectors required using table 1.

Finding a table value under the column marked $jq = 1.2$, whose value is less than 0.000001, the corresponding row value under the column marked number of teams shows the minimum number of inspection groups is 9. Therefore, the number of additional inspection groups is $9 - 7 = 2$ groups.

By increasing the number of inspection workers by only four members, the rate of failure to secure the network will be reduced from one in ten thousand to one in a million given uncontrolled incursions. The "Northeast Blackout of 2003" suggests that taking preventative measures/checks is very important (NYISO, 2004). The example shows how the proposed method can be used to plan the required inspection groups for such preventive checks.

IMPLEMENTING STEPS

Due to different geographic environments of the border, the difficulty encountered in each patrol may be different. When tracking down illegal crossers, some agents may be equipped with cars, others may need to walk and pass through mountain areas, deserts, or canyons, resulting in a variety of difficulties. To capture this difference, we use time as a unit to measure the work load each patrol team performs to track down illegal crossers or patrol the assigned area(s). In other words, the working load or inspection load the patrol team performs in searching for illegal crossers or patrolling its area can be measured in terms of the time spent in performing such duties.

To implement the proposed approach, a step-by-step algorithm is summarized below. Let r be the duty time of a border patrol team. The unit for r can be an hour or a day. The patrol teams work in shifts and change after every r.

Step 1: Divide the border into m sections and calculate the expected work load to be performed for each patrol section J (for J = 1, 2, …, m) given a certain time period r, then the total work load expected for the entire border during r is:

$$\text{Work-load} = \sum_{J=1}^{m} TS_J * q_J + \sum_{J=1}^{m} T_J .$$

Where, T_J is the time used in inspecting section J when no illegal crossing occurred. TS_J is the average time spent in handling or tracking one illegal crossing occurring in section J, and q_J is the average number of times illegal crossings occurred in section J in the past.

Step 2: Calculate yearly work load f:

$$f = \frac{8760}{r} \left[\sum_{J=1}^{m} TS_J * q_J + \sum_{J=1}^{m} T_J \right] \text{ hours}$$

Step 3: Determine the number of patrol teams required yearly given a desired threshold (e.g., the expected rate of the assigned patrol area being out of control should be less than one in 10,000):

Using Table 1 to find a table value under the column marked the value of f, the nearest small value that is less than the desired threshold. Then find the corresponding value in the row marked the "No. of Teams".

DISCUSSION AND CONCLUSIONS

According to President George W. Bush, the United States has not been in complete control of its border for decades (Media, 2006). Therefore illegal immigration has been on the rise. Recently a bill has been signed into law to plan for 700 miles of new fencing along the US-Mexico border to curb illegal crossings. In addition to needing different detection devices and drawing attention to immigration law, the U.S. border counties have expressed a desire to expand the number of patrol agents along the border. The goal of this chapter is to introduce an approach to making border patrolling more effective and efficient when determining total or additional forces. Specifically, we examine how to determine the minimum required patrol teams or additional forces in order to reduce the rate of the border being out of control or the patrol teams neglecting their duties to an acceptable minuscule level. The method is simple and easy to use. For convenience, we have transformed the results of the calculations into a table, which shows the different expected inspection load (e.g., patrolling miles or duration) associated with the number of required patrol teams, and their patrol effectiveness achieved.

The method can be applied to different areas without being constrained by border geographic conditions. It also has a wide variety of potential applications such as protecting critical infrastructure (for example, energy networks, gas pipelines, reservoirs, etc.) and securing the coastline. Since planning and organizing an effective and efficient inspection and patrol system is necessary and important to a nation's security, the proposed model can provide scientific backup for such planning.

In our model, we assume that border patrol is conducted by teams and illegal crossings are counted by the number of occurrences rather than the number of illegal crossers, and the patrol teams handle the number of incidents. However, when an illegal crossing occurs, the number of illegal crossers may not be just a single person but groups. Since it is difficult to know the size of the groups in advance (unless the patrol team has intelligence), it is likely that the number of members on a patrol team would need to vary by the number of points along the border at which illegal crossings are most likely to occur based on border's geographic conditions. In the meantime, we also assume that the illegal border-crossing events occur independently, which may be realistic in many cases. However, if the illegal crossers share information with each other or are organized by the same smuggler crime group, the independence assumption may be violated. In these cases, correlation among multiple illegal crossings can be added to the model. We leave these extensions for future research.

Table 1. The number of teams with associate effectiveness of Inspection2

No. of Teams	jq (or f): Inspection load					
	0.1	0.2	0.3	0.4	0.5	0.6
1	0.004679	0.017523	0.036936	0.061552	0.090204	0.121901
2	0.000155	0.001148	0.003599	0.007926	0.014388	0.023115
3	3.85E-06	5.68E-05	0.000266	0.000776	0.001752	0.003358
4	7.67E-08	2.26E-06	1.58E-05	6.12E-05	0.000172	0.000394
5	1.27E-09	7.49E-08	7.83E-07	4.04E-06	1.42E-05	3.89E-05
6	1.82E-11	2.13E-09	3.34E-08	2.29E-07	1.00E-06	3.29E-06
7	2.24E-13	5.32E-11	1.25E-09	1.14E-08	6.22E-08	2.45E-07
8	0	1.18E-12	4.14E-11	5.04E-10	3.44E-09	1.62E-08
9	0	2.31E-14	1.24E-12	2.01E-11	1.71E-10	9.67E-10
10	0	0	3.29E-14	7.28E-13	7.73E-12	5.25E-11
11	0	0	0	2.35E-14	3.09E-13	2.61E-12
12	0	0	0	0	0	1.15E-13
13	0	0	0	0	0	0

No. of Teams	jq (or f) : Inspection load					
	0.7	0.8	0.9	1	1.2	1.4
1	0.155805	0.191208	0.227518	0.264241	0.337373	0.408167
2	0.034142	0.047423	0.062857	0.080301	0.120513	0.166502
3	0.005753	0.00908	0.013459	0.018988	0.033769	0.053725
4	0.000786	0.001411	0.002344	0.00366	0.007746	0.014253
5	9.00E-05	0.000184	0.000343	0.000594	0.0015	0.003201
6	8.88E-06	2.07E-05	4.34E-05	8.32E-05	0.000251	0.000622
7	7.69E-07	2.05E-06	4.82E-06	1.02E-05	3.70E-05	0.000107
8	5.93E-08	1.81E-07	4.77E-07	1.13E-06	4.86E-06	1.63E-05
9	4.13E-09	1.43E-08	4.25E-08	1.11E-07	5.76E-07	2.25E-06
10	2.61E-10	1.04E-09	3.45E-09	1.00E-08	6.22E-08	2.83E-07
11	1.52E-11	6.87E-11	2.57E-10	8.32E-10	6.17E-09	3.27E-08
12	8.11E-13	4.19E-12	1.77E-11	6.36E-11	5.66E-10	3.49E-09
13	3.86E-14	2.27E-13	1.13E-12	4.50E-12	4.82E-11	3.46E-10
14	0	0	6.41E-14	2.81E-13	3.81E-12	3.21E-11
15	0	0	0	0	2.66E-13	2.78E-12
16	0	0	0	0	0	2.11E-13
17	0	0	0	0	0	0

continued on the following page

Table 1. continued

No. of Teams	*jq* (or *f*): Inspection load					
	1.6	1.8	2	2.5	3	3.5
1	0.475069	0.537163	0.5939942	0.712703	0.800852	0.864112
2	0.216642	0.269379	0.3233236	0.456187	0.57681	0.679153
3	0.078813	0.108708	0.1428765	0.242424	0.352768	0.463367
4	0.023682	0.036407	0.052653	0.108822	0.184737	0.274555
5	0.00604	0.010378	0.0165636	0.042021	0.083918	0.142386
6	0.001336	0.002569	0.0045338	0.014187	0.033509	0.065288
7	0.00026	0.000562	0.0010967	0.004247	0.011905	0.026739
8	4.54E-05	0.00011	0.0002374	0.00114	0.003803	0.009874
9	7.14E-06	1.94E-05	4.65E-05	0.000277	0.001102	0.003315
10	1.02E-06	3.12E-06	8.31E-06	6.16E-05	0.000292	0.001019
11	1.35E-07	4.63E-07	1.36E-06	1.26E-05	7.14E-05	0.000289
12	1.65E-08	6.33E-08	2.07E-07	2.38E-06	1.61E-05	7.60E-05
13	1.87E-09	8.07E-09	2.93E-08	4.20E-07	3.40E-06	1.86E-05
14	1.98E-10	9.60E-10	3.87E-09	6.92E-08	6.70E-07	4.26E-06
15	1.96E-11	1.07E-10	4.80E-10	1.07E-08	1.24E-07	9.18E-07
16	1.82E-12	1.13E-11	5.61E-11	1.56E-09	2.16E-08	1.87E-07
17	1.49E-13	1.11E-12	6.18E-12	2.15E-10	3.57E-09	3.58E-08
18	0	9.61E-14	6.42E-13	2.80E-11	5.59E-10	6.53E-09
19	0	0	5.83E-14	3.48E-12	8.31E-11	1.13E-09
20		0	0	4.07E-13	1.18E-11	1.87E-10
21		0	0	4.14E-14	1.57E-12	2.95E-11
22		0	0	0	1.81E-13	4.44E-12
23		0	0	0	0	6.34E-13
24		0	0	0		7.78E-14
25		0	0	0		0

continued on the following page

Table 1. continued

No. of Teams	*jq* (or *f*): Inspection load					
	4	4.5	5	5.5	6	6.5
1	0.908422	0.938901	0.959572	0.973436	0.982649	0.988724
2	0.761897	0.826422	0.875348	0.911624	0.938031	0.956964
3	0.56653	0.657704	0.734974	0.798301	0.848796	0.88815
4	0.371163	0.467896	0.559507	0.642482	0.714944	0.776328
5	0.21487	0.29707	0.384039	0.471081	0.55432	0.630959
6	0.110674	0.168949	0.237817	0.313964	0.393697	0.473476
7	0.051134	0.086586	0.133372	0.190515	0.25602	0.327242
8	0.021363	0.040257	0.068094	0.105643	0.152763	0.208427
9	0.008132	0.017093	0.031828	0.053777	0.083924	0.122616
10	0.00284	0.006669	0.013695	0.025251	0.042621	0.066839
11	0.000915	0.002404	0.005453	0.010988	0.020092	0.03388
12	0.000274	0.000805	0.002019	0.004451	0.008827	0.016027
13	7.63E-05	0.000252	0.000698	0.001685	0.003628	0.0071
14	1.99E-05	7.37E-05	0.000226	0.000599	0.0014	0.002956
15	4.89E-06	2.03E-05	6.90E-05	0.0002	0.000509	0.00116
16	1.13E-06	5.27E-06	1.99E-05	6.32E-05	0.000175	0.00043
17	2.48E-07	1.30E-06	5.42E-06	1.89E-05	5.69E-05	0.000151
18	5.16E-08	3.02E-07	1.40E-06	5.37E-06	1.76E-05	5.05E-05
19	1.02E-08	6.72E-08	3.45E-07	1.45E-06	5.18E-06	1.61E-05
20	1.92E-09	1.42E-08	8.11E-08	3.75E-07	1.46E-06	4.89E-06
21	3.46E-10	2.88E-09	1.82E-08	9.24E-08	3.91E-07	1.42E-06
22	5.97E-11	5.58E-10	3.91E-09	2.18E-08	1.01E-07	3.95E-07
23	9.87E-12	1.04E-10	8.07E-10	4.94E-09	2.48E-08	1.05E-07
24	1.56E-12	1.85E-11	1.60E-10	1.08E-09	5.89E-09	2.71E-08
25	2.35E-13	3.17E-12	3.05E-11	2.25E-10	1.34E-09	6.69E-09
26	3.04E-14	5.13E-13	5.58E-12	4.55E-11	2.96E-10	1.59E-09
27	0	7.09E-14	9.65E-13	8.86E-12	6.28E-11	3.66E-10
28		0	1.42E-13	1.66E-12	1.29E-11	8.13E-11
29		0	0	2.95E-13	2.54E-12	1.74E-11
30			0	4.44E-14	4.75E-13	3.60E-12
31				0	7.51E-14	7.05E-13
32					0	1.16E-13
33					0	0

continued on the following page

Table 1. continued

No. of Teams	*jq* (or *f*): Inspection load					
	7	7.5	8	8.5	9	9.5
1	0.992705	0.995299	0.996981	0.9980671	0.998766	0.999214
2	0.970364	0.979743	0.986246	0.9907168	0.993768	0.995836
3	0.918235	0.940855	0.95762	0.9698909	0.978774	0.98514
4	0.827008	0.867938	0.900368	0.925636	0.945036	0.959737
5	0.699292	0.758564	0.808764	0.8504027	0.884309	0.911472
6	0.550289	0.621845	0.686626	0.7438221	0.793219	0.835051
7	0.401286	0.475361	0.547039	0.6144029	0.676103	0.731337
8	0.270909	0.338033	0.407453	0.476895	0.544347	0.608177
9	0.169504	0.223592	0.283376	0.3470263	0.412592	0.478174
10	0.098521	0.137762	0.184114	0.236638	0.294012	0.354672
11	0.05335	0.079241	0.111924	0.151338	0.196992	0.24801
12	0.027	0.042666	0.063797	0.0909171	0.124227	0.16357
13	0.012811	0.021565	0.034181	0.0514111	0.073851	0.101864
14	0.005717	0.01026	0.017257	0.0274254	0.041466	0.059992
15	0.002407	0.004608	0.008231	0.0138334	0.022036	0.033473
16	0.000958	0.001959	0.003718	0.0066127	0.011106	0.017727
17	0.000362	0.00079	0.001594	0.0030024	0.00532	0.008928
18	0.00013	0.000303	0.00065	0.0012975	0.002426	0.004284
19	4.44E-05	0.000111	0.000253	0.0005347	0.001056	0.001962
20	1.45E-05	3.87E-05	9.40E-05	0.0002106	0.000439	0.000859
21	4.53E-06	1.29E-05	3.34E-05	7.94E-05	0.000175	0.000361
22	1.35E-06	4.13E-06	1.14E-05	2.87E-05	6.68E-05	0.000145
23	3.89E-07	1.27E-06	3.73E-06	9.96E-06	2.45E-05	5.61E-05
24	1.07E-07	3.75E-07	1.17E-06	3.32E-06	8.65E-06	2.09E-05
25	2.85E-08	1.07E-07	3.55E-07	1.07E-06	2.94E-06	7.47E-06
26	7.31E-09	2.92E-08	1.04E-07	3.31E-07	9.64E-07	2.58E-06
27	1.81E-09	7.74E-09	2.93E-08	9.92E-08	3.05E-07	8.62E-07
28	4.32E-10	1.98E-09	7.97E-09	2.87E-08	9.34E-08	2.78E-07
29	9.98E-11	4.90E-10	2.10E-09	8.03E-09	2.77E-08	8.68E-08
30	2.23E-11	1.17E-10	5.37E-10	2.18E-09	7.93E-09	2.63E-08
31	4.84E-12	2.72E-11	1.33E-10	5.72E-10	2.21E-09	7.70E-09
32	1.01E-12	6.13E-12	3.19E-11	1.46E-10	5.95E-10	2.19E-09
33	2.01E-13	1.33E-12	7.43E-12	3.61E-11	1.56E-10	6.06E-10
34	3.33E-14	2.74E-13	1.67E-12	8.68E-12	3.97E-11	1.63E-10
35	0	4.72E-14	3.56E-13	2.02E-12	9.82E-12	4.26E-11
36		0	6.34E-14	4.43E-13	2.35E-12	1.08E-11
37			0	8.08E-14	5.30E-13	2.65E-12

continued on the following page

Table 1. continued

38				0	9.95E-14	6.14E-13
39					0	1.18E-13
40						0

No. of Teams	jq (or f): Inspection load					
	10	15	20	25	30	35
1	0.999501	0.999995	1	1	1	1
2	0.997231	0.999961	1	1	1	1
3	0.989664	0.999789	0.999997	1	1	1
4	0.970747	0.999143	0.999983	1	1	1
5	0.932914	0.997208	0.999928	0.999999	1	1
6	0.869859	0.992368	0.999745	0.999994	1	1
7	0.779779	0.981998	0.999221	0.999977	0.999999	1
8	0.66718	0.962554	0.997913	0.999925	0.999998	1
9	0.54207	0.930146	0.995005	0.999779	0.999993	1
10	0.41696	0.881536	0.989188	0.999414	0.999978	0.999999
11	0.303224	0.815248	0.978613	0.998584	0.999936	0.999998
12	0.208444	0.732389	0.960988	0.996856	0.999832	0.999993
13	0.135536	0.636782	0.933872	0.993533	0.999593	0.999981
14	0.083458	0.534346	0.895136	0.987598	0.999079	0.999951
15	0.04874	0.43191	0.843487	0.977707	0.998053	0.999882
16	0.027042	0.335877	0.778926	0.962252	0.996127	0.999729
17	0.014278	0.251141	0.702972	0.939525	0.99273	0.999414
18	0.007187	0.180528	0.618578	0.907959	0.987067	0.998802
19	0.003454	0.124781	0.529743	0.866425	0.978127	0.997675
20	0.001588	0.082971	0.440907	0.814508	0.964715	0.995703
21	0.0007	0.053106	0.356302	0.752701	0.945557	0.992417
22	0.000296	0.032744	0.279389	0.682467	0.919431	0.987187
23	0.00012	0.019465	0.212507	0.606124	0.885354	0.97923
24	4.69E-05	0.011165	0.156773	0.526602	0.842758	0.967626
25	1.77E-05	0.006185	0.112185	0.447079	0.791643	0.95138
26	6.42E-06	0.003312	0.077887	0.370614	0.732663	0.92951
27	2.25E-06	0.001716	0.052481	0.299814	0.667131	0.90116
28	7.64E-07	0.000861	0.034334	0.236599	0.596918	0.865723
29	2.51E-07	0.000418	0.021818	0.182104	0.524283	0.822955
30	7.98E-08	0.000197	0.013475	0.136691	0.451648	0.773058
31	2.46E-08	9.03E-05	0.008092	0.100068	0.381357	0.716722
32	7.37E-09	4.02E-05	0.004727	0.071456	0.315459	0.655105

continued on the following page

Table 1. continued

33	2.14E-09	1.74E-05	0.002688	0.04978	0.255551	0.589754
34	6.06E-10	7.30E-06	0.001489	0.033842	0.202692	0.522481
35	1.67E-10	2.99E-06	0.000804	0.022458	0.157383	0.455208
36	4.46E-11	1.19E-06	0.000423	0.014552	0.119627	0.389804
37	1.16E-11	4.63E-07	0.000217	0.009211	0.089013	0.327934
38	2.95E-12	1.75E-07	0.000109	0.005696	0.064844	0.27095
39	7.25E-13	6.49E-08	5.32E-05	0.003444	0.046253	0.21981
40	1.68E-13	2.34E-08	2.54E-05	0.002036	0.03231	0.175062
41	3.24E-14	8.27E-09	1.19E-05	0.001177	0.022107	0.136863
42	0	2.85E-09	5.43E-06	0.000666	0.01482	0.10503
43		9.61E-10	2.42E-06	0.000369	0.009735	0.07912
44		3.17E-10	1.06E-06	0.0002	0.006269	0.058509
45		1.02E-10	4.54E-07	0.000106	0.003958	0.042479
46		3.24E-11	1.90E-07	5.54E-05	0.00245	0.030282
47		1.00E-11	7.83E-08	2.83E-05	0.001488	0.021199
48		3.02E-12	3.15E-08	1.42E-05	0.000887	0.014576
49		8.84E-13	1.25E-08	6.95E-06	0.000519	0.009846
50		2.43E-13	4.83E-09	3.35E-06	0.000298	0.006534
51		5.44E-14	1.84E-09	1.59E-06	0.000168	0.004261
52		0	6.86E-10	7.36E-07	9.31E-05	0.002732
53		0	2.51E-10	3.36E-07	5.07E-05	0.001722
54		0	9.05E-11	1.51E-07	2.71E-05	0.001067
55		0	3.20E-11	6.64E-08	1.43E-05	0.00065
56		0	1.11E-11	2.87E-08	7.38E-06	0.00039
57		0	3.79E-12	1.22E-08	3.75E-06	0.00023
58		0	1.27E-12	5.13E-09	1.88E-06	0.000134
59		0	4.10E-13	2.11E-09	9.25E-07	7.64E-05
60		0	1.24E-13	8.56E-10	4.48E-07	4.30E-05
61		0	3.03E-14	3.42E-10	2.14E-07	2.38E-05
62			0	1.34E-10	1.01E-07	1.30E-05
63			0	5.20E-11	4.65E-08	6.99E-06
64			0	1.98E-11	2.12E-08	3.70E-06
65			0	7.42E-12	9.53E-09	1.93E-06
66			0	2.74E-12	4.22E-09	9.95E-07
67			0	9.88E-13	1.84E-09	5.05E-07
68			0	3.45E-13	7.92E-10	2.53E-07
69				1.12E-13	3.36E-10	1.25E-07
70				2.92E-14	1.41E-10	6.07E-08
71				0	5.81E-11	2.91E-08

continued on the following page

Table 1. continued

72				0	2.36E-11	1.38E-08
73				0	9.48E-12	6.46E-09
74				0	3.74E-12	2.98E-09
75				0	1.45E-12	1.36E-09
76					5.40E-13	6.11E-10
77					1.87E-13	2.72E-10
78					5.15E-14	1.19E-10
79					0	5.16E-11
80					0	2.21E-11
81						9.32E-12
82						3.87E-12
83						1.58E-12
84						6.19E-13
85						2.25E-13
86						6.45E-14
87						0

No. of Teams	jq (or f): Inspection load					
	40	45	50	60	70	80
1	1	1	1	1	1	1
2	1	1	1	1	1	1
3	1	1	1	1	1	1
4	1	1	1	1	1	1
5	1	1	1	1	1	1
6	1	1	1	1	1	1
7	1	1	1	1	1	1
8	1	1	1	1	1	1
9	1	1	1	1	1	1
10	1	1	1	1	1	1
11	1	1	1	1	1	1
12	1	1	1	1	1	1
13	0.999999	1	1	1	1	1
14	0.999998	1	1	1	1	1
15	0.999995	1	1	1	1	1
16	0.999986	0.999999	1	1	1	1
17	0.999965	0.999998	0.9999999	1	1	1
18	0.99992	0.999996	0.9999998	1	1	1
19	0.999824	0.99999	0.9999995	1	1	1

continued on the following page

Table 1. continued

20	0.999632	0.999976	0.9999988	1	1	1
21	0.999266	0.999947	0.999997	1	1	1
22	0.998601	0.999887	0.9999929	1	1	1
23	0.997445	0.99977	0.999984	1	1	1
24	0.995517	0.999551	0.9999655	1	1	1
25	0.992434	0.999156	0.9999284	1	1	1
26	0.987689	0.998473	0.9998571	0.999999	1	1
27	0.980661	0.997334	0.9997252	0.999999	1	1
28	0.97062	0.995503	0.9994895	0.999997	1	1
29	0.956771	0.992663	0.9990832	0.999993	1	1
30	0.938306	0.988402	0.998406	0.999986	1	1
31	0.914479	0.982218	0.9973137	0.999972	1	1
32	0.884696	0.97352	0.9956071	0.999945	1	1
33	0.848596	0.961661	0.9930212	0.999897	0.999999	1
34	0.806124	0.945964	0.9892185	0.999812	0.999999	1
35	0.757586	0.925782	0.9837861	0.999666	0.999997	1
36	0.703654	0.900556	0.9762411	0.999424	0.999994	1
37	0.645349	0.869874	0.9660451	0.99903	0.999989	1
38	0.583976	0.833541	0.9526293	0.998408	0.999979	1
39	0.521029	0.791618	0.9354296	0.997452	0.999961	1
40	0.458082	0.744455	0.91393	0.996017	0.99993	0.999999
41	0.39667	0.69269	0.8877109	0.993918	0.999877	0.999999
42	0.338183	0.637228	0.8564978	0.990919	0.999789	0.999998
43	0.283776	0.579187	0.8202034	0.986734	0.999645	0.999996
44	0.234315	0.519826	0.7789598	0.981027	0.999417	0.999992
45	0.19035	0.460465	0.7331335	0.973418	0.999061	0.999985
46	0.152119	0.402395	0.6833224	0.963493	0.99852	0.999974
47	0.119583	0.346796	0.6303318	0.950823	0.997714	0.999955
48	0.092469	0.294671	0.5751333	0.934986	0.996539	0.999922
49	0.070335	0.246802	0.5188083	0.915593	0.994859	0.999869
50	0.052628	0.20372	0.4624833	0.892322	0.992509	0.999785
51	0.03874	0.165706	0.4072627	0.864944	0.989282	0.999652
52	0.028057	0.132809	0.354166	0.833354	0.984939	0.999447
53	0.019995	0.104878	0.3040747	0.797592	0.979202	0.999139
54	0.014022	0.081602	0.257694	0.757857	0.971766	0.998682
55	0.009679	0.062558	0.2155296	0.714509	0.962301	0.998017
56	0.006576	0.047255	0.1778829	0.668064	0.950471	0.997067
57	0.004399	0.035174	0.1448594	0.619176	0.935942	0.995734
58	0.002898	0.0258	0.1163909	0.568601	0.918407	0.993895

continued on the following page

Table 1. continued

59	0.00188	0.018651	0.0922651	0.517169	0.897603	0.991402
60	0.001201	0.013289	0.0721602	0.465738	0.873332	0.988078
61	0.000756	0.009334	0.0556808	0.415149	0.845479	0.983719
62	0.000469	0.006463	0.0423909	0.366192	0.814033	0.978094
63	0.000287	0.004412	0.0318434	0.319567	0.779093	0.970951
64	0.000173	0.00297	0.0236032	0.275855	0.740877	0.962023
65	0.000103	0.001972	0.0172646	0.235506	0.699721	0.951033
66	6E-05	0.001291	0.0124626	0.198826	0.656071	0.937713
67	3.47E-05	0.000834	0.008879	0.165977	0.610467	0.921809
68	1.97E-05	0.000532	0.006244	0.136993	0.563521	0.903098
69	1.11E-05	0.000334	0.0043346	0.11179	0.515895	0.881403
70	6.15E-06	0.000207	0.0029707	0.090187	0.468269	0.85661
71	3.36E-06	0.000127	0.0020103	0.071931	0.421314	0.828674
72	1.81E-06	7.68E-05	0.0013433	0.056717	0.375663	0.797634
73	9.67E-07	4.59E-05	0.0008864	0.044213	0.331889	0.763617
74	5.08E-07	2.7E-05	0.0005778	0.034075	0.29048	0.726842
75	2.64E-07	1.57E-05	0.000372	0.025964	0.251832	0.687616
76	1.35E-07	9.05E-06	0.0002366	0.019561	0.216235	0.646325
77	6.86E-08	5.14E-06	0.0001487	0.014571	0.183874	0.603425
78	3.43E-08	2.88E-06	9.232E-05	0.010733	0.154832	0.559425
79	1.7E-08	1.6E-06	5.665E-05	0.007818	0.129099	0.514869
80	8.28E-09	8.76E-07	3.436E-05	0.005632	0.106583	0.470312
81	4E-09	4.74E-07	2.06E-05	0.004012	0.087124	0.426305
82	1.91E-09	2.54E-07	1.221E-05	0.002827	0.070513	0.383372
83	8.98E-10	1.34E-07	7.153E-06	0.001971	0.056503	0.341991
84	4.18E-10	7.02E-08	4.144E-06	0.001359	0.044829	0.30258
85	1.93E-10	3.63E-08	2.374E-06	0.000927	0.035215	0.265487
86	8.78E-11	1.86E-08	1.345E-06	0.000626	0.027389	0.230982
87	3.95E-11	9.38E-09	7.541E-07	0.000418	0.021093	0.199254
88	1.76E-11	4.69E-09	4.181E-07	0.000276	0.016084	0.17041
89	7.75E-12	2.32E-09	2.293E-07	0.000181	0.012145	0.144483
90	3.37E-12	1.14E-09	1.245E-07	0.000117	0.009081	0.121436
91	1.44E-12	5.51E-10	6.683E-08	7.48E-05	0.006724	0.101175
92	6.05E-13	2.64E-10	3.552E-08	4.75E-05	0.004931	0.083558
93	2.45E-13	1.25E-10	1.868E-08	2.98E-05	0.003581	0.068402
94	9.13E-14	5.87E-11	9.725E-09	1.85E-05	0.002576	0.055504
95	2.69E-14	2.73E-11	5.012E-09	1.14E-05	0.001835	0.044643
96	0	1.25E-11	2.557E-09	6.94E-06	0.001295	0.035591
97		5.68E-12	1.292E-09	4.19E-06	0.000906	0.028126

continued on the following page

Table 1. continued

98		2.54E-12	6.46E-10	2.5E-06	0.000627	0.022033
99		1.11E-12	3.2E-10	1.48E-06	0.00043	0.017108
100		4.68E-13	1.569E-10	8.69E-07	0.000293	0.013169
101		1.82E-13	7.623E-11	5.04E-07	0.000197	0.010048
102		5.53E-14	3.667E-11	2.9E-07	0.000132	0.007601
103		0	1.746E-11	1.65E-07	8.7E-05	0.0057
104		0	8.23E-12	9.34E-08	5.71E-05	0.004238
105		0	3.833E-12	5.23E-08	3.71E-05	0.003124
106			1.759E-12	2.9E-08	2.39E-05	0.002283
107			7.9E-13	1.59E-08	1.52E-05	0.001655
108			3.414E-13	8.68E-09	9.64E-06	0.001189
109			1.357E-13	4.69E-09	6.05E-06	0.000847
110			4.208E-14	2.51E-09	3.76E-06	0.000599
111			0	1.33E-09	2.32E-06	0.00042
112			0	7E-10	1.42E-06	0.000292
113			0	3.65E-10	8.6E-07	0.000201
114				1.89E-10	5.17E-07	0.000137
115				9.67E-11	3.08E-07	9.32E-05
116				4.92E-11	1.82E-07	6.27E-05
117				2.48E-11	1.07E-07	4.18E-05
118				1.24E-11	6.22E-08	2.77E-05
119				6.12E-12	3.59E-08	1.82E-05
120				2.99E-12	2.05E-08	1.19E-05
121				1.44E-12	1.17E-08	7.66E-06
122				6.8E-13	6.57E-09	4.92E-06
123				3.08E-13	3.67E-09	3.13E-06
124				1.28E-13	2.04E-09	1.98E-06
125				4.11E-14	1.12E-09	1.24E-06
126				0	6.12E-10	7.72E-07
127				0	3.32E-10	4.76E-07
128					1.79E-10	2.92E-07
129					9.53E-11	1.78E-07
130					5.05E-11	1.07E-07
131					2.65E-11	6.43E-08
132					1.38E-11	3.83E-08
133					7.16E-12	2.26E-08
134					3.67E-12	1.33E-08
135					1.86E-12	7.73E-09
136					9.3E-13	4.47E-09

continued on the following page

Table 1. continued

137					4.54E-13	2.57E-09
138					2.12E-13	1.46E-09
139					9.1E-14	8.3E-10
140					3.01E-14	4.67E-10
141					0	2.61E-10
142					0	1.45E-10
143					0	7.96E-11
144					0	4.36E-11
145					0	2.37E-11
146					0	1.28E-11
147					0	6.83E-12
148						3.62E-12
149						1.9E-12
150						9.82E-13
151						4.95E-13
152						2.39E-13
153						1.05E-13
154						3.6E-14
155						0

Meanwhile, to seal the border, the authorities have planned to build metal fences along the entire border between Mexico and the U.S.. It would cost billions to build and tens of billions more to maintain. To reduce the costs, an alternative approach of establishing a "virtual fence" using information technology is proposed (Smith & Epstein, 2008). The idea is to connect a web of radar, infrared cameras, ground sensors, and airborne drones to extend the eyes and ears of the border patrol law enforcement. This requires efforts to assemble beam images and information from radar, cameras, and Wi-Fi transmitters to a command center in Tucson and to laptops installed in 50 patrol cars. The challenge is image identification and understanding. Wind and rain can affect the cameras' image quality, and current image processing technology is unable to distinguish between mesquite bushes and clusters of people or animals. Early tests suggest that there is a difficulty of quickly integrating infrared images, radar scans, and ground sensor readings when a target is discovered. Thus the integrated information could not arrive at the patrol cars in time for agents to pursue targets.

If the problem can be resolved, the virtual fence can be deployed along the whole border. Some specialists estimate that the border patrol would need extra 100,000 guards to go after all the migrants spotted by this technology.

REFERENCES

Carroll, S., & Gonzalez, D. (2005). Napolitano taps disaster funds for border counties. The Arizona Republic, August 16, 2005. Retrieved August 16, 2005, from http://www.azcentral.com/arizonarepublic/news/articles/0816borderemergency16.html.

CNN. (2006). Bush calls for 6,000 troops along border. May 16, 2006. Retrieved May 17, 2006, from http://www.cnn.com/2006/POLITICS/05/15/immigration/

CNN. (2005). Border emergency declared in New Mexico. Retrieved August 13, 2005, from http://www.cnn.com/2005/US/08/12/newmexico.

DHS Portfolios. (2005). DHS Portfolios: Border and Transportation Security. Retrieved November 21, 2005, from http://www.dhs.gov/dhspublic/interapp/editorial/editorial_0545.xml

Ding, W. (2007). A mathematical approach to limit illegal border-crossings: With applications in protecting critical infrastructure. *Defense & Security Analysis*, *23*(4), 359-377.

Media. (2005). Napolitano declares border emergency. Associated Press. Retrieved August 15, 2005, from http://www.azcentral.com/news/articles/0815borderemergency15.html.

Media. (2006). Bush signs 700 miles of border fence into law. Retrieved October 26, 2006, from http://www.usbc.org/.

New York Independent System Operator [NYISO] (2004), NYISO interim report on the August 14, 2003 blackout. Retrieved January 15, 2004, from http://www.hks.harvard.edu/hepg/Papers/NYISO.blackout.report.8.Jan.04.pdf

Smith, G., & Epstein, K. (2008). On the border: the virtual fence isn't working. *Business Week*, February 18, 2008, 45-48.

ENDNOTES

[1] This part is modified and expanded from an article published by *Defense and Security Analysis*, 2007 (Ding, 2007).

[2] Only part of *jq* (or *f*) are listed here. If users need to use different values of *jq* (or *f*) other than those listed, please contact the author for a computer program.

Chapter XII
Weaponizing the Internet and the YouTube War

INTRODUCTION

In the war against terrorist enemies, the United States currently is using a traditional defensive approach: engaging in formal military ground battles with adversaries such as al-Qaeda. By conducting a formal military operation, powerful military forces ideally should defeat terrorists, break up terrorist cells, remove their home bases, disperse leaders, and severely degrade the terrorist groups' ability to wage attacks against the United States.

A traditional military war normally involves two parties with known geographical locations and concentrated battle areas. A victory occurs when an enemy is defeated. However, the war on terrorism represents an opposite situation: without geographic concentration. Modern terrorists operate across national borders and have access to funding and advanced technology with global reach. Terrorists such as al-Qaeda lack geographic homes, which mean the battlefield is geographically dispersed. Furthermore, in addition to using conventional weapons, they increasingly use modern information technology, particularly the Internet, to wage their battles. They ride the back of the Web and use advanced communications to distribute their thoughts or views, gather support, recruit new members, and move immense financial funds from one place to another. According to Weimann (2006), many terrorist groups have their own Web sites on the Internet, which they use to teach their members to prepare computer viruses, worms, Trojan horses, sniffers, and other malicious programs that multiply and cause potentially severe damages. They thus consider the capabilities of the Web as offensive mass weapons that can undermine worldwide actions.

The modern Internet penetrates all levels of society, such that information flows continuously and seamlessly across political, ethnic, and religious divides. Because of the global nature of cyberspace, it provides a new platform on which terrorists can wage battles. In this chapter, we examine the role of the Internet as a battlefield and analyze the course of war in cyberspace. We model the Internet structure and determine that the Internet needs a self-immunization mechanism that can self-detect illegal or criminal activities online.

A NEW BATTLEFIELD

Manpower and weaponry are two necessary and critical components in any type of war. In a traditional ground battle, the more troops and the better equipment, the greater the chances of winning the battle. However, if the Internet serves as a staging ground for a war, the number of solders and the status of their weaponry may not be decisive factors for winning the war. Using an inexpensive computing device, one person can access hundreds of thousands of people indirectly and anonymously through the mass connection of the Internet. Thus, war on the Internet appears relatively safe and of little risk compared with traditional ground battles. Little input may lead to great expectations, and the advantages of the Internet thus undoubtedly attract terrorist organizations.

To battle against terrorists (e.g., al Qaeda) who lack a geographical base but use the global Internet, we need to understand the role of the Internet as a battlefield.

Internet as Propaganda Medium

The Internet plays a key role for the strategy of terrorism. When the Internet is in place, reaching target audiences and broadcasting messages that the terrorist organization wants to transmit becomes easier than ever before. Conventional print and broadcast media suffer constraints with regard to who selects the message, such that a person or organization cannot directly control the dissemination of messages. With the Internet, not only can someone freely disseminate his or her message directly to many readers, but that person also completely controls the content of the message. With little or no regulation or censorship, or other forms of government control, the Internet allows terrorist groups such as al-Qaeda to concentrate their propaganda efforts. They develop Web sites to post their news, thoughts, views, and announcements. From these sites, visitors can download products in different data formats, such as films, video, audio clips, photographs, and books. Furthermore, they can use different data formats and languages to target different audiences for different purposes.

To potential supporters, they transmit messages of power to raise the morale of the target audience, despite their technological inferiority, limited membership, and lack of resources. These Web sites distribute education and training materials and provide step-by-step instructions for communicating with cell members. On Web forums, they discuss topics of interest and tactics.

A completely opposite message gets distributed to another target audience—the enemy or public who fights against them. Terrorists use Web sites to highlight their success and attempt to cause their enemy public to feel vulnerable, anywhere and anytime. For example, al-Qaeda consistently claims on its Web sites that the destruction of the World Trade Center caused concrete damages to the U.S. economy. Moreover, since September 11, 2001, their Web sites have frequently posted announcements of impending attack on U.S. targets. These warnings receive considerable media coverage, which helps generate a widespread sense of fear and insecurity among the target population (Talbot, 2005).

To those who are not directly involved in the conflict and observe events from the sidelines, terrorist Web site offer information in different languages and aim to gain sympathy for their causes.

Internet as a Recruiting and Fund-Raising Tool

The Internet offers a great opportunity and platform to build social networks among anonymous people anywhere and everywhere, even if they never see each other physically. Social networks have become a ubiquitous feature of online life. Online chat rooms, cybercafes, MySpace, Facebook, LinkedIn, user nets, and other such sites are attracting more and more people, especially young people, and keeping them online. Furthermore, advanced technology associated with information feeds, a form of virtual word of mouth, enables people to receive news and information automatically, without logging in to an online account. These technologies benefit people and society but also offer a convenient tool that terrorists may use to reach out to potential recruits.

Much like other Web sites, terrorist sites provide interactive business functions, such as sign-in forms and shopping carts. In addition to a Web page through which visitors can make credit card donations, they publish banking information, including the accounts into which donations can be deposited. Using clickstream information, terrorist organizations can determine who visits their Web sites and which pages they view. Technology also enables them to identify users who express sympathy or support, whom they then ask for donations.

Internet as a Training Base

The Internet represents an almost unlimited digital library, a sea of knowledge that contains a vast variety of information. If a user wants to discover how to set up a Web site and maintain a Web server, for example, he or she can get help readily from the Internet. Powerful search engines provide detailed "know-how" information, including step-by-step tutorials and functions for hands-on testing. Therefore, without physically going to a school or training facility, anyone can obtain school-quality education from the Internet. Information technology thus has changed the nature of education.

Terrorist groups do not want to miss the chance associated with such readily available information. By distributing training materials over the Internet rather than using real classrooms, they can reach their audience inexpensively and at the same time make them virtually impossible to track. For example, persons interested in establishing their own terrorist cells can find instructional materials from terrorist Web sites, which outline step-by-step instructions for communicating with cell members, defining tactics, and undertaking necessary procedures. Users also can view instructional films and download training manual for everything from kidnapping officials to building nuclear devices (Ulph, 2005). Although these virtual combat classrooms do not render physical training camps obsolete, they offer significant benefits through advanced multimedia technology.

Internet as a Weapon

The power of the Internet penetrates all levels of society and changes everyday life. It is hard to determine whether the Internet is misused; the ease of use and access to information has fostered new categories of criminal activities, commonly referred to as cyber attacks. By releasing computer viruses, worms, and other type of malicious codes, malicious actors intentionally seek to exploit the vulnerabilities of the targeted system to achieve a wide range of political or economic effects.

In some cases, the line between terrorist activities online and terrorist activities on the battlefield is so blurred that it becomes virtually impossible to distinguish them. For example, in November 2005, the information bureau of the Army of the Victorious Sect (AVS), a Sunni insurgent group operating in Iraq, announced an open competition for the design of the organization's new official Web site. The winner would not only enjoy the implementation of the winning design but also would receive an unusual prize: "The winner will fire three long-range rockets from any location in the world at an American military base in Iraq by pressing a button [on his computer] with his own blessed hand, using technology developed by the jihad fighters, Allah willing" (MEMRI, 2005).

Taking into account current cyberterrorism trends, we may surmise that terrorist groups will exist only in virtual space at some point in time. They will coordinate through the Internet to prepare attacks against countries with developed computer networks, because national boundaries have little meaning in cyberspace.

Although the Internet infrastructure officially consists of software and hardware, these elements form a global cyberspace that remains open to the world and available to anyone, anywhere, assuming they have the capability to exploit those opportunities. In next section, we examine the structure of the Internet and show that the inherent vulnerability of the Internet infrastructure permits malicious activities to flourish and perpetrators to remain anonymous.

UNDERSTANDING VULNERABILITIES THROUGH MODELING THE STRUCTURE OF THE INTERNET

The Internet is a publicly accessible network of interconnected computer networks. Although these interconnected networks look complicated, the fundamental structure of the Internet has a simple format: a series of layers. These layers define the basic network functions and are self-executable (autonomous) entities. Each layer relies on the layer below to execute more primitive functions and provides services to its upper counterpart. Different protocols (or rules) in each layer govern how communication occurs between two adjacent layers. When a user requests access to information on a Web server through a personal computer (PC), for example, the PC communicates with the server through a network. All information exchanged goes through these layers. We use an example to illustrate how the Internet works and, specifically, the working principle of these layers. Our goal is to show that the functions of the Internet are highly engineered, which creates inherent vulnerabilities that are difficult to overcome.

The Problem

Suppose a user sends a request through her PC to access a company's Web page, such as www.google.com. This request and its corresponding response go through the following stages:

Stage 1: The application layer. A browser in the user's PC activates the application layer to communicate the client program loaded on the user's PC to the Web server application program. At the application layer, the standard protocol for the Web is HTTP (Hypertext Transfer Protocol), which functions to govern requests and responses between the browser and the Web server application programs. For example, it allows the browser on the user's PC to appear as a standard set of codes, called Hypertext Markup Language (HTML), and decides how text and graphics should be displayed.

At the application layer, the user begins to do something useful, such as browse a Web site, send e-mail, or transfer a file between a server and a client computer. The application layer thus contains a range of protocols that directly serve the user, including Telnet (for remote log-ins), file transfer protocol (FTP), simple mail transfer protocol (for e-mail), HTTP for the Web, and so forth. The requested message then moves to the next stage (transport layer) for processing.

Stage 2: The transport layer. At the transport layer, the goal is to ensure that the user's computer (or other computing devices) and the Web server (or a host computer) can work together, regardless of the vendor or make of the two computers. Before the message is sent to the next layer, the transport layer divides it into sequence of manageable and basic blocks, referred to as data packets. Each packet is self-contained; its header contains complete address information about the destination and return site. The packets for each message, whether an e-mail message, a large file transfer, or a complicated Web transaction, are numbered and can be sent separately, so that they can be reassembled in the correct sequence at the destination.

The transport layer also manages data flow control, which automatically adapts the rates at which packets are transmitted depending on whether it detects congestion. If a particular link of a given path is busy, some packets might take an alternate route. The layer also acknowledges successful transmissions and requests retransmission if packets are damaged or arrive in error, meaning that it provides checks to ensure that each packet is error-free when delivered (i.e., error recovery function).

The standard for the transport layer is the transmission control protocol (TCP), which assumes that the next stage down (i.e., Internet layer) will move data packets to their destinations without a problem.

Stage 3: The Internet layer. At the Internet layer, the packets are routed to the destination host (e.g., Web server). Because each packet contains complete address information, routers along the packet's path need only inspect the header of the packet to determine its next-hop destination and forward it across several subnets or single networks to its destination. The protocol for routing packets is the Internet protocol, or IP. It first translates the network address and names into their physical equivalents, then uses one or more routers connected by single networks to do the job. A typical example may be as follows: Send this packet to computer number 123.456.78.90 via computer 987.654.32.10, which is on a network one hop away.

A router is network hardware that links a network to other networks. Using a routing table(s)—a log of the pattern of traffic coming from neighboring routers—routers can determine whether to take a certain route or select an alternative path for the packet if the default route is down. Every few seconds, each router on the network consults the router to which it is directly connected (its neighbor). By comparing notes, the router can decide which way to send packets to each of the hundreds of routers on the Internet.

The routers do not keep track of which packets belong to which active connections, which implies a route can forget about a packet as soon as it has been forwarded.

Stage 4: The data link layer and the physical layer. At this stage, the goal is to decide how packets should progress through the route using the physical medium, such as cable or physical wiring. To achieve this goal, this stage employs two layers: the data link layer and the physical layer. The data link layer addresses the actual transfer of data between two computers located on the same network. It also handles the physical transfer, framing (assembly of data into a single unit or block), and error detection. A typical example of the data link layer reads: Send this packet to computer number 123.456.78.90, which can be seen right next door.

The physical layer converts bits into signals for outgoing messages and signals into bits for incoming messages, using modems and telephone network standards to transmit message signals to the destination. Modems only link a user host to the first router. The protocol between the user's PC and the first router is the point-to-point protocol.

Stage 5: This stage consists of generating a response. When the signals arrive at the receiving end, the data link layer picks up the raw data (incoming message) from the physical layer and converts it into frames for delivery to the Internet layer. At the Internet layer, the frames are encapsulated into IP packets, sent to the transport layer. At the transport layer, the received IP packets get de-encapsulated and checked for errors, after which the contents move to the upper layers, where the message is checked to determine which host computer should receive it. Meanwhile, the message is converted into a format that the receiving application can understand. When the message reaches the application layer of the Web server, it prompts an acknowledgment and response. The homepage of the company—www.google.com in our example—then displays on the user's monitor.

This example shows that information communication processes among computers across the Internet are fully engineered. When the user hits a send button, a sequence of actions associated with the message or request, governed by protocols, automatically are executed without human interference. Such self-implementation and management functions, despite their many benefits, create a fundamental vulnerability, in that they lack self-awareness, or the capability to recognize the contents of packets. This vulnerability is vital, because it makes malicious activities possible and feasible. Let's return to our example to see how this vulnerability occurs at each stage.

In Stage 1, when the user types a request using a Web browser, the application layer activates and launches an appropriate protocol to handle the user's request. This layer does not provide a function to identify the content of the request, nor does it inspect whether the request contains harmful codes or information. Therefore, an invisible hole emerges that an attacker can exploit. As a result of this hole, computers increasingly are becoming infected with malicious software, such as bot, which creates networks of zombie computers, or botnets. If a Web site is infected, visitors to its pages sometimes can be infected merely by viewing them. Installing firewalls and antivirus software on users' computers may prevent conventional threats, such as worms and viruses, but these security tools do not inspect data downloaded through browsers. Therefore, in the current system design, any malicious code or inappropriate materials/requests can easily pass through the application layer. To overcome this system drawback, current approaches attempt to develop filters that (1) screen users' search query terms against predefined keyword lists or (2) check whether requests come from a specified "black list."

In Stage 2, which divides the user's request into packets at the transport layer, again, no function exists for detecting content. The TCP controls the transmission, but it does not care about whether the content of the request is harmful. Thus, the drawback continues to exist and has not been resolved.

In Stage 3, the packets arrive at the Internet layer, and the IP is activated. Because the IP is designed to support the easy attachment of hosts to networks, it provides little support for identifying the contents of each packet header field. Moreover, routers only check the address information in each packet's header part, which creates an opportunity for attackers to send one or more carefully crafted packets that can exploit the targeted system. One of the well-known attacks that often occurs at this layer pertains to a denial of service attack (DoS).

A DoS attack aims to disrupt the service provided by a network or server. It can be launched as two types, according to Hussain et al. (2003). The first type aims to crash a system by sending one or more carefully crafted malicious codes, commonly referred to as hacking. The second type involves sending large volumes of packets to occupy a significant portion of the available bandwidth, resulting in system congestion. This second type, also called a bandwidth attack, cannot be prevented easily because the targeted systems are connected to the public Internet. At present, no protocol or mechanism is available to govern users' ability to send large amounts of useless messages, and it is difficult for a server to check the validity of messages. Extensive research into DoS attacks suggests remedies such as developing patches to cover known holes in certain software or methods to detect or trace senders' IP addresses (Abdelsayed et al., 2003; Chang, 2002; Dean et al., 2002; Mahajan et al., 2002; Mirkovic et al., 2002).

In Stage 4, once the packets pass through the Internet layer, they receive green lights for the rest of their journey to reach the destination (Web server). Both the data link and the physical layers are designed to perform actual data transmission, and they are not responsible for guarding the system.

Finally, when the user's request arrives at the destination (server) in Stage 5, by default, the server processes any incoming requests and performs tasks related to requests such as accessing a database, displaying information, performing a business transaction, and so on. Because those network layers do not verify the contents of a request, any protection against an incoming threat depends largely on the response capability of the server. Commonly deployed defense mechanisms against cyber attacks include (1) antivirus software as well as network and application firewalls, (2) intrusion detection systems, and (3) patches on security holes for certain software. However, the mere installation of a network security device is not a substitute for maintaining and updating network defenses. In a recent Computer Security Institute survey, 90 percent of responders reported using antivirus software on their network systems, 89 percent had installed computer firewalls, and 60 percent employed intrusion detection systems. Yet of those who had installed antivirus software, 85 percent of the systems had been damaged by different types of computer viruses and malicious codes (CERT, 2006).

In addition, firewalls allow free passage to codes or programs downloaded through the browser, so certain malicious codes (for example, a bot) can install themselves on users' computers. Many Web users thus are the victims of "drive-by" downloads of bots from innocent Web sites, corrupted to exploit their browser vulnerabilities.

The current Internet infrastructure serves as a platform that offers ease of use and a source to generate service requests, but because of these characteristics, it is also very difficult for the network and a server to check the validity of requests and identify the contents of requests. Thus, it becomes difficult to protect both the network and the server from malicious requests that waste network resources and infect the server. Furthermore, packet routing relies on the capacity of each available route; false routes therefore can create black holes that absorb traffic destined for a particular block of address space. Because routers do not keep track of which packets belong to which active connections, if a packet contains malicious codes, it is difficult to pinpoint its source. For example, some malicious codes can appear to come from known and trusted sources, such as colleagues or well-known banks.

Possible Solutions

Management practices implemented to overcome weaknesses in the current Internet infrastructure basically focus on improving the functions of the Internet layer, by developing tools and methods to improve the reliability and secure use of key protocols, as well as ensure the security of routers that direct the flow of data. For example, the current IP is version 4 (IPv4), yet many organizations and countries have moved to an updated version, IPv6. To address the lack of source address verification in packet routing, new technology attempts to provide forged source address filtering to defeat DoS attacks. However, these efforts do not amount to a real solution, which requires enabling the Internet to implement self-awareness mechanisms that identify harmful contents.

Table 12.1. Internet infrastructure: Inherent vulnerabilities and possible solutions

Network Layers	Vulnerabilities	Solutions
Application layer	Lack ability to identify the contents/meaning of a request	1. Firewalls 2. Antivirus software 3. Intrusion detection systems 4. Security patches
Transport layer	No function to detect the contents of a packet	
Internet layer	Same as above	
Data link layer	Same as above	
Physical layer	Same as above	

WHY THE TASK OF COUNTERING CYBER ATTACKS IS NOT EASY

As shown in Table 12.1, vulnerabilities exist in each network layer. In the application layer, invisible holes can emerge that an attacker can exploit. The resulting outcome is that computers suffer the risk of infection, which can turn them into zombie computers or botnets. Existing approaches to fight against this threat rely on installing firewalls and intrusion detection systems that (1) screen users' search query terms against predefined keyword lists or (2) check whether requests come from a specified "black IP list."

In the transport and Internet layers, no function can identify the contents of each data packet. Instead, a new threat emerges because the protocols in these two layers only check the address information in each packet, creating an opportunity for attackers to send one or more carefully crafted packets that appear to come from known and trusted sources, such as colleagues or banks. This new threat reflects well-know denial of service (DoS) attacks. A potential solution to this threat would develop software that patches the hole or detects and traces the senders' IP address.

As mentioned before, current protections against an incoming threat depend on the methods used to overcome the existing shortcomings of current Internet structures. Commonly deployed defense mechanisms against cyber attacks include (1) antivirus software with network and application firewalls, (2) various intrusion detection systems, and (3) patches of security holes for certain software and operating systems. The effectiveness of antivirus software and firewalls relies on their abilities to detect the latest viruses, malwares, spyware, and so on. If responders or defenders are unaware of a hole in the software or operating systems, it is impossible to design corresponding patches to cover the hole. Therefore, the defense mechanism associated with using patches depends on how quickly those patches can be developed to cover the known holes.

In contrast, DoS attacks generate traffic flows that flood the network, thereby cutting off access to the service or host. The key element in an intrusion detection system involves learning both normal and abnormal traffic patterns. However, network intrusions typically occur in seconds or perhaps up to an hour, driven by automated deterministic processes or a person who seeks an exploitable weakness.

Therefore, the dynamics of these deterministic processes remain hidden, which makes designing an effective intrusion system with a dynamic property extremely challenging.

A cyber attack has several special characteristics compared with traditional battles:

1. Cyber attacks are covert, and the attacked victim (or response side) is unaware of when an attack will occur. The network remains open to attackers, but the response side cannot see its opponents and know only that opponents are hiding somewhere on the Internet.

2. Attackers are scattered around the world. They can access the network and launch an attack against a target computer or network at any time and from anywhere without any geographic boundaries.

3. Unless it obtains intelligence in advance, the response side remains in a passive position and realizes the occurrence of an attack only when it discovers computers or networks that do not function properly. Other than installing firewalls on the Internet, the response side cannot create a patch before it knows about the security hole, nor can it develop antivirus programs before it knows how viruses function. Moreover, the attacked side does not know the number of security holes or their location in advance.

4. It is very difficult to define anomalies in the massive number of traffic patterns. Attacks frequently change network locations and addresses, so tracing the source is a massive, "needle-in-a-haystack" job.

These characteristics indicate that countering cyber attacks is not an easy job, as the following simple analytic model also demonstrates.

Let $A(t)$ be the power of attackers at time t, which represents their capability to launch an attack, such as sending large volumes of data packets to occupy the network or issuing malicious codes to steal information or damage the target computers or network.

Let $D(t)$ denote the defensive power of the responders at time t, which includes the protection and prevention capabilities the responder side has deployed, including anti-virus/spam software, firewalls, various intrusion detection programs, and security patches. Let $P(t)$ represent newly increased attack power, or a reinforcement at time t, such as a new virus, new hackers, and so on. Then, $Q(t)$ is the newly increased defensive power at time t, reflecting the number of new patches developed, the improved functions in firewalls and intrusion detection systems, the newly updated anti-virus software, and so forth.

The rate at which an attack reduces its power (e.g., the attack reveals its Internet location/IP address and gets destroyed, the virus/malicious code gets prevented) is jointly proportional to the level of ability of the defensive power used by the response side and the quality of the attack. The rate at which the response side loses its defensive ability is proportional to the quality of the attacking power. If a time clock starts when an attack is launched, then the combative behavior between the attackers and defenders can be modeled as follows:

$$\frac{dA}{dt} = -gA \cdot D + P(t), \text{ and} \qquad\qquad (12\text{-}1)$$

$$\frac{dD}{dt} = -cA + Q(t),$$

(12-2)

where $A(t = 0) = A_0$, or the attacking power before launching an attack, and $D(t = 0) = D_0$, which represents the existing defensive power.

The greater A_0, the more vulnerable the Internet is, and the lower D_0, the weaker are the defensive approaches and capabilities. In these equations, g and $c > 0$ indicate the respective defensive/attacking effectiveness per attack. Quantitatively, g represents the average loss or destroy rate of the attackers that depends on the successful defensive power possessed by the responder side, and c indicates the average damage caused by a successful attack, such that damage refers to the average number of computers or the size of the network infected per attack.

Equations (12-1) and (12-2) are nonlinear because of the $A \times D$ term in equation (12-1). Quantitatively, it is difficult to derive a solution, but we can approximate a solution that reveals the variations in attacking and defensive capabilities over time. In turn, we can identify the intuitive qualitative behavior about the model system.

Quantitative Analysis

Consider a situation in which P(t) and Q(t) are both constant. The system becomes

$$\frac{dA}{dt} = -gA \cdot D + P, \text{ and}$$

(12-3)

$$\frac{dD}{dt} = -cA + Q.$$

(12-4)

If we set the right side of both equations to 0, we can solve for critical points. That is,

$$-gA \cdot D + P = 0, \text{ and}$$

(12-5)

$$-cA + Q = 0$$

(12-6)

Solving these two simultaneously, we find $A = \dfrac{Q}{c}$ and $D = \dfrac{Pc}{gQ}$. Therefore, the critical point is

$(A_c, D_c) = (\dfrac{Q}{c}, \dfrac{Pc}{gQ})$.

Next let u $=A - A_c$ and v $= D - D_c$. We can rewrite equations (12-3) and (12-4) as follows:

$$\frac{du}{dt} = \frac{\partial u}{\partial A} \cdot \frac{dA}{dt}$$
$$= \frac{\partial}{\partial A}(A - A_c) \cdot \frac{dA}{dt} = \frac{dA}{dt}$$
$$= -gA \cdot D + P,$$

and

$$\frac{dv}{dt} = \frac{\partial v}{\partial D} \cdot \frac{dD}{dt}$$
$$= \frac{\partial}{\partial D}(D - D_c) \cdot \frac{dD}{dt} = \frac{dD}{dt}$$
$$= -cA + Q.$$

Substituting u $=A - A_c$ and v $= D - D_c$ into these equations, we get

$$\frac{du}{dt} = -g(u + A_c)(v + D_c) + P, \text{ and}$$
$$\frac{dv}{dt} = -c(u + A_c).$$

Then, substituting $A_c = \frac{Q}{c}$ and $D_c = \frac{Pc}{gQ}$ into the equations yields

$$\frac{du}{dt} = -guv - \frac{Pc}{Q}u - \frac{gQ}{c}v, \text{ and} \tag{12-7}$$

$$\frac{dv}{dt} = -cu. \tag{12-8}$$

The linear approximate solutions for equation (12-7) and (12-8) in turn are

$$u(t) = \frac{1}{2X}[c \cdot P \cdot e^{tM} - c \cdot P \cdot e^{tN} + e^{tM}X + e^{tN}X] \cdot K_1 + \frac{gQ^2}{cX}[e^{tM} - e^{tN}] \cdot K_2, \text{ and}$$

$$v(t) = \frac{cQ}{X}[e^{tM} - e^{tN}] \cdot K_1 + \frac{1}{2X}[-c \cdot P \cdot e^{tM} + c \cdot P \cdot e^{tN} + e^{tM}X + e^{tN}X] \cdot K_2,$$

where X $= \sqrt{c^2P^2 + 4gQ^3}$,

$$M = \frac{-c^2P - cX}{2cQ},$$

$$N = \frac{-c^2P + cX}{2cQ},$$

$$K_1 = u(t = 0) = A_0 - A_c, \text{ and}$$

$$K_2 = v(t = 0) = D_0 - D_c.$$

Furthermore, we can measure g and c using $g = N_D \dfrac{R_D}{R_A}$ and $c = N_A S_A$.

In this system, N_D is the number of times the attacks do not achieve their expected goal, such as when the attackers' IP address gets detected or their malicious code loses its function because of anti-virus software or patches. N_A is the number of attachs lunched and S_A represents the number of times that attacks hit the target successfully. R_A measures the average size or range of the network or number of computers affected after one successful attack, and R_D measures the average number of attacking computers or attackers discovered per detective action.

Thus, the linear approximate solutions for equations (12-3) and (12-4) are

$$A(t) = u(t) + A_c = u(t) + \frac{Q}{c}, \text{ and} \tag{12-9}$$

$$D(t) = v(t) + D_c = v(t) + \frac{Pc}{gQ}. \tag{12-10}$$

Qualitative Behavior

This solution shows the variation in the attacking and defensive parties over time; we also consider its intuitive qualitative behavior. When both P(t) = 0 and Q(t) = 0, equations (12-1) and (12-2) indicate what happens at the moment that an attack occurs. During that particular period, no newly developed defensive power exists or can be used; instead, protection depends on already installed defense components. The combat behavior during this period therefore can be described as

$$\frac{dA}{dt} = -gA \cdot D, \text{ and} \tag{12-11}$$

$$\frac{dD}{dt} = -cA. \tag{12-12}$$

Rewriting equations (12-11) and (12-12) yields

$$\frac{\dfrac{dD}{dt}}{\dfrac{dA}{dt}} = \frac{dD}{dA} = \frac{-cA}{-gA \cdot D} = \frac{c}{gD}.$$

If we expand this expression, we obtain

$$gD \times dD = c \times dA.$$

Then, we integrate both sides and find

$$\int_{D_0}^{D(t)} g \cdot D \cdot dD = \int_{A_0}^{A(t)} c \cdot dA,$$

which we solve to get

$$\frac{1}{2} g [D^2(t) - D_0^2] = c[A(t) - A_0],$$

or

$$\frac{1}{2} g D^2(t) - \frac{1}{2} g D_0^2 = c A(t) - c A_0.$$

That is,
$$gD^2(t) = 2cA(t) - 2cA_0 + gD_0^2. \tag{12-13}$$

If we let $M = gD_0^2 - 2cA_0$, then equation (12-13) becomes

$$gD^2(t) = 2cA(t) + M. \tag{12-14}$$

Equation (12-14) represents a family of parabolic curves. Its corresponding phase portrait is depicted in Figure 12.1, which displays the combat situation between the defenders and attackers when an attack occurs.

We also can rewrite equation (12-7) as

$$D(t) = \sqrt{\frac{2c}{g} A(t) + \frac{M}{g}}.$$

When $M > 0$, A will become 0 if D moves to $D(t) = \sqrt{\frac{M}{g}}$ (in other words, when $D(t) = \sqrt{\frac{M}{g}}$,

$A(t) = 0$ at time t). This situation implies that defenders have successfully prevented the attack.

From $M = gD_0^2 - 2cA_0$, we can infer that $gD_0^2 - 2cA_0$ when $M > 0$. That is,

$$D_0 > \sqrt{\frac{2cA_0}{g}}.$$

Figure 12.1. The fight between defenders and attackers: A phase graph

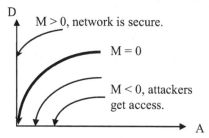

Therefore, when $D_0 > \sqrt{\dfrac{2cA_0}{g}}$, defenders have the capability to prevent the attacks and protect the network.

Yet what if M < 0? From equation (12-14), we know

$$A(t) = \frac{gD^2(t)}{2c} - \frac{M}{2c}.$$

Hence, when A decreases and becomes $A(t) = -\dfrac{M}{2c}$, D must become 0, which implies that attackers

have successfully avoided the prevention and gained access to the targeted network.

If M = 0, then $gD_0^2 - 2cA_0 = 0$. Thus, $D_0^2 = \dfrac{2c}{g}A_0$.

Summary

These analyses show that countering cyber attacks is not an easy task because attackers are scattered around the world and attacks are covert. To protect against an adversary three times as numerous, it is not sufficient for a defender to be three times as effective; instead, defenders must be three times larger.

As mentioned previously, one of the most important ways terrorists use the Internet is as a medium for propaganda, that is, a new forum to foster global awareness of their beliefs. They also use the Web to provide information about how to build chemical and explosive weapons. For example, according to Weimann (2006), many terrorist sites post *The Terrorist' Handbook* and *The Anarchist Cookbook*, two well-known manuals that offer detailed instructions for how to construct a wide range of bombs. Such information may be sought by not only terrorist organizations but also disaffected individuals prepared to use terrorist tactics to advance their idiosyncratic ideals. A search for the keywords "terrorist handbook" on the Google search engine returns approximately 276,000 matches. Although these matches include Web sites that simply contain the word "handbook," many of them also offer violent materials.

Completely removing terrorist sites is a difficult job, because these sites almost always reappear at other Web addresses. Web sites are dynamic (Talbot, 2005): They suddenly emerge, frequently modify their formats, and then disappear or seem to disappear because they change their Web addresses, even though they retain much of the same content. Keeping track of such Web sites is a massive job. Some observers suggest that allowing the Web sites to remain may help analysts gain intelligence and discover terrorist plots, whereas others recommend eradicating the sites to prevent their influence over people and avoid offering a forum for those interested in learning, thinking about, and discussing violent contents.

If authorities wish to prevent the Internet from being used as a staging ground for terrorism, both Internet surveillance and flexible online content filters may be needed.

Online content filtering is not a new topic. In the late 1990s, the Bertelsmann Foundation (1999) issued a multiparty report on "Self-regulation of Internet Content." The report addresses issues pertaining to Internet content, including protection of vulnerable parties, finding and evaluating information, and detecting electronic crimes. Following this report, the software and online industries have become increasingly involved in developing technical capabilities for self-regulating systems. Some researchers develop software packages that use a blacklist or keyword list approach to block objectionable Internet materials. Others create Web content labeling schemes for content rating, similar to the existing rating system for movies (Lasica, 1997; Miller et al., 1996; Resnick, 1997; Weinberg, 1997). However, these methods remain far from perfect; existing filtering tools often throw out the good with the bad, and content ratings lack universal schemes acceptable to everyone.

Because society at large promotes free speech, the great challenge in content filtering involves who gets to decide what constitutes acceptable content, and on what basis. Different people likely have different opinions about whether access to a particular Web page should be restricted, and a simple scale may not be able to reflect those differences fully. In next section, we instead adopt an example to show that a flexible and adaptive content filtering method that meets to each user's taste is achievable.

AN EXAMPLE APPLICATION

Conceptual Idea

When our hypothetical user reads a Web page, she recognizes and understands the contents and hence is able to capture the thematic property that the page exhibits. We further assume that this thematic property can be described as an abstract concept, expressed by a function that consists of a set of markers, which are specific words or phrases that indicate characteristics of certain contents. In such a setting, understanding a page's content becomes a procedure by which the user forms a concept based on the page. We propose designing an algorithm that can generate a concept which represents a page's thematic property by conducting sentiment analysis to identify markers on each page.

The general procedure consists of two steps: generating exemplars and forming a concept. Exemplars refer to the set of pages that reflect a person's preferences. By learning from these exemplars, the algorithm forms a concept. That is, we "tell" the machine that all these exemplars contain types of content X that we consider objectionable. Any page containing such content belongs to the category X. This method is (1) flexible, in that we can change the exemplars at any time; (2) customizable, which reflects the preference of a particular user who can provide user-specific exemplars; and (3) comprehensive, in that it applies to all sites.

To determine whether the proposed method is effective, we use the specific domain of filtering pornographic content on the Web to illustrate the method. Many parents prefer to prevent their children from accessing age-inappropriate content on the Internet.

Current methods of text-based filtering include combinations of (1) blacklisting "bad" or whitelisting "good" sites, (2) blocking sites that include "bad" words, and (3) applying a rating to the Web site, whether determined by the site creator or a third party. These methods all suffer deficiencies. Because the variety and extent of material available to computer users is so vast and changes so rapidly, the blacklist approach may suffer from incompleteness. For instance, if an unacceptable Web page does not appear on the blacklist, the system will accept the page even though it should be blocked. Alternatively, the keywords list method may block good sites that include "bad" keywords, such as medical or educational sites. Finally, a rating-based system is neither comprehensive, because it can rate only a small percentage of Web sites, nor efficient, due to the growing volume of Web sites and the frequency with which they get updated and changed (Jacob et al., 2007).

Civil liberty groups also argue that parents or guardians must be able to guide children's (or users') online behavior in a manner that is consistent with their values and world perspective, without losing the freedom they require to be autonomous adults. Unfortunately for many parents and guardians, none of the techniques outlined in the previous paragraph seem adequate to meet these requirements. Different people have different opinions about whether a particular Web page should be blocked or not, and those differences cannot be reflected fully by any simple scale. For example, Lee et al. (2002) use neural networks to filter pornographic Web pages but do not even attempt to customize the filtering to fit the value judgments of a responsible guardian. Hence, we require a flexible method that can adapt to each guardian's taste.

To overcome these deficiencies, we develop an adaptable e-guardian system that enables flexible access management for Web pages. We consider a situation in which an individual or institution, "the guardian," has a legitimate desire to control a user's access to sites that contain certain types of objectionable material. However, the guardian wants the user to have full and ready access to sites with nonobjectionable material. The adaptive e-guardian system therefore is designed to understand both the guardian's requirements and the user's needs. The guardian's requirements include opinions about the type of pages that should or should not be viewed by users. Because different guardians have different opinions, the system's multi-agent mechanism adapts to reflect these unique values. Users also may opt out and view the blocked pages, though if they do so, the system issues a warning and sends a record of the activity to the guardian.

Figure 12.2. The e-guardian system

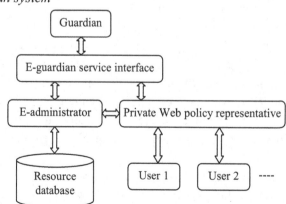

Through several experiments conducted to test this system, we find that it achieves better performance than several popularly used blocking software applications.

The System

System Structure. To use the system, the guardian first sends a service request that pages need to be examined through the service interface. The system then asks the guardian to provide the necessary information to determine the guardian's specifications. This information may indicate the type of contents or pages for which the guardian wants restricted access.

Figure 12.2 illustrates the structure of the proposed e-guardian system. It consists of five major components: users, a guardian, a private Web policy representative, an e-administrator, and a resource database.

User An individual, such as a child, using a computer to access information that the system is intended to regulate.

Guardian An individual, family, school, library, organization, business, or other entity that has acquired the system and has an interest in regulating the access of users to content through the computers it controls.

E-administrator A management subsystem that performs administrative tasks, such as receiving the guardian's input, querying the resource database to obtain a training data set according to the guardian's specific set of rules, providing a monitoring report to the guardian, and generating billing statements.

Private Web Policy Representative (PWPR) Generated by the system when a guardian uses the e-guardian service. This private Web policy representative, residing on the guardian's computer (e.g., a home PC if the guardian is a family, a server if the guardian is a business site), is trained to represent the guardian's preferences by examining each Web page that users want to access, making judgments about the contents of those pages, and taking action in response to those judgments.

Resource database An exemplar data set that represents the guardian's opinion, used to customize a private policy representative. Usually it contains two types of data resources: data sets rated by a trusted individual or organization (namely, a third-party rater) other than the guardian, and data sets generated by the system with the aid of the guardian.

Note that only the guardian interacts with the e-administrator. Individual users whose information access is being regulated only interact with the PWPR. In contrast, the resource database interacts directly with the e-administrator, not the individual PWPR. Presumably, many copies of the PWPR would be installed in different places, with one (or more) trained for each guardian. Likewise, multiple users in the guardian's organization may interact with each PWPR.

Operational Decisions. Once the guardian orders the service, the e-administrator combines inputs from the guardian to produce a guardian-specific PWPR that represents the guardian when evaluating Web pages. The system has a default PWPR trained by a third party's data. The system shows the guardian the performance of the default PWPR, and if the guardian is satisfied with this performance, no further training is required, and the guardian can install the default PWPR immediately. If the guardian finds the default PWPR insufficient, the system can automatically collect Web pages according to the guardian's requirements and thereby generate a customized PWPR for that guardian. We demonstrate how the system produces a PWPR for a particular guardian in the next section.

The PWPR thus is trained to filter content requested by users. Each time a user requests a page, the PWPR classifies the page as not-objectionable (page is displayed), clearly objectionable (page is

Figure 12.3. A flow chart of categorization processing

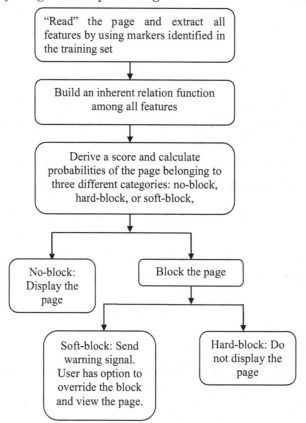

hard blocked), or potentially objectionable (page is soft blocked). The procedure is illustrated in Figure 12.3.

Finally, the PWPR notifies the guardian of filtering activities, such as a user overriding soft blocks, and reports a log of activity to the e-administrator to support billing, as well as to update of training data sets provided by the guardian and secure a repository of information about blocking.

Generating a Private Web Policy Representative. The PWPR filtering module represents the guardian in interactions with individual users to filter content and take action in response to a user's decision to override a blocking action. In this section, we describe the customization of a PWPR to represent each individual guardian's preference.

To customize a PWPR, the guardian provides information about preferences toward types and actions of blocking and choices of training data sets (third-party defined or own training set automatically collected by the system) for each criterion. The training set includes a set of pages and an associated classification (e.g., blocked or not blocked). The guardian can specify hard blocks (i.e., suggest hard blocking any page judged to meet a criterion), pure soft block (i.e., suggest soft blocking any page judged to meet a criterion), or general soft block (i.e., suggest hard blocking any page judged with a certain degree of confidence to meet a criterion; otherwise, soft block). The first two variants represent special cases of the third in which the degrees of confidence are set extremely low and extremely high, respectively.

After receiving this information, the system identifies features based on the training set and produces guardian-specific model parameters, namely, a classification scheme. On the basis of this classification scheme (e.g., should or should not be blocked), the system can judge new pages with regard to whether they meet this criterion.

Many approaches and techniques, such as neural networks, Bayesian nets, decision trees, supervised/unsupervised learning, rule- and example-based learning in artificial intelligence, and machine learning, can help design an intelligent classification system (Boley et al., 1999; Center, 1999; Cheeseman and Stutz, 1996; Craven et al., 1997; Lee et al., 2002; Leiberman, 1995; Maes and Kozierok, 1993; Menhaj and Delgosha, 2001; Midine et al., 1994; Salton and McGill., 1993). Because some techniques perform better than others, depending on the training sets and criteria, we adopt a multi-agent mechanism to customize a PWPR. That is, given a training set, whether from a third party's data or the own training set automatically collected by the system, several raw PWPRs train simultaneously using the same data set but different techniques. For example, one PWPR may be trained with a decision tree approach, another by a statistical classification technique (Caulkins et al., 2006), and the third with neural networks.

By comparing the performances of these PWPRs, the system can choose the PWPR with the best performance to serve as the customized PWPR. We use two indices to measure each PWPR's performance: the false positive rate and the false negative rate. For a given Web page, if the guardian considers it inappropriate but the PWPR decides to let the Web page be viewed, it represents a false positive error. Conversely, if the guardian says a Web page is suitable but the PWPR does not permit the user to view it, we refer to it as a false negative error. Because it uses a multi-agent mechanism to customize several PWPRs simultaneously and chooses the best one, the e-guardian system can be more flexible, adopt the latest machine learning technology, and deploy the PWPR that is best suited to reflect the values of a particular guardian.

Furthermore, by examining the content of the training data evaluated by the guardian, each trained PWPR comes to know the guardian's evaluation criteria. This procedure continues until the guardian believes that the PWPR's judgment is acceptable.

Empirical Study of the System

In this section, we present an empirical study in which the PWPR is trained using a decision tree approach. As we mentioned previously, the PWPR can be trained using different learning techniques through a multi-agent mechanism. Therefore, we compare the performance of the e-guardian system with several existing software applications, such as X-Stop (www.xstop.com), I-Gear, and Net Nanny.

Determining Data Sets. To train the PWPR, the system needs to have an exemplar data set. The issue here is how many Web pages are required so as to achieve an acceptable performance. Below we conduct a simple analysis to derive the exemplar data size.

Suppose the content of a Web page is represented by features. If we let x be the content of a page and $y_1, y_2, ..., y_i$ (for i = 1, 2, ..., n) be features, then $x = (y_1, y_2, ..., y_i, ..|$ for i = 1, 2, ..., n). Consider the whole Internet (W) as a population, if the frequency of each y_i (for i = 1, 2, ..., n) acrosss the whole Internet population is $F_w(yi, W)$, whereas in a sample with size N (where N > 0), the frequency is $F_N(y_i, N)$, then the error $e(y_i, N)$ can be defined as the difference of the frequencies

$$e(y_i, N) = |\, F_w(y_i, W) - F_N(y_i, N)|.$$

Therefore, the probability that the error level is greater than ε can be computed as

$$P[e(y_i, N) > \varepsilon] = P[|F_w(y_i, W) - F_N(y_i, N)| > \varepsilon]$$
$$= P[N \times |F_w(y_i, W) - F_N(y_i, N)| > N \times \varepsilon],$$

where ε is the tolerant error level.

According to Chernoff's bound theory (Chernoff, 1952; Hagerup and Rub, 1989), $P[e(y_i, N) > \varepsilon]$ can be described as a bound expression, such that

$$P[e(y_i, N) > \varepsilon] \leq 2e^{-2\varepsilon^2 N}.$$

In our e-guardian system, because the PWPR's decision to show or block a Web page is expressed with a binary variable, such that decision = 1 if the Web page is inferred to have objectionable content and 0 otherwise, the value of a decision generated by the PWPR must exhibit a Binomial distribution. Suppose the guardian trusts the performance of the e-guardian system, in which case trust can be described as

$$Trust = P[e(y_i, N) \leq \varepsilon]$$
$$\geq 1 - 2e^{-2\varepsilon^2 N}. \tag{12-5}$$

The sample size (N) can be calculated using this formula after we set the values for error and trust. For example, assume the guardian trusts the performance of the trained PWPR at a 95% level (i.e., the guardian believes that 95% of results generated by the trained PWPR correctly reflect his or her opinion), and the tolerant error level ε equals 0.05; then, the sample size will be

$$N \geq -\frac{1}{2\varepsilon^2} \ln(\frac{1-trust}{2}) \geq -\frac{1}{2*(0.05)^2} \ln(\frac{1-0.95}{2}) = 738.$$

Based on this principle, we randomly collect a training set of 750 Web pages from google.com. The guardian believes that 375 pages contain nonobjectionable contents but the remaining 375 pages are objectionable. The real training performance of the PWPR using a decision tree approach shows that it achieves accuracy of 94.67% (i.e., proportion of the total number of predictions that are correct); therefore, the sample size selection based on equation (12-5) appears reasonable.

Table 12.2. Comparison of the e-guardian with several software applications

Data Set	Software	False Positive Rate	False Negative Rate
Test sample 1,030 pages (836 bad, 194 good)	e-guardian	0.129	0.128
	Net Nanny	0.32	0.127
	X-Stop	0	0.562
	I-Gear	0	0.613

To collect test sample, we type nine search terms (sex, adult, lingerie, penthouse, swingers, abortion, breast, and legs) from a list of the "top 100 sex words" used in Internet searches (www.searchword.com), as well as the terms "gender study" and "women in film," into the Google search engine individually. For every search, we randomly select one from every five pages in the list of search results returned by Google, yielding 1,030 Web pages. For all training and test data sets, an independent rater, acting in the role of a guardian, supplied his opinion of whether these Web pages should be blocked or not.

Results. We use the test sample to compare the performance of the e-guardian system with several popular existing software applications, such as Net Nanny, X-Stop, and I-Gear, in terms of two performance indices: false positive rate and false negative rate. The results appear in Table 12.2.

According to Net Nanny's frequently asked questions (www.netnanny.com/ Support/NNFAQ.asp), Net Nanny monitors all online activities with a screening list. A Web page whose URL appears on this list gets blocked. We downloaded Net Nanny's 30-day evaluation version, which offers the same functionality as the commercial applications, and applied it to our test data. The false positive rate of the e-guardian system is low, which indicates that the system blocks most Web pages the rater considers objectionable. In comparison, the false negative rate of the e-guardian system is moderate (12.8% vs. 12.7%). Net Nanny allows users to view 87% of the good pages, but it also lets almost one-third of the bad pages through.

To develop the screening list (i.e., blacklist), human beings have to read every Web page. This approach is expensive, and it cannot cover all Web pages on the Internet, nor is the screening list updated daily. In contrast, our e-guardian system adapts to individual guardians' judgments and categorizes Web pages. It avoids the cost of hiring human raters (e.g., 100% coverage of unlabeled sites), is easy to use, and suffers no time lag.

We next compare the e-guardian with X-Stop and I-Gear (http://www.symantec.com/ urlabs/public/index.html), both of which use a keyword library, an "allowed list," and a blocked sites list. They update their lists of blocked sites daily and their libraries weekly (http://update.xstop.com/), then block any page that contains words in their libraries or that appears on the blocked sites list. Both X-Stop and I-Gear block 100% of the bad pages in the test data, because their URLs appear on the blocked site list. But they both also block half of the good pages, because these sites contain words that appeared in their libraries. Our e-guardian system has much lower false negative error than either X-Stop or I-Gear, though the false positive rate is slightly higher.

This result shows that the e-guardian system, in which the PWPR receives training using a decision tree approach, provides better performance than several other popular existing software applications.

Discussion. Our proposed system contains a private Web policy representative (PWPR) that can be trained through a multi-agent mechanism to represent a particular guardian's preference. To overcome a time lag issue (i.e., the total time it takes to rate or label a new page or create structures such as blocked lists, plus the time taken to make this information available for use in filtering), we design the PWPR to "read" the actual content of the page at the time of the request and make a judgment, which means it will never be out of date. Because it builds a quantitative model to represent the theme of each requested page, it can filter unwanted sites without blindly blocking all sites that contain suspect words or content.

For flexibility, the e-guardian supports two types of blocking: soft and hard. For soft-blocked sites, the PWPR warns the user that the page may violate the guardian's standards, then gives the user two choices: (1) "Do not display the page" and (2) "Show the page." Thus, the user may override a soft block and view the questionable page, but doing so prompts a report from the PWPR to the guardian. In this sense, it provides automatic filtering with flexible blocking, rather than purely automatic blocking. This flexibility offers great value in application domains in which civil liberties strongly protect free access to information (e.g., public libraries). It is also valuable when the user is trustworthy and has time-critical needs for access to information. A business, for example, may worry that hard blocking would deny critical information to employees working on deadline and/or demoralize employees by treating them like children.

However, the system also suffers several limitations. First, the prototype cannot assess languages other than English. Second, the adaptable system requires training, which we undertake by identifying a set of pages as either acceptable or unacceptable. Customized training may be more time consuming than an individual guardian who tolerates for some applications. However, guardians may adopt the values of a surrogate guardian that already has provided training to the system. Although this option reduces the capacity of the system to reflect each guardian's idiosyncratic tastes, it may enable more widespread adoption. Third, the system only focuses on primary Web pages; a recursive algorithm might be added to the process to trace each hidden link on the primary Web page. These limitations mark avenues for further research.

CONCLUSION

Cyber security remains a key component in critical infrastructure protection. Most attention and efforts have focused on methods that may improve existing Internet protocols or developing patches to cover vulnerabilities created by the design or implementation of software, hardware, and networks. In this chapter, we show that the functions of the Internet are highly engineered, which creates inherent vulnerabilities that are difficult to overcome. As technology evolves and new systems get introduced though, additional vulnerabilities may emerge. The radical solution may be to initiate a design that enables the Internet to gain self-awareness mechanisms that can identify harmful contents.

REFERENCES

Abdelsayed, S., Glimsholt, D., Leckie, C., Ryan, S., & Shami, S. (2003). An efficient filter for denial-of-service bandwidth attacks. In *Proceedings of the 46th IEEE global Telecommunications Conference,* pp. 1353-1357.

Bertelsmann Foundation (1999). Self-regulation of Internet content. Retrieved October 4, 1999 from http://www.stiftung.bertelsmann.de/internetcontent/english/download/Memorandum.pdf.

Boley, D., Gini, M., Gross, R., Han, E. H., & etc al. (1999). Partitioning-based clustering for web document categorization. *Decision Support Systems, 27*, 329-341.

Caulkins, J. P., Ding, W., Duncan, G., Krishnan, R., & Nyberg, E. (2006). A method for managing access to web pages: filtering by statistical classification (FSC) applied to text. *Decision Support System, 42*(1), 144-161.

Center, J. L. Jr. (1999). Bayesian classification using an entropy prior on mixture models. In *Proceedings of the 19th International Workshop on Bayesian Inference and Maximum Entropy Methods in Science and Engineering*, pp. 42-70.

CERT (2006). CERT/CC statistics. Retrieved September 8, 2007, from http://www.cert.org/stats/cert_stats.html.

Chang, R. K. C. (2002). Defending against flooding-based distributed denial-of-service attacks: A tutorial. *IEEE Communication Management*, *40*(10), 42-51.

Cheeseman, P. & Stutz, J. (1996). Bayesian classification (AutoClass): theory and results. In Fayyad, U. M., Piatetsky Shapiro, G., Smyth, P, & Uthurusamy, R. (Eds.), *Advances in Knowledge Discovery and Data Mining*. Menlo Park, CA: AAAI Press, 158-180.

Chernoff, H. (1952). A measure of asymptotic efficiency for tests of a hypothesis based on the sum of observations. *Annual Mathematical Statistics*, *23*, 493-507.

Craven, M., Freitag, D., McCallum, A.., Mitchell, T., & et al. (1997). Learning to extract symbolic knowledge from the World Wide Web. *Technical Report*, Pittsburgh: Carnegie Mellon University.

Dean, D., Franklin, M., & Stubblefield, A. (2002). An algebraic approach to IP traceback. *ACM Transactions on Information System Security*, *5*(2), 119-137.

Hagerup, T. & Rub, C. (1989). A guided tour of Chernoff bounds. *Information Processing Letters*, *33*, 305-308.

Hussain, A., Heidemann, J., & Papadopoulos, C. (2003). A Framework for classifying denial of service attacks. In *Proceedings of ACM SIGCOMM* (pp.99-110), Karlsruhe, Germany, August 25-29, 2003.

Jacob, V., Krishnan, K., Ryu, Y. U.(2007). Internet content filtering using isotonic separation on content category ratings. *ACM Transactions on Internet Technology*, *7*(1), 1-19.

Lasica, J. (1997). Ratings today, censorship tomorrow. *Salon Magazine*, July.

Lee, P. Y., Hui, S. C., & Fong, A. C. M. (2002). Neural network for web content filtering. *IEEE Intelligent Systems, 17*(5), 48-57.

Lieberman, H. (1995). Letizia: An agent that assists Web browsing. In *Proceedings of the International Joint Conference on Artificial Intelligence*, Montreal, 1995.

Maes, P., & Kozierok, R. (1993). Learning interface agent. In *Proceedings of the 11th national Conference on Artificial Intelligence*. Boston: MIT Press.

Mahajan, R., Bellovin, S. M., Floyd, S., Ioannidis, J., Paxson, V., & Shenker, S. (2002). Controlling high bandwidth aggregates in the network. *ACM Computer Communication Review*, *32*(3), 62-73.

MEMRI (2005). Islamist website design contest: Winners fires missiles U.S. Army base in Iraq. The Middle East Media Research Institute, Special Dispatch 1038, December 1, 2005. Retrieved March 7, 2006, from http://memri.org/bin/articles.cgi?Page=archives&Area=sd&ID=SP103805.

Menhaj, M. B., & Delgosha, F. (2001). A soft probabilistic neural network for implementation of Bayesian classifiers. In *Proceedings of International Joint Conference on Neural Networks*, 454-458.

Midine, D., Spiegelhalter, D. J, & Taylor, C. C. (1994). *Machine Learning, Neural and Statistical Classification* (edited collection), New York: Ellis Horwood.

Miller, J., Resnick, P., & Singer, D. (1996).Rating service and rating systems (and their machine readable descriptions). Retrieved December 4, 1998, from http://w3.org/PICS/services.html.

Mirkovic, J., Prier, G., & Reiher, P. (2002). Attacking DDoS at the source. In *Proceedings of ICNP 2002*. Paris, France, 312-321.

Resnick, P. (1997). Filtering information on the Internet. *Scientific American*, March.

Salton, G., & McGill, M. J. (1993). *Introduction to Modern Information Retrieval*, New York: McGraw-Hill.

Talbot, D. (2005). Terror's server. *Technology Review*, 46-52. February.

Ulph, S. (2005). A guide to Jihad on the Web. *Jamestown Foundation Terrorism Monitor*, *2*(7), March 31.

Weimann, G., (2006). *Terror on the Internet*. Washington DC: United States Institute of Peace Press.

Weinberg, J. (1997). Rating the net. Retrieved December 4, 1998, from http://www.msen.com/~weinberg/rating.htm.

Chapter XIII
Containing Financial Contagion at the Source

Credit is the air that financial markets breathe and when the air is poisoned there's no place to hide.
— Charles R. Morris,
The Trillion Dollar Meltdown, 2008

THE PROBLEM, A FLAWED ASSUMPTION WITH FLAWED METHODS

The world financial market is currently in turmoil because of the recent housing and credit crisis. From January to November 2007, more than 1 million homes in the United States entered foreclosure. Not only are homeowners losing their homes, but paying renters are being evicted as lenders reclaim properties. Depending on the state, 48–69% of foreclosed loans come from the subprime market. Subprime refers not to interest rates but to borrower quality, determined by low credit scores, little credit history, or unstable income with limited assets. Because of the increased risk associated with loaning to them, those borrowers cannot get favorable rates and often take out loans with short-term introductory rates. These loans generally get packaged by Wall Street into residential-backed securities and structured into slices or tranches that can be priced and rated from AAA to BBB– on the basis of the credit risk inherent in each tranche. When these mortgages adjust to market rates, the borrower no longer qualifies for the existing loan and can no longer pay it back. Because techniques such as gifted down payments and no requirements to prove income were the only way to move these borrowers into mortgages, many were lured into a false sense of prosperity for which they were neither prepared nor equipped and for which they are now suffering through foreclosure.

The subprime mortgage market bubble eventually led to a credit crunch, causing a chain reaction in which the twin engines of America's credit system—the capital markets and banks—both misfired. A recent U.S. banks report suggests that bank failures could rise beyond historical norms (Pimlott et al., 2008). The resulting effect has spread from Wall Street to the broader economy. If the International Monetary Fund is correct, the resulting credit crash could be the most expensive in history, measured in dollar terms at $945 billion (Guha, 2008; Strauss, 2008). The impact is so devastating that pressing questions arise: How might we avoid such credit crashes or contain the spread of credit crises at their source?

Although credit crashes do not emerge randomly, the core of the problem lies with misjudgments by the investment community (Greenspan, 2008). Many researchers believe that three trends have conspired to create the recent credit crash: First, residential mortgages, leveraged buyouts, and other loans have gravitated away from banks toward global capital markets. Subprime mortgage-based securities appear underpriced at their original issuance, which allows banks to evade the requirement to reserve capital and thereby push them and their off-balance sheet vehicles to achieve much higher leverage. Second, the securitization of mortgages has encouraged careless lending, such that households borrow more than they are able to pay back. Third, investment portfolio managers' increased reliance on credit ratings from rating agencies has resulted in a flawed image of reality that depicts prosperous mortgage markets and apparently risk-free investments (Crook, 2008). Credit-rating agencies have admitted that the golden ratings they awarded to many mortgage-linked "structured" products were erroneous, particularly those of collateralized debt obligations (*The Economist*, 2008).

Undoubtedly, the financial market turmoil has laid bare the weaknesses and flaws of the current approach to credit evaluation. After being badly harmed by the sharp rise in U.S. mortgage delinquencies, credit rating agencies, particularly the three main actors—Moody's, Standard & Poor's, and Fitch—are reviewing their methods. Officially, a higher rating should indicate stronger business performance, with less chance of bankruptcy. Any development of models or methods for rating in turn is based on certain economic theories. At the heart of the present approach to credit evaluation are estimates of risk and value that consider risk a multidimensional concept. Although commonly expressed numerically as the product of probability and expected consequences associated with an adverse event, risk generally is defined as a triplet comprised of a scenario, the probability of that scenario, and its associated consequences. In the context of risk analysis for loan evaluation, for example, a lender usually investigates the borrower's ability to meet the obligation should a loan application be granted. Thus, the scenario may involve a potential delay or inability to provide debt payment. The assessment procedure attempts to evaluate the possibilities of the occurrence of default, and its expected consequence should be a default or delinquency.

Although real-world risk evaluation models are very complex, a simple format can express their core theme:

Risk <= Market Threat × Capability × Consequence,

where market threat describes the set of adverse circumstances that, if they occurred in a market, would affect a borrower's operation and payment ability; capability measures a borrower's survival ability or resistibility if influenced by a market threat; and consequence indicates possible outcomes of an adverse event. A borrower or lender in this context refers to people or an individual firm.

When a lender provides a loan to a borrower, it does not want to lose the money, yet in ever-changing competitive markets, a market threat can occur at any time. Therefore, the lender must assess the possibility of a market threat and the borrower's survival ability in response to that threat. The borrower's survival ability is a multidimensional concept to which many factors may contribute, analogous to the concept of "health." For example, to evaluate whether a person is healthy, physicians examine a set of concrete medical indexes, such as blood pressure, heartbeat, and basic organ functions. Similarly, to determine a borrower's financial health, or survival ability in a competitive market, the lender needs a set of concrete financial indexes. In most situations, assets, capital, operating management, earnings, and liquidity represent the important factors that constitute the basic index set. Depending on the types of analytical models used, some lenders may adopt a broader set with more indexes, whereas others may use fewer.

Given the uncertainty of a market threat, risk evaluation necessitates different financial indexes to predict the probability of business failure in lending or investment decisions. Many approaches and complex analytical models have attempted to formulate financial indexes in recent decades. Although these models adopt different assumptions, they share one fundamental and key assumption: the possible market outcomes follow known probability distributions that do not change over time. That is, if the variables of interest have probabilities, the probabilities are known to modelers in advance. For example, suppose someone plans to build a model to describe a firm's operating performance and forecast its earning trend. Using this modeling assumption, the modeler would specify that the present state of the firm's performance follows a single and known probability distribution. In such a setting, possible earning states at a given future date can be obtained as a calculable probability of each such future state's occurrence, conditional on the present state. From this point of view, the setting implicitly indicates that the modeler has perfect foresight. In reality, however, perfect foresight is very difficult to achieve. How can we predetermine future changes on the basis of each calculable probability, conditional on the present state? This fundamental assumption clearly is incorrect, yet it continues to be used widely in economic, financial, and management models, largely because this assumption is implicitly embraced by a famous economic and decision theory, namely, rational expectation theory.

A Flawed Assumption

Rational expectation theory characterizes how rational persons make decisions. Rather than making a general decision, a decision maker attempts to make an optimal one and therefore must satisfy two basic decision conditions: he/she needs complete information about the situation, and he/she must have the computation capability to handle the complete information set.

These two conditions are not easy to meet when theory applies to real-world modeling and decision making. The second condition might be relaxed or achieved through advanced computing technology, but the first condition is challenging. Having *complete* information implies that the decision maker knows every property of the target situation over time, including the past, the present, and the future. Whatever change that might take place in the future therefore must be knowable and known in the present.

In economic and financial modeling, this first condition takes on the character of an implicit assumption: it is possible to prespecify economic changes over time. As Frysman & Goldberg (2007) show, the contemporary approach to economic analysis of market outcomes is fundamentally flawed because of its reliance on rational expectation theory.

Models for credit evaluation are not exceptional. According to Ray McDaniel, president of Moody's, at the 2008 World Economic Forum in Davos (Tett, 2008), some of the key assumptions that have supported existing analysis and modeling simply failed.

Flawed Methods: Sample Selection Bias and Problems with Data Aggregation

As mentioned previously, the heart of credit evaluation is risk assessment. In many circumstances, this evaluation becomes a process for examining borrowers' performance and identifying if a chance exists that a borrower (e.g., a firm) will become financially distressed or fail in response to a market threat. A review of research dedicated to predicting business failure in the past 35 years suggests that most models rely on statistical methods and suffer from two major flaws: potential sample selection bias and problems with data aggregation (Balcaen & Ooghe, 2006). Statistical modeling requires a large sample to provide sufficient data for model estimation (also called "model training" in data mining and machine learning). Following this principle, contemporary models for predicting business failure and credit rating often use cross-sectional data of firms for their sample and assume that the variables of interest follow a known, single distribution that does not change over time. According to this paradigm, each model gets estimated on the basis of cross-sectional data. The obtained parameters and/or estimated model then may be applied to a target firm to obtain a risk prediction. Because the values of the parameters are estimated from a group of sample firms, the model reflects an aggregate outcome. Thus, these models are aggregate-level models.

However, these models fail to take into account that, even if two firms belong to the same industry type and have similar asset sizes, each has its own inherent characteristics, and the selected variables of interest pertaining to each individual firm may follow different probability distributions. Moreover, a firm's risk of insolvency changes over time due to changes in the competitive nature of the market, corporate strategy, and/or technology adoptions. Therefore, the values of the parameters estimated from a group of sample firms may not account for each firm's intrinsic heterogeneity accurately, even if the firms' observed characteristics, such as financial indexes, are incorporated. In addition, almost all aggregate-level models use a single observation (e.g., one annual account) for each firm in the estimation samples and ignore past information about each firm's performance. This situation indicates that a firm's time-series performance is also ignored (Dirickx and van Landeghem, 1994; Kahya and Theodossiou, 1996; Theodossiou, 1993). The classification results of aggregate-level models therefore largely depend on sample selection, as well as the choice of the various assumed probability distributions used in an estimation (e.g., Balcaen & Ooghe, 2006; Benos & Papanastasopoulos, 2005; Cooke et al., 1987; Simon, 1997; Zmijewski, 1984).

A New Approach

Credit evaluation or business failure prediction calls for a new approach that can capture each individual firm's intrinsic heterogeneity and time-series behavior, and that, at the same time, can overcome the sample selection problem and polish the flawed rational expectation theory (Larson, 2008). In this chapter, we develop a new approach that provides a more accurate early prediction of a firm's insolvency so as to avoid risk. The proposed method uses only a single firm's time-series data to compute the likelihood of its insolvency for credit evaluation, without considering any other firm's information, which avoids the sample selection problem completely.

In addition, to overcome the flawed rational expectation theory, instead of assuming known probability distributions of the variables of interest (BarNiv & McDonald, 1992; Beneish, 1997; Campbell, 1996; Merton, 1974; Shumway, 2001; Zmijewski, 1984), the proposed method estimates them on the basis of each individual firm's own data. That is, the model identifies an unknown number of probability distributions of the individual firm's profitability ratio through adaptive learning. Because each firm's earning trend and profitability may change over time due to constantly changing markets, different firms may have different distributions of profitability, and the underlying distribution exhibited in a firm's own data may not follow a single distribution but rather exhibit multiple modes. Thus, the proposed model implements a real-time estimation of each individual firm's possible multiple data-generating processes to determine the actual distribution(s) exhibited in its data. In the meantime, the model updates the underlying estimated distribution with the firm's new data in each time period and thus captures the firm's past and current behavior. This is completely different from the conventional approach which assumes the probability distribution does not change over time.

Finally, unlike most current models that use extensive sets of financial ratios as part of their predictor variables, the proposed model only uses two pieces of critical information from the individual firm as model variables—the firm's operating earnings and interest payments for debt—to make a prediction.

Managerially, the proposed model is simple to implement and requires only a single firm's information, which is easily available, unlike Merton models, for example, that suffer implementation difficulty due to the invisibility of the firm's value process and computational complexity (Das & Sundaram, 2000). Economically, the cost of collecting samples for estimation for aggregate-level models also can be avoided with the proposed model.

To validate the proposed model, we conduct an empirical study in which we apply the model to a real-world data set and compare it with three conventional aggregate-level models. The empirical results show that the proposed model predicts insolvency two to five years prior to actual bankruptcy with high accuracy (i.e., 92.65% predictive accuracy for two years ahead and 77.45% accuracy for five years in advance), with a probability cutoff point of 0.5. For the comparisons with conventional aggregate-level models, we select three benchmark models: the Z-score model with a multivariate discriminant analysis (Altman, 1968, 2000; Altman et al., 1977), the well-known machine learning decision tree algorithm C4.5 (Quinlan, 1993), and conditional probability models such as the Probit model (BarNiv & McDonald, 1992; Beneish, 1997; Campbell, 1996; Zmijewski, 1984). The Z-score model is widely used by both academics and practitioners, and many other studies have treated it as a benchmark for comparison with a "new and improved" model (Altman & Narayanan, 1997; Balcaen & Ooghe, 2006, Holmen, 1988). We choose C4.5 because it is popularly used in machine learning and data mining literature for classification tasks (Quinlan, 1993). Recently, academic studies also have applied conditional probability models (e.g., Probit/Logit analyses) and other statistical models, such as hazard models, to forecast bankruptcy (Dimitras et al., 1991; Jones, 1987; Shumway, 2001; Zavgren, 1983; Zmijewski, 1984). However, Shumway (2001) demonstrates that the hazard model performs better than the Z-score model but does not outperform a conditional probability model (Probit/Logit model). Therefore, we use the Probit model as another benchmark for comparison in this study.

The comparison results show that the overall predictive accuracy one year prior to actual bankruptcy for the proposed model is 95.10%, much better than each of the three benchmark approaches (Z-score: 70.59%, C4.5: 78.85%, Probit: 81.73%) with a probability cutoff point of 0.5 for both the proposed model and the Probit model. The proposed model signals a firm's vulnerability to insolvency as early as five years prior to actual bankruptcy with 77.45% accuracy (Z-score: 59.80%, C4.5: 66.35%, Probit: 67.31%). The prediction results generated by the proposed model remains similar if different classification cutoff points are used. Therefore, the proposed method, which uses only an individual firm's data, can provide a more accurate signal of the firm's risk of potential bankruptcy far in advance.

The remainder of this chapter is organized as follows: we first briefly examine existing models on prediction firm's health. Next, we introduce formulation of the proposed model and its learning procedure. We then describe the empirical performance of the proposed method and offer some discussion of the managerial implications.

BRIEF REVIEW OF THE EXISTING APPROACHES

At present, credit evaluation adopts two distinct approaches: qualitative and quantitative approaches. Qualitative approach is based on the experience of a lender, his/her knowledge of the bank's loan policy and overall impression of the borrower. The most common example using qualitative approach is the "credit scoring method" used in credit card application (Cohen & Hammer, 1966; Eisenrietch, 1981; Orgle, 1970). In applying for a credit card, each applicant needs to fill an application form. Then points are assigned to each item based on the answers given in the application form. The credit officer assigns weights to some items which they consider as significant. The total points for an application are then compared to some critical levels which are predetermined from senior managers' experience or lending institution's policy. The credit is approved or rejected is based on whether the point score of the application is above or below this predetermined "cut off" point. In the absence of a rigorous theoretical framework, this procedure is sensible.

Quantitative approach refers to the evaluation method that is based on statistical or econometric models. In this chapter, we focus on quantitative approach.

The management and finance literature includes many models for predicting a firm's health, which can be grouped into two broad categories according to the analysis they adopt (Benos and Papanastaso-poulos, 2005). The first category adopts a fundamental analysis with econometric methods of model estimation. Examples in this category include Z-score models that use multivariate discriminant analysis, conditional probability models such as Logit/Probit, classification models using decision trees, models that employ Bayesian reasoning, and hazard models using survival functions and linear regression (e.g., Altman, 1983, 2000; BarNiv & McDonald, 1992; Breiman et al., 1984; Diamond, 1976; Eidleman, 1995; Jarrow & Turnbull 1995; Sarkar & Sriram 2001; Shumway, 2001). The object of these models is to find and estimate selected financial ratios/indexes that are important for assessing or forecasting a firm's potential risk of insolvency from cross-sectional data (i.e., from a group of similar firms). The working procedure of these models can be summarized as a three-step framework: Step one collects two sets of sample firms, of which set one is a group of financially healthy firms and set two is a group of failed firms matched to set one along dimensions such as asset size, growth, and industry type. Step two involves model estimation through statistical regression or very sophisticated econometric techniques to obtain coefficients or parameters (i.e., weights attached to the selected independent variables). Before the estimation, important factors that may affect the firm's performance, such as the firm's financial ratios, are identified to indicate significant differences between the two sets of sample firms. A model incorporating these factors as independent variables is then estimated on the basis of the sample data of the two groups, and the parameters of the model are obtained after the estimation. Step three uses the estimated model and obtained parameters to classify the firms in the test sample as bankrupt or not. The features of this category are that the parameters of interest are estimated and determined by aggregate cross-sectional data, and that during model estimation in step two, the variables of interest are assumed to follow a single known distribution. For example, in the popular Z-score model, the variables in every group are assumed to follow a multivariate normal distribution, and the covariance matrices are assumed to be equal for every prior defined group. Even though empirical studies show that defaulted firms in particular violate the normality assumption (Benos & Papanastasopoulos, 2005), in the past 30 years, Z-score and conditional probability models, such as Logit/Probit, have dominated the literature on business bankruptcy prediction (Balcaen & Ooghe, 2006). Recently, Shumway (2001) proposed a hazard model to capture a firm's past performance using its time-series data. His research indicates that the hazard model performs better than the Z-score model but does not outperform the Logit model in terms of insolvency prediction.

The second category of models is referred to as Merton, or structural, models, which adopt contingency claim analyses. The object of Merton models is to view corporate liabilities as contingent claims on the assets of the firms (Black & Cox, 1976; Black & Scholes, 1973; Collin-Dufresne & Goldstein, 2001; Geske, 1977; Longstaff & Schwartz, 1995; Merton, 1974). In a typical Merton model, the determination of whether a firm will default depends on the values of two variables: the firm's forward asset, an option value of the assets of the firm at time T, and the firm's outstanding debt at time T, which is an estimated face value of a single debt payment at time T. The firm defaults if the value of the firm's forward assets is less then the promised debt repayment at time T. To use the Merton models, researchers must determine the current market value of the firm's assets, the volatility of the assets, the firm's forward assets, its outstanding debt, and debt maturity. Due to the volatility of options, the market value and volatility of the firm are estimated from the stock's market value, volatility, and the book value of liabilities. Obtaining these values requires statistical estimation of a group of sample firms, called reference entities (Black & Cox, 1976; Collin-Dufresne & Goldstein, 2001; Geske, 1977; Hull et al., 2004; Longstaff & Schwartz, 1995). From this point of view, the Merton models are also aggregate-level models. Similarly, they assume the variable of interest (i.e., the value of the firm, projected to a given future date T) follows a single known distribution of a log-normal diffusion process with constant volatility during the estimation (Merton, 1974). According to the literature, Merton models suffer important practical weaknesses (Das & Sundaram, 2000); specifically, they are difficult to implement because the firm's value process is unobservable and computationally complex.

Methodologically, models in these two categories can all be considered aggregate-level models and share two common potential drawbacks, though they adopt different analyses and select different variables for model building. First, the parameters of interest in the models are statistically estimated by cross-sectional data and not specific to an individual firm. Therefore, the prediction decision for a firm is dominated exogenously by parameters obtained from a group of firms (e.g., Grice & Ingram, 2001; Platt & Platt, 1991; Sarkar & Sriram, 2001). Simon (1997) points out that such data are too aggregated to reveal much about each individual firm's own characteristics. In addition, the estimation samples consist of a group of firms in which each firm is represented by a single observation, which alone is unable to account for the firm's time-series performance behavior because insolvency takes time and represents a process (Balcaen & Ooghe, 2006). Heckman (1979) and Zmijewski (1984) both examine the effects of sample selection on model estimation and show that aggregate-level models are very sensitive to sample selection. For example, if firms in the estimation sample set do not represent the same type of industries as those in the test sample set, aggregate-level models are inappropriate, because the prediction results may not be accurate. Second, these types of models subjectively assume the distributions of the variables involved in the model do not change over time but remain the same for future samples. Thus, the known probability distributions of the model variables get applied during model estimation, which may be too strong and incorrect, as we show subsequently.

This chapter presents a new methodology that can resolve these two issues. We show that this method provides a more accurate early prediction of insolvency than current aggregate-level models, and even more important, it can adapt to each individual firm by incorporating the individual firm's time-series performance to capture its own characteristics.

AN ADAPTIVE LEARNING MODEL

To construct the model, we follow the definition of financial distress offered by Wruck (1990) and that provided by corporate finance theory (Ross et al., 2004), according to which financial distress[1] is a situation in which (1) a firm's operating cash flow is insufficient to meet its current obligations (e.g., trade credits, interest expenses) or can meet them only with difficulty or (2) a firm has a negative net worth (i.e., value of assets is less than the values of debts). A recent report by Clarke & Dean (2001; Clarke et al., 2003) on corporate collapse analysis concludes that the ultimate cause of a firm's failure seems to be a lack of cash to pay debts on time, which seems like a good starting place for senior managers who need to assess the health of their own firms. Lawson (2002) summarizes the suggestions of various insolvency experts and senior managers and notes out that cash flow is of critical importance and that a firm's on-time payment ability is key to its ability to remain solvent. If a firm's periodical (e.g., monthly, quarterly, yearly) earnings before taxes are insufficient to pay basic debts in a timely manner, the firm is in trouble and its managers may need to start thinking of rescue plans. Glen (2004) also reviews empirical evidence regarding a sample of more than 6,000 real sector firms in 41 countries and their ability to service debt for the period 1994–2001. His results show that cash flow must be available to make interest payments; otherwise, debt pushes the firm from vulnerability to insolvency. Previous research also indicates that the only statistically significant variables in predicting insolvency are those that measure the firm's profitability and leverage (Shumway, 2001). Therefore, in the proposed model, instead of assuming the availability of complete information about the individual firm's operation, we use only two pieces of vital information as model variables: operating earnings and interest payments for debt. Instead of assuming known probability distributions of the firm's earning trends or other factors, the model estimates them. Instead of considering all financial ratios pertaining to the firm's performance, such as working capital, total assets, retained earnings, market value equity, book value, sale level, and so forth, we are only interested in whether the firm can make its interest payments on time.

Let a firm's total assets be TA_j and its operating earnings after depreciation but before interest expenses and income taxes be OE_j at time j (where $j = 1, 2, ..., J$. The unit j can be a month, quarter, or year)[2]. The firm's profitability rate ω_j is defined as $\omega_j = OE_j/TA_j$, which measures the true productivity of the firm's assets, independent of any tax and interest expenses. Suppose each time the firm has to pay income taxes and interest payments for securing all its short- and long-term debts or loans (if the firm has debts), the earnings, R_j, after these payments in each time period will be

$$R_j = OE_j - Tax_j - IntExp_j. \tag{13-1}$$

which can be rewritten as $R_j + Tax_j = OE_j - IntExp_j$, where Tax_j denotes the income taxes the firm needs to pay at time j, and $IntExp_j$ represents the timely required expenses that the firm must pay to secure all its different short- and long-term debts. If the firm is a financial services institution, $IntExp_j$, could be the periodic (e.g., monthly) interest expenses that the firm must pay on customers' deposits, its own short- and long-term debts, and any other borrowings. Obviously, the income taxes and timely required expenses are nonnegative, such that $Tax_j \geq 0$ and $IntExp_j \geq 0$. To meet timely payments, the firm must have enough operating earnings to pay them, that is, $OE_j - IntExp_j \geq 0$.

When $OE_j - IntExp_j > 0$, the firm has the capacity to meet its timely required payments. If $OE_j - IntExp_j = 0$, the firm's earnings at time j are just enough to cover the timely required payments for securing the debts, and $R_j + Tax_j = 0$. Because the income taxes are not negative (i.e., $Tax_j \geq 0$), this scenario implies nonpositive earnings after all payments (i.e., $R_j \leq 0$), so the firm's earnings surplus at time j equals 0.

However, when $OE_j - IntExp_j < 0$, then $R_j + Tax_j < 0$, which implies that $R_j < 0$ (because $Tax_j \geq 0$). In other words, the firm loses money in its business. When a firm experiences consistent operating losses, that is, $OE_j - IntExp_j < 0$ occurs continually (e.g., several months or quarters), the firm is unlikely to have the capacity to meet timely interest payments, not including the payment of income taxes plus the repayment of principals. Therefore, $OE_j - IntExp_j < 0$ may signal that a firm is likely to be financially distressed, and the firm's operating income is insufficient to satisfy current obligations such as interest expenses.

Because a firm's ultimate existence is based on the earning power of its assets, the firm's profitability rate, $\omega_j (= OE_j/TA_j$, for $j = 1, 2, ..., J)$, appears instead of OE_j in the model to capture the true productivity of the firm's assets, independent of any taxes and interest expenses. Previous studies have shown that profitability rate, ω_j, can be very helpful in assessing firm performance (Altman, 2000). Hence, we rewrite the signaling indicator $OE_j - IntExp_j \leq 0$ as $\omega_j - \dfrac{IntExp_j}{TA_j} \leq 0$ (for $j = 1, 2, ..., J$).

Because the firm's profitability rate ω_j changes over time, a firm may face a risk that the value of ω_j will fall below the value of $\dfrac{IntExp_j}{TA_j}$, suggesting the firm could be financially distressed. Therefore, on must calculate the probability, such that the value of ω_j is less than the value of $\dfrac{IntExp_j}{TA_j}$ at time $j + 1$, given the firm's previous data records about ω_j and $\dfrac{IntExp_j}{TA_j}$ for $j = 1, 2, ..., J$. If ω_j follows a distribution $f(\omega)$, the risk of financial distress a firm may face at time $j + 1$ can be predicted using equation (13-2).

$$P(-\infty < \omega_j < \frac{IntExp_j}{TA_j}) = \int_{-\infty}^{\frac{IntExp_j}{TA_j}} f(\omega)d\omega, \tag{13-2}$$

where $P(a)$ is the probability of the occurrence of event a and $f(\omega)$ is the density function of ω that, at this point, can be any type of distribution.

Theoretically, equation (13-2) can measure the probability that a firm enters a region in which $\omega_j < \dfrac{IntExp_j}{TA_j}$ and predict its risk of potential insolvency at time $j + 1$. Hence, $P(-\infty < \omega_j < \dfrac{IntExp_j}{TA_j})$ serves as an indicator of the potential risk of insolvency the firm may face at time $j + 1$, denoted as FDRISK. The firm's profitability rate ω_j is assumed to follow a distribution $f(\omega)$, which is unknown and will be estimated empirically. As we show in the empirical study, however, it may come from multiple distributions and exhibit multiple modes (see Figure 13.2). In such a case, we use a more general expression to obtain FDRISK, as given in equation (13-5) and introduced in next section.

The idea behind equation (13-2) is illustrated in Figures 13.1a and 13.1b. Figure 13.1a shows a bankrupt firm's quarterly profitability rate and interest payments to total assets (i.e., $\dfrac{IntExp_j}{TA_j}$) from the first quarter of 1997 through the third quarter of 2000. Given this firm's historical data (i.e., profitability rate and $\dfrac{IntExp_j}{TA_j}$), the predicted probability (i.e., FDRISK) that the firm may face an insolvency risk and go into bankruptcy may be calculated using equation (13-2), as displayed in Figure 13.1a. This firm's quarterly profitability rate drops below its quarterly payments-to-total assets ratio after the third quarter of 1999, and the predicted risk for insolvency in quarter 3 of 2000 therefore is 57.62%. This firm filed an actual bankruptcy petition in the fourth quarter of 2000, suggesting that the predicted result generated by the proposed model is correct.

Figure 13.1b, however, shows a different situation in which a non-bankrupt firm suffered two years of negative profits from the fourth quarter of 2000 through the fourth quarter of 2002 but did not actually become bankrupt. The predicted FDRISK in quarter 4 of 2000 is 7% and in the third quarter of

Figure 13.1 Firm's Profitability Rate (ω), $\dfrac{IntExp_j}{TA_j}$, and FDRISK

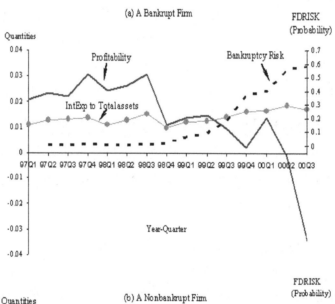

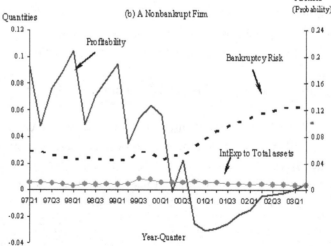

Note: Both the profitability rate and the IntExp to Total assets use the left-hand side vertical line as their Y-axis; the Risk of Financial Distress (FDRISK) uses the right-hand side vertical line as its Y-axis.

2003 is 12.33%, which does not predict bankruptcy if a cutoff point of 0.5 is used. Again, the prediction generated by the proposed model is consistent with the actual data.

Although both firms suffered negative profits in some periods, the proposed model (i.e., equation 13-5) can capture each firm's time-series performance behavior to provide different predictive values of FDRISK on the basis of each firm's own data.

To apply equation (13-2) to calculate a firm's FDRISK, one must determine an appropriate distribution of the profitability rate (ω). Because a firm's earning trend and profitability rate change over time due to constantly changing markets, the distribution might not be singular but rather exhibit multiple modes. Thus, the assumption of a single underlying distribution or data-generating process may be too strong. To capture possible multiple underlying data-generating processes in the data, the proposed model assumes an unknown number of distributions that are empirically determined from each individual firm's own data. In the next section, we show how the model learns to estimate the distribution(s) of a firm's profitability rate on the basis of its own data.

Learning to Recognize a Possible Distribution Type with Single Mode or Multiple Modes

To calculate the degree of insolvency risk, FDRISK, the model needs to know the distribution of a firm's profitability rate ($f(\omega)$) with its parameters (i.e., $\overline{\omega}$ and σ^2). There are many different ways to estimate the possible distribution that target data may exhibit (Newbold, 1994), but frequency histograms usually provide a good beginning heuristic. We therefore have developed a computer program—an algorithm for determining a possible probability distribution type given a time-series data set—that reads an individual firm's data as input and suggests the possible distribution type and its frequency histogram as output. Using this program to process each individual firm in the empirical data set, we can identify the possible distribution type for each firm. Then, the model must consider whether the distribution exhibits a single mode or multiple modes. For example, using the empirical data as input, the outputs show that the sample histograms of many companies' profitability rates look like mound-shaped distributions, but the histograms of some companies' profitability rates clearly exhibit multiple modes (see examples in Figure 13.2).

Let Y denote a distribution type. For example, Y can represent a normal, a chi-square, or any other distribution. Suppose that the distribution of the profitability rate ($f(\omega)$) is a mixture of type Y distributions. Mathematically,

$$\omega_j = \overline{\omega_n} + \varepsilon_{jn}, \varepsilon_{jn} \sim Y[0, \sigma_n^2], \text{ with probability } P_n, \text{ such that } \sum_{n=1}^{N} P_n = 1, \tag{13-3}$$

where ε_{jn} is the error term of distribution n at time j. Equation (13-3) indicates that the profitability rate (ω) follows a mixture of N distributions of type Y with different means and standard deviations (i.e., $\overline{\omega_n}$ and σ_n).

Next, we use a Bayesian approach to determine the possible number of distributions that each particular firm's data may follow. In other words, the total number of distributions, N, of type Y is determined using the Bayes factors (Allenby et al., 1998; Kass & Raferty, 1995; Li et al., 2002; Montgomery et al., 2004). We provide an example of the procedure in the next section. For identification purpose, assume $\overline{\omega_1} \le \overline{\omega_2} \le \cdots \le \overline{\omega_N}$. The likelihood is given by

Figure 13.2. Sample histograms of the profitability rate (ω)

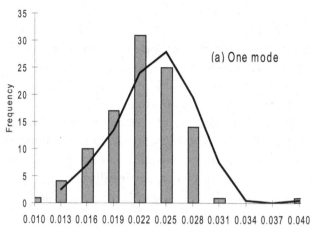

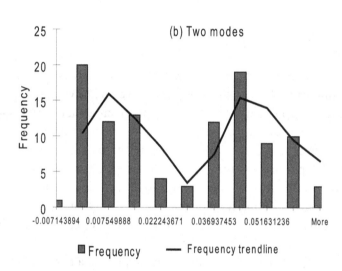

$$L = \prod_{j=1}^{J}(\sum_{n=1}^{N} P_n \times f_n(\omega_j \mid \overline{\omega}_n, \sigma_n^2)),$$ (13-4)

where $f_n(\omega_j \mid \overline{\omega}_n, \sigma_n^2)$ is the type Y density function n with mean $\overline{\omega}_n$ and standard deviation σ_n.

Given the mixture setup, the potential risk of insolvency (i.e., equation (13-2)) can be rewritten as

$$\text{FDRISK} = \sum_{n=1}^{N} P_n \cdot f_n(\omega_j \mid \overline{\omega}_n, \sigma_n^2) = \sum_{n=1}^{N} [P_n \cdot \int_{-\infty}^{\frac{IntExp_j}{TA_j}} f_n(\omega_j \mid \overline{\omega}_n, \sigma_n^2) d\omega]$$ (13-5)

Equation (13-5) thus is the final model used to predict a firm's risk of insolvency at time $j + 1$. Corresponding Markov Chain Monte Carlo (MCMC) algorithms to estimate P_n, $\overline{\omega}_n$, and σ_n^2 on the basis of different distribution types Y have been developed, but due to space limitations, we offer only two algorithms, used for the normal and t distributions, in Appendix A for illustration purposes.

Figure 13.3 contains a flow chart displaying the process of equation (13-5). Given an individual firm, the model reads its interest payments, total assets, and operating income after depreciation but before interest expenses and income taxes, prior to the time period j, to calculate the firm's profitability rates. The model then determines a possible distribution type Y that the profitability rates may exhibit. Subsequently, it identifies the number of distributions through a learning procedure and predicts FDRISK for $j + 1$. Finally, the model updates (i.e., $j = j + 1$) with the arrival of the firm's new data, reestimates the underlying distribution(s) on the basis of the firm's historical data and new arrivals, and recomputes the firm's FDRISK. This procedure repeats as often as necessary.

Figure 13.3. Flow chart of the proposed method

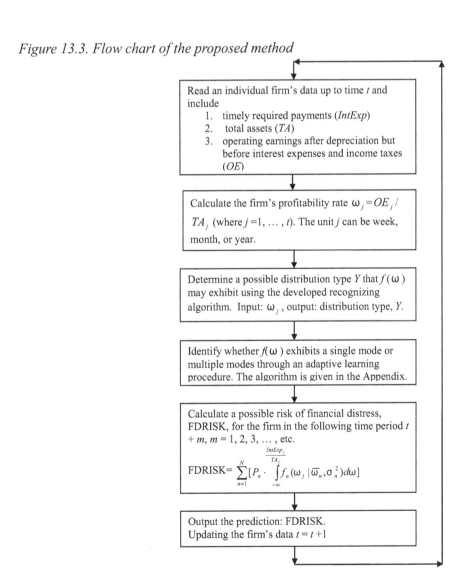

Procedure for Identifying the Number of Distributions

As we mentioned previously, a Bayesian approach, specifically, MCMC (Gelfand & Smith, 1990), appears in the proposed model to estimate the total number of distributions N of type Y. In addition, it estimates the individual firm-level parameters (i.e., $\overline{\omega}_n$, σ_n^2, and P_n) for each firm in each time period. Given input ω_j from the past up to the current period, we allow a "burn-in" period of 10,000 iterations to ensure convergence and capture the final 10,000 iterations to compute the posterior moments. For exposition purpose, the examples in Figure13-2 illustrate the procedure of how to identify the number of distributions. Figure 13-2 shows two histograms of two firms' profitability rates: a single mode in Figure 13.2a and two modes in Figure 13.2b. Due to space limits, we discuss only the estimation results for the last quarter of 2002 for these two firms, which we refer to as Firm 1 and Firm 2.

These two firms have a normal distribution, according to the program developed for determining distribution type. To identify the appropriate number of distributions (i.e., N), following standard practice in the Bayesian mixture model literature (Kass & Raferty, 1995; Li et al., 2002; Montgomery et al., 2004), the computer program affiliated with the proposed model starts with one distribution, and then tests two, three, and so forth. The best case (here, the appropriate number of distributions) is chosen on the basis of the Bayes factors[3]. The main estimation results for Firms 1 and 2 in Figure 2 appear in Tables 1a and 1b, respectively.

Consider Firm 1. Its histogram exhibits a clear bell shape with one mode. In the last two rows of Table 13.1a, we provide the log marginal density of models with a mixture of one, two, three, or four normal distributions. Log marginal density in Bayesian statistics is equivalent to the log likelihood in a traditional frequentist approach; the higher, the better. When comparing the proposed model with only one normal distribution with those with two, three, or four normal distributions, the log of the Bayes factors are 9.97, 10.60, and 10.58, respectively, which confirms that the proposed model with only one normal distribution fits the data best and is therefore preferred. The support for this claim can be found in the estimates in the top half of Table 13.1a. When $N = 2$, the estimates of the two membership probabilities (i.e., P_n) and both of the two distribution means are not significantly different from 0 at the 95% probability interval level. When $N = 1$, however, both the distribution mean and the variance are highly significant at the 95% probability interval level, which supports the presence of a single mode in the firm's sample histogram.

The histogram that reflects Firm 2 exhibits a combination of two bell shapes with two modes (Figure 13-2b). When the proposed model with two normal distributions is compared with those with one, three, or four normal distributions, the log of the Bayes factors are 2.65, 2.07, and 3.93, respectively. Therefore, the proposed model with two normal distributions fits the data best and is preferred in this case. The estimates in the top half of Table 13.1b again support this result. When $N = 2$, the estimates of the two membership probabilities (i.e., P_n) and one distribution mean are significantly different from 0 at the 95% probability interval level, which supports the presence of the two modes in the firm's sample histogram.

Example Illustrating the Use of the Proposed Model

In this section, we use a bankrupt firm as an example to illustrate how to apply the proposed model. The actual data from the firm's financial statements appear in Table 13.2, though for the purposes of illustration, Table 13.2 only displays data from the fourth quarter of 1997 to the third quarter of 2000.

Table 13.1a. Parameter estimates and log marginal densities for firm 1

Parameters		$\overline{\omega}_n$	σ_n^2	P_n	
N = 1		0.025* (0.005)	0.505 (0.036)	1.000 (0.000)	
N = 2	Dist. 1	0.022 (0.136)	0.696 (0.159)	0.508 (0.295)	
	Dist. 2	0.024 (0.120)	0.704 (0.159)	0.492 (0.295)	
Number of Distributions		N = 1	N = 2	N = 3	N = 4
Log-Marginal Density		-58.78	-68.75	-69.38	-69.36

The parameter estimates are posterior means with posterior standard deviations in parentheses

Table 13.1b. Parameter estimates and log marginal densities for firm 2

Parameters		$\overline{\omega}_n$	σ_n^2	P_n	
N = 1		0.024* (0.003)	0.227 (0.028)	1.000 (0.000)	
N = 2	Dist. 1	0.004 (1.404)	1.072 (0.294)	0.334 (0.026)	
	Dist. 2	0.044 (0.003)	0.224 (0.027)	0.666 (0.026)	
Number of Distributions		N = 1	N = 2	N = 3	N = 4
Log-Marginal Density		-18.58	-15.93	-18.00	-19.86

The parameter estimates are posterior means with posterior standard deviations in parentheses

This firm filed an actual bankruptcy petition in the fourth quarter of 2000. The data in Table 13.2 also include ratios used for some aggregate-level models, such as Z-score, C4.5 decision tree algorithm, and the Probit model. The proposed model uses "Total Assets (TA)" and "Operating Earnings after depreciation but before interests and income taxes (OE)" as inputs to compute the firm's profitability rate (ω_j) for each time period, then estimates the firm's $\overline{\omega}_n$, σ_n^2, and P_n from its profitability rate data. By incorporating the firm's interest payments in each time period, the model generates predicted FDRISK values for the subsequent period. For example, the predicted FDRISK listed in quarter 2 of 2000 is 55.90%, which means the firm has a 55.90% chance of becoming insolvent in quarter 3 of 2000. This firm's bankruptcy petition suggests that the prediction generated by the proposed model is correct at a cutoff point of 0.5. In contrast, two aggregate-level models, the Z-score model and C4.5, predict insolvency incorrectly; they both suggest the firm is healthy. (Note that because it is not a manufacturing firm, the firm would be classified as bankrupt if its Z-score were less than 1.1 and non-bankrupt if its Z-score were greater than 2.6. For the C4.5 decision tree algorithm, the firm would be predicted to go bankrupt if the value of C4.5 were 1; otherwise, the firm would be classified as non-bankrupt).

Table 13.2. Example: A bankrupt firm's data

QTR	Year	Working Capital*	Book Value* of Total Debt	Market Value Equity*	Earnings Before Interest & Tax*	Retained Earnings*
4	1997	72.652	7.1492	19.625	3.315	8.657
1	1998	104.413	7.5185	17	3.716	9.873
2	1998	111.404	7.7706	17.5	4.857	11.18
3	1998	97.36	8.0237	9.625	5.559	12.492
4	1998	165.096	7.994	8.25	2.658	12.462
1	1999	242.22	8.0087	7.625	4.618	12.818
2	1999	306.253	8.2422	8.875	5.864	14.04
3	1999	417.989	8.0482	4.3125	4.739	13.015
4	1999	444.634	4.0294	4.75	1.031	-8.106
1	2000	454.071	3.7757	3.0625	7.019	-9.617
2	2000	376.061	1.0338	0.6875	-0.567	-23.677
3	2000	346.905	0.7782	0.15	-13.243	-24.89

QTR	CYR	Operating Income After Depreciation Before Interest & Tax*	Interests Pay (IntExp)*	Total Assets* (TA)	IntExp/TA
4	1997	3.315	1.48	108.977	0.0136
1	1998	3.716	1.67	154.084	0.0108
2	1998	4.857	2.37	187.443	0.0126
3	1998	5.559	2.74	182.735	0.015
4	1998	2.658	2.4	248.884	0.0096
1	1999	4.618	4.03	338.756	0.0119
2	1999	5.864	5	405.873	0.0123
3	1999	4.739	6.94	508.077	0.0137
4	1999	1.031	8.25	512.888	0.0161
1	2000	7.019	8.45	518.862	0.0163
2	2000	-0.567	8.22	443.88	0.0185
3	2000	-13.243	6.65	396.465	0.0168

QTR	CYR	Sales*	Profitability Rate	FDRISK	Z-score	C4.5	Probit
4	1997	13.585	0.03042	0.00963	7.7191	0	0.0124
1	1998	14.205	0.02412	0.00031	7.1904	0	0.0212
2	1998	19.549	0.02591	0.00046	6.6321	0	0.0301
3	1998	21.248	0.03042	0.00494	5.182	0	0.0145
4	1998	18.04	0.01068	0.01472	5.6702	0	0.0357
1	1999	19.442	0.01363	0.06135	5.9052	0	0.0442
2	1999	22.619	0.01445	0.08874	6.2904	0	0.0631
3	1999	22.239	0.00933	0.1822	6.1056	0	0.1128
4	1999	29.221	0.00201	0.37629	6.8868	0	0.2574
1	2000	23.709	0.01353	0.39991	6.623	0	0.3298
2	2000	25.069	0.00128	0.55903	6.0735	0	0.4499
3	2000	19.567	-0.0334	0.57623	5.5132	0	0.451

The unit is million dollars.

EMPIRICAL TESTING

A real-world data set was randomly collected from two resources: *The Wall Street Journal Index* (WSJD) and *Standard & Poor's Compustat* (i.e., *Compustat*'s *Annual Industrial and Research Files*. The *Compustat* research file contains companies deleted from its annual active industrial file because of bankruptcy and identifies bankrupt firms with a 02(03) code in files. Only firms that filed any type of bankruptcy between January 2000 and December 2003 and appear in both the *Compustat* and WSJD are included in the bankrupt group. The total number of firms identified as bankrupt is 1,175, regardless of industry type or asset size. We randomly selected one out of every 10 firms, yielding 117 firms in the bankrupt group, of which 102 provide the accounting data required to estimate aggregate-level models. Thus, our final bankrupt group includes 102 firms. In line with previous research, we also collected 102 healthy firms as a non-bankrupt group for the model estimation of the aggregate-level models. These 102 healthy (non-bankrupt) firms were randomly selected from the population of *Compustat* firms for which Standard & Poor's (S&P) ratings on short- and long-term domestic issuer credit ratings are available and better than "CCC." The S&P short- and long-term domestic issuer credit ratings reflect S&P's current opinion of the firm's capacity and willingness to meet its short- or long-term financial commitments (i.e., short-term credit/debts = maturates of one year or less; long-term credit/debts = maturates of more than one year) as they come due. Firms in the non-bankrupt group did not file petitions for bankruptcy during the same period and remained in existence at the time of the analysis (i.e., the end of 2004). Assignments to the bankrupt versus non-bankrupt group merely serve to compare the models, as we describe in next section. However, because the proposed model is at the individual firm level, it does not need any other firm's data for estimation and prediction.

The financial statements for each firm in the two groups were collected for each year from *Compustat*; it is assumed that these annual financial statements are correct. For the bankrupt group, we collect data for each firm beginning from the date that a firm's financial statement became available in *Compustat* to the date it petitioned for bankruptcy. For the non-bankrupt group, we collect each firm's financial statements from the date the firm's financial statement became available in *Compustat* to the period of the analysis. Table 13.3 presents the characteristics of the bankrupt and non-bankrupt firms as two groups. Note that these firms represent different industries.

Overall Results of the Proposed Model

A computer system to implement the procedure of the proposed model displayed in Figure 13.3 was developed using the programming language C++. This system processes each firm's time-series data and calculates its profitability rate for each time period. Then the distribution(s) of the profitability rate for each firm is identified, and finally, the system generates the individual FDRISK for each firm using equation (13-5).

We first examine the predictive ability of the system for firms using data up to time period j to make predictions about the firms in the following period ($j + 1$). To do so, the system generates 204 FDRISK values, each of which represents a firm. To make a comparison with other aggregate-level models, the proposed model enforces a rule of a 0.5 probability cutoff point for each FDRISK[4]. If a firm's FDRISK is greater than or equal to 0.5, the system predicts the firm will go bankrupt. Otherwise, the firm is classified as non-bankrupt. Table 13.4 presents the overall predictive results one year in advance for the whole data set. We measure these predictions using predictive accuracy, or the proportion of the

Table 13.3. Sample characteristics: Bankrupt and non-bankrupt firms

Industry Classification	Total Sample	
	Bankrupt Group (102)	Non-Bankrupt Group (102)
Manufacturing	**44**	**48**
Non-manufacturing	**58**	**54**
Mining	16	3
Transportation	11	3
Information technology	9	16
Utility	1	18
Wholesale/retail trade	2	3
Finance/real estate	7	7
Health care & social assistance	4	-
Services	8	4

Table 13.4. Overall predictive accuracy for whole data set (204 firms)

Years in Advance	Proposed Model*			Z-Score Model**		
	Correct	Type I	Type II	Correct	Type I	Type II
1	95.10% (**98.04%**)	7.84% (**0.98%**)	1.96% (**2.94%**)	70.59% (77.45%)	27.45% (31.37%)	31.37% (13.73%)
2	92.65% (**97.06%**)	13.73% (**0.98%**)	0.98% (**4.96%**)	66.18% (70.10%)	41.18% (49.02%)	26.47% (10.78%)
3	89.22% (**94.61%**)	21.57% (**4.90%**)	0.00% (**5.88%**)	54.90% (61.27%)	56.86% (60.78%)	33.33% (16.67%)
4	84.31% (**93.14%**)	31.37% (**7.84%**)	0.00% (**5.88%**)	58.33% (63.24%)	62.75% (65.69%)	20.59% (7.84%)
5	77.45% (**91.18%**)	45.10% (**11.76%**)	0.00% (**5.88%**)	59.80% (61.27%)	64.71% (70.59%)	15.69% (6.86%)

*Using 0.5 as a cutoff point for the proposed model (0.15 as cutoffs for those in parentheses)
**Using 2.675 as cutoff score (1.81 as cutoffs for those in parentheses) for manufacturing firms; 1.1 for non-manufacturing firms

total number of predictions that are correct. We also include Type I and Type II error measurements in Table 13.4, which occur when a bankrupt firm is classified as non-bankrupt or a non-bankrupt firm is classified as bankrupt, respectively.

The proposed model is highly accurate, with a 95.10% overall correct classification rate. The Type I error rate is only 7.84%, and the Type II error rate is even lower at 1.96%.

Decision makers (e.g., a firm's manager, auditor, credit examiners) may choose different cutoffs they consider appropriate, depending on the extent of the firm's ability to tolerate insolvency risks. Table 13.5 presents an analysis of the predictive accuracy by year for the proposed model when using various cutoff points, as well as of the Type I and Type II errors by year. As the cutoff point increases, predictive accuracy decreases. The decreased Type II errors suggest that the non-bankrupt firms are more likely to indicate lower FDRISK values, whereas the bankrupt firms exhibit higher FDRISK values. If the Type I and II error rates represent criteria to evaluate the prediction performance, taking 15% as a

Table 13.5. Predictive accuracy using alternative cutoffs for the proposed model

Cutoff	1 Year	2 Years	3 Years	4 Years	5 Years
5%	88.24% (0.98%, 22.55%)	89.71% (0.98%, 19.61%)	89.22% (1.96%, 19.61%)	90.69% (3.92%, 14.71%)	90.20% (6.86%, 12.75%)
10%	94.61% (0.98%, 9.8%)	93.14% (0.98%, 12.75%)	93.14% (2.94%, 10.78%)	90.69% (7.84%, 10.78%)	89.71% (9.8%, 10.78%)
15%	98.04% (0.98%, 2.94%)	97.06% (0.98%, 4.9%)	94.61% (4.9%, 5.88%)	93.14% (7.84%, 5.88%)	91.18% (11.56%, 4.9%)
20%	97.55% (1.96%, 2.94%)	96.57% (2.94%, 3.92%)	94.12% (7.84%, 3.92%)	92.65% (11.76%, 2.94%)	90.69% (15.69%, 2.94%)
25%	97.55% (1.96%, 2.94)	96.57% (3.92%, 2.94%)	94.12% (8.82%, 2.94%)	91.67% (13.73%, 2.94%)	89.71% (18.63%, 1.96%)
30%	97.06% (3.92%, 1.96%)	95.59% (6.86%, 1.96%)	94.12% (9.8%, 1.96%)	91.18% (16.67%, 0.98%)	87.75% (23.53%, 0.98%)
35%	96.57% (4.9%, 1.96%)	95.10% (7.84%, 1.96%)	93.63% (11.76%, 0.98%)	90.69% (18.63%, 0.0%)	86.27% (27.45%, 0.0%)
40%	96.57% (4.9%, 1.96%)	94.12% (9.8%, 1.96%)	92.65% (13.73%, 0.98%)	88.73% (22.55%, 0.0%)	82.84% (34.31%, 0.0%)
45%	95.59% (6.86%, 1.96%)	93.63% (11.76%, 0.98%)	91.18% (16.675, 0.98%)	88.24% (23.53%, 0.0%)	81.37% (37.25%, 0.0%)
50%	95.10% (7.84%, 1.96%)	92.65% (13.73%, 0.98%)	89.22% (21.57%, 0.0%)	84.31% (31.37%, 0.0%)	77.45% (45.1%, 0.0%)
55%	95.10% (8.82%, 0.98%)	91.18% (16.67%, 0.98%)	87.75% (24.51%, 0.0%)	82.84% (34.31%, 0.0%)	75.00% (50.0%, 0.0%)
60%	94.12% (10.78%, 0.98%)	91.18% (16.67%, 0.98%)	86.76% (26.47%, 0.0%)	81.86% (36.27%, 0.0%)	73.53% (52.94%, 0.0%)
65%	92.16% (14.71%, 0.98%)	89.22% (20.59%, 0.98%)	85.78% (28.43%, 0.0%)	80.88% (38.24%, 0.0%)	71.57% (56.86%, 0.0%)
70%	90.20% (18.63%, 0.98%)	86.76% (25.49%, 0.98%)	84.31% (31.37%, 0.0%)	79.41% (41.18%, 0.0%)	69.61% (60.78%, 0.0%)
75%	90.20% (19.61%, 0.98%)	86.27% (27.45%, 0.0%)	82.35% (35.29%, 0.0%)	77.45% (45.10%, 0.0%)	66.18% (67.65%, 0.0%)
80%	87.75% (24.51%, 0.0%)	83.82% (32.35%, 0.0%)	78.43% (43.14%, 0.0%)	73.04% (53.92%, 0.0%)	64.71% (70.59%, 0.0%)
85%	86.76% (26.47%, 0.0%)	81.86% (36.27%, 0.0%)	76.47% (47.065, 0.0%)	70.10% (59.8%, 0.0)	60.78% (78.43%, 0.0%)
90%	84.80% (30.39%, 0.0%)	77.45% (45.1%, 0.0%)	71.57% (56.85%, 0.0%)	66.67% (66.67%, 0.0%)	58.33% (83.33%, 0.0%)
95%	80.39% (39.22%, 0.0%)	73.04% (53.92%, 0.0%)	66.18% (67.65%, 0.0%)	61.27% (77.45%, 0.0%)	55.39% (89.22%, 0.0%)

Notes: The first number in the cells is the predictive accuracy. The two numbers in the parenthesis in each cell are Type I and Type II error rates, respectively.

cutoff point seems to be appropriate for the proposed model, because the error rates (Type I = 0.98% and Type II = 2.94%) are relatively small compared with those that occur with other cutoffs. Because different firms may have different tolerance capacities, we do not recommend a specific cutoff for FDRISK for each firm but instead use a cutoff of 50%, similar to what many researchers have adopted when making comparisons among models.

Comparison with Aggregate-Level Models

As we mentioned previously, the Z-score model, C4.5 decision tree algorithm, and Probit model serve as three benchmark aggregate-level models for comparison against the proposed model. The procedures for each model are explained next.

Altman's Z-Score Model

Using a multivariate discriminant analysis, Altman (1968, 2000) derived a model consisting of a linear combination of five financial ratios that discriminate between bankrupt and non-bankrupt firms. Due to industry differences (i.e., manufacturing vs. non-manufacturing, publicly traded vs. privately held), the Z-score model has three variations:

$$Z = 1.2\,X_1 + 1.4\,X_2 + 3.3\,X_3 + 0.6\,X_4 + 1.0\,X_5, \qquad \text{for public manufacturing firms}$$
$$Z' = 0.717\,X_1 + 0.847\,X_2 + 3.107\,X_3 + 0.420\,X_4 + 0.998\,X_5, \qquad \text{for private firms, and}$$
$$Z'' = 6.56\,X_1 + 3.26\,X_2 + 6.72\,X_3 + 1.05\,X_4, \qquad \text{for public non-manufacturing firms}$$

where X_1 is the working capital/total assets, X_2 is the retained earnings/total assets, X_3 is the earnings before interest and taxes/total assets, X_4 is the market value equity/book value of the total debt, X_5 is the sales/total assets, and Z (Z' or Z'') is the overall Z-score index. Due to lack of a private firm database, the comparison herein focuses on publicly traded firms with both Z and Z'' models. Altman's Z-score model suggests that the lower the observed Z (Z'') score, the greater the risk of bankruptcy.

Because the Altman models already provide parameter values for the variables of interest, one can apply them directly to the data set to get Z (Z'') scores. Therefore, we apply the Z model to a subset of data containing only manufacturing firms in both the bankrupt and non-bankrupt groups. We then use the Z'' model for non-manufacturing firms in both groups and derive the Z-score for each firm in each year. Among manufacturing firms, firms are classified as bankrupt if their Z scores are less than 2.675 (Altman, 1968). Altman (2000) suggests the lower bound of the zone of ignorance, 1.81, as a more realistic cutoff Z score than 2.675, so we also include this alternative cutoff (1.81) in the comparison. Non-manufacturing firms are classified as bankrupt if Z'' is less than 1.1 and non-bankrupt if Z'' is greater than 2.6. The range 1.1–2 6 is considered the zone of ignorance. For consistency, we use the lower bound of the zone of-ignorance, 1.1, as a cutoff point for non-manufacturing firms. That is, a firm is bankrupt if its Z'' score is less than 1.1; otherwise, it is classified as non-bankrupt.

Results generated by the Z-score model appear in Table 13.4, along with the Type I and Type II error rates. The Altman model correctly predicts 70.59% of the total sample with a 2.65 cutoff score for manufacturing and a 1.1 score for non-manufacturing firms, yielding a Type I error of 27.45% and a Type II error of 31.37%. When using 1.81, the lower bound of the zone of ignorance, as the cutoff score for manufacturing firms, the Altman model correctly classifies 77.45% of the total firms, with a Type

I error of 31.37% and a lower Type II error of 13.73%. Clearly, the proposed model outperforms the Altman model.

C4.5 and Probit Models

The well-known machine learning induction algorithm, C4.5, has been popularly used in data mining for classification tasks. It can induce classification rules in the form of decision trees from a set of given examples (Quinlan, 1993). Probit analysis is also widely used to predict a firm's financial performance (Balcaen & Ooghe, 2006; BarNiv & McDonald, 1992; Campbell, 1996; Zmijewski, 1984), in which context it outperforms state-of-art models such as the hazard model (Shumway, 2001). To use both the C4.5 and Probit models, researchers must calibrate and estimate them first to generate decision rules and obtain parameters or coefficients, respectively. Therefore, we randomly select 50 bankrupt and 50 non-bankrupt firms from the overall data set to form a calibration data set. The remaining 104 firms, consisting of 52 bankrupt and 52 non-bankrupt firms, serve as test cases, which I refer to as the holdout sample. The calibration data set is employed to (1) induce a decision tree using C4.5 and (2) estimate parameters using Probit analysis (Greene, 1997).

For the calibration data set, we collected each firm's most recent yearly financial statement for predicting the firm's performance in the subsequent period (e.g., for the bankrupt firms, if a firm filed a bankruptcy petition in 2002, the most recent yearly financial statement was 2001). The resultant calibration data set consists of 100 records, each representing a single firm. Overall, the calibration data are collected in time period t to estimate a model, and the estimated model makes predictions about the firms in the subsequent period $(t + 1)$. For consistency, we use the same independent variables (or financial ratios) used in the Altman's Z-score model for the C4.5 and Probit models. That is, we calculate X_1, X_2, X_3, X_4, and X_5 for each firm in the calibration data set from which C4.5 generates a classification tree, then use the generated classification tree to examine the holdout test sample. In the Probit model, the five variables serve as independent variables, the calibration data set helps us estimate the coefficients of these five variables, and the dependent variable functions as a binary index of bankruptcy.

The prediction results using the calibration samples for both C4.5 and Probit models appear in Appendix B. With a 0.02 overall classification error rate, C4.5 performs quite well, as does the Probit model, with a 96% correct prediction rate, a Type I error rate of 6%, and a Type II error rate of 2%. Both models' calibration performance compares favorably with the calibration performance in many previous studies (Altman, 2000; Shumway, 2001; Zmijewski, 1984).

To compare these models' predictive ability with that of the proposed model, we use the holdout sample. Table 13.6 displays the predictive results. Again, we employ the 0.5 cutoff for both the proposed and the Probit models.

The C4.5 and Probit models correctly classify 78.85% and 81.73% of the holdout sample, respectively. Both have the same 26.92% Type I error rate, but the Probit model has a lower Type II error rate (9.62%) than C4.5 (15.38%). However, the proposed model's 93.26% correct prediction rate, as well as its lower 9.61% Type I error rate and 3.85% Type II error rate, make it more accurate. In contrast, the Z-score model correctly classifies 68.69% of the holdout sample, for a Type I error of 37.25% and a Type II error of 25%. Therefore, the proposed individual-level model clearly outperforms all three benchmark models—Altman's Z-score, C4.5, and Probit—in terms of predictive ability. Using a single observation for each firm in aggregate-level models is not sufficient to capture the firm's characteristics, so the proposed model uses each individual firm's time-series data to capture the time dimension of the firm's potential insolvency and make a prediction.

Table 13.6. Comparison with C4.5 and probit model in holdout sample

Years in Advance	Proposed Model*		C4.5		Probit Model*		Z-score**	
	Correct	Type I / Type II	Correct	Type I / Type II	Correct	Type I / Type II	Correct	Type I / Type II
1	93.26%	9.61% / 3.85%	78.85%	26.92% / 15.38%	81.73%	26.92%/ 9.62%	68.69% (70.71%)	37.25% / 25% (45.1% /12.5%)
2	88.46%	23.07% / 0.0%	75.00%	34.62% / 9.62%	76.92%	30.77%/ 15.38%	66.67% (69.79%)	44.68% / 24.49% (48.93%/12.24%)
3	82.69%	34.61% / 0.0%	70.19%	40.38% / 19.23%	71.15%	38.46%/ 19.23%	65.63% (64.58%)	47.83% / 34% (54.35%/0.18%)
4	78.84%	38.46% / 3.85%	68.27%	42.31% / 21.15%	69.23%	42.31% /19.23%	63.83% (67.02%)	48.89% / 22.45% (55.56%/ 12.24%)
5	76.92%	46.15% / 0.0%	66.35%	50% / 17.31%	67.31%	51.92% /13.46%	61.29% (65.59%)	56.81% / 16.33% (63.63% / 8.16%)

* Using 0.5 as a cutoff point for the proposed model and the Probit model.
** Using 2.675 as cutoff score (1.81 as cutoff point is used for those in parentheses)

Early Discovery in Five Years

Managers and investors also likely are interested in whether the proposed model can provide early indicators of a firm's insolvency for a period of time longer than one year prior to bankruptcy. Using an individual firm's data over time to identify and provide reliable signals of the firm's insolvency could facilitate corrective actions by managers before it becomes too late.

Tables 13.4 and 13.6 display forecasting results for five years in the future, as created by the proposed model, Altman's model, C4.5, and the Probit model. Note that we use the holdout sample in Table 13.6. The results in both tables suggest that the proposed model provides an accurate early signal up to five years in advance with a predictive accuracy of 77.45% (Z-score: 59.80.%, C4.5: 66..35%, Probit: 67.31%). The C4.5 and Probit models have similar prediction results that are less accurate than the proposed model. Not surprisingly, as the time span of the prediction increases, the relative predictive ability of all four models decreases.

DISCUSSION AND CONCLUSION

The goal of this study is to improve current models on predicting risk of individual firm insolvency for credit evaluation. The proposed method, which uses only individual firm's data and does not employ data from any other firm, is comprehensive, in that it applies to all firms regardless of industry type or asset size. In contrast, aggregate-level models require a cross-sectional sample of firms to obtain the required parameters to make a prediction. The proposed model also is adaptive to each individual firm, captures the firm's time-series performance behavior, and updates during each time period when new data arrive. In contrast, the aggregate-level models cannot account for firms' time-series behavior because they use only a single observation to represent each firm.

The prediction performance of the proposed model, as illustrated in Tables 13.4 and 13.6, is based on a decision rule that if a firm's FDRISK value is greater than or equal to a probability score of 0.5, the firm is classified as going bankrupt; otherwise, it is financially healthy. However, the observation of FDRISK values across the sample set for both bankrupt and non-bankrupt firms suggests that the non-bankrupt firms in the sample set exhibit lower FDRISK values that range between 0.1% and 12%, whereas the bankrupt firms display higher FDRISK values, usually greater than 14%. In Table 13.5, we provide different cutoffs with the corresponding Type I and II error rates to detail the accuracy of the probability predictions by the proposed model. If the Type I and II error rates are the criteria used to evaluate the prediction performance, taking 15% as a cutoff point seems appropriate for the proposed model because the Type I and II error rates are relatively small compared with those associated with other cutoffs (error rates for one year ahead are 0.98% and 2.94%, respectively).

Readers may also wonder if the proposed method is computationally intensive, because it functions at the individual firm level. As we demonstrate in the empirical study however, computational intensity is minimized by the simplicity of the proposed model and available computer technology. The estimation of the distribution type(s) with single (or multiple) mode(s) can be completed within minutes for any firm.

The proposed method therefore has some important managerial implications. Because of its individual-level and adaptive properties, the costs of collecting sample firms for model estimation can be saved. It is also simple to implement. Therefore, managers can use this model as a safeguard to oversee the performance of a firm over a series of years and measure the firm's progress to recognize poor performance in its early stages. They can also use the model to determine the firm's acceptable borrowing level with the firm's current tolerant FDRISK (i.e., the maximum amount of loan/debt the firm can borrow given its FDRISK). For example, suppose a firm's current FDRISK is 10% and the firm's managers agree that the firm can bear this risk value. Also suppose the firm wants to enlarge its business by applying for a loan. How much can the firm borrow under the current 10% risk? If D_t is the amount of the loan that the firm can borrow at time t with an interest rate i_t, then on the basis of equation (13-5), the managers can run the system to calculate the firm's loan amount, D_t, given $FDRISK_t$, as

$$D_t = \frac{A \cdot TA_t - IntExp_t}{i_t - A},$$

(13-6)

where TA_t is the firm's total asset value at time t before borrowing loan D_t and $IntExp_t$ is the firm's current required payment before borrowing D_t to secure all previous debts. In addition,

$A = \sum_{n=1}^{N} [(InverseY(\text{FDRISK}_t)) \cdot P_n]$, where $InverseY(\cdot)$ is the inverse of the cumulative distribution

function of type Y, and P_n is the estimated membership probability of distribution n of type Y.

Similarly, lenders, credit officers, and investors can use equation (13-6) to evaluate a request for financing or refinancing from a firm and determine whether the firm's payment ability is below a predefined threshold (i.e., FDRISK).

Rather than predicting bankruptcy, the proposed model can also be applied to help identify healthy firms. For example, following the proposed method, *Business Week* has adopted equation 13-1 (i.e., the firm's earnings before interests and taxes OE_j, the firm's profitability rate ω_j, and the firm's asset value TA_j) and selected a list of firms from *Standard & Poor's Compustat* to identify companies that are the best performers relative to their peers in 2008 (*Business Week*, 2008).

The proposed model also has some limitations. To examine the firm's capacity to make its timely required payments, the proposed model requires the individual firm's historical and current operating data to estimate and identify the distribution of its profitability rate. Therefore, the model cannot be applied directly to a completely new start-up firm because that firm lacks operating earnings data. The proposed model needs at least two data observations to estimate the variance of the firm's distribution(s) of profitability rate to be able to compute the likelihood of insolvency the firm may suffer. However, once the new firm has existed for two time periods, whether two days, two weeks, or two months, the proposed model can be used to compute the firm's potential risk of insolvency.

REFERENCES

Allenby, G. M., Arora, N., & Ginter, J. L. (1998). On the heterogeneity of demand. *Journal of Marketing Research, 35*, 384 – 389.

Altman, E. I. (1968). Financial ratios, discriminant analysis and prediction of corporate bankruptcy. *Journal of Finance, 23*(9), 589-609.

Altman, E. I. (1983). *Corporate financial distress: A complete guide to predicting, avoiding and dealing with bankruptcy.* New York: Wiley & Son.

Altman, E. I. (2000). Predicting financial distress of companies: Revisiting the Z-score and ZETA models. Working paper. Stern School of Business, New York University.

Altman, E. I. (2003). Quantitative techniques for the assessment of credit risk. *AFP Exchange, 23*(2), 7-13.

Altman, E. I., Haldeman, R. G., & Narayanan, P. (1977). Zeta analysis: A new model to identify bankruptcy risk of corporations. *Journal of Banking Finance, 1*(6), 29-54.

Altman, E. I., & Narayanan, P. (1997). An international survey of business failure classification models. *Financial Markets, Institutions and Instruments, 6*(2), 1-57.

Balcaen, S., & Ooghe, H. (2006). 35 Years of studies on business failure: An overview of the classic statistical methodologies and their related problems. *The British Accounting Review, 38*, 63-93.

Balcaen, S., & McDonald, J. B.(1992). Identifying financial distress in the insurance industry: A synthesis of methodological and empirical issues. *The Journal of Risk and Insurance, 59*(4), 543-573.

Beneish, M. D. (1997). Detecting GAAP violation: Implications for assessing earnings management among firms with extreme financial performance. *Journal of Accounting and Public Policy, 16*(3), 271-301.

Benos, A., & Papanastasopoulos, G. (2005). Extending the Merton model: A hybrid approach to assessing credit quality. Working paper, Department of Banking and Financial Management, University of Piraeus, Greece.

Black, F., & Cox, C. J. (1976). Some effects of bond and indenture provisions. *Journal of Finance, 31*, 351-367.

Black, F., & Scholes, M. (1973). Pricing of options and corporate liabilities. *Journal of Political Economy*, *81*, 637-659.

Breiman, L. J., Friedman, J. H., Olshen, R. A., & Stone, C. J. (1984). *Classification and regression trees*. Belmont, CA: Wadsworth.

Business Week (2008). The best 50 performers. *Business Week*, April 7, 2008.

Campbell, S. V. (1996). Predicting bankruptcy reorganization for closely held firms. *Accounting Horizons*, September, 12-25.

Clarke, F. L., Dean, G.W.D., & Oliver, K. G. (2003). *Corporate collapse: Accounting, regulatory and ethical failure*. Cambridge, England: Cambridge University Press.

Clarke, F. L., & Dean, G. W. D. (2001). Corporate collapses analyzed. In CCH Australia Limited (et.) *Collapse Incorporated: Tales, safeguards & responsibilities of corporate Australia* (71-98). Sydney, Australia.

Cohen, K. J, & Hammer, F. S. (1966). Analytical methods in banking. Horwood IL: Richard Irwin, Inc.

Collin-Dufresne, P., & Goldstein, R. (2001). Do credit spreads reflect stationary leverage ratio? *Journal of Finance*, *5*, 1929-1957.

Cooke, R., Medel, M., & Thijs, W. (1987). Calibration and information in expert resolution: A classical approach. Report 87-31, Faculty of Mathematics and Informatics, Delft University of Technology.

Crook, C. (2008). Regulation needs more than tuning. *Financial Times*, 9, April 7, 2008.

Das, S. R. and Sundaram, R. K. (2000). A discrete-time approach to arbitrage-free pricing of credit derivatives. *Management Science*, *46*(1), 46-62.

Diamond, H.S., Jr. (1976). Pattern recognition and the detection of corporate failure. unpublished PhD dissertation, New York University.

Dimitras, A., Zanakis, S., & Zopoudinis, C. (1996). A survey of business failure with an emphasis on failure prediction methods and industrial applications. *European Journal of Operational Research*, *90*(3), 487-513.

Dirickx, Y., & van Landeghem, C. (1994). Statistical failure prevision problems. *Tijdschrift voor Economie en Management*, *39*(4), 429-462.

Eidleman, G. J. (1995). Z scores –A guide to failure prediction. *The CPA Journal*, *65*(2), 52-53.

Eisentiech, D. C. (1981). Credit analysis: trying it all together. *Journal of Commercial Bank Lending*, *12*, 2-13.

Gelfand, A. E., & Smith, A. F. M. (1990). Sampling-based approaches to calculating marginal densities. *Journal of the American Statistical Association*, *85*(410) 398-409.

Geske, R. (1977). The valuation of corporate liabilities as compound options. *Journal of Finance & Quantitative Analysis*, *4*, 541-552.

Glen, J. (2004). Debt and firm vulnerability. Working paper, International Finance Corporation.

Greene, W. H. (1997). *Econometric analysis* (3rd edition). Upper Saddle River, NJ: Prentice Hall.

Greenspan, A. (2008). The Fed is blameless on the property bubble. *Financial Times*, *9*, April 7, 2008.

Grice, J. S., & Ingram, R. W. (2001). Tests of the generalizability of Altman's bankruptcy prediction model. *Journal of Business Research*, *54*, 53-61.

Guha, K. (2008). IMF points to high cost of global credit crisis. *Financial Times*, 4, April 7, 2008.

Heckman, J. J. (1979). Sample selection bias as a specification error. *Econometrica*, *47*(1), 153-161.

Holmen, J. S. (1988). Using financial ratios to predict bankruptcy: An evaluation of classic models using recent evidence. *Akron Business and Economic Review*, *19*(1), 52-63.

Hull, J., Nelken, I., & White, A. (2004). Merton's model, credit risk, and volatility skews. Working paper, University of Toronto.

Jarrow, R., & Turnbull, S. (1995). Pricing derivatives on financial securities subject to credit Risk. *Journal of Finance*, *50* (1), 53-86.

Jones, F. L. (1987). Current techniques in bankruptcy prediction. *Journal of Account Literatures*, *6*, 131-164.

Kahya, E., & Theodossiou, J. O. (1996). Predicting corporate financial distress: A time-series CUSUM methodology. Presented at *the Third Annual Conference of the Multinational Finance Association*, June, 1-38.

Kass, R., & Raferty, A. (1995). Bayes factors. *Journal of the American Statistical Association*, *90*(430), 773-795.

Larsen, P. T. (2008). EU warning systems need strengthening. *Financial Times*, 8, April 2, 2008.

Lawson, M. (2002). Early warning signs. *The Australian Financial Review*. May. Retrieved May 3, 2004, from http://www.afrboss.com.au/magazine.asp?rgid=2&listed_months=26.

Li, S., Liechty, J. C., & Montgomery, A. (2002). Modeling category viewership of Web users with multivariate count models. Working Paper, Tepper School of Business, Carnegie Mellon University.

Longstaff, F., & Schwartz, S. E. (1995). A simple approach to valuing risky fixed and floating rate debt. *Journal of Finance*, *51*(3), 789-819.

Merton, C. R. (1974). On the pricing of corporate debt: The risk structure of interest rates. *Journal of Finance*, *29*, 449-470.

Montgomery, A., Li, S. Srinivasan, K., & Liechty, J. C. (2004). Modeling online browsing and path analysis using clickstream data. *Marketing Science*, *23*(4), 579-595.

Morris, C. R. (2008). The trillion dollar meltdown: Easy money, high rollers, and the great credit crash. Public Affairs.

Newbold, P. (1994). *Statistics for business and economics* (4ᵗʰ edition). Upper Saddle River, NJ: Prentice Hall.

Oakley, D. (2008), Distressed debt levels rise to five-year peak. *Financial Times, 25*, April 8, 2008.

Orgle, Y. E. (1970). A credit scoring model for commercial loans. *Journal of Money, Credit & Banking, 2*, 435-445.

Pimlott, D., Guha, K, Chung, J., & White, B. (2008), Regulator fears wave of bank failures. *Financial Times*, 1, April 23, 2008.

Platt, H. D., & Platt, M. B. (1991). A note on the use of industry-relative ratios in bankruptcy prediction. *Journal of Banking Finance, 15*, 1183-1194.

Quinlan, J. R. (1993). *C4.5: Programs for machine learning*. San Mateo, CA: Morgan Kaufmann Publishers.

Ross, S. A., Randolph, W.W., & Jaffe, J, F. (2004). *Corporate finance* (7ᵗʰ Edition). New York, NY: McGraw-Hill Companies.

Sarkar, S., & Sriram, R. S. (2001). Bayesian models for early warning of bank failures. *Management Science, 47*(11), 1457-1475.

Shumway, T. (2001). Forecasting bankruptcy more accurately: A simple hazard model. *Journal of Business, 74*(1), 101-124.

Simon, H. A. (1997), *Models of bounded rationality: Empirical grounded economic reason*. Cambridge, MA: The MIT Press.

Strauss, D. (2008), OECD predicts subprime losses to hit $420 bn. *Financial Times, 4*, April 16, 2008.

Tett, G. (2008), Ratings agencies move to quell critics. *Financial Times*. January 31, 2008

The Economist (2008). Credit-rating agencies: Restructured products. *The Economist*, February 9ᵗʰ-15ᵗʰ, 80.

Theodossiou, J. O (1993). Predicting shifts in the mean of a multivariate time series process: An application in predicting business failures. *Journal of the American Statistical Association, 88*(422), 441-449.

Wruck, K. H. (1990). Financial distress, reorganization, and organizational efficiency. *Journal of Financial Economics, 27*, 419-444.

Zavgren, C. (1983). The prediction of corporate failure: the start of the art. *Journal of Accounting Literature, 2*(1), 1-37.

Zmijewski, M. E. (1984). Methodological issues related to the estimation of financial distress prediction models. *Journal of Accounting Research, 22*, 59-82.

ENDNOTES

[1] According to bankruptcy literature (Zmijewski, 1984), financial distress also may be defined as the act of filing a petition for bankruptcy, such that a firm is identified as bankrupt if it has filed a bankruptcy petition and non-bankrupt if it has not. Therefore, we use the terms "financially distress," "insolvency," and "bankruptcy" interchangeably.

[2] Because the proposed model is an individual-level model, all the variables and parameters are firm specific. For notational simplicity, we drop the firm subscript for the rest of the paper and assume it is understood.

[3] See Kass & Raferty (1995) for a discussion of Bayes factors. A fit statistic for a Bayesian model comparison can be generated by taking the log of the ratio of the posterior marginal densities of the two competing models, assuming the priors for the two models are equally likely. Here, posterior marginal density is defined as the harmonic mean of the likelihood over the sample period. Specifically, if the log of this ratio is greater than 2, it provides decisive evidence of the better fit of the model in the numerator relative to that in the denominator. In this model, one can simply take the absolute value of the difference between the two competing models' log marginal densities to obtain the log of the Bayes factor.

[4] The probability score of 0.5 used in the proposed model is based on the literature, in which most researchers adopt 0.5 as a cutoff when making comparisons with other alternative models. According to Zeijewski (1984), a 0.5 probability cutoff assumes a symmetric loss function. The group error rates would change if different probability cutoffs were used, but the comparisons across estimation samples and techniques would not be affected.

APPENDIX A: MARKOV CHAIN MONTE CARLO ALGORITHMS

We use a MCMC approach, specifically the Gibbs sampler, to estimate the parameters with possible multiple modes (Gelfand & Smith, 1990). We ran the MCMC algorithm for 20,000 iterations and discard the first 10,000 iterations as the "burn-in" period to ensure convergence. With the second 10,000 iterations, we estimate the parameters of interest. The MCMC algorithm appears below.

A1. When the distribution type Y is determined to be normal distribution

Step 1: Set priors for parameters to be estimated.
Diffuse priors are set for the mean $\overline{\omega}_n$, the standard deviation σ_n, and the membership probability P_n for distribution n.

$\overline{\omega}_n \sim Normal(\overline{\overline{\omega}}, \sigma_\omega^2)$ with $\overline{\overline{\omega}} = 0$ and $\sigma_\omega^2 = 100$.

$\sigma_n^2 \sim InverseGamma(\alpha, \beta)$ with $\alpha = 1$ and $\beta = 1$.

$P_n \sim Dirichlet(\alpha_1, ..., \alpha_N)$ with $\alpha_n = 1$ for $n = 1, ..., N$.

Step 2: Let number of distributions, N, be 1. That is, N = 1.

Step 2.1: Draw random draws of $\overline{\omega}_n$ from the full conditional distribution:

$$\overline{\omega}_n \mid \sigma_n, P_n, C_j \sim Normal(B \cdot A, B) \cdot I(\overline{\omega}_1 \leq \overline{\omega}_2 \leq \cdots \leq \overline{\omega}_N),$$

where $A = \sum_{j=1}^{J} \frac{1}{\sigma_n^2} \omega_j I(C_j = n) + \frac{1}{\sigma_\omega^2} \overline{\overline{\omega}}$ and $B = (\sum_{j=1}^{J} \frac{1}{\sigma_n^2} I(C_j = n) + \frac{1}{\sigma_\omega^2})^{-1}$.

$I(C_j = n)$ is an indicator function, such that it is equal to 1 if $\overline{\omega}_n$ follows the normal distribution n at time j and equal to 0 otherwise. C_j denotes the membership of different normal distributions.

Step 2.2: Draw random draws of σ_n^2 from the full conditional distribution:

$$\sigma_n^2 \mid \overline{\omega}_n, P_n, C_j \sim InverseGamma(\alpha + 0.5 \cdot \sum_{j=1}^{J} I(C_j = n), \quad \beta + [\sum_{j=1}^{J} (\omega_j - \overline{\omega}_n)^2 \cdot I(C_j = n)] / 2)$$

Step 2.3: Draw random draws of C_j from the full conditional distribution:

$$C_j \mid \overline{\omega}_n, \sigma_n^2, P_n \sim Multinomial(\pi_1, \pi_2, ..., \pi_N)$$

where $\pi_n = \dfrac{L(H_j \mid n) \cdot P_n}{\sum_{k=1}^{N} L(H_j \mid k) \cdot P_k}$ and $L(H_j \mid n)$ is the conditional likelihood at time j given

distribution membership $C_j = n$.

Step 2.4: Draw random draws of P_n from the full conditional distribution:

$$P_n \mid \overline{\omega}_n, \sigma_n^2, C_j \sim Dirichlet(\alpha_1 + \sum_{j=1}^{J} I(C_j = 1), \; \alpha_2 + \sum_{j=1}^{J} I(C_j = 2), ..., \; \alpha_N + \sum_{j=1}^{J} I(C_j = N))$$

Step 2.5: Repeat Step 2.1–2.4 until the algorithm converges.

Step 2.6: Compute the log of marginal density.

Step 3: If the log of marginal density increases, then

$N = N + 1$; repeat Step 2.1–2.6,
otherwise, stop.

Step 4: Output N and the estimated parameters under each distribution.

A2. When the Distribution Type Y is Determined to be *t* Distribution

We have $f_n(\omega_j \mid K_n) = t(K_n) = \dfrac{\Gamma((K_n+1)/2)}{\sqrt{K_n \pi}\,\Gamma(K_n/2)} \cdot (1 + \dfrac{\omega_j^2}{K_n})^{-(\frac{K_n+1}{2})}$, where K_n is the degree of freedom (a positive integer) for the nth *t* distribution with mean $\overline{\omega}_n = 0$ and variance $\sigma_n^2 = \dfrac{K_n}{K_n - 2}$. The likelihood becomes:
$L = \prod_{j=1}^{J} (\sum_{n=1}^{N} P_n \times f_n(\omega_j \mid K_n))$.

Step 1: Set priors for parameters to be estimated.

Diffuse priors are set for the degree of freedom K_n and the membership probability P_n for distribution n.
$K_n \sim Geometric(q) = q(1-q)^{K_n-1}$ with $q = 0.1$, $E(K_n) = 1/q$, and $var(K_n) = (1-q)/q^2$.
$P_n \sim Dirichlet(\alpha_1, ..., \alpha_N)$ with $\alpha_n = 1$ for $n = 1, ..., N$.

Step 2: Let number of distributions, N, be 1. That is, $N = 1$.

Step 2.1: Draw random draws of K_n from its full conditional distribution:

$$K_n \mid P_n, C_j \propto \left[\prod_{j=1}^{J} f_n(\omega_j \mid K_n) \times I(C_j = n) \right] \cdot (1-q)^{K_n-1},$$

where $I(C_j = n)$ is an indicator function equal to 1 if $\overline{\omega}_n$ follows the *t* distribution n at time j and equal to 0 otherwise. C_j denotes the membership of different *t* distributions.

Because there is no conjugate posterior full-conditional distribution for K_n, we employ a random-walk Metropolis-Hasting algorithm to generate K_n. At iteration r, we generate a candidate as $\ln(K_n^c) = \ln(K_n^{(\gamma-1)}) + \tau$, $\tau \sim N[0, \sigma_\tau^2]$, where σ_τ^2 is chosen to achieve a reasonable acceptance rate. The acceptance probability is given by $\min\left\{\dfrac{p(K_n^c \mid P_n, C_j)}{p(K_n^{(r-1)} \mid P_n, C_j)}, 1\right\}$, where $p(.\mid.)$ is as given previously. To make sure K_n is a positive integer, let $K_n = \text{int}(K_n^c)$ when K_n^c is accepted.

Step 2.2: Draw random draws of C_j from its full conditional distribution:

$$C_j \mid K_n, P_n \sim Multinomial\,(\pi_1, \pi_2,...,\pi_N),$$

where $\pi_n = \dfrac{L(H_j \mid n) \cdot P_n}{\displaystyle\sum_{k=1}^{N} L(H_j \mid k) \cdot P_k}$ and $L(H_j \mid n)$ is the conditional likelihood at time j given distribution membership $C_j = n$.

Step 2.3: Draw random draws of P_n from its full conditional distribution:

$$P_n \mid \overline{\omega}_n, \sigma_n^2, C_j \sim Dirichlet(\alpha_1 + \sum_{j=1}^{J} I(C_j = 1), \alpha_2 + \sum_{j=1}^{J} I(C_j = 2),..., \alpha_N + \sum_{j=1}^{J} I(C_j = N))$$

Step 2.4: Repeat Steps 2.1–2.3 until the algorithm converges.

Step 2.5: Compute the log of marginal density.

Step 3: If the log of marginal density increases, then

N = N + 1; repeat Steps 2.1–2.5,
otherwise stop.

Step 4: Output N and the estimated parameters under each distribution.

APPENDIX B: CALIBRATION RESULTS FOR DECISION TREE C4.5 AND THE PROBIT MODEL

B1. Calibration Performance for C4.5

We use the calibration data set to train C4.5 to generate induced decision trees on the basis of the five variables. We then apply the decision tree to the holdout sample. The calibration results are as follows:

C4.5 rule generator

Read 100 cases (5 attributes) from training data

Processing tree 0, final rules from tree 0:

Rule 1:
    X2 <= -0.0158
    -> class 1 [96.8%]

Rule 2:
    X3 <= -0.0045
    -> class 1 [96.4%]

Rule 5:
    X2 > -0.0158
    X4 > 0.9526
    -> class 0 [94.6%]

Rule 4:
    X1 > 0.0275
    X2 > -0.0158
    X3 > -0.0045
    -> class 0 [92.2%]

Default class: 1 (bankrupt)

Tested training data (100), errors 2 (2.0%) <<

```
(1)  (0)   classified as
-----  -----
 49    1     (1): class 1 (bankrupt) ----> Type I error rate 2%
  1   49     (0): class 0 (healthy) ----> Type II error rate 2%
```

Interpretation: The preceding table is called a confusion matrix. Both the rows and columns have the same headers, but there is a distinction between them:

- The rows of the table are the classes available for use in the classification process.
- The columns of the table are the classes chosen during classification.
- The cell in which a particular row and column intersect may contain a number or not.
  - o   If the cell does not contain a number, no tested instances under that cell's row class have been classified by its corresponding column class.
  - o   A number in a cell represents the number of instances of the row class that have been classified as members of the corresponding column class.
  - o   Misclassifications occur when the row and column classes of a cell do not match.

Evaluation on test data (holdout sample 104, 2 years in advance):
Tested holdout sample (104), errors 23 (22.1%) <<

```
(1)   (0)   classified as
----- -----
 34    18   (1): class 1 (bankrupt)
  5    47   (0): class 0 (healthy)
```

Interpretation: This table indicates that 34 instances of the known class "bankrupt firm" are correctly classified by the generated rules as members of class "bankrupt," and 47 instances of the known class "healthy firm" are correctly classified. However, 18 instances represent incorrect predictions that should be "bankrupt," and 5 instances are incorrect predictions that should be "healthy."

B2. Calibration Performance for the Probit Model

The size of the calibration sample is 100.

Prediction	Frequency
Correct	96
Actually Bankrupt but predicted non-bankrupt	3
Actually Healthy but predicted bankrupt	1

Compilation of References

Abdelsayed, S., Glimsholt, D., Leckie, C., Ryan, S., & Shami, S. (2003). An efficient filter for denial-of-service bandwidth attacks. In *Proceedings of the 46th IEEE global Telecommunications Conference,* pp. 1353-1357.

Agency for Toxic Substances and Disease Registry [ATSDR] (2006). *Educational material—toxicological profile guidelines.* U.S. Department of Health and Human Services. Retrieved January 12, 2007, from http://www.atsdr.cdc.gov

Air Transport Association [ATA], (2002). Passenger traffic down 8.7 percent in May. Press release June 18, 2002. Retrieved January 8, 2003, from http://www.airlines.org/public/news/display2asp?nid=5539.

Alen, M. T., Stoney, C. M., Owens, J. F., & Matthews, K. A.(1993). Hemodynamic adjustments to laboratory stress: the influence of gender and personality. *Psychosomatic Medicine, 55,* 505-517.

Allenby, G. M., Arora, N., & Ginter, J. L. (1998). On the heterogeneity of demand. *Journal of Marketing Research, 35,* 384 – 389.

Altman, E. I. (1968). Financial ratios, discriminant analysis and prediction of corporate bankruptcy. *Journal of Finance, 23*(9), 589-609.

Altman, E. I. (1983). *Corporate financial distress: A complete guide to predicting, avoiding and dealing with bankruptcy.* New York: Wiley & Son.

Altman, E. I. (2000). Predicting financial distress of companies: Revisiting the Z-score and ZETA models. Working paper. Stern School of Business, New York University.

Altman, E. I. (2003). Quantitative techniques for the assessment of credit risk. *AFP Exchange, 23*(2), 7-13.

Altman, E. I., & Narayanan, P. (1997). An international survey of business failure classification models. *Financial Markets, Institutions and Instruments, 6*(2), 1-57.

Altman, E. I., Haldeman, R. G., & Narayanan, P. (1977). Zeta analysis: A new model to identify bankruptcy risk of corporations. *Journal of Banking Finance, 1*(6), 29-54.

Asaeda, G. (2002). The day that the START triage system came to a STOP: observations from the World Trade Center Disaster. *Academic Emergency Medicine, 9*(3), 255-256.

ASME (1987). American standard safety code for elevators, escalators, dumbwaiters and moving walks, A17.1, *American Society of Mechanical Engineers,* New York.

Association of American Railroads [AAR] (2004). *Railroads: the safe way to move.* Washington, DC: Association of American Railroads. Retrieved December 12, 2004, from http://www.aar.org/pubcommon/documents/policy/safe_way_to_move.pdf.

Attention (2007). *Merriam-Webster online.* Retrieved May 5, 2007, from http://www.m-w.com/dictionary/attention.

Auf der Heide, E. (2006). The importance of evidence-based disaster planning. *Annals of Emergency Medicine, 47*(1), 34-49.

Averill, J., Mileti, D., Peacock, R., et al., (2005), *Occupant behavior, egress, and emergency communications* (Tech.

Rep. No.1-7). Maryland, United States: National Institute of Standards and Technology, September 2005.

Aylwin, C. J., Konig, T. C., Brenan, N. W., & et al. (2006). Reduction in critical mortality in mass casualty incidents: analysis of triage, surge, and resource use after the London bombings on July 7, 2005. *Lancet, 368*(9554), 2219-2225.

Bai, Y., Lin, C. C., Chen, J. Y., Chue, C. M., & Chou, P. (2004). Survey of stress reactions among health care workers involved with the SARS outbreak. *Psychiatry Service, 55*, 1055-1057.

Baker, E. I. (1991). Evacuation behavior in hurricanes. *International Journal of Mass Emergencies and Disasters, 9*(2), 287-310.

Baker, E. I. (1979). Predicting response to hurricane warnings: a reanalysis of data from four studies. *Mass Emergencies, 4*, 9-24.

Balcaen, S., & McDonald, J. B.(1992). Identifying financial distress in the insurance industry: A synthesis of methodological and empirical issues. *The Journal of Risk and Insurance, 59*(4), 543-573.

Balcaen, S., & Ooghe, H. (2006). 35 Years of studies on business failure: An overview of the classic statistical methodologies and their related problems. *The British Accounting Review, 38*, 63-93.

Bartholomew, R. E., & Victor, J. S. (2004). A social-psychological theory of collective anxiety attacks: the "Mad Gasser" reexamined. *The Sociological Quarterly, 45*(2), 229-248.

Bashir, Z., Lafronza, V., Fraser, M. R., et al. (2003). Local and state collaboration for effective preparedness planning. *Journal of Public Health Management Practice, 9*(5), 344-351.

Baskin, S. I., & Brewer, T. G. (2004). Cyanide poisoning. In *Textbook of Military Medicine: Medical Aspects of Chemical and Biological Warfare*, Chapter 10. Retrieved January 12, 2005, from http://www.vnh.org/MedAsp-ChemBioWar/chapters/chapter_10.htm.

Baskin, S. I., Horowitz, A. M., & Nealley, E. W. (1992). The antidotal action of sodium nitrite and sodium thiosulfate against cyanide poisoning. *Journal of Clinical Pharmacology, 32*, 368-375.

Baum, A., Gatchel, R. J., & Schaeffer, M. A. (1983). Emotional, behavioral, and physiological effects of chronic stress at Three Mile Island. *Journal of Consulting and Clinical Psychology, 51*, 565-572.

BBC (2005). Police deny stampede 'inaction'. Retrieved August 8, 2007, from http://news.bbc.co.uk/go/pr/fr/-/2/hi/south_asia/4211839.stm.

Beament, J. (2003). *How we hear music*. Rochester, NY: Boydell Press.

Begier, E. M., Sockwell, D., Branch, L. M., et al (2003). The national capitol region's emergency department syndromic surveillance system: do chief complaint and discharge diagnosis yield different results? *Emerging Infect Disease, 9*, 393-396.

Beneish, M. D. (1997). Detecting GAAP violation: Implications for assessing earnings management among firms with extreme financial performance. *Journal of Accounting and Public Policy, 16*(3), 271-301.

Benos, A., & Papanastasopoulos, G. (2005). Extending the Merton model: A hybrid approach to assessing credit quality. Working paper, Department of Banking and Financial Management, University of Piraeus, Greece.

Bertelsmann Foundation (1999). Self-regulation of Internet content. Retrieved October 4, 1999 from http://www.stiftung.bertelsmann.de/internetcontent/english/download/Memorandum.pdf.

Black, F., & Cox, C. J. (1976). Some effects of bond and indenture provisions. *Journal of Finance, 31*, 351-367.

Black, F., & Scholes, M. (1973). Pricing of options and corporate liabilities. *Journal of Political Economy, 81*, 637-659.

Bleich, A., Dycian, A., Koslowsky, M., Solomon, Z., & Wiener, M. (1992). Psychiatric implications of missile attacks on a civilian population: Israeli lessons from the Persian Gulf War. *Journal of the American Medical Association, 268*, 613-615.

Boley, D., Gini, M., Gross, R., Han, E. H., & etc al. (1999). Partitioning-based clustering for web document categorization. *Decision Support Systems, 27*, 329-341.

Bolton, D. O'Ryan, D., Udwin, O., Boyle, S., & Yule, W. (2000). The long-term psychological effects of a disaster experienced in adolescence: II: General psychopathology. *Journal of Child Psychology and Psychiatry, 41*(9), 513-523.

Boring, E. G. (1933). *Dimensions of consciousness.* New York: Appleton-Century-Crofts, Inc.

Breiman, L. J., Friedman, J. H., Olshen, R. A., & Stone, C. J. (1984). *Classification and regression trees.* Belmont, CA: Wadsworth.

Briere, J., & Elliott, D. M. (2000). Prevalence, characteristics, and long-term sequelae of natural disaster exposure in the general population. *Journal of Traumatic Stress, 13*(4), 661-679.

Brownstein, J. (2007). ER wait time problems widespread. ABC News Medical Unit. June 28, 2007.

Bundesen, C. (2002). A general theory of visual attention. In L. Bäckman & C. von Hofsten (Eds.), *Psychology at the turn of the millennium: Vol. 1. Cognitive, biological, and health perspectives*, 179–200. Hove, UK: Psychology Press.

Bundesen, C. (1990). A theory of visual attention. *Psychological Review, 97*, 523-547.

Burkle, F. M. (1996). Acute-phase mental health consequences of disasters: implications for triage and emergency medical services. *Annals of Emergency Medicine, 28*, 119-128.

Business Week (2008). The best 50 performers. *Business Week*, April 7, 2008.

Campbell, S. V. (1996). Predicting bankruptcy reorganization for closely held firms. *Accounting Horizons*, September, 12-25.

Cannon, W. B. (1932). *The wisdom of the body.* New York: Norton.

Carroll, S., & Gonzalez, D. (2005). Napolitano taps disaster funds for border counties. The Arizona Republic, August 16, 2005. Retrieved August 16, 2005, from http://www.azcentral.com/arizonarepublic/news/articles/0816borderemergency16.html.

Caulkins, J. P., Ding, W., Duncan, G., Krishnan, R., & Nyberg, E. (2006). A method for managing access to web pages: filtering by statistical classification (FSC) applied to text. *Decision Support System, 42*(1), 144-161.

Center, J. L. Jr. (1999). Bayesian classification using an entropy prior on mixture models. In *Proceedings of the 19th International Workshop on Bayesian Inference and Maximum Entropy Methods in Science and Engineering*, pp. 42-70.

CERT (2006). CERT/CC statistics. Retrieved September 8, 2007, from http://www.cert.org/stats/cert_stats.html.

Chang, R. K. C. (2002). Defending against flooding-based distributed denial-of-service attacks: A tutorial. *IEEE Communication Management, 40*(10), 42-51.

Chaubey, A., & Malhotra, B. D. (2002). Mediated biosensors. *Biosense and Bioelectronics, 17*, 441-456.

Cheeseman, P. & Stutz, J. (1996). Bayesian classification (AutoClass): theory and results. In Fayyad, U. M., Piatetsky Shapiro, G., Smyth, P, & Uthurusamy, R. (Eds.), *Advances in Knowledge Discovery and Data Mining.* Menlo Park, CA: AAAI Press, 158-180.

Chen, W. Y., & Bokka, S.(2005). Stochastic modeling of nonlinear epidemiology. *Journal of Theoretical Biology, 234*, 455-470.

Chernoff, H. (1952). A measure of asymptotic efficiency for tests of a hypothesis based on the sum of observations. *Annual Mathematical Statistics, 23*, 493-507.

Citizen Guidance (2001). *Citizen guidance on the Homeland Security Advisory System.* Retrieved January 3, 2003, from http://www.dhs.gov/dhspublic/.

Clare, L., & Halligan, P. (2006). Pathologies of awareness: Bridging the gap between theory and practice, The Special Issue of the *Journal of Neuropsychological Rehabilitation*, August.

Clark, L. (2002). Panic: Myth or reality? *Contexts*, Fall, 21-26.

Clark, L. (2003). Conceptualizing responses to extreme events: The problem of panic and failing gracefully. In L. B. Clark (ed.) *Terrorism and Disaster: New Threats, New Ideas. Research in Social Problems and Public Policy* (11) (pp. 123-141). Amsterdam: Elsevier.

Clarke, F. L., & Dean, G. W. D. (2001). Corporate collapses analyzed. In CCH Australia Limited (et.) *Collapse Incorporated: Tales, safeguards & responsibilities of corporate Australia* (71-98). Sydney, Australia.

Clarke, F. L., Dean, G. W. D., & Oliver, K. G. (2003). *Corporate collapse: Accounting, regulatory and ethical failure*. Cambridge, England: Cambridge University Press.

CNN (2005). Anger over India stampede deaths. Retrieved August 8, 2007, from http://edition.cnn.com/2005/WORLD/asiapcf/01/26/india.stampede.ap/index.html

CNN. (2005). Border emergency declared in New Mexico. Retrieved August 13, 2005, from http://www.cnn.com/2005/US/08/12/newmexico.

CNN. (2006). Bush calls for 6,000 troops along border. May 16, 2006. Retrieved May 17, 2006, from http://www.cnn.com/2006/POLITICS/05/15/immigration/

CNN (2003). *Major power outage hits New York, other large cities*. Retrieved August 14, 2003, from http://www.cnn.com/2003/US/08/14/power.outage/.

Cohen, K. J, & Hammer, F. S. (1966). Analytical methods in banking. Horwood IL: Richard Irwin, Inc.

Coiera, E. (2003). *The Guide to Health Informatics* (2nd Edition). Arnold: London.

Collin-Dufresne, P., & Goldstein, R. (2001). Do credit spreads reflect stationary leverage ratio? *Journal of Finance*, 5, 1929-1957.

Congressional Research Services [CRS] (2004). Homeland Security Advisory System: Possible issues for congressional oversight. *Congressional Research Services*. Washington , DC, January 29, 2004.

Conte, C. (2005). Are we ready yet? *Outlook*, October, A2-A6.

Cooke, R., Medel, M., & Thijs, W. (1987). Calibration and information in expert resolution: A classical approach. Report 87-31, Faculty of Mathematics and Informatics, Delft University of Technology.

Cordesman, A. (2000). *The risks and effects of indirect, covert, terrorist and extremist attacks with weapons of mass destruction*. September. Washington DC: Center for Strategic and International Studies (CSIS).

Craven, M., Freitag, D., McCallum, A.., Mitchell, T., & et al. (1997). Learning to extract symbolic knowledge from the World Wide Web. *Technical Report*, Pittsburgh: Carnegie Mellon University.

Crook, C. (2008). Regulation needs more than tuning. *Financial Times*, 9, April 7, 2008.

Cross, J. (1979, April). *The association between previous residence and hurricane hazard perception and adjustments*. Paper presented at the 75th Annual Meeting of the Association of American Geographers, Philadelphia, PA.

Cutter, S. L. (1995). *Living with risk*. New York: Edward Arnold Publisher.

Daeemen, W., & Hoogendoor, S. P. (2003). Controlled experiments to derive walking behavior. *European Journal of transport and Infrastructure Research*, 3(1), 39-59.

Das, S. R. and Sundaram, R. K. (2000). A discrete-time approach to arbitrage-free pricing of credit derivatives. *Management Science*, 46(1), 46-62.

Davis, T. (2004). Public confidence down the drain: The federal role in ensuring safe drinking water in the District of Columbia. Open statement presented at a hearing before the House Committee on Government Reform, March 5, 2004. Washington, DC.

Dean, D., Franklin, M., & Stubblefield, A. (2002). An algebraic approach to IP traceback. *ACM Transactions on Information System Security, 5*(2), 119-137.

Demartino, R. M. (2002), Bioterrorism: what are we afraid of and what should we do? Paper presented to *the Biosecurity 2002 Conference*, November. Las Vegas.

DHS Portfolios. (2005). DHS Portfolios: Border and Transportation Security. Retrieved November 21, 2005, from http://www.dhs.gov/dhspublic/interapp/editorial/editorial_0545.xml

Diamond, H.S., Jr. (1976). Pattern recognition and the detection of corporate failure. unpublished PhD dissertation, New York University.

Dimitras, A., Zanakis, S., & Zopoudinis, C. (1996). A survey of business failure with an emphasis on failure prediction methods and industrial applications. *European Journal of Operational Research, 90*(3), 487-513.

Ding, W. (2002). *A Study of Collaborative Scientific Discovery.* Unpublished doctoral dissertation, Carnegie Mellon University, USA.

Ding, W. (2007). A mathematical approach to limit illegal border-crossings: With applications in protecting critical infrastructure. *Defense & Security Analysis, 23*(4), 359-377.

Dirickx, Y., & van Landeghem, C. (1994). Statistical failure prevision problems. *Tijdschrift voor Economie en Management, 39*(4), 429-462.

Drabek, T. E. (1999). Shall we leave? A study on family reactions when disaster strikes. *Emergency Management Review, 1*, 25-29.

Eidleman, G. J. (1995). Z scores –A guide to failure prediction. *The CPA Journal, 65*(2), 52-53.

Eisentiech, D. C. (1981). Credit analysis: trying it all together. *Journal of Commercial Bank Lending, 12*, 2-13.

Elveback, L. R. & et al. (1976). An influenza simulation model for immunization studies. *American Journal of Epidemiology, 103*, 152-165.

Elveback, L. R. & et al. (1976). An influenza simulation model for immunization studies. *American Journal of Epidemiology, 103*, 152-165.

Entman, R. M. (1993). Framing: Toward clarification of a fractured paradigm. *Journal of Communication, 43*(4), 51-8.

Federal Guidance (2001). *Guidance for federal departments and agencies.* Retrieved January 3, 2003, from http://www.dhs.gov/dhspublic/.

Felitti, V. (2003). The relationship of adverse childhood experiences to adult health status. Presented at the *Snowbird Conference of the Child Trauma Treatment Network*, DVD published by the National Child Traumatic Stress Network. The Intermountain West, September 2003.

Felitti, V., Anda, R., Nordenberg, D., Williamson, D., Spitz, D., Edwards, V., Koss, M., & Marks, J. (2004). Relationship of childhood abuse and household dysfunction to many of the leading causes of death in adults: The adverse childhood experiences study. *American Journal of Preventive Medicine, 14*(4), 245-258.

Ferguson, N. M., Cummings, D. A. T., Cauchemez, A., et al. (2005). Strategies for containing an emerging influenza pandemic in southeast Asia. *Nature*, August, 1-7.

Festinger, L. (1954). A theory of social comparison processes. *Human Relations.* 117-140.

Financial Times (2008). Cascade that can help avert disaster. *Financial Times*, January 20, 2008.

Fischer, H. W., Stine, G. F., Stoker, B. L., Trowbridge, M. L., & Drain, E. M. (1995). Evacuation behavior: why do some evacuate, while others do not? A case study of the Ephrata Pennsylvania (USA) evacuation. *Disaster Prevention and Management, 4*(4), 30-36.

Fischhoff, B. (2003). Assessing and communicating the risks of terrorism. In *Science and technology in a vulnerable world* (pp. 51-64). American Association for the Advancement of Science. MA: Washington, DC.

Fischhoff, B., Gonzalez, R. M., Small, D. A., & Lerner, J. S. (2003). Judged terror risk and proximity to the World Trade Center. *Journal of Risk and Uncertainty, 26*, 131-151.

Franz, D. R., Jahrling, P. B., Friedlander, A. M., et al. (1997). Clinical recognition and management of patients exposed to biological warfare agents. *Journal of American Medical Association, 278*, 399-411.

Freudenburg, W. R., Coleman, C. L., Gonzalez, J., & Hegeland, C. (1996). Media coverage of events: analyzing the assumptions. *Risk Analysis, 16*, 31-42.

Fruin, J. J. (1971). *Pedestrian planning and design.* Metropolitan Association of Urban Designers and Environmental Planners, New York, USA.

Fujiyama T., & Tyler, N. (2004, January). Pedestrian speeds on stairs–an initial step for a simulation model. In *Proceedings of the 36th Universities' Transport Studies Group Conference*, Newcastle upon Tyne, UK.

Fung, H. T., Kam, C. W., & Yau, H. H. (2002). A follow up study of electromagnetic interference of cellular phones on electronic media equipment in the emergency department. *Emergency Medicine, 14*, 315-319.

Garrett, L. (2005). The next pandemic? *Foreign Affairs, 84*(4), 3-23.

Gaynor, M., Seltzer, M., Moulton, S., & Freedman, J. (2005). A dynamic, data-driven, decision support system for emergency medical services. *Lecture Notes in Computer Science, 3515*, 703-711.

Gelfand, A. E., & Smith, A. F. M. (1990). Sampling-based approaches to calculating marginal densities. *Journal of the American Statistical Association, 85*(410) 398-409.

General Accounting Office (2004). Homeland Security–Risk communication principles may assist in refinement of the Homeland Security Advisory System. *The U.S. General Accounting Office report on the Homeland Security Advisory System.* Retrieved December 12, 2004, from http://www.gao.gov/cgi-bin/getrpt?gao-04-538T.

Geske, R. (1977). The valuation of corporate liabilities as compound options. *Journal of Finance & Quantitative Analysis, 4*, 541-552.

Giordano, F. R., & Weir, M. D. (1994). *Differential equations: A modeling approach. Reprinted with correction.* New York: Addison-Wesley Publishing Company.

Glen, J. (2004). Debt and firm vulnerability. Working paper, International Finance Corporation.

Goffman, E. (1971). *Relations in public: microstudies in the public order.* New York: Basic Books.

Goffman, E. (1974). *Frame analysis: An essay on the organization of experience.* London: Harper and Row.

Greene, W. H. (1997). *Econometric analysis* (3rd edition). Upper Saddle River, NJ: Prentice Hall.

Greenspan, A. (2008). The Fed is blameless on the property bubble. *Financial Times, 9*, April 7, 2008.

Grice, J. S., & Ingram, R. W. (2001). Tests of the generalizability of Altman's bankruptcy prediction model. *Journal of Business Research, 54*, 53-61.

Guha, K. (2008). IMF points to high cost of global credit crisis. *Financial Times, 4*, April 7, 2008.

Gurr, N., & Cole, B. (2002). *The new face of terrorism: Threats from weapons of mass destruction.* London: Tauris Publishers.

Guttelling, J. M. & Wiegman, O. (1996). *Exploring risk communication.* Dordrecht: Klewer Academic Publishers.

Hagerup, T. & Rub, C. (1989). A guided tour of Chernoff bounds. *Information Processing Letters, 33*, 305-308.

Hankin, B. D., & Wright, R. A. (1958). Passenger flow in subway. *Operational Research Quarterly, 9*, 81.

Harper, F. T., Musolino, S. V., & Wente, W. (2007). Realistic radiological dispersal device hazard boundaries and ramifications for early consequence management decisions. *Health Physics, 93*(1), 1-16.

Heckman, J. J. (1979). Sample selection bias as a specification error. *Econometrica, 47*(1), 153-161.

Heinke, D., & Humphreys, G. W. (2003). Attention, spatial representation, and visual neglect: simulating emergent attention and spatial memory in the selective attention for identification model (SAIM). *Psychological Review, 110*, 29–87.

Hermand, D., Karsenty, S., Py, Y., Guillet, L., & Chauvin, B. et al. (2003). Risk target: an interactive context factor in risk perception. *Risk Analysis, 23*, 821-833.

Heurgren-Carlstrom, G., & Malmberg, E. (2003). Online information resources of toxicology in Sweden. *Toxicology, 190*(1-2), 63-73.

Hoffer, E. (1955). *The passionate state of mind*, aphorism 33. New York: Harper.

Hoffman, F. (2002). A member of the Hart-Rudman Commission, *Intellibridge report*.

Holmen, J. S. (1988). Using financial ratios to predict bankruptcy: An evaluation of classic models using recent evidence. *Akron Business and Economic Review, 19*(1), 52-63.

Homeland Security Council [HSC]. (2006). *National strategy for pandemic influenza: Implementation plan.* Washington DC: US Homeland Security Council.

Homeland Security Council [HSC]. (2006). *National strategy for pandemic influenza: Implementation plan.* Washington DC: US Homeland Security Council.

Houts, P., Cleary, P., & Hu, T. (1988). *The Three Mile Island crisis: psychological, social and economic impacts on the surrounding population.* University Park: Pennsylvania State University Press.

Hull, J., Nelken, I., & White, A. (2004). Merton's model, credit risk, and volatility skews. Working paper, University of Toronto.

Hussain, A., Heidemann, J., & Papadopoulos, C. (2003). A Framework for classifying denial of service attacks. In *Proceedings of ACM SIGCOMM* (pp.99-110), Karlsruhe, Germany, August 25-29, 2003.

Irnich, W. E., & Tobisch, R. (1999). Mobile phones in hospitals. *Biomedical Instrument and Technology*, Jan/Feb, 28-34.

Isobe, M., Adachi, T, & Nagatani, T. (2004). Experiment and simulation of pedestrian counter flow. *Physica, A*(336), 638-650.

Isom, G. E., & Johnson, J. D. (1987). Sulfur donor in cyanide intoxication. In Ballantyne, B. M., & Marrs, T. C. (Eds.), *Clinical and experimental toxicology of cyanides* (pp. 413-426). Bristol: Wright.

Jacob, V., Krishnan, K., Ryu, Y. U. (2007). Internet content filtering using isotonic separation on content category ratings. *ACM Transactions on Internet Technology, 7*(1), 1-19.

Jaeger, C. C., Renn, O., Rosa, E. A., & Webler, T. (2001). *Risk, uncertainly, and rational action.* Earthscan Publications Ltd.

Jarrow, R., & Turnbull, S. (1995). Pricing derivatives on financial securities subject to credit Risk. *Journal of Finance, 50* (1), 53-86.

Jones, F. L. (1987). Current techniques in bankruptcy prediction. *Journal of Account Literatures, 6*, 131-164.

Kahya, E., & Theodossiou, J. O. (1996). Predicting corporate financial distress: A time-series CUSUM methodology. Presented at *the Third Annual Conference of the Multinational Finance Association*, June, 1-38.

Kammerer, C. A., & Mazelis, R. (2006). Trauma and retraumatization. Retrieved Decemebr 12, 2006, from http://www.gainscenter.samhsa.gov/atc/pdfs/papers/trauma.pdf.

Karesh, W. B., & Cook, R. A. (2005). The human-animal link. *Foreign Affairs, 84*(4), 38-50.

Kasperson, J. X., Kasperson, R. E., Pidgeon, N., & Slovic, P. (2003). The social amplification of risk: Assessing fifteen years of research and theory. In N. Pidgeon, R. E. Kasperson, & P. Slovc (Eds.), *The social amplification of risk* (pp. 13-46). Cambridge, England: Cambridge University Press.

Kasperson, R. & Stallen, P. J. M. (1991). *Communication risk to the public: International perspectives.* Boston: Klewer.

Kass, R., & Raferty, A. (1995). Bayes factors. *Journal of the American Statistical Association, 90*(430), 773-795.

Keim, M. E. (2006). Terrorism involving cyanide: the prospect of improving preparedness in the prehospital setting. *Prehospital and Disaster Medicine, 21*(2), s56-s60.

Keinan, G., Friedland, N., & Ben-Porath, Y. (1987). Decision-making under stress: scanning of alternatives under physical threat. *Acta Psychologica, 64*, 219-228. North Holland: Elsevier Science Publishers.

Kermack, W. O., & McKendrick, A. G. (1927). A contribution to the mathematical theory of epidemics. *Proceedings of the Royal Society of London*, A, *115*(772), 700-721.

Kiang, N. Y. S. (1969). *Discharge patterns of single auditory fibers*. MIT Research Monograph 35, Cambridge, MA.

Klahr, D., & Dunbar, K. (1988). Dual space search during scientific reasoning. *Cognitive Science, 12*, 1-48.

Klote, H.H., Alvord, D.M., Levin, B.M., & Groner, N. E. (1992). Feasibility and design considerations of emergency evacuation by elevators (Tech. Rep. No. 4870). Maryland, United States: National Institute of Standards and Technology.

Kohlmann, E. (2006). The real online terrorist threat. *Foreign Affairs, 85*(5), 115-120.

Koopman, C., Classen, C. C., Cardena, E., & Spiegel, D. (1995). When disaster strikes, acute stress disorder may follow. *Journal of Traumatic Stress, 8*(1), 29-46.

Krug, R. M. (2003). The potential use of influenza virus as an agent for bioterrorism. *Antiviral Research, 57*, 147-150.

Kuligowski, E. (2003, May). Elevators for occupant evacuation and fire department access. In *Proceedings of the CIB-CTBUH International Conference on Tall Buildings*, 8-10, Malaysia.

Lam, W. H. K., & Cheung, C. Y. (2000). Pedestrian speed/flow relationships for walking facilities in Hong Kong. *Journal of transportation Engineering*. ASCE, *126*(4), 343-349.

Lam, W. H. K., Morrall, J. F., & Ho, H. (1979). Pedestrian flow characteristics in Hong Kong. *Transportation Research Record, 1487*, 56-62.

Landauer, R. (1991). Information is physical. *Physics Today, 44*, 23-29.

Langley, P., Simon, H.A., Bradshaw, G.L., & Zytkow, J.M. (1987). *Scientific Discovery*. Cambridge, MA: MIT Press.

Larsen, P. T. (2008). EU warning systems need strengthening. *Financial Times*, 8, April 2, 2008.

Lasica, J. (1997). Ratings today, censorship tomorrow. *Salon Magazine*, July.

Laurent, J. F., Richter, F., & Michel, A. (1999). Management of victims of urban chemical attacks: the French approach. *Resuscitation, 42*, 141-149.

Lawson, M. (2002). Early warning signs. *The Australian Financial Review*. May. Retrieved May 3, 2004, from http://www.afrboss.com.au/magazine.asp?rgid=2&listed_months=26.

Lee, P. Y., Hui, S. C., & Fong, A. C. M. (2002). Neural network for web content filtering. *IEEE Intelligent Systems, 17*(5), 48-57.

Leppard, D., Hastins, C., & Berry, J. (1998). Killer germs on sale for just 600 pounds. *The London Sunday Times*, p8, November 22, 1998.

Lerner, J. S., Gonzalez, R. M. Small, D. A., & Fischhoff, B. (2003). Effects of fear and anger on perceived risks of terrorism: A national field experiment. *Psychological Science, 14*, 144-150.

Li, S., Liechty, J. C., & Montgomery, A. (2002). Modeling category viewership of Web users with multivariate count models. Working Paper, Tepper School of Business, Carnegie Mellon University.

Lieberman, H. (1995). Letizia: An agent that assists Web browsing. In *Proceedings of the International Joint Conference on Artificial Intelligence*, Montreal, 1995.

Lipton, E. (2005). U.S. report lists possibilities for terrorist attacks and likely toll, *The New York Times*.

Retrieved March 17, 2005, from http://www.nytimes.com/2005/03/16/politics/16home.htm

Logan, G. D. (2002). An instance theory of attention and memory. *Psychological Review, 109*, 376–400.

Lomranz, J., Hobfoll, S., Johnson, R., Eyal, N., & Zermach, M. (1994). A nation's response to attack: Israelis' depressive reactions to the Gulf War. *Journal of Traumatic Stress, 7*, 59-73.

London Time (2004). London's dirty-bomb plot, October 11, 2004. Retrieved February 11, 2008, from http://www.time.com/time/magazine/article/0,9171,995357,00.html.

London Time (2006). Why liquid explosives may be terror's secret weapon, August 10, 2006. Retrieved February 11, 2008, from http://www.time.com/time/nation/article/0,8599,1225032,00.html.

Longini, I. M., Nizam, A., Xu, S. F., et al. (2005). Containing pandemic influenza at the source. *Science, 309*, 1083-1087.

Longstaff, F., & Schwartz, S. E. (1995). A simple approach to valuing risky fixed and floating rate debt. *Journal of Finance, 51*(3), 789-819.

Lonigan, C. J., Shannon, M. P., Finch, A. J., Daugherty, T. K., & Taylor, C. M. (1991). Children's reactions to a natural disaster: Symptom severity and degree of exposure. *Advances in Behavior Research and Therapy, 13*, 135-154.

Los Angeles Times (2008). How the U.S. seeks to avert nuclear terror. Retrieved January 6, 2008, from http://www.latimes.com/news/printedition/front/la-na-nuke-6jan06,1,6779317.story?ctrack=5&cset=true

Luce, R. D. (1963). Detection and recognition. In R. D. Luce, R. R. Bush, & E. Galanter (Eds.), *Handbook of mathematical psychology*, 103–89. New York: Wiley.

Lundgren, R. (1994). *Risk communication: A handbook for communicating environmental, safety and health risks*. Columbus, Ohio: Battelle Press.

Machiavelli, N. (1514). *The prince*. Cambridge, England: Cambridge University Press.

Madjid, M, Lillibridge, S. Mirhaji, P., & Casscells, W. (2003). Influenza as a bioweapon, *Journal of the Royal Society of Medicine, 96*, 345-346.

Maes, P., & Kozierok, R. (1993). Learning interface agent. In *Proceedings of the 11th national Conference on Artificial Intelligence*. Boston: MIT Press.

Mahajan, R., Bellovin, S. M., Floyd, S., Ioannidis, J., Paxson, V., & Shenker, S. (2002). Controlling high bandwidth aggregates in the network. *ACM Computer Communication Review, 32*(3), 62-73.

Maniscalco, P. M., Christen, H. T., Rubin, D. L., & Kim, P. (1998). Terrorism. Part I: calibrating your risks and response. *Journal of Emerging Medical Service, 23*, 38-51.

Maunder, R. G., Lancee, W. J., Balderson, K. E., Bennett, J. P., Borgundvaag, B., Evans, S., & Fernandes, C. M. B. et al. (2006). Long-term psychological and occupational effects of providing hospital healthcare during SARS outbreak. *Emerging Infectious Diseases, 12*(12), 1924-1932.

McCarthy, M. (2001). Attacks provide the first major test of USA's national antiterrorist medical response plans. *Lancet, 358*, 941.

McCarthy, M. (2005). Building an enduring capability for homeland security science and technology. *DHS Technology Conference*, Boston, MA.

Media (2006). *New 9/11 tapes show communication confusion*. Retrieved August 17, 2006, from http://www.msnbc.msn.com/id/14375089/page/2/

Media (2006). *The new tapes reveal communication confusion*. August 16, 2006.

Media. (2005). Napolitano declares border emergency. Associated Press. Retrieved August 15, 2005, from http://www.azcentral.com/news/articles/0815borderemergency15.html.

Media. (2006). Bush signs 700 miles of border fence into law. Retrieved October 26, 2006, from http://www.usbc.org/.

Melin, L. (2002). Terrorist profiles: An analysis based on 920 chemical incidents. *The ASA Newsletter, 91,* 2-4. Applied Science and Analysis, Inc.

Meltzer, M. I., Cox, N. J., & Fukuda, K. (1999). The economic impact of pandemic influenza in the United States: Priorities for intervention. *Emerging Infectious Diseases, 5*(5), 659-671.

MEMRI (2005). Islamist website design contest: Winners fires missiles U.S. Army base in Iraq. The Middle East Media Research Institute, Special Dispatch 1038, December 1, 2005. Retrieved March 7, 2006, from http://memri.org/bin/articles.cgi?Page=archives&Area=sd&ID=SP103805.

Menhaj, M. B., & Delgosha, F. (2001). A soft probabilistic neural network for implementation of Bayesian classifiers. In *Proceedings of International Joint Conference on Neural Networks,* 454-458.

Merton, C. R. (1974). On the pricing of corporate debt: The risk structure of interest rates. *Journal of Finance, 29,* 449-470.

Michalowski, J. J., Rubin, S., Slowinski, R., & Wilk, S. (2003). Mobile clinical support system for pediatric emergencies. *Decision Support Systems, 36,* 161-176.

Midine, D., Spiegelhalter, D. J, & Taylor, C. C. (1994). *Machine Learning, Neural and Statistical Classification* (edited collection), New York: Ellis Horwood.

Milby, T. H. & Baselt, R. C. (1999). Hydrogen sulfide poisoning: clarification of some controversial issues. *American Journal of Industry Medicine, 35,* 192-195.

Mileti, D. S. (1999). *Design for future disasters: a sustainable approach for hazards research and application in the United States.* Washington, DC: Joseph Henry Press.

Mileti, D. S. Sorensen, J., Vogt, B., & Sutton, J. (2003). *Warning America. Report to the Federal Emergency Management Agency.* Boulder, CO: National Hazards

Center, Institute of Behavioral Science, University of Colorado.

Mileti, D. S., & O'Brien, P. (1992). Warning during disaster: normalizing communication risk. *Social Problems, 39*(1), 40-55.

Miller, J., Resnick, P., & Singer, D. (1996).Rating service and rating systems (and their machine readable descriptions). Retrieved December 4, 1998, from http://w3.org/PICS/services.html.

Minsky, M. L. (1975). A Framework for Representing Knowledge. In P. H. Winston (ed.), *The Psychology of Computer Vision.* New York: McGraw-Hill.

Mirkovic, J., Prier, G., & Reiher, P. (2002). Attacking DDoS at the source. In *Proceedings of ICNP 2002.* Paris, France, 312-321.

Montgomery, A., Li, S. Srinivasan, K., & Liechty, J. C. (2004). Modeling online browsing and path analysis using clickstream data. *Marketing Science, 23*(4), 579-595.

Morris, C. R. (2008). The trillion dollar meltdown: Easy money, high rollers, and the great credit crash. Public Affairs.

Morse, A. (2002). Bioterrorism preparedness for local health departments. *Journal of Community Health and Nurse, 19*(4), 203-211.

Mould, R. F. (2000). *Chernobl record. The Definitive history of the Chernobyl catastrophe.* Bristol, Institute of Physics Publishing.

Musse, S., Babski, C., Capin, T., & Thalmann, D. (1998), Crowd modeling in collaborative virtual environments, In *Proceedings of ACM Virtual Reality Software Technology.* 115-123. Taiwan.

National Research Council [NRC], (2006). *Facing hazards and disasters: Understanding human dimensions.* Committee on Disaster Research in the Social Sciences: Future Challenges and Opportunities. Washington DC, US: National Academies Press.

National Research Council [NRC], (2006). *Facing hazards and disasters: Understanding human dimensions.*

Committee on Disaster Research in the Social Sciences: Future Challenges and Opportunities. Washington DC, US: National Academies Press.

Navin, F. P. D., & Wheeler, R. J. (1969). Pedestrian flow characteristics. *Traffic Engineering,* June, 30-36.

New York Independent System Operator [NYISO] (2004), NYISO interim report on the August 14, 2003 blackout. Retrieved January 15, 2004, from http://www.hks.harvard.edu/hepg/Papers/NYISO.blackout.report.8.Jan.04.pdf

Newbold, P. (1994). *Statistics for business and economics* (4th edition). Upper Saddle River, NJ: Prentice Hall.

Newell, A., & Herbert A. S. (1972). *Human problem solving.* Englewood Cliffs, NJ: Prentice Hall.

Nickell, L. A., Crighton, E. J., Tracy, C. S., Al Enazy, H., Bolaji, Y., & Hanjrah, S. et al. (2004). Psychosocial effects of SARS on hospital staff: survey of a large tertiary case institution. *Canadian Medical Association Journal, 170,* 793-798.

Nigg, J. M. (1993). Risk communication and warning systems. In *Proceedings of the International Conference on Natural Risk and Civil Protection,* 209-236. Commission of European Communities, Belgirate, Italy.

Norris, F. H., Friedman, M. J., & Watson, P. J. (2002). 60,000 disaster victims speak: Part II. Summary and implication of disaster mental health research. *Psychiatry, 65*(3), 240-260.

Norris, F. H., Friedman, M. J., Watson, P. J., Byrne, C. M., Diaz, E., & Kaniasty, K. (2002b). 60,000 disaster victims speak. Part I. An empirical review of the empirical literature, 1981-2001. *Psychiatry, 65*(3), 207-239.

Norris, F. H., Friedman, M. J., Watson, P. J., Byrne, C. M., Diaz, E., & Kaniasty, K. (2002). 60,000 disaster victims speak. Part I. An empirical review of the empirical literature, 1981-2001. *Psychiatry, 65*(3), 207-239.

North, C. A., Nixon, S. J., Shariat, S., Mallonee, S., McMillen, J. C., Spitznagel, E. L., & Smith, E. M. (1999). Psychiatric disorders among survivors of the Oklahoma City bombing. *Journal of the American Medical Association, 282*(8), 755-762.

North, C. S., Kawasaki, A., Spitznagel, E. L., & Hong, B. A. (2004). The course of PTSD, major depression, substance abuse, and somatization after a natural disaster. *The Journal of Nervous and Mental Disease, 192*(10), 1-7.

NSW. (2000). *Disaster mental health response handbook.* Institute of Psychiatry and Center for Mental Health, North Sydney: NSW Health.

O'Flaherty, C. A., & Parkinson, M. H. (1972). Movement in a city centre footway. *Traffic Engineering and Control,* February, *434.*

O'Toole, T. (2000). *Biological weapons: National security threat & public health emergency.* Washington DC: Center for Strategic and International Studies (CSIS).

Oakley, D. (2008), Distressed debt levels rise to five-year peak. *Financial Times, 25,* April 8, 2008.

Ohbu, S., Yamashina, A., Takasu, N., Yamguchi, T., Murai, T., & et al. (1997). Sarin poisoning on Tokyo subway. Retrieved February 12, 2005, from http://www.sma.org/smj/97june3.htm.

Okumera, T., Suzuki, K., Fukuda, A., & et al. (1998). The Tokyo subway Sarin attack: Disaster management. Part 2: Hospital response. *Academy of Emergency Field, 5,* 618-624.

Older, S. J. (1968). Movement of pedestrians on footways in shopping streets. *Traffic Engineering and Control, 10*(4), 160-163.

Orgle, Y. E. (1970). A credit scoring model for commercial loans. *Journal of Money, Credit & Banking, 2,* 435-445.

Osterholm, M. T., (1999). The medical impact of a bioterrorism attack. *Postgraduate Medicine, 106,* 121-124.

Parks, B. (2003). Transforming the grid to revolutionize electric power in North America. U.S. Department of Energy. In *Proceedings of Edison Electric Institute's*

Fall 2003 Transmission, Distribution and Metering Conference, October 13, 2003.

Pawlak, R., & Melchor, J. (2005). Long-term stress can impair short-term memory. *Proceedings of the National Academy of Sciences*, December 5.

Perreault, L., & Metzger, J. (1999) A pragmatic framework for understanding clinical decision support. *Journal of Healthcare Information Management, 13*(2), 5-21.

Pimlott, D., Guha, K, Chung, J., & White, B. (2008), Regulator fears wave of bank failures. *Financial Times*, 1, April 23, 2008.

Platt, H. D., & Platt, M. B. (1991). A note on the use of industry-relative ratios in bankruptcy prediction. *Journal of Banking Finance, 15*, 1183-1194.

Powers, M. J., & Ban, J. (2004). *Bioterrorism: Threats and preparedness*. Retrieved January 12, 2005, from http://www.nae.edu/nae/bridgecom.nsf/weblinks/CGOZ-58NLKB?OpenDocument.

PPW (2004). The Homeland Security Advisory System: Threat codes & public responses. *PPW testimony before the House Subcommittee on National Security, Emerging Threats and International Relations*. Retrieved November 18, 2004, from http://www.Partnershipfor-PublicWarning.org.

Predtechenskii, V. M., & Milinskii, A. I. (1978). *Planning for foot traffic flow in buildings*. New Delhi: Amerind Publishing Company, Inc .

Proulx, G. (2001), As of year 2000, what do we know about occupant behavior in fire? *The Technical Basis for Performance Based Fire Regulations*, United Engineering Foundation Conference, 127-129, San Diego, January 7-11, 2001.

Public Survey (2001), Survey project on American's response to biological terrorism. *International Communications Research*, Harvard School of Public Health and Robert Wood Johnson Foundation. October 24-28, 2001.

Pushkarev, B., & Zupan, J. M. (1975). *Urban space for pedestrians*. Cambridge, MA: The MIT Press.

Quarantelli, E. I., & Dynes, R. R. (1977). Response to social crisis and disaster. *Annual Review of Sociology, 3*, 23-49.

Quinlan, J. R. (1993). *C4.5: Programs for machine learning*. San Mateo, CA: Morgan Kaufmann Publishers.

Ratcliff, R. (1978). A theory of memory retrieval. *Psychological Review, 85*, 59–108.

Ratcliff, R., van Zandt, T., & McKoon, G. (1999). Connectionist and diffusion models of reaction time. *Psychological Review, 106*, 261–300.

Reeves, A., & Sperling, G. (1986). Attention gating in short-term visual memory. *Psychological Review, 93*, 180–206.

Regnier, E. (2008), Public evacuation decisions and hurricane track uncertainty. *Management Science, 54*(1), 16-28.

Relman, D. A., & Olson, J. E. (2001). Bioterrorism preparedness: What practitioners need to know. *Infectious Medicine, 18*(11), 497-515.

Resnick, P. (1997). Filtering information on the Internet. *Scientific American*, March.

Reuters (2008), *U.S. aims to give wake-up alerts on storms*. February 12, 2008.

Reuters (2008). ER waits dangerously long in U.S.. Retrieved January 16, 2008 from http://content.healthaffairs.org/cgi/content/abstract/hlthaff.27.2.w84/

Ropeik, D. & Slovic, P. (2003). Risk communication: A neglected tool in protecting public health. *Risk in Perspective*, 11(2), Harvard Center for Risk Communication, Cambridge, MA.

Ross, S. A., Randolph, W.W., & Jaffe, J, F. (2004). *Corporate finance* (7th Edition). New York, NY: McGraw-Hill Companies.

Rubinson, L., Nuzzo, J. B., Talmor, D. S., & et al. (2005). Augmentation of hospital critical care capacity after attacks or epidemics: recommendations of the working group on emergency mass critical care. *Critical Care Medicine, 33*(10), Supplements.

Salton, G., & McGill, M. J. (1993). *Introduction to Modern Information Retrieval*, New York: McGraw-Hill.

Sargent, T. J. (1993). *Bounded Rationality in Macroeconomics*, Oxford: Oxford University Press.

Sarkar, S., & Sriram, R. S. (2001). Bayesian models for early warning of bank failures. *Management Science, 47*(11), 1457-1475.

Schlenger, W. E., Caddell, L., Ebert, B. K., & Jordan, K. M. (2002). Psychological reactions to terrorist attacks: findings from the national study of Americans' reactions to September 11. *Journal of the American Medical Association, 288*, 581-588.

Sharan, P., Chaudhary, G., Kavathekar, S. A., & Saxena, S. (1996). Preliminary report of psychiatric disorders in survivors of a severe earthquake. *American Journal of Psychiatry; 153*, 556-558.

Shepard, R. N.(1957). Stimulus and response generalization: A stochastic model relating generalization to distance in psychological space. *Psychometrika, 22*, 325–45

Shih, S-I., & Sperling, G.(2002). Measuring and modeling the trajectory of visual spatial attention. *Psychological Review, 109*, 260–305.

Shumway, T. (2001). Forecasting bankruptcy more accurately: A simple hazard model. *Journal of Business, 74*(1), 101-124.

Simon, H. A. (1997), *Models of bounded rationality: Empirical grounded economic reason.* Cambridge, MA: The MIT Press.

Simon, H. A. (1997). *Models of Bounded Rationality: Empirical Grounded Economic Reason*, Cambridge, MA: The MIT Press.

Sjöberg, L. (2000). Factors in risk perception. *Risk Analysis, 20*(1), 1-11.

Sjöberg, L. (2004). The perceived risk of terrorism. *SSE/EFL Working paper series in Business Administration* (No 2002:11). Stockholm School of Economics, Stockholm, Sweden.

Slociv, P. (1987). Perception of risk. *Science, 236*(17), 280-285.

Slovic, P., Fischoff, B., & Lichtenstein, S. (1980). Facts and fears: understanding perceived risk. In D. Schwing & R. Albers (Eds.) *Societal risk assessment: how safe is safe enough?* (pp. 181-216). New York: Plenum.

Slovic, P., Fischoff, B., & Lichtenstein, S. (1979). Rating the risks. *Environment, 21*, 3, 14-20.

Smith, G., & Epstein, K. (2008). On the border: the virtual fence isn't working. *Business Week*, February 18, 2008, 45-48.

South Carolina Emergency Management Division (2005). *Graniteville train accident situation reports.* Retrieved December 10, 2005, from http://www.scemd.org.

Stein, B. D., Tanielian, T. L., Eisenman, D. P., Keyser, D. J., & Burnam, M. A. (2004). Emotional and behavioral consequences of bioterrorism: planning a public health response. *The Milbank Quarterly, 82*(3), 413-455.

Straus, S. E., Wilson, K., Rambaldini, G., Rath, D., Lin, Y., Gold, W. L., & Kapral, M. K. (2004). Severe acute respiratory syndrome and its impact on professionalism: quantitative study of physicians' behavior during an emerging healthcare crisis. *BMJ, 329*, 83.

Strauss, D. (2008), OECD predicts subprime losses to hit $420 bn. *Financial Times, 4*, April 16, 2008.

Strauss, D. (2008). OECD predicts subprime losses to hit $420 billion. *Financial Times*, April 16, 2008.

Styles, E. (2006). *The psychology of attention.* 2nd ed. United Kingdom: Psychology Press.

Sunstein, C. R. (2003). Terrorism and probability neglect. *Journal of Risk and Uncertainty, 26*, 121-136.

Talbot, D. (2005). Terror's server. *Technology Review*, 46-52. February.

Tam, C. W., Pang, E. P., Lam, L. C., & Chiu, H. F. (2004). Severe acute respiratory syndrome (SARS) in Hong Kong in 2003: stress and psychological impact among frontline healthcare workers. *Psychological Medicine, 34*, 1197-1204.

Tam, C. W., Pang, E. P., Lam, L. C., & Chiu, H. F. (2004). Severe acute respiratory syndrome (SARS) in Hong Kong in 2003: stress and psychological impact among frontline healthcare workers. *Psychological Medicine, 34*, 1197-1204.

Terrorism Research Center [TRC] (2005). *News release.* Retrieved December 10, 2005, from http://www.Terrorism.com.

Tett, G. (2008), Ratings agencies move to quell critics. *Financial Times.* January 31, 2008

The 9/11 Commission Report (2004). *Final Report of the National Commission on Terrorist Attacks upon the United States.* Authorized Edition, New York: W.W. Norton & Company.

The Economist (2008). Credit-rating agencies: Restructured products. *The Economist*, February 9th-15th, 80.

The New York Times. (1938). Radio listeners in panic, taking war drama as fact. October 31. Retrieved January 12, 2005, from http://members.aol.com/jeff1070/wotw.html.

The Partnership for Public Warning [PPW] (2002). Developing a unified all hazards public warning system. A report by the workshop on *Effective Hazard Warnings*, February, 2002. Retrieved January 3, 2003, from http://www.PartnershipforPublicWarning.org/.

The President's Commission Report (1980). *The Accident at Three Mile Island*, Authorized Edition. Retrieved August 17, 2007, from http://www.pddoc.com/tmi2/kemeny/

Theodossiou, J. O (1993). Predicting shifts in the mean of a multivariate time series process: An application in predicting business failures. *Journal of the American Statistical Association, 88*(422), 441-449.

Toshiyuki, A. (1993). Prediction system of passenger flow. In R. A. Smith & J. F. Dickie (Eds.), *Engineering for crowd safety* (pp. 249-258). Amsterdam: Elsevier.

Trettin, L., & Musham, C. (2000). Is trust a realistic goal of environmental risk communication? *Environment and Behavior, 32*(3), 410-426.

Trust for America's Health [TFAH] (2007). Ready or not? 2007. Retrieved December 12, 2007, from http://healthamericans.org/reports/bioterro07/.

U.S. Agency for Toxic Substances and Disease Registry [ATSDR] (2001). *Hazardous Substances Emergency Events Surveillance System biennial report, 1999–2000.* Atlanta, GA: US Department of Health and Human Services, Agency for Toxic Substances and Disease Registry.

U.S. Army Medial Research Institute for Infectious Diseases [Army] (1998). *Medial Management of Biological Casualties Handbook.* 3rd ed. Fort Detrick, Frederick, MD: USAMRIID.

U.S. Centers for Disease Control and Prevention [CDC] (2000). Biological and chemical terrorism: strategic plan for preparedness and response, *MMWR, 49*, 1-14.

U.S. Centers for Disease Control and Prevention [CDC] (2006). *Bioterrorism overview.* Retrieved December 4, 2007, from http://www.bt.cdc.gov/bioterrorism/.

U.S. Department of Defense [DOD] (2008). *Electronic surveillance system for the early notification of community-based epidemics (ESSENCE).* Retrieved January 10, 2008, from http://www.geis.ha.osd.mil/geis/surveillanceactivities/essence/essence.asp.

U.S. Centers for Disease Control and Prevention [CDC] (2006). *Fact sheet: Overview of influenza surveillance in the Untied States.* Retrieved December 4, 2007, from http://www.cdc.gov/flu/.

U.S. Congressional Research Services [CRS] (2004). *Homeland Security Advisory System: possible issues for congressional oversight.* January 29, 2004. Washington, DC: Congressional Research Services.

U.S. Center of Disease Control and Prevention [CDC] (2008). Overview of influenza surveillance in the United States. Retrieved March 10, 2008, from http://www.cdc.gov/flu/weekly/fluactivity.htm.

U.S. Centers for Disease Control and Prevention [CDC] (2003). Recognition of illness associated with exposure to chemical agents–United States, *MMWR, 52*, 938-940.

U.S. Department of Homeland Security [DHS] (2001). *The Homeland Security Advisory System.* Retrieved January 3, 2003, from http://www.dhs.gov/.

U.S. Department of State [DOS] (2002). *Patterns of global terrorism 2001.* Retrieved December 12, 2007, from http://www.state.gov/documents/organization/10319.pdf.

U.S. Department of State [DOS] (2003). *Patterns of global terrorism 2002.* Retrieved December 12, 2007, from http://www.state.gov/documents/organization/20177.pdf.

U.S. Department of State [DOS] (2004). *Patterns of global terrorism 2003.* Retrieved December 12, 2007, from http://www.state.gov/documents/organization/31912.pdf.

U.S. Department of Transportation [DOT] (1999). *Biennial report on hazardous materials transportation, calendar years 1996–1997.* Washington, DC: U.S. Department of Transportation. Retrieved May 15, 2003, from http://hazmat.dot.gov/pubs/biennial/96_97biennial.rpt.pdf.

U.S. Department of Transportation [DOT] (1998). *Hazardous materials shipments.* Washington, DC: U.S. Department of Transportation. Retrieved May 15, 2003, from http://hazmat.dot.gov/pubs/hms/hmship.pdf.

U.S. Environmental Protection Agency [EPA] (2005). *Norfolk Southern Graniteville derailment.* Washington, DC: Environmental Protection Agency.

U.S. Environmental Protection Agency [EPA] (2005). *Smoke detectors and radiation.* Retrieved January 11, 2005, from www.epa.gov/radiation/sources/smoke_alarm.htm.

U.S. Federal Emergency Management Agency [FEMA] (2004). DHS lunches digital emergency alert system pilot for the national capital region. New Release, October 21, 2004. Retrieved October 23, 2004, from http://www.fema.gov/news/newsrelease_print.fema?id=14924.

U.S. Federal Emergency and Management Agency [FEMA] (2008). *National Response Framework.* Retrieved March 16, 2008, from http://www.fema.gov/NRF.

U.S. General Accounting Office [GAO] (1997). *Combating terrorism: threat and risk assessments can help priorities and target program investments.* Retrieved April 5, 2006, from http://www.gao.gov/docsearch/repandtest.html/GAO-NSIAD-98-74.pdf

U.S. General Accounting Office [GAO] (2000). *Combating terrorism: Linking threats to strategies and resources.* July 26, 2000. Retrieved April 5, 2006, from http://www.gao.gov/docsearch/repandtest.html/GAO-T-NSIAD-00-218.pdf.

U.S. General Accounting Office [GAO] (1997). *Combating terrorism: Threat and risk assessments can help priorities and target program investments.* Retrieved April 5, 2006, from http://www.gao.gov/docsearch/repandtest.html/GAO-NSIAD-98-74.pdf

U.S. General Accounting Office [GAO] (2003). Hospital Preparedness. Retrieved December 18, 2007 from http://www.gao.gov/cgi-bin/getrpt?GAO-03-924.

U.S. General Accounting Office [GAO] (2004). *Homeland Security–Risk communication principles may assist in refinement of the Homeland Security Advisory System.* Retrieved January 3, 2005, from http://www.gao.gov/cgi-bin/getrpt?gao-04-538T.

U.S. General Accounting Office [GAO] (2007). *Combating nuclear terrorism: Federal efforts to respond to nuclear and radiological threats and to protect key emergency response facilities could be strengthened.* November 15, 2007. Retrieved December 22, 2007, from http://www.gao.gov/docsearch/repandtest.html/GAO-08-285T.pdf.

U.S. Homeland Security Council [HSC] (2007), *National Strategy for Homeland Security.* Washington DC: Homeland Security Council.

U.S. Homeland Security Council [HSC] (2006). *National strategy for pandemic influenza: Implementation plan.* Retrieved August, 2006, from http://www.whitehouse.gov/homeland/pandemic-influenza-implementation.html

U.S. National Center for Injury Prevention and Control [NCIPC] (2007). In a moment's notice: surge capacity for terrorist bombings. Atlanta (GA): U.S. Centers for Disease Control and Prevention.

U.S. National Research Council [NRC] (2002). *Making the nation safer: The role of science and technology in countering terrorism.* Washington, DC: National Academies Press.

Udwin, O., Boyle, A., Yule, W., Bolton, D., & O'Ryan, D. (2000). Risk factors for long-term psychological effects of a disaster experienced in adolescence: Predictors of post traumatic stress disorder. *Journal of Child Psychology and Psychiatry, 41*(8), 969-979.

Ulph, S. (2005). A guide to Jihad on the Web. *Jamestown Foundation Terrorism Monitor, 2*(7), March 31.

UNDP/UNICEF (2002). The human consequences of the Chernobyl nuclear accident: a strategy for recovery. *A Report Commissioned by UNDP and UNICEF with the support of UN-OCHA and WHO.* Retrieved February 10, 2005, from http://www.reliefweb.int/library/documents/2002/undp_rus_25jan.pdf.

Ursano, R. J., Grieger, T. A., & McCarroll, J. E. (1996). Prevention of posttraumatic stress: Consultation, training, and early treatment. In B. A. Van der Kolk, A.C. McFarlane, & L. Weisaeth (Eds.), *Traumatic stress: The effects of overwhelming experience on mind, body, and society,* 441-462, New York: Guilford Press.

US Centers for Disease Control and Prevention [CDC]. (2003). Severe cute respiratory syndrome. Retrieved January 4, 2004, from http://www.cdc.gov/ncidod/sars

USA Today (May 23, 2006). Editorial: In Katrina disaster, human error claimed heavy toll. Retrieved May 24, 2006, from http://www.usatoday.com/news/opinion/editorials/2006-05-23-our-view x.htm.

Viscusi, W. K., & Zeckhauser, R. J. (2003). Sacrificing civil liberties to reduce terrorism risks. *Journal of Risk and Uncertainty, 26,* 99-120.

Vitter, D. (March 2, 2006). *Vitter statement on Katrina Video.* Retrieved March 10, 2006, from http://vitter.senate.gov/?module=pressroom/pressitem&ID=0a46a873-6bed-486d-8f77-eadc3f36c7b4.

Walters, J., & Kettl, D. (2005). The Katrina breakdown–coordination and communication problems between levels of government must be addressed before the next disaster strikes. *Governing,* December. Retrieved March 2, 2006, from http://www.governing.com/articles/12disast.htm.

Washington Post. (2005). Bird flu called global human threat. Sec. A16. Retrieved February 26, 2005, from http://www.washingtonpost.com/wp-dyn/articles/A46424-2005Feb23.html.

Way, J. L. (1984). Cyanide intoxication and its mechanism of antagonism. *Annual Review of Pharmacology Toxicology, 24,* 451-481.

Weidmann, U. (1993). *Transport technik der fussgaener.* ETH, Schriftenreihe Ivt-Berchte, 90, Zuerich (In German).

Weimann, G., (2006). *Terror on the Internet.* Washington DC: United States Institute of Peace Press.

Weinberg, J. (1997). Rating the net. Retrieved December 4, 1998, from http://www.msen.com/~weinberg/rating.htm.

Wilson, M. (2002). Personal communication. FBI NICS information officer. July 15, 2002.

Wruck, K. H. (1990). Financial distress, reorganization, and organizational efficiency. *Journal of Financial Economics, 27,* 419-444.

Yamori, K. (2001). Going with the flow: micro-macro dynamics in the macrobehavioral patterns of pedestrian crowds. *Psychological Review, 105*(3), 530-557.

Zamiska, N. (2005). Asian countries gear up to tackle bird-flu threat. *The Wall Street Journal,* October 3, 2005. Retrieved October 3, 2005, from http://online.wsj.com/article/SB112829683236458056.html/.

Zavgren, C. (1983). The prediction of corporate failure: the start of the art. *Journal of Accounting Literature, 2*(1), 1-37.

Zmijewski, M. E. (1984). Methodological issues related to the estimation of financial distress prediction models. *Journal of Accounting Research, 22,* 59-82.

About the Author

Amy Wenxuan Ding is an assistant professor at University of Illinois, USA. She received a PhD in Information Technology and Cognitive Science from Carnegie Mellon University, USA. She specializes in computational intelligence, mathematical description of natural intelligence, and advanced methods of modeling, simulation, and decision making. She has published numerous papers at various top-tiered academic journals. Currently she is an associate editor of the *Journal of Defense Modeling and Simulation*, and serves on the editorial boards of the *International Journal of Social and Humanistic Computing* and *International Journal of Electronic Banking*.

Index